Teaching
Jewish American Literature

Teaching Jewish American Literature

Edited by
Roberta Rosenberg
and
Rachel Rubinstein

The Modern Language Association of America
New York   2020

MLA and the MODERN LANGUAGE ASSOCIATION are trademarks owned
by the Modern Language Association of America. For information about
obtaining permission to reprint material from MLA book publications, send
your request by mail (see address below) or e-mail (permissions@mla.org).

Library of Congress Cataloging-in-Publication Data
Names: Rosenberg, Roberta, editor. | Rubinstein, Rachel, 1972– editor.
Title: Teaching Jewish American literature / edited by Roberta Rosenberg
  and Rachel Rubinstein.
Description: New York : The Modern Language Association of
  America, 2020. | Series: Options for teaching, 1079-2562 ; 49 |
  Includes bibliographical references. | Summary: "Offers pedagogical
  techniques for teaching Jewish American fiction, poetry, drama, graphic
  novels, children's literature, and digital texts, including considerations
  of religious and secular Jewish culture, race and multicultural contexts,
  immigration, the Holocaust, gender and sexuality, multilingual literary
  traditions, and humor. Gives syllabus suggestions for undergraduate and
  graduate courses"— Provided by publisher.
Identifiers: LCCN 2019054064 (print) | LCCN 2019054065 (ebook) |
  ISBN 9781603294720 (hardcover) | ISBN 9781603294454 (paperback) |
  ISBN 9781603294461 (EPUB) | ISBN 9781603294478 (Kindle)
Subjects: LCSH: American literature—Jewish authors—Study and teaching
  (Higher) | American literature—Jewish authors—History and criticism.
Classification: LCC PS153.J4 T43 2020 (print) | LCC PS153.J4 (ebook) |
  DDC 810.9/8924073071—dc23

Options for Teaching 49
ISSN 1079-2562

Cover illustration of the print and electronic editions: Panel 5 of Fran Gallun,
The Book: An Installation, 2001. Gouache, acrylic, ink, and collage on Arches
paper. Photo by Lance Schnatterly.

Published by The Modern Language Association of America
85 Broad Street, suite 500, New York, New York 10004-2434
www.mla.org

Contents

Part III: Multilingual and Transnational Approaches

Part IV: Gender and Sexuality Approaches

Part V: Multidisciplinary and Digital Humanities Approaches

Part VI: New Approaches and Key Texts

Part VII: Resources

Roberta Rosenberg and Rachel Rubinstein

Introduction

In the January 2003 special issue of *PMLA*, *America: The Idea, the Literature*, Paul Giles calls for a "critical transnationalism" that would reveal the "cultural jagged edges, structural paradoxes, or other forms of apparent incoherence" that add to our cultural understanding of America's position in the global community (65). Indeed, the "transnational turn" in American studies, Donald E. Pease writes, "has effected the most significant reimagining of the field since its inception" (40). Jewish American literature, however, has not been fully recognized as fundamental to these conversations, despite the groundbreaking work of a growing cadre of scholars. Jewish literatures in the Americas—Canada, the Caribbean, and Latin America, in addition to the United States—offer an opportunity to think transnationally and hemispherically in a way that responds to and exemplifies the call for a critical transnationalism in the teaching of American literatures.

As we reassert the importance of Jewish American literature in the context of the new American studies (among other fields), the development of Jewish studies as an academic discipline suggests additional contexts for reevaluating this diverse body of work. Jewish studies developed in nineteenth-century western Europe, pioneered by reformist Jewish intellectuals who applied the analytical tools of Western scholarship to Jewish religious texts. The discipline's early focus was on biblical exegesis, and it aimed to displace Christian scholars as the Western authorities on Hebrew scripture. In her essay "Jewish Studies as Counterhistory," Susannah Heschel contends that the work of contemporary multiculturalists bears remarkable similarities to that of the early scholars of *Wissenshaft Das Judentums* ("Judaic studies"), who sought to destabilize the dominant Christian metanarrative of history largely by making Jews "the subjects of their own self-defined historical narratives" (105). As Judaic studies moved into the American academy in the twentieth century, however, it maintained a bias toward European intellectual and religious history and philosophy. But the last thirty years have brought greater visibility to social history, women's history, and the development of Yiddish, Judeo-Spanish, Judeo-Arabic, and other vernacular traditions in diasporas around the world.

If American literary scholarship has increasingly interrogated the boundaries and meanings of "America," so too has Jewish studies developed its own reflexive and critical stance. In "placing" and "displacing" Jewish studies within literary studies, Leslie Morris charts the movement of Jewish studies from a "parochial and Germanic perch" to a "transdisciplinary position . . . encompassing some of the central issues in the humanities (nationhood, identity, mediality, textuality)." Morris defines the future of Jewish studies as the future of literary studies as a whole, from historical philology to an emphasis on border zones, and argues that this definition enables "a rethinking of traditional textual studies" (765). Morris observes, however, that when Jewish literature intersects with literary studies in both English and foreign language departments, it is often limited "to explorations of Jewish content or themes in literary works or simply literature by Jewish writers" (770).

This narrowly defined notion of Jewish literature may have led Irving Howe, in his introduction to the 1977 anthology *Jewish-American Stories*, to predict the demise of Jewish American literature once the latest immigrant generation assimilated and lost its Jewish "difference." Howe viewed Jewish American literature as a fixed "regional literature" (16) that spoke only to the initiated—"incomprehensible to a reader who lacked some memory or impression" of Jewish immigrant culture narrowly defined (5). As Benjamin Schreier argues in *The Impossible Jew* (2–3), older, traditional studies of Jewish American literature echo Howe's theory, privileging a homogenizing, representational, and historicist definition of Jewish literature as nationalist or regional.

Many contemporary scholars, however, share Morris's expansive, postmodern definition of Jewish and Jewish American literature. Julian Levinson, in *Exiles on Main Street*, observes that "Jewishness can be formed in dialogue with American literary culture, its vocabulary, conceptual categories, and implicit politics" (5). Hana Wirth-Nesher, in her introduction to the recent and field-defining *Cambridge History of Jewish American Literature*, contends that Jewish American writing is a "dynamic and mutable discourse, in which the terms 'Jewish' and 'American' interact and signify in ways that are sometimes discrepant, sometimes complementary, and always dialectical" (2). Wirth-Nesher argues that Jewish American literature "deserves to be recognized as an inherent component of the dynamic field of American literature" (3).

Our approach in this volume follows the movement in literary and cultural scholarship away from assumptions of a fixed and stable identity and toward what Jonathan Freedman characterizes as a more diverse "klezmerical" perspective. Just as klezmer music incorporates and transforms the artistry of other peoples, Freedman argues, "klezmerical" Jewish American literature should reject essentialist strictures and instead move toward "a tradition of dynamic innovation . . . new configurations of ethnic belonging, new aesthetic forms in which to express them and ultimately new vessels for delineating and interrogating the experience of a multiracial, multiethnic modernity at large" (22). In fact, Freedman describes his "profound disagreement" with any narrow definition of Jewishness that "stresses the need for purity, consistency, essence, limits, boundaries in defining what is and is not Jewish" (35).

In the introduction to their anthology *Insider/Outsider: American Jews and Multiculturalism*, the editors agree with many of the abovementioned contemporary literary scholars that Jewish literature provides the "longest-standing case of a group whose self-definition was always part of a multicultural context" and that "Jews constitute a liminal border case, neither inside nor outside—or, better, both inside and outside" (Biale et. al, 8). For these postmodern critics, an analysis of Jewish American literature can "open up multicultural theory in new and interesting ways" (8). The editors of the anthology *The New Diaspora: The Changing Landscape of American Jewish Fiction* likewise describe the present-day "great flowering of Jewish culture in a dozen languages" as reminiscent of an earlier, historic migration period in America, from the 1880s to the 1920s (Aarons et al. 10). Victoria Aarons and her coeditors define the new Jewish American writing as "a richly diverse body of pluralistic fiction" as well as a burgeoning new transnational literature by authors from countries as varied as Egypt, France, Guatemala, Hungary, Iran, Russia, and South Africa (2). Aarons and her coeditors, therefore, view Jewish American fiction not as a narrow, white, privileged discourse but rather as part of a "larger global movement . . . [that] reflects both [Jews'] commonality with other cultures and their distinctive history" (3).

Jewish American literature also serves as a gateway into the study of Jewish and American postmodernities. Shaul Magid, taking his inspiration from David Hollinger's theories of the "postethnic," asks the following provocative questions of American literary texts in a "post-Judaic" age: "How much 'American' is in American Judaism? How much 'Jewishness' is in America? How much has 'Jewishness' changed in contemporary America? And how much has America changed?" (1). In her essay "Reflections on Editing: *Jewish American Literature: A Norton Anthology*," Hilene Flanzbaum, one of W. W. Norton's editors, also sees this complex cultural hybridity when she notes that "to study the actual experiences of American Jews may be one of the rare instances where deconstruction does come fairly close to describing what is actually happening. . . . Questioning, redefining, and challenging . . . a continual process of simultaneously making and shattering meaning." Rather than presenting Jewish American literature as a homogenous, nationalistic American literature, Flanzbaum describes Jewish experience as "in continual flux between deconstruction and reconstruction . . . for the last 340 years" (65). Although Flanzbaum sees a long-standing tradition for Jewish literature in America, she also theorizes that contemporary Jewish American literature has more in common with many of its better-known multicultural literary counterparts.

Shira Wolosky makes a similar case for thinking about Jewish American literature in her essay "On Contemporary Literary Theory and Jewish American Poetics" by tracing the impact of Jewish literary theorists like John Hollander, Harold Bloom, and Sacvan Bercovitch on both Jewish hermeneutics and contemporary American literary theory (257). Tresa Grauer echoes Wolosky, Aarons et. al., and Flanzbaum in her essay "Identity Matters: Contemporary Jewish American Writing" when she theorizes that the thematic premises of contemporary and Jewish American literatures are complementary: "[I]n contemporary discourse, both the individual and the collective are understood to be comprised of multiple identifications (and disidentifications); our allegiances, ambivalences, and attentions can be said to shift depending on the various social positions that we occupy" (Grauer 271).

Although the last twenty years have thus seen a wave of paradigm-shifting scholarship in Jewish American literary studies, the gap between this innovative reevaluation of the field and the state of classroom practice calls for new pedagogical resources and interventions. A more diverse, comparative, informed, and nuanced view of Jewish American literature in our pedagogy can better represent the most exciting work in the field, as well as respond to the increasingly complex identities and backgrounds of our students, who may or may not identify as Jewish. Jennifer Glaser speaks to this gap between theory and classroom practice in her review essay "The Politics of Difference and the Future of American Jewish Literary Study." Glaser praises the new work of the scholars Jonathan Freedman, Julian Levinson, and Anita Norich and calls for greater attention to the "need to maintain Jewish literature as a viable subject of study in the English department." She also argues that without this rethinking and reframing the discipline will be "increasingly consigned to the role of the sickly cousin to other diasporic traditions" (483).

Given what we see to be the resonances and complementary preoccupations of the most original and creative scholarship in ethnic, American, and Jewish American literary studies, it is dismaying to note the last's underrepresentation in English and American studies departments' curricula and in discussions of pedagogy. At a December 2009 MLA convention session titled "Does the English Department Have a Jewish Problem?" Josh Lambert provided statistics to support Glaser's pessimistic, anecdotal assessment. Lambert noted that according to *U.S. News & World Report*, only two of the top twenty English departments had a tenure-track faculty member in Jewish American literature, while five others had teachers with an interest in but no publications or training in the field. The only area of Jewish studies well represented by trained scholars was Holocaust studies, with six scholars. At the same time, English departments had experts in many ethnic American literatures, including African American, Asian American, Chicano, Latinx, and Native American literatures. Scott Jaschik notes this imbalance in his article "The Lost Tribe," in which he argues that "English departments that would never allow themselves to be without experts in the literatures of many racial and ethnic groups in the U.S. don't think twice about failing to have a knowledge base in Jewish American literature. . . . Discussions about multicultural literature that ought to include Jewish writers simply don't." In other words, as Biale argues of Jews in post–World War II America, Jewish American literary studies finds itself "doubly marginal: marginal to the majority culture, but also marginal among minorities" (Biale 27).

Although there may be a dearth of trained scholars who teach Jewish American literature, the study of the Holocaust is well represented in the academy. Teachers at all levels benefit from institutions dedicated to teaching the Holocaust, including the United States Holocaust Memorial Museum and Israel's Yad Vashem Holocaust Remembrance Center. Other organizations, such as Facing History and Ourselves, provide materials on Holocaust education for K–12 teachers. In addition, excellent scholarly sources on teaching the Holocaust in Jewish American literature include Alan L. Berger's *Crisis and Covenant: The Holocaust in American Jewish Fiction* and Berger and Gloria L. Cronin's *Jewish American and Holocaust Literature: Representation in the Postmodern World.* Emily Budick has also provided scholars with chapters titled "The Holocaust in the Jewish American Literary Imagination," in *The Cambridge Companion to Jewish American Literature,* and, more recently, "The Ghost of the Holocaust in the Construction of Jewish American Literature," in *The Cambridge History of Jewish American Literature.*

While Jewish American literature is often absent from the curriculum, according to Lambert, as reported by Jaschik, four of the top twenty English departments offered courses in Holocaust studies, since many of these academic programs are endowed by outside donors with a specific interest in this area. Donor support extends to teacher education and K–12 offerings of Holocaust literature. Holocaust literature may, as a result, be seen as the de facto substitute for Jewish American literature. At the 2009 MLA convention session, Lambert called it "fascinating and unfortunate . . . that the genocide of Jews can seem more worthy of attention than the culture of Jews themselves" (qtd. in Jaschik).

The MLA session inspired a special issue of *MELUS* devoted to new scholarship and pedagogies in Jewish American literature, coedited by Lori Harrison-Kahan and Lambert and titled *The Future of Jewish American Literary Studies.* A number of scholars contributed to the special issue's section on pedagogy, addressing the teaching of Jewish American literature within ethnic and American literature classes, the teaching of Jewish American literature by enthusiasts with no training or expertise, and the teaching of Jewish American identities in and through performance.

Through their efforts, Harrison-Kahan and Lambert hoped to initiate a national discussion of "identity and the nation, representation and marginalization, and cultural traditions and literature aesthetics" that might help to "shape the future study and teaching of American and ethnic American literature" (177). Likewise, in his contribution to the issue, "Teaching Jewish American Literature as Global Ethnic American Literature," Dean Franco argues that including Jewish American literature in the American literature curriculum "can challenge the very frameworks by which we understand a reified national literature," thereby providing alternative narratives often missing from the traditional canon. In particular, Jewish literature provides a case history of themes often thought of as the purview of an American multicultural literature from which Jewish American literary texts are often excluded. Franco posits that Jewish American literature reveals "representations of diaspora, trauma, and memory and the role of narrative for stabilizing or undoing myths of cultural identity" as well as "a transnational/comparative approach [that] can permit a sustained focus on the political, aesthetic, and philosophical implications of ethnic American literature" (184).

This perspective is not necessarily shared, however, by scholars in many of the major ethnic American literatures. Unlike African American studies, Chicano studies, and Native studies, Jewish studies generally and Jewish American literary studies specifically are no longer viewed as a form of reparation tied to a particular community's lack of access to or underrepresentation in the academy. Indeed, as Rachel Rubinstein describes in her essay "Not Just 'White Folks': Teaching Jewish American Literature as Multi-ethnic and Multiracial," it is "increasingly difficult . . . to teach Jewish literature, both as part of a multi-ethnic literary curriculum and as a multi-ethnic literary tradition, on a radical campus where Jewishness is associated with whiteness, privilege, and an oppressive nation-state" (180).

The uncritical association of Jewishness in America with white privilege is problematized by Karen Brodkin, Eric Goldstein, Michael Rogin, and others who have persuasively demonstrated in cultural, sociological, and historical terms how Jews in the United States were both subjected to and actively participated in their own racial formation and re-formation in a new national context. In "Reading Jewishness as a Marker of Ethnoracial and Cultural History" Helene Meyers maintains that Jewish American literature both decenters American literature as "Christian-centered" (185) and illustrates Eric Goldstein's argument in *The Price of Whiteness*, that, in Goldstein's words, "whiteness sat uneasily with many central aspects of Jewish identity" (1). What Brodkin, Goldstein, and Rogin describe as the whiteness or the whitening of American Jews masks the contemporary reality of a profoundly diverse Jewish population in America and the world. In her essay "Teaching about Jewishness in the Heartland," the anthropologist Misha Klein thus argues that her course Anthropology of Jews and Jewishness acts as a "lens" through which students can begin to understand core concepts of multiculturalism: "race, ethnicity, identity, kinship, migration, diaspora and transnationalism; gender and sexuality, religion and ritual, food-ways, language, national identity and globalization" (89). This neglected diversity of Jewish identities and creative expression, in turn, drives the variety of pedagogical approaches that we highlight in the present volume.

Teachers and scholars of Jewish American literature must grapple with the continuing influence that global conflicts exercise on local understandings of race, power, and privilege. Several contributors to our volume explicitly and thoughtfully engage the entwined histories of Jews and Arabs, Israel and Palestine in their pedagogies. Others do so obliquely, through inclusive syllabi that implicitly challenge exclusive associations of Jews with whiteness, the West, and Europe, while also acknowledging the realities of contemporary access and privilege in today's higher education. It is our hope that offering further tools and resources for instructors of Jewish American literature may positively and productively shape the conversations on college campuses concerning these always charged, and sometimes deeply painful, issues.

Therefore, the goal of *Teaching Jewish American Literature* is to reintegrate Jewish literary studies into the academy, English department offerings, and literature and language programs, expanding the study of Jewish American texts and cultures while creating new audiences for stand-alone courses and comparative studies. Our emphasis is on teaching Jewish American literature as a global and multilingual literature. Foundational to this effort is the reframing of Jewish immigration to America as a history that is not limited to the turn of the twentieth century or the geographical boundaries of the present-day United States. Jewish American literature represents another version of the American Atlantic in world literature, as it introduces transnational and multilingual elements into American literature in English. As Sarah Phillips Casteel asks in her essay "Landscapes: America and the Americas": "What would it mean to reimagine the study of Jewish American literature as the study of Jewish literatures of the Americas? What kinds of conceptual as well as geographical and linguistic shifts would a hemispheric reframing of the field entail?" (413). *Teaching Jewish American Literature* not only meets the needs of teachers and scholars but also creates an environment for this rethinking of the present ways the literature is taught. The volume provides crucial academic and pedagogical background for faculty members teaching Jewish American studies without expert or scholarly knowledge in either Jewish or American studies, and it provides scholars in the field with the most current thinking and theory. We also hope that it opens lines of communication with scholars from both world literatures and American multicultural studies.

The thirty-four essays and the resources for teaching in this volume, therefore, create an important link between Jewish American literature, American and diasporic literatures, Jewish literary and religious contexts, and contemporary literary and critical theory. We are attentive to the ways in which Jewish American literature speaks to both the postmodern preoccupation with multicultural identity politics and literary critical modes of interpretation as well as to students' interest in traditional culture and religion. Authors provide religious and ritual contexts as well as a focus on Jewish languages (Yiddish, Ladino, and Hebrew) for nonspecialists. The resources section provides new or untrained teachers and advanced scholars with additional places to find information on religious ritual, history, and cultural customs, as well as critical, theoretical, and archival materials.

The historical and contemporary multilingualism of Jewish literature and of Jewish literary scholarship across the Americas offers fascinating case studies for Americanists working to expand the monolingual American literary canon. Many of our contributors move beyond English-language texts and therefore, out of necessity, must teach texts in translation. *Jewish-American Literature: A Norton Anthology* is an invaluable resource of translated texts for classroom use, as Kathryn Hellerstein describes in her essay, but other contributors ask students to engage with texts in the original source language, as in Joanna Meadvin and Katherine Trostel's course on Ladino literature. When authors describe how they use non-English language sources in their teaching, they make sure to address the availability and accessibility of particular translations. The resources section in this volume includes a curated bibliography of non-English-language primary sources in translation.

Though many contemporary students and scholars note that the teaching of Jewish American literature tends to overemphasize early-twentieth-century eastern European immigrant experiences and narratives, much of that teaching still neglects the abundant Yiddish cultural materials that were created in the Americas. Only a small proportion of Yiddish American literature has been translated into either English or Spanish, and much that has been translated is currently out of print. A number of our contributors describe integrating Yiddish-language materials into their courses, drawing upon a growing number of translations and republications of Yiddish literature. For recent discussions of translations of Yiddish literatures in the United States, Latin America, and Canada, see Alan Astro, *Yiddish South of the Border*; Rebecca Margolis, "Yiddish Translation in Canada: A Litmus Test of Continuity"; and Rachel Rubinstein, "Is Yiddish Literature the Next Big Thing?" A smaller cohort of eastern European Jewish writers produced a body of writing in Hebrew in America, texts that only recently have attracted the attention of scholars and translators, such as Alan Mintz, Michael Weingrad (*American Hebrew Literature*; *Letters*), and Stephen Katz. Critically annotated, bilingual translations, such as those in Marc Shell and Werner Sollors's edited collection *Multilingual Anthology of American Literature*, are potential models for the kinds of resources needed to teach Jewish American literature as a polyphonic literature.

Structure of the Book

The latest edition of *The Heath Anthology of American Literature* (Lauter), a multivolume anthology frequently used in university literature survey courses and one that prides itself on its linguistic, ethnic, gender, and racial inclusivity, nonetheless introduces its first Jewish-authored text, Emma Lazarus's "The New Colossus" (1883), only in volume C, followed by works by Mary Antin and Abraham Cahan. The identification of Jewish American literature with late-nineteenth-century eastern European mass migration to urban centers of the northeastern United States has become so reflexive that the Heath editors never mention that Lazarus herself was not an immigrant, that she was Sephardic (descended from Iberian Jews) as well as Ashkenazi (with origins in central or eastern Europe), or that these lines of descent have meaning in Jewish American literary history.

Our volume seeks to view Jewish American literature from its earliest Atlantic-world origins, and therefore we begin part 1, "Reframing Jewish American Histories, Rethinking Canons," with Laura Leibman's discussion of teaching the earliest Jewish cultural production in the Americas and its engagement with race and racialization. In this way we hope to reorient received narratives of Jewish American literature and set up a new paradigm for thinking about and teaching it. All the essays in the first part make diverse interventions into often-unquestioned assumptions about

Jewish American literature. Kathryn Hellerstein, along with Leibman, discusses teaching texts beyond those associated with the period of major eastern European migration, using *Jewish American Literature: A Norton Anthology*'s more expansive contents as a way to introduce students not only to early Jewish American literature but to multilingual literary texts translated from Yiddish, Hebrew, Ladino, and German. To interrupt the notion of Jewish American literature as chronicling the abandonment of parochial traditionalism in favor of a secular American pluralism, Louis Gordon foregrounds an alternative canon, including works by such writers as Ludwig Lewisohn, Herman Wouk, Irving Fineman, and Dara Horn, whose protagonists maintain their commitments to Jewish spiritual and ritual practice. Similarly, Lucas Wilson provokes students at a Christian college to consider how the Canadian novel *The Second Scroll* reappropriates biblical themes and tropes in its post-Holocaust theological critique of the New Testament. Lori Lefkovitz considers Dara Horn and Nicole Krauss as representatives of a cadre of contemporary American writers who deploy a distinctive Jewish idiom to explore fate (*bashert*) and contingency. In their work, long-ago, faraway, pre-Holocaust events ultimately determine the circumstances and self-understanding of young Jewish American characters, for whom storytelling proves a therapeutic, redemptive antidote to the vagaries of Jewish history. Part 1 introduces themes that resonate throughout the volume and significant resources for educators to craft courses that accurately represent the historical breadth and ethnic, racial, linguistic, and religious complexity of Jewish American literature.

Critiques of comparative or multicultural literary pedagogies in the American university have focused on their tendencies to flatten or universalize difference and their potential for touristic and superficial engagements, exacerbated by what are often English-only approaches. Cognizant of these possible pitfalls and engaging these debates, parts 2 and 3 of our volume examine Jewish American literature as both a multiethnic and a multilingual tradition that our contributors also teach within comparative American multicultural curricula.

Part 2, "Comparative Teaching Approaches," concentrates on Jewish American literature in juxtaposition with other American literatures, arguably the most common context in which students are introduced to the subject. Dean Franco proposes teaching specific comparative clusters of texts by Jewish American, Asian American, Chicano, Native American, and African American writers to examine synchronically how literary texts engage with prevailing social theories of difference, thus staging exemplary comparisons to suggest how teachers can prompt conversations about the critical and theoretical stakes of pluralism. Meri-Jane Rochelson and Donna Aza Weir-Soley design their team-taught comparative course on Jewish and Caribbean literatures to highlight the common patterns typical of immigrant generations while maintaining the sense of distinctiveness within cultures; through coteaching, they model a pedagogy of "intellectual collaboration and . . . mutuality and respect." Sarah Casteel's course on black-Jewish literary relations innovates on familiar terrain by adopting a comparative diasporas approach and a transnational framework, expanding beyond the borders of the United States and challenging what she calls "methodological nationalism" in the teaching of ethnic minority literatures. Jodi Eichler-Levine describes comparative approaches to teaching children's and young adult literature by juxtaposing Jewish, African American, Arab American, and Latinx texts in order to examine ideas of intergenerational cultural transmission and intercultural encounters. In addition, Eichler-Levine introduces her students to the critical interpretation of a genre that often evokes emotional reactions rather than analysis. Through close readings of meaning-laden and "ideologically charged" fictional objects, Sasha Senderovich's discussion of teaching contemporary Soviet-born Jewish American authors challenges accepted chronologies of Jewish literature in America (from immigration a century ago to assimilation in the postwar period) and easy dichotomies between the Soviet Union and the United States. Finally, Nadia Mohammed describes teaching *Daispo/Renga*, a poetry volume written collaboratively by the Jewish American poet Marilyn Hacker and the Palestinian American poet Deema K. Shihab, to Iraqi students who are only exposed to Jewishness in literature classrooms through the troubling stereotypes of *The Merchant of Venice* and *Oliver Twist*. In this context, *Daispo/Renga* simultaneously invokes American racial and religious politics, the Israeli-Palestinian conflict, and Iraqi social and political upheavals since 2003 and introduces students to "concepts of racial discrimination, otherness, and gender expectations" through a deliberate strategy of "engaged pedagogy."

Part 3, "Multilingual and Transnational Approaches," includes Ilan Stavans's description of Jews beyond America, an inclusive, multilingual, international course that spans texts from the Bible and Spanish medieval poetry to an Arabic Haggadah, to the television show *Transparent*, and to Jewish salsa music. Considering Jewish literature as world literature, Naomi Sokoloff argues that "Jewish literature, transnational and multilingual as it is, may fit well into curricular frameworks that emphasize translation studies and the global circulation of culture." Sokoloff's pedagogical approach focuses on contemporary American engagements with traditional Jewish prayer, and she characterizes the approach as fruitfully cross-disciplinary in a broadly humanistic context. Hana Wirth-Nesher, in a similarly expansive manner, suggests that "living as a Jew has always meant inhabiting more than one language." She organizes her teaching around what she calls a linguistic approach, examining the traces of other languages and idioms in Jewish American literature as well as translation into and out of English. Continuing the focus on language, Joanna Meadvin and Katharine Trostel have designed a course in Jewish literature at a designated Hispanic-serving institution by exploring themes of exile, diaspora, and trauma through the lens of Ladino—"a language minor to both national and Jewish literary canons." Incorporating texts by Sephardic Jewish immigrants to Latin America as well as contemporary Latin American texts that invoke Ladino, the course culminates in a creative assignment that asks students to plumb their own linguistic histories and resources and write a piece in a language other than (Standard) English. Justin Cammy likewise unsettles both the linguistic and geographic boundaries of Jewish American literature by introducing his students to an immigrant Francophone Jewish novel of Montreal, Regine Robin's *La Québécoite* (translated as *The Wanderer*), using the novel's rich postmodern play and its invocations of French, Canadian, and Yiddish intertexts as an opportunity to interrogate ideas about literary nationalism, linguistic and literary purity, and hybrid, border-crossing identities.

In this volume we challenge what many in the Jewish American world are now terming "Ashke-normativity," articulated by Dalia Kandiyoti in her 2012 essay "What Is the 'Jewish' in 'Jewish American Literature'?" In part 3 of this volume Kandiyoti observes that contemporary Jewish American studies overwhelmingly consists of eastern European or Ashkenazi studies—all other histories, experiences, identifications, and narratives are minoritized. Kandiyoti's contribution thus offers readings of Sephardic literary texts in comparative contexts, arguing for an intervention "not only in Jewish American studies but also in related fields such as Latinx, trans-American, and Arab American studies, in which Jewish, Muslim, and Latinx convergences or common destinies seldom appear."

Part 4, "Gender and Sexuality Approaches," takes up another feature of Jewish American literature in need of revision and expansion, as observed in Daniel Boyarin, Daniel Itzkovitz, and Anne Pellegrini's essay collection *Queer Theory and the Jewish Question*, which explores the "complex of social arrangements and processes through which modern Jewish and homosexual identities emerged as traces of each other" (1). The "long-standing" idea that "Jews embodied non-normative sexual and gender categories" (Boyarin et al. 1) informs the pedagogical approaches of part 4. Many of the contributors in this part also build upon the multicultural, transnational, and multilingual approaches of our earlier sections; for instance, Yaron Peleg analyzes authors from Sholem Aleichem to David Grossman to Philip Roth in an examination of the twentieth-century discourse of Jewish masculinity across eastern Europe, the United States, and Israel. Corinne Blackmer, likewise, puts four key texts by Sholem Asch, Sigmund Freud, Gertrude Stein, and Adrienne Rich into conversation with one another in the context of queer and feminist theory's intersections with Jewishness. Judith Lewin's courses on Jewish women's writing seek to "dislodge" student assumptions about what constitutes Jewish literature while also interrogating recurring intersectional issues in Jewish women's writing. Zohar Weiman-Kelman describes how using Irena Klepfisz's poems invoking Yiddish in her Jewish American literature course at the University of Haifa serves to destabilize notions of language, gender and sexuality, and race. She contends that the course has helped her students—primarily Palestinian citizens of Israel—investigate themes of linguistic and queer struggle and their own theoretical, poetic, and political points of identification and critique. In his teaching of the contemporary feminist Jewish graphic artists Aline Kominsky-Crumb and Diane Noomin, Peter Antelyes models an approach that situates these artists at the historical and cultural intersections of Jews, gender, and comics history and explores issues from "visibility and representation to insider/outsider perspectives to the contested links between Jewishness and feminism." Finally, Linda Schlossberg, when teaching Tony Kushner's *Angels in America* in an LGBTQ literature course, asks students to identify moments that "stage powerful links between 1950s and 1980s America, particularly in terms of cultural anxieties surrounding Jews, queerness, and communism."

Part 5, "Multidisciplinary and Digital Humanities Approaches," highlights the multidisciplinary nature of Jewish American literary studies, particularly classes that focus on innovations in the digital humanities. Jewish cultural and artistic production in America historically has spanned textual, visual, performative, musical, and digital media. Indeed, we argue that Jewish American literature is a particularly rich site for digital humanities approaches, given its profound inter- and multidisciplinarity and the abundance and variety of digitally archived and accessible materials. Judah Cohen uses American musical theater to challenge students to think about the twinned construction of Jewish and African American identities on stage through minstrelsy, impersonation, self-exoticization, and nostalgia, while introducing students to the complexities of the study of performance. Jennifer Caplan designs an interdisciplinary course in Jewish American humor, one that she describes as an ever-dynamic experience, given the constant rate at which new material is emerging in this multimedia field.

Laini Kavaloski's course Digital Jews examines the transnational context of contemporary Jewish cultural production (including fiction but extending to museums, blogs, Web sites, and other cultural forms), eventually asking students to create their own digital media platforms, based on their readings, as tools for critical analysis, writing, literary exploration, and game design. Temma Berg's examination of legends of the golem draws students from the English department, Judaic studies, and women, gender, and sexuality studies, as the course readings range from medieval legend through contemporary science fiction. Berg charges students with writing their own midrash (adaptation or interpretation) of the golem story, which she argues is an unusually resilient and flexible signifier. Mindful of what other scholars have identified as "Holocaust fatigue" in today's students, Jennifer Lemberg focuses on contemporary Jewish American narratives of post-Holocaust return in relation to other narratives of return (such as those of war veterans and those of the repatriation of Native artifacts and bodies). "Jewish American narratives dedicated to mapping geographical and temporal distances," writes Lemberg, "offer insights into this 'paradigm' that may be useful in examining the memory work of other communities, and, conversely, attending to the presence of returns in other literatures deepens our understanding of Jewish American texts."

Part 6, "New Approaches and Key Texts," is organized around pedagogical approaches to a few key authors and texts: Abraham Cahan's *Yekl*, Israel Zangwill's *The Melting Pot*, Anzia Yezierska's *Bread Givers*, and Philip Roth's "Goodbye, Columbus." While several of our sections move from broad historical and theoretical reflections to considerations of single texts or clusters of texts, the literature analyzed in this part represents some of the most frequently taught and anthologized works of Jewish American literature. However, we by no means intend to argue that these are the most exemplary or canonical or key texts in the field. For instance, the film *The Jazz Singer*, Henry Roth's *Call It Sleep*, Bernard Malamud's *The Magic Barrel* and *The Tenants*, and Art Spiegelman's *Maus I* and *II*, among others, certainly could have been included as key Jewish American literary texts. Indeed, the four texts we chose to focus on can be said to reinscribe the conventional, "Ashke-normative" narrative of eastern European immigration, Lower East Side poverty, Americanization, upward mobility, and assimilation that so many of our contributors seek to complicate and revise in their teaching. For this reason, we feature a multiplicity of approaches to each text: the primary aim of this part is not to privilege a few texts but rather to model how a single text can be opened up to reveal complex historical, theoretical, and pedagogical possibilities, in universities in the United States and abroad. Thus, John Wharton Lowe describes his teaching of *Yekl* in relation to realism, naturalism, regionalism, narratives of self-invention, and American humor. Karen Skinazi and Lori Harrison-Kahan describe how they each teach *The Melting Pot* in relation to broader national tropes of the melting pot and to other texts about race and ethnicity. Judy Phagan, Sarah Gleeson-White, Lucas Thompson, and Catherine Rottenberg examine Yezierska's *Bread Givers* in illuminating comparisons with other immigration narratives, Yezierska's own later work, such canonical works as *The Great Gatsby*, and other works of world literature. Josh Lambert introduces a discussion among Rachel Gordan, Benjamin Schreier, Bettina Hoffman, and Julian Levinson on Philip Roth's novella "Goodbye, Columbus," the title story in the author's National Book Award–winning debut, in different disciplinary contexts: history, sociology, religion, literature, and film. Schreier reflects on the versatility of the text and its usefulness in a variety of contexts, Gordan suggests how the text can be used to inform the study of the social and religious history of the American 1950s, Hoffmann describes her use of the text in an American studies program in Germany, and Levinson explains how showing a scene from the end of the 1969 film adaptation can enrich students' understandings of the novella.

Two decades ago, an introductory university course in Jewish American literature might have looked like the following: The semester would begin with Abraham Cahan's *Yekl* and Emma Lazarus's poem "The New Colossus," then continue with Mary Antin's *Promised Land* and Anzia Yezierska's *Bread Givers*. The 1930s would be analyzed through, perhaps, Henry Roth's *Call It Sleep* and Michael Gold's *Jews without Money*, while Philip Roth, Bernard Malamud, and Saul Bellow would represent the postwar period. The twentieth century would be rounded out with an examination of Holocaust memory and fiction in Cynthia Ozick's *The Shawl* and Art Spiegelman's *Maus I* and *II.* For many of us who continued to study in the field, courses like this one served as the gateways to a rich and revelatory literature. As the contributors to this volume demonstrate, however, the possibilities for the classroom in the twenty-first century are now even broader and more varied. The goal of this volume is to present an expanded perspective on teaching Jewish American literature, one that both appreciates and illustrates the deep history and linguistic and ethnic variety of a literature influenced by diverse cultures as Jews have migrated around the world.

Finally, we are respectful of many of the traditional themes and common preoccupations discernible in a literature written by what Hana Wirth-Nesher describes as a "transnational people . . . a people who shared religion, kinship, language, history, and/or a repertoire of texts" ("Introduction" 9). In seeking a balance between these approaches to teaching Jewish American literature, we hope to cultivate "new literary voice[s], telling a story that has not yet been told" or heard in the academy (Lambert, "Since 2000" 636). With this volume, we look to contribute to the ongoing development of Jewish American literary practice both in and outside the classroom.

Works Cited

Aarons, Victoria, et al., editors. *The New Diaspora: The Changing Landscape of American Jewish Fiction.* Wayne State UP, 2015.

Antin, Mary. *The Promised Land.* Houghton Mifflin, 1912.

Astro, Alan, editor. *Yiddish South of the Border: An Anthology of Latin American Yiddish Writing.* U of New Mexico P, 2003.

Berger, Alan L. *Crisis and Covenant: The Holocaust in American Jewish Fiction.* State U of New York P, 1985.

Berger, Alan L., and Gloria L. Cronin. *Jewish American and Holocaust Literature: Representation in the Postmodern World.* State U of New York P, 2004.

Biale, David. "The Melting Pot and Beyond." Biale et al., pp. 17–33.

Biale, David, et al., editors. *Insider/Outsider: American Jews and Multiculturalism.* U of California P, 1998. ✓

Boyarin, Daniel, et al., editors. *Queer Theory and the Jewish Question.* Columbia UP, 2003.

Brodkin, Karen. *How Jews Became White Folks and What That Says about Race in America.* Rutgers UP, 1998.

Budick, Emily. "The Ghost of the Holocaust in the Construction of Jewish American Literature." Wirth-Nesher, *Cambridge History*, pp. 343–61.

———. "The Holocaust in the Jewish American Literary Imagination." Wirth-Nesher and Kramer, pp. 212–30.

Cahan, Abraham. *Yekl: A Tale of the New York Ghetto.* D. Appleton, 1896.

Casteel, Sarah Phillips. "Landscapes: America and the Americas." Wirth-Nesher, *Cambridge History*, pp. 413–31.

Flanzbaum, Hilene. "Reflections on Editing: *Jewish American Literature: A Norton Anthology.*" *The Massachusetts Review*, vol. 44, nos. 1–2, Spring–Summer 2003, pp. 63–69.

Franco, Dean. "Teaching Jewish American Literature as Global Ethnic American Literature." Harrison-Kahan and Lambert, pp. 183–84.

Freedman, Jonathan. *Klezmer America: Jewishness, Ethnicity, Modernity.* Columbia UP, 2008.

Giles, Paul. "Transnationalism and Classic American Literature." *PMLA*, vol. 118, no. 1, Jan. 2003, pp. 62–77.

Glaser, Jennifer. "Review Essay: The Politics of Difference and the Future(s) of American Jewish Literary Studies." *Prooftexts*, vol. 29, no. 3, Fall 2009, pp. 474–84.

Gold, Michael. *Jews without Money.* Horace Liveright, 1930.

Goldstein, Eric. *The Price of Whiteness: Jews, Race, and American Identity.* Princeton UP, 2008.

Grauer, Tresa. "Identity Matters: Contemporary Jewish American Writing." Wirth-Nesher and Kramer, pp. 269–84.

Harrison-Kahan, Lori, and Josh Lambert, editors. *The Future of Jewish American Literary Studies.* Special issue of *MELUS*, vol. 27, no. 2, Summer 2012.

Heschel, Susannah. "Jewish Studies as Counterhistory." Biale et al., pp. 101–15.

Hollinger, David. *Postethnic America.* Basic Books, 1995.

Howe, Irving, editor. *Jewish-American Stories.* New American Library, 1977.

Jaschik, Scott. "The Lost Tribe." *Inside Higher Education*, 28 Dec. 2009, www.insidehighered.com/news/2009/12/28/lost-tribe.

The Jazz Singer. Directed by Alan Crosland, adapted by Alfred A. Cohn, and starring Al Jolson. Warner Bros. Pictures, 1927.

Kandiyoti, Dalia. "What Is the 'Jewish' in 'Jewish American Literature'?" *Studies in American Jewish Literature*, vol. 31, no. 1, Spring 2012, pp. 48–60.

Katz, Stephen. *Red, Black and Jew: New Frontiers in Hebrew Literature.* U of Texas P, 2009.

Klein, Misha. "Teaching about Jewishness in the Heartland." *Shofar: An Interdisciplinary Journal of Jewish Studies*, vol. 32, no. 4, Summer 2014, pp. 89–104.

Lambert, Josh, participant. "Does the English Department Have a Jewish Problem?" Special session. MLA Annual Convention, 27 Dec. 2009, Philadelphia Marriott.

———. "Since 2000." Wirth-Nesher, *Cambridge History*, pp. 622–41.

Lauter, Paul et. al., editors. *The Heath Anthology of American Literature.* 7th ed., Wadsworth Publishing, 2013. 5 vols.

Lazarus, Emma. "The New Colossus." *The Heath Anthology of American Literature*, edited by Paul Lauter et al., 7th ed., vol. C, p. 834.

Levinson, Julian. *Exiles on Main Street: Jewish American Writers and American Literary Culture.* Indiana UP, 2008.

Magid, Shaul. *American Post-Judaism: Identity and Renewal in a Postethnic Society.* Indiana UP, 2013.

Malamud, Bernard. *The Magic Barrel.* Farrar, Straus and Giroux, 1958.

———. *The Tenants.* Farrar, Straus and Giroux, 1971.

Margolis, Rebecca. "Yiddish Translation in Canada: A Litmus Test of Continuity." *TTR: Traduction, terminologie et redaction,* vol. 19, no. 2, January 2006, pp. 149–89.

Meyers, Helene. "Reading Jewishness as a Marker of Ethno-racial and Cultural History." Harrison-Kahan and Lambert, pp. 185–86.

Mintz, Alan. *A Sanctuary in the Wilderness: A Critical Introduction to American Hebrew Poetry.* Stanford UP, 2011.

Morris, Leslie. "Placing and Displacing Jewish Studies: Notes on the Future of a Field." *PMLA,* vol. 125, no. 3, pp. 764–66.

Ozick, Cynthia. *The Shawl.* Reprint ed., Vintage Books, 1990.

Pease, Donald E. "How Transnationalism Reconfigured the Field of American Studies: The Transnational/Diaspora Complex." *American Studies as Transnational Practice,* edited by Pease and Yuan Shu, Dartmouth College P, 2015, pp. 39–63.

Rogin, Michael. *Blackface, White Noise: Jewish Immigrants in the Hollywood Melting Pot.* U of California Press, 1996.

Roth, Henry. *Call It Sleep.* Robert O. Ballou, 1934.

Roth, Philip. *"Goodbye Columbus" and Five Short Stories.* Modern Library, 1966.

Rubinstein, Rachel. "Is Yiddish Literature the Next Big Thing?" *The Forward,* 10 Dec. 2010, forward.com/culture/133698/is-yiddish-literature-the-next-big-thing/.

———. "Not Just 'White Folks': Teaching Jewish American Literature as Multi-ethnic and Multiracial." Harrison-Kahan and Lambert, pp. 180–82.

Schreier, Benjamin. "The Failure of Identity: Toward a New Literary History of Philip Roth's Unrecognizable Jew." *Jewish Social Studies,* vol. 17, no. 2, Winter 2011, pp. 101–35.

———. *The Impossible Jew: Identity and the Reconstruction of Jewish American Literary History.* New York UP, 2015.

Shell, Marc, and Werner Sollors, editors. *Multilingual Anthology of American Literature: A Reader of Original Texts with English Translations.* New York UP, 2000.

Spiegelman, Art. *Maus I: A Survivor's Tale: My Father Bleeds History.* Pantheon Books, 1986.

———. *Maus II: A Survivor's Tale: And Here My Troubles Began.* Pantheon Books, 1991.

Weingrad, Michael. *American Hebrew Literature: Writing Jewish National Identity in the United States.* Syracuse UP, 2011.

———, editor and translator. *Letters to America: Selected Poems of Reuven Ben-Yosef.* Syracuse UP, 2015.

Wirth-Nesher, Hana, editor. *The Cambridge History of Jewish American Literature.* Cambridge UP, 2016.

Wirth-Nesher, Hana, and Michael P. Kramer, editors. *The Cambridge Companion to Jewish American Literature.* Cambridge UP, 2003.

————. "Introduction: Jewish American Literatures in the Making." Wirth-Nesher and Kramer, pp. 1–18.

Wolosky, Shira. "On Contemporary Literary Theory and Jewish American Poetics." Wirth-Nesher and Kramer, pp. 250–68.

Yezierska, Anzia. *Bread Givers*. Doubleday Page, 1925.

Zangwill, Israel. *The Melting-Pot: Drama in Four Acts*. Macmillan, 1910.

Part I

Reframing Jewish American Histories, Rethinking Canons

Laura Arnold Leibman

Using Early Jewish American
Literature to Teach about Race

As the Dutch battled the Portuguese for control of Recife in the 1640s
and 1650s, Rabbi Isaac Aboab da Fonseca watched his more than fifteen
hundred congregants wither from hunger and disease. Yet rather than de-
spairing at the sight of the Brazilian community's suffering, Aboab wrote
a poem praising God and comparing the Portuguese attackers to Haman
from the story of Esther (Leibman 36, 40–44). Aboab also racialized the
dispute, disparaging the Portuguese leader as an "evil man" whose "mother
was of Negro descent, a man who did not know his father's name"
(Schorsch, "American Jewish Historians" 113).

Aboab was not alone in tangling his experience in the early American
colonies with race. Students encountering early Jewish American literature
through the lens of *Jewish American Literature: A Norton Anthology* may
easily get the misimpression that Jews' whiteness was self-evident prior to
the United States Civil War. Yet studying early America complicates this
understanding of Jews and race. In some colonies—such as Suriname—
multiracial Jews made up as much as ten percent of the Jewish community.
In other locations, even European Jews fell between the racial categories
of white and black (Ben-Ur and Roitman 205; Snyder 154, 159). Moreover,
Euro-American Jews often posited their whiteness vis-à-vis multiracial Jews

and racialized others. Studying Jews and race in early Jewish American literature, therefore, can help students understand the shifting nature of race in American literary history.

This essay provides an alternative way to begin Jewish American literature classes, one that focuses more on Jews and race. It includes resources for three class sessions that move from the early colonial era to the early nineteenth century and focus on three intertwined questions: What is a Jew? What did race mean to early Americans? What makes this American literature? The lessons underscore how understandings of Jews and race have changed over time.

The lessons employ a dialogical approach designed to raise questions rather than answer them. As Paulo Freire notes, active models of education rely on dialogue, since "[w]ithout dialogue there is no communication and without communication there can be no true education" (qtd. in Perry 109). To encourage students to ask questions, each lesson contains texts and images with conflicting perspectives. The works are juxtaposed in order to open debate: they are what Freire refers to as problem posing (79–80; Perry 109–10). To take a problem-posing approach to early Jewish American literature, I recommend three dialogues: one on the Inquisition, one on Jews and slavery, and one on Jews and the body politic.

Dialogue 1: Out of the Inquisition's Flames

Jewish American Literature: A Norton Anthology is one of the few collections of Jewish American literature that take readers from the colonial era to the present. Hence the anthology is a popular choice for course assignments. The collection begins with a 1656 petition requesting rights for Jews in New Amsterdam, later New York (Chametzky 24–25). Diane Matza's *Sephardic-American Voices* similarly begins the journey of American literature in the United States with an early-nineteenth-century text from Charleston, South Carolina. Instead of these anthologies, I recommend beginning with earlier texts that address the Spanish colonies and the Inquisition. The critic Dalia Kandiyoti argues that scholars limit Jewish American studies when they envision "America" as ending at the border of the United States (50–51). Beginning the study of Jewish American literature with the writings of the conversos (forced converts and their descendants) in New Spain immerses students in key questions about who and what is an American Jew and how race was understood differently in the colonies than it is today. Early American Jews used literary forms to understand traumatic events such as imprisonment, torture, and death by burning. For classes that continue up through the postmodern era, these early literary representations of trauma can be usefully compared to later writings on the Holocaust.

This first lesson places two texts and three images in dialogue. The texts are the spiritual autobiography, or *Vida* (life), of Luis de Carvajal the Younger (1595) and Miguel de Barrios's "Sonnet for Tomás Tremiño de Sobremonte" (1683–84).[1] Carvajal's and de Barrios's works are read alongside three images: Francisco Rizi's *Auto-da-fé in the Plaza Mayor of Madrid* (1683) and photographs of the gravestone of Elijah Nahamias de Crasto (1692) and that of Abraham and Isaac Senior (1727).

Carvajal's *Vida*, de Barrios's sonnet, and the accompanying images start a dialogue about Jewishness. Irving Zeitlin and others have argued that it was only when Jews were granted emancipation starting in the 1790s that Christians in Europe generally began to conceptualize Jews as "an anthropologically inferior 'race'" rather than a "religious despised caste" (179). But the Inquisition's understanding of Jewish difference held that even descendants of converted Jews remained tainted by their Jewish ancestry for generations (Schorsch, *Swimming* 5–6, 467). Judaism remained in the blood of these descendents regardless of their beliefs or status as Jews according to Jewish law. This understanding of Jewish difference as an "immutable essentialist characteristic" makes the Inquisition a crucial step in the history of race making (Rodrigue 195).

The first dialogue suggests that there is no easy answer to who and what is a Jew. Is anyone with any Jewish blood considered Jewish? Does behavior or belief make a person Jewish? Reading Carvajal's text prompts students to think about who gets to decide what constitutes Jewishness. Some conversos arrested by the Inquisition self-identified as devout Catholics. Yet as Carvajal's *Vida* makes clear, even members of the writer's own family are "blind" to the Jewish religion (59).[2] When people today call all conversos who were imprisoned by the Inquisition "Jews," they are using the Inquisition's definition and evidence.

Rizi's *Auto-da-fé* helps students visualize how the Inquisition publicly defined Jewishness on behalf of those convicted and question what it means to use sources that were extracted from people during or following torture. Rizi's painting depicts the ritual public penance of condemned heretics in Madrid's Plaza Mayor. Most of the condemned were descendants of Jews who had been forced to convert to Catholicism. The painting positions the viewer as an "observer in an imaginary balcony," overlooking the scene and facing King Charles II and his court, thereby giving the viewer "a kind of parallel authority over the proceedings" (Rawlings 3). The painting thus encourages students to think about their own role as participants in history making.

De Barrios's poem, published the same year as Rizi's painting was made, reveals how Jews used literature to understand oppression. Although based mainly in Amsterdam, de Barrios also lived in the Caribbean. Discussion of him can be used to raise the question, What makes someone an American author? Moreover, throughout his life de Barrios floated between New Christian and Jewish identities. His elegy for Tomás Treviño de Sobremonte, a New Christian burnt at the stake in Mexico City in 1649, reclaims Spanish baroque poetics to highlight Jews' crucial role in redemption.

De Barrios's poem tells the story of Treviño's imprisonment and subsequent execution in an auto-da-fé. Throughout the poem, de Barrios compares Treviño to the biblical figures of Job, Isaac, and Elijah. Like Isaac when he is bound (in the Akeidah scene; *Jewish Study Bible*, Gen. 22:1–19), Treviño faces his fate unafraid and even brings the wood for the sacrifice. De Barrios's comparison of Treviño to Isaac would have resonated with Jews in Amsterdam and in the Dutch colonies, as the Akeidah scene was one of the most popular biblical motifs on Jewish gravestones in the Dutch-speaking world during this era (fig. 1).

In his final lines de Barrios compares Treviño to the prophet Elijah, who ascends to heaven in a chariot of fire. As in 2 Kings 2:11–13, a mantle falls to the ground behind Treviño as a "cloak of dust" that coats the earth. De Barrios transforms the ashes of Treviño's body from a symbol of despair into Elijah's cloak, a symbol of redemption for the next generation. Jewish gravestones depicting Elijah use the same biblical allusions as de Barrios's poem. Gravestones like that of Elijah Nahamias de Crasto help students visualize biblical stories, and reveal how de Barrios's contemporaries interpreted their own struggles (fig. 2). By using poetry to bear witness to trauma, de Barrios provides an important antecedent to Emma Lazarus's poem "1492," as well as to later Jewish American poets writing about the Holocaust, such as Philip Levine ("On a Drawing," "The Survivor"), Denise Levertov ("From 'During the Eichmann Trial'"), and Anthony Hecht ("It," "More Light"). De Barrios's invocation of the Inquisition as a site of trauma and identity creation connects his work to later non-Jewish Caribbean writers who use the trope of 1492 to mark not only the Jews' expulsion from Spain but also the "onset of European colonization" of the Americas (Casteel 10–12).

Figure I. Gravestone of Abraham and Isaac Senior; 1727, Beit Haim Cemetery, Ouderkerk aan de Amstel, Netherlands; photographed by Laura Arnold Leibman, 2012. Courtesy of the *Jewish Atlantic World Database*.

Figure 2. Gravestone of Elijah Nahamias de Crasto; 1692, Beit Haim Cemetery, Blenheim, Curaçao; photographed by Laura Arnold Leibman, 2012. Courtesy of the *Jewish Atlantic World Database*.

Dialogue 2: Jews and Slavery

The second dialogue comes from the late eighteenth century and shifts students' attention to the Caribbean, where before the 1820s most Jews in the Americas lived. The dialogue continues questioning Jewish American geography and tackles one of the most controversial subjects in early Jewish American studies: slavery. Jews' relation to the slave trade was hotly debated in the 1990s and became a central feature in Jewish and black tensions during that decade. In this lesson students compare

Figure 3. Pierre Jacques Benoit; *Voyage à Surinam*; Société des Beaux-Arts, 1839. Courtesy of the John Carter Brown Library at Brown University, https://jcb.lunaimaging.com/luna/servlet.

Jewish and non-Jewish representations of Jewish slavery using, respectively, David Cohen Nassy's 1788 *Essai historique sur la colonie de Surinam (Historical Essay on the Colony of Surinam)* and John Gabriel Stedman's *Narrative, of a Five Years' Expedition against the Revolted Negroes of Surinam* (1795).[3] The two texts come from Dutch Suriname, home to the second largest Jewish community in early America. The texts are complemented by two visual sources about Jews and race in the early Caribbean: Pierre Jacques Benoit's *Jewish Shopkeeper from Suriname* (fig. 3), and the Jewish Jamaican artist Isaac Mendes Belisario's "Koo, Koo, or Actor-Boy" (fig. 4).

Stedman's and Nassy's texts provide overlapping but often conflicting visions of Jews and race in Suriname. Slavery was particularly brutal in Suriname, yet the colony was also home to the first Afro-Jewish prayer group in the Americas. For Stedman, Jews epitomize slavery's evils: Jews are particularly cruel masters and play an active role in the suppression of Maroons, descendants of runaway slaves (56, 66, 322). Whereas Stedman was a British mercenary working for hire in the Dutch colony, Nassy came from an influential Jewish Surinamese family and hence portrays Jewish

Figure 4. Isaac Mendes Belisario; "Koo, Koo, or Actor-Boy"; from *Sketches of Character in Illustration of the Habits, Occupation and Costume of the Negro Population in the Island of Jamaica,* 1837–38. Courtesy of the British Museum, 2006,0929.48.

life differently from Stedman. Surinamese Jews are ideal Dutch citizens who suffered persecution by the Spanish and experienced prejudice in Suriname: even slaves insulted Jews by calling them "*Smous*" (Nassy 104). Nassy provides a complicated perspective on relationships between European and multiracial Jews in the colony, particularly conflicts with the Afro-Jewish prayer group, of which his son was a leader. Taken together, the texts help students delve further into eighteenth-century debates about race and what constitutes a Jew. The readings from Suriname clarify that some colonial Jews were multiracial.

Both Stedman and Nassy racialize Jews vis-à-vis people with African ancestry. Benoit's and Belisario's images underscore Jews' precarious connection to whiteness. In *Voyage à Surinam*, Benoit always places Jews in the context of other nonwhite peoples. In his depiction of the shopkeeper Isak Abraham Levy, Benoit uses gestures to draw visual parallels between Jews and monkeys, Amerindians, and people of African descent. These parallels underscore Jews' place in the colony's racial hierarchies.

The Jewish Jamaican artist Isaac Mendes Belisario is more ambivalent about the relationship between Jews and people of African ancestry. "Koo, Koo, or Actor-Boy" is taken from his collection *Sketches of Character* (1837–38). The vibrant print depicts a scene from the Junkanoo celebration, a festival in which slaves and former slaves parodied whites. *Sketches of Character* was published on the eve of emancipation in Jamaica, when both Jewish men and free men of color were about to achieve the right to vote and partake in government. Behind Actor-Boy's head is a sign for the store of "M. Q. Henriques," a prominent Sephardic shopkeeper in Kingston. Scholars have hotly debated whether Belisario's famous lithographs reinforce or subvert the racial divide in the colony. Students can engage in this debate using evidence from the image, analyzing the ways in which Jews were objects and subjects of race making in the colonies. Thinking about race making as something done both to and by Jews helps students move beyond seeing Jews as solely victims or oppressors.

Stedman's and Nassy's texts also help students question what makes something literature. Although written as historical accounts, these texts benefit from literary analysis, particularly a discussion of narrators and narration. Archival research has found no basis for the stereotype that Surinamese Jews were the cruelest slave owners (Stedman 322; Hoogbergen 37–38). If students had only these two primary texts, would they reach the same conclusion? It is worth asking students which narrator they find more reliable, Stedman or Nassy, and why. Students sometimes find

Stedman's discussion of the traumatic violence of slavery disconcerting: Stedman places graphic depictions of atrocities beside mundane descriptions of flora and fauna. Why does Stedman treat traumatic events so differently from Nassy's treatment of them?

Dialogue 3: Jews and the Body Politic

The third dialogue centers on national dramas in nineteenth-century New York and Philadelphia. During the 1790s to 1830s, Jews throughout the Americas sought political emancipation, including the rights to vote and to hold public office. Even as emancipation promised Jewish political equality, non-Jewish artists, writers, and thinkers increasingly depicted early American Jews as inherently different. Indeed, during the emancipation era, race and gender were increasingly seen as located in Jews' physical bodies rather than in their religious practices. Early Jewish American writers engaged with these new embodied messages of Jewishness through their literary works. To better understand this newly embodied Jewishness and Jews' response to it, students read two emancipation-era American plays that think about Jews, race, and the body politic: one play by Susanna Rowson, a non-Jewish playwright who lived in the United States, and the other by the Jewish playwright Mordecai Manuel Noah. The plays are read alongside images from the Barbary Wars and a depiction of a female soldier from the era.

Rowson's play *Slaves in Algiers* (1794) reveals early concerns in the United States about including Jews in the body politic. The play features three women enslaved in North Africa during tensions leading up to the Barbary Wars (1801–05 and 1815–16): one Christian, one Jew, and one Muslim. Throughout the play, Jews serve as foils to Christian virtue, and Rowson repeatedly suggests Judaism runs counter to the national spirit of the United States. Images from the University of Michigan's exhibit *The Barbary Wars at the Clements* reveal how Rowson's stereotypes were part of a larger pattern of depicting non-Christians as barbarous enemies who threatened the new nation.

Noah's *She Would Be a Soldier; or, The Plains of Chippewa: An Historical Drama in Three Acts* (1819) similarly uses the oppression of women to talk about the body politic of the United States.[4] Noah aimed to highlight the virtues of American men in his "national play." Set during the Battle of Chippewa (1814), Noah's play crosses boundaries through cultural and gendered cross-dressing, and critics have hotly debated why Noah uses the cross-dressing motif. Is his intent to call "into question all national boundaries and power relations" (Kleinman 211)? Or does Noah use the motif to solidify existing categories of manhood and race?

To understand how cross-dressing might reinforce gender binaries, students examine Thomas Rowlandson's satirical print *She Will Be a Soldier*, of 1798 (fig. 5). The female soldier was a popular motif during this era, and people born biologically female did successfully present as men and serve as soldiers during both the French and American Revolutions. Men's depictions of cross-dressing or transgender soldiers, however, often portray the figures as inherently female and with hats that ineffectively disguise them as men. Rowlandson's drawings reinforce the point that early depictions of gender crossing were not inherently subversive. Since Noah depicts the British disguised as Native Americans, students might also ponder whether Noah's drama questions or reinforces racial categories. These questions will remind students of the questions raised by Belisario's "Koo, Koo, or Actor-Boy"; for instance, the actual Junkanoo celebration satirizes whites, but is Belisario's depiction equally satirical?

Figure 5. Thomas Rowlandson; *She Will Be a Soldier*; 1798. Courtesy of the British Museum, 1878,0713.2777.

Students may notice that no Jews appear in Noah's play. Early Jewish American playwrights often avoided explicitly Jewish themes and characters. Students should be pushed to consider why. Is it important for Jewish American literature to have Jewish characters or themes? In considering this question, students once again question who counts as a Jew and what counts as Jewish authorship and as Jewish American literature.

This essay proposes that teachers can more effectively teach about early American Jews and race by placing early Jewish American literature in dialogue with other textual and visual representations of Jews from the era. Adding Jews to the discussion changes how we teach religion and the canon of early American literature. While scholars have examined at length how Puritans envisioned themselves as "the New Israelites," early American scholarship has tended to neglect writings by actual Jews.[5] Early Jewish American literature—like literature by early Muslim Americans—destabilizes the notion that Christianity is the only truly American religion, and disputes the idea that non-Christian religions were brought to North America solely by recent immigrants.

A dialogic approach to writings by early American Jews also enhances our understanding of Jewish American literary history by undermining the equation of Jewishness with either Ashkenazi Jews or whiteness. Today multiracial Jews make up twelve percent of Jewry in the United States, with nearly 87,000 nonwhite, Hispanic, or multiracial Jewish households in the New York area alone (UJA-Federation of New York 2). Texts by early Sephardic American and multiracial Jewish authors and early dialogues by Jews and non-Jews about Jews and slavery likewise provide an important precursor to discussions about tensions between Jews and blacks in the twentieth century. Nassy's historical essay, which talks about the first Afro-Jewish prayer group in the Americas, further reminds students that, even in the colonial era, *Jewish* and *white* were not synonyms. Early American dialogues about the Inquisition, slavery, and the body politic help students see that contemporary questions about Jews, race, and national identity are part of an ongoing conversation.

Notes

1. Seymour Liebman refers to the *Vida* as Carvajal's "memoirs" (see Carvajal). For a copy and translation of de Barrios's poem, see Leibman 46–47.

2. For a history of the criticism of Carvajal's text as well as an astute analysis of the theme of Jewish identity, see Ronnie Perelis's "Blood and Spirit" and *Narratives from the Sephardic Atlantic*.

3. In addition to paperback editions, *Narrative, of a Five Years' Expedition against the Revolted Negroes of Surinam* can be found online at the *Internet Archive*, archive.org/details/narrativeoffivey01sted/page/n6. Relevant selections are also in Hoberman et al. 390–93.

4. Relevant selections can be found in Hoberman et al. 406–14.

5. For Puritans' self-fashioning as New Israelites, see Conforti 45.

Works Cited

The Barbary Wars at the Clements. William L. Clements Library, University of Michigan, clements.umich.edu/exhibits/online/barbary/barbary-introduction.php. Accessed 25 May 2017.

Ben-Ur, Aviva, and Jessica V. Roitman. "Adultery Here and There: Crossing Sexual Boundaries in the Dutch Jewish Atlantic." *Dutch Atlantic Connections, 1680–1800*, edited by Gert Oostindie and Jessica V. Roitman, Brill, 2014, pp. 185–223.

Carvajal, Luis de the Younger. "Memoirs." *The Enlightened: The Writings of Luis de Carvajal, el Mozo*, edited and translated by Seymour B. Liebman, U of Miami P, 1967, pp. 55–84.

Casteel, Sarah Phillips. *Calypso Jews: Jewishness in the Caribbean Literary Imagination*. Columbia UP, 2016.

Chametzky, Jules. *Jewish American Literature: A Norton Anthology*. W. W. Norton, 2001.

Conforti, Joseph A. *Imagining New England Explorations of Regional Identity from the Pilgrims to the Mid-Twentieth Century*. U of North Carolina P, 2001.

Fishman, Charles, editor. *Blood to Remember: American Poets on the Holocaust*. Time Being Books, 2007.

Freire, Paulo. *Pedagogy of the Oppressed*. Translated by Myra Bergman Ramos, 30th anniversary ed., Continuum International Publishing, 2000.

Hecht, Anthony. "It Out-Herods Herod. Pray You, Avoid It." Fishman, p. 171.

———. "More Light! More Light!" Fishman, p. 172.

Hoberman, Michael, et al., editors. *Jews in the Americas: 1776–1826*. Routledge, 2017.

Hoogbergen, Wilhelmus S. *De Boni-Oorlogen: 1757–1860*. Centrum voor Caraïbische Studies, 1985.

The Jewish Study Bible: Featuring the Jewish Publication Society Tanakh Translation. Edited by Adele Berlin, Marc Z. Brettler, and Michael Fishbane, Oxford UP, 2004.

Kandiyoti, Dalia. "What Is the 'Jewish' in 'Jewish American Literature'?" *Studies in American Jewish Literature*, vol. 31, no. 1, 2012, pp. 48–60.

Kleinman, Craig. "Pigging the Nation, Staging the Jew in M. M. Noah's *She Would Be a Soldier*." *American Transcendental Quarterly*, vol. 10, no. 3, 1996, pp. 201–19.

Leibman, Laura Arnold. "Poetics of the Apocalypse: Messianism in Early Jewish American Poetry." *Studies in American Jewish Literature*, vol. 33, no. 1, 2014, pp. 35–62.

Levertov, Denise. "From 'During the Eichmann Trial.'" Fishman, pp. 273–76.

Levine, Philip. "On a Drawing by Flavio." Fishman, p. 277.

———. "The Survivor." Fishman, p. 278.

Matza, Diane, editor. *Sephardic-American Voices: Two Hundred Years of Literary Legacy.* Brandeis UP, 1996.

Nassy, David Cohen. *Historical Essay on the Colony of Surinam, 1788.* Translated by Simon Cohen, edited by Jacob R. Marcus and Stanley F. Chyet, American Jewish Archives, 1974.

Noah, Mordecai Manuel. *She Would Be a Soldier; or, The Plains of Chippewa: An Historical Drama in Three Acts: Performed for the First Time on the Twenty-First of June, 1819.* Longworth's Dramatic Repository, 1819. 2nd series, no. 48940, Early American Imprints. *Internet Archive,* www.archive.org /stream/shewouldbeasoldi29231gut/29231.txt.

Perelis, Ronnie. "Blood and Spirit: Paternity, Fraternity and Religious Self-Fashioning in Luis de Carvajal's Spiritual Autobiography." *Estudios interdisciplinarios de América Latina y el Caribe,* vol. 23, no. 1, 2012, pp. 77–98.

———. *Narratives from the Sephardic Atlantic: Blood and Faith.* Indiana UP, 2016. Indiana Series in Sephardi and Mizrahi Studies.

Perry, Patricia H. *A Composition of Counterpoints: Roads of Reflection from Freire to Elbow.* Peter Lang, 2000.

Rawlings, Helen. "Representational Strategies of Inclusion and Exclusion in José del Olmo's Narrative and Francisco Rizi's Visual Record of the Madrid *Auto de Fe* of 1680." *Romance Studies,* vol. 29, no. 4, 2013, pp. 223–41.

Rizi, Francisco. *Auto-da-fé in the Plaza Mayor of Madrid.* 1683. Museo Nacional del Prado, Madrid, www.museodelprado.es/en/the-collection/art -work/auto-da-fe-in-the-plaza-mayor-of-madrid/8d92af03-3183-473a-9997 -d9cbf2557462.

Rodrigue, Aron. "The Jew as the Original 'Other.'" *Doing Race: Twenty-One Essays for the Twenty-First Century,* edited by Hazel Markus and Pula Moya, W. W. Norton, 2010, pp. 187–98.

Rowson, Susanna. *Slaves in Algiers; or, A Struggle for Freedom: A Play, Interspersed with Songs, in Three Acts.* Wrigley and Berriman, 1794. Early American Imprint Collection, Text Creation Partnership, 2003–05, name.umdl.umich.edu /N21056.0001.001.

Schorsch, Jonathan. "American Jewish Historians, Colonial Jews and Blacks, and the Limits of 'Wissenschaft': A Critical Review." *Jewish Social Studies,* vol. 6, no. 2, 2000, pp. 102–32.

———. *Swimming the Christian Atlantic: Judeoconversos, Afroiberians and Amerindians in the Seventeenth Century.* Brill, 2009.

Snyder, Holly. "Customs of an Unruly Race: The Political Context of Jamaica Jewry, 1670–1831." *Art and Emancipation in Jamaica: Isaac Mendes Belisario and His Worlds,* edited by T. J. Barringer et al., Yale UP, 2007, pp. 151–61.

Stedman, John Gabriel. *Stedman's Surinam: Life in an Eighteenth-Century Slave Society: An Abridged, Modernized Edition of Narrative of a Five Years Expedition against the Revolted Negroes of Surinam.* Edited by Richard Price and Sally Price, Johns Hopkins UP, 2013.

UJA-Federation of New York. *Special Study on Nonwhite, Hispanic, and Multiracial Jewish Households.* Berman Jewish Databank, June 2014.

Zeitlin, Irving M. *Jews: The Making of a Diaspora People.* Polity Press, 2010.

Louis Gordon

Expanding the Jewish American Literary Canon for Hebrew Day School Students

Teachers of Jewish American literature will invariably encounter students who do not identify with the Jewish American experience as a flight from traditional Judaism toward a more universal existence. Indeed, students from more traditional homes or a Hebrew day school background may find that this dominant narrative does not capture their own experiences or perspectives on Jewish life. This is not necessarily a recent phenomenon but one rooted in the historical divide between adherents of the Haskalah, a Jewish enlightenment movement that swept through European Jewish life in the nineteenth century, and those who sought to maintain long-standing Jewish religious traditions. This tension has manifested in more modern times through the rise of the *baal teshuva*, or return to Judaism, movement, whose followers are Jews who have rejected their secular upbringing and embraced Orthodox Jewish tradition.

In his essay collection *The Wicked Son*, the playwright David Mamet articulates the disenchantment of the traditionalists with the assimilationist narratives that have dominated Jewish American literature. While analyzing the negative attitudes toward Jewish tradition held by Gabe Wallach, the assimilated protagonist of Philip Roth's 1962 novel *Letting Go*, Mamet critiques Wallach's notion that "the world of the immigrant generation is a horror tale of close escapes and non-escapes from poverty, of intellectual and social gaffes, and of communal misery" (37). Mamet queries, "[W]ho is this Gabe Wallach, this modern man, so scornful of tradition, of filial respect, as to mock, not with loving irony but with vicious sarcasm, the ways of his forbears?" (38).

While the tension between assimilation and tradition may always be a theme in Jewish literature, this essay introduces teachers at Hebrew day schools to the works of writers who, from the early days of Jewish American literature forward, have sought to counter the rejection of traditional Jewish ideas in their own prose. Along with Josh Lambert, who graduated from a Canadian Hebrew day school and has argued for the inclusion of secular Jewish writers in the day school curriculum (Lambert, "Finding"), I would contend that the educational experience is only enhanced by reading the traditionalists alongside such better-known authors as Bernard Malamud, Saul Bellow, and Philip Roth. The inclusion of traditional writers adds both sensitivity and depth to students' understanding of a point of view that is too often ignored, while illustrating that the Jewish American literary canon is composed of often divergent perspectives. While Lambert has noted that the superior Jewish education possessed by some Jewish American writers who debuted after 1997 has helped them create a more Jewishly grounded literature, he does not explicitly link this phenomenon to the large increase in the number of students attending Hebrew day schools in the 1990s (Lambert, "Since 2000" 623, 626–27).[1] The inclusion of traditionalists in curricula is particularly important because if present demographic trends continue, the number of writers with day school backgrounds will continue to rise, and Jewish literary criticism should respond to the needs of these more observant students. In addition, the works of the traditionalists may speak more to the better-educated students of today's era than to their parents. For these reasons, I would like to discuss some of the traditional authors who might add breadth and depth to a day school curriculum: Ludwig Lewisohn, Irving Fineman, Herman Wouk, and a host of contemporary writers.

Ludwig Lewisohn

While Lewisohn has been the subject of relatively little scholarship in recent decades, he was the most prominent Jewish American man of letters of the first half of the twentieth century. Lewisohn's Zionist and religiously oriented writings are particularly astonishing in the light of the fact that after emigrating from Germany he grew up in the Methodist Church, where he came to accept Jesus as his personal savior (Lewisohn, *Up Stream* 50–51). Nevertheless, Lewisohn's supposedly "Semitic" features betrayed his origins, and after being told of the difficulties he would face as a Jew in academia, he eventually abandoned his efforts to assimilate. In an interview conducted while he was living in exile in France in the late 1920s, Lewisohn noted, "Once I was a Jew, like many others, sorrowfully and half rebelliously; today, again like many others, I am a Jew seemingly, gladly, almost with a sense of consecration" (qtd. in Strauss 10).

A formidable artistic achievement, Lewisohn's *The Island Within* is worthwhile reading for day school and other students since it deals directly with the issues of assimilation into a majority culture. The novel traces the story of a German Jewish family from its religious roots in Poland to assimilation in New York City. The descendants of Braine, the family matriarch, rapidly assimilate to the dominant American culture. Yet her grandson, Arthur Levy, a doctor who married a gentile and fathered a son, cannot escape the anti-Jewish sentiment he perceives in American society. Levy reclaims his Jewish heritage after a distant cousin, a rabbi, provides him with a document written by a common ancestor; the document details the 1096 martyrdom of the Jews of Mainz at the hands of crusaders. At the novel's end, Levy is determined that his son not be embarrassed about his Jewish identity, "for if history has an ethical direction its symbol is not the clansman or the warrior, but he who passively defends an idea and thus sacrifices an ineffable Name" (343).

While *The Island Within*'s steadfast affirmation of the richness of Jewish tradition will likely resonate with today's more traditional students, the novel was perhaps ahead of its time. A formative exercise for day school students reading the novel would be to compare it with Myron Kaufmann's bestselling *Remember Me to God*, which features a protagonist from a traditional Jewish family who unsuccessfully tries to convert to Christianity, and which was published almost thirty years after Lewisohn critiqued such assimilation efforts in *The Island Within*. Reading the two novels together offers day school students important insights into two divergent responses to the dilemma of the Jew in a secular American society and validates students' acceptance of their Jewish religious identity over assimilation.

Irving Fineman

While Lewisohn may have been the first Jewish American writer to challenge the assimilationist narrative, he was not the only writer—even in the 1930s—to produce work with particular relevance to day school students. In a 1966 essay in *Tradition*, Fineman, a novelist who had taught literature at Bennington College, protested that when he started writing books in the 1930s "he was troubled by the image of the Jews" in such novels as Michael Gold's *Jews without Money* and Henry Roth's *Call It Sleep*. To Fineman, these writers seemed to be "grossly misrepresentative in the light of his own experience" ("Image" 29–30). Fineman noted that, like Abraham Cahan's famous protagonist David Levinsky in *The Rise of David Levinsky*, his own father had been a talmudic scholar who immigrated to the United States; however, unlike Levinsky, his father did not make it to the "affluent upper West Side," most likely because he "would not, no matter how bitter the struggle, sacrifice his Judaism" (30–31).

Fineman was "prompted, almost in protest," to present his own image of the Jew in his third novel, *Hear, Ye Sons* ("Image" 32), which recounts the early years in Russia of Jacob, a sixty-eight-year-old Jewish American lawyer who is at once familiar and yet different from many of the classic Jewish immigrant protagonists. Jacob tells of growing up in a Russian shtetl and attending the classic religious study hall known as a beth hamidrash. In response to the critiques of the sometimes-disastrous matchmaking found in Sholem Aleichem's *Tevye the Dairyman*, and its cinematic reworking in *Fiddler on the Roof*, Fineman gives Jacob a successful arranged marriage to a dark-haired beauty named Ruth, prompting Jacob to proclaim, "God was good" (*Hear* 141). Today's yeshiva students can consider the episode as a rejoinder to those who proclaim that everything about the old religion and its social and religious rituals was bad.

Jacob is later drafted into the Russian military, but after refusing to violate Yom Kippur he deserts the army and flees the country. After his escape he visits the Alexandrow (Alexander) Rebbe in Poland, who blesses him, saying, "[Y]ou have been destined to carry across the sea some seeds of our holy Torah, to plant them in the new land where thousands of Jews have gone" (289). Though Fineman could not have intended this in 1933, the depiction is a literary tribute to the Alexander Hasidim, who were virtually destroyed a decade later in the Holocaust. The scene can also be used to teach how literature preserves the legacy of a decimated Jewish culture, a lesson that will resonate in Hebrew day schools that present the Holocaust in the context of the larger secular curriculum.

Teachers may find it particularly appropriate for students studying the Talmud and Jewish philosophy alongside Jewish American literature to examine Fineman's literary assessment of Norman Mailer for using a "a scrap of primitive medical lore" to epitomize the Talmud in *The Naked and the Dead* and of Bernard Malamud for depicting Morris Bobber's "masochistic tolerance" as a Jewish trait in *The Assistant* ("Image" 36, 40). While these criticisms accurately demonstrate a lack of classical or textual Jewish knowledge on the part of two of the twentieth century's greatest Jewish writers, more traditional students will also find it fascinating that Fineman saved his greatest criticism for Wouk, who would later emerge as the Jewish American novelist most sympathetic to Jewish tradition. Fineman argued that Wouk's depiction of the young, privileged protagonist and her friends in *Marjorie Morningstar* "is the most thoroughly vulgar depiction of Jews in our fiction" ("Image" 38).

Contemporary day school students will not find it surprising that, as Fineman bemoaned, he and Lewisohn have had little influence on the subsequent generation of creative writers and critics ("Image" 33). Teachers may wish to contrast Fineman's critique with Louis Harap's *Creative Awakening: The Jewish Presence in Twentieth-Century American Literature, 1900–1940s*, since Harap pronounced Lewisohn a "reactionary" (59) and reduced Fineman to "an apologist for obscurantist aspects of Orthodox life" (122). Teachers could ask students why and how critics have reached such strikingly divergent opinions about the same texts. The exercise will allow students who deal with religious texts on a regular basis to apply the same type of complex analysis to mainstream American literature.

At the same time, day school instructors can encourage students to assess the impact of Fineman on Wouk, who did not feature observant Jewish characters in his fiction until after Fineman's essay was published. Indeed, for yeshiva students or students at more conservative Jewish institutions, Fineman's stinging words are easily both literary criticism and an exercise in *mussar*, or ethical preaching, which Wouk possibly took to heart in creating the most formidable account of *teshuva* ("return") in Jewish American literature.

Herman Wouk

Wouk's *War and Remembrance* interweaves another narrative of religious conversion and *teshuva* with the story of the American naval commander Pug Henry and the larger sweep of events during World War II. Henry's son is married to the Jewish Natalie, who is working for her uncle, Professor Aaron Jastrow, in Italy while her husband is at sea. Jastrow is a famous author and former yeshiva student from Oswiecim, Poland, who converted to Catholicism as a sixteen-year-old. When war breaks out, however, Jastrow and his niece wind up in a concentration camp, where he reclaims his faith. Jastrow writes that Reb Laizar at the Oswiecim yeshiva "slapped me out of my Jewish identity, as it were, and an SS Officer kicked me back into it" (772). Jastrow dons phylacteries for the first time in fifty years and teaches a Talmud class to several young boys, noting, "[T]he Talmud speaks across two thousand years to teach my boys, as its last word to them, the gulf between ourselves and the Germans" (908). The episode gives day school teachers the opportunity to discuss the unique dilemma of students who deal with both rigid religious authority and anti-Semitism.

Wouk's satirical novel *Inside, Outside* should also be considered an appropriate selection for more mature day school students. The first part of the novel presents the recollections of an aging Orthodox Jewish advisor to President Richard Nixon named Israel David Goodkind, who recounts his own battle to preserve Judaism in the face of the temptations of assimilation. Goodkind also details his friendship with a Philip Roth–like character named Peter Quat, who is the author of controversial books, such as *The Smelly Melamed*, that feature unflattering and vulgar Jewish characters.

Ruth Wisse has noted that "Wouk's satire of Roth is only a shade less devastating than Roth's own lifelong mockery of American Jews." *Inside, Outside* should be read in conjunction with Roth's *The Counterlife*, as together they offer day school students competing perspectives on such themes as the role of Israel in Jewish life, intermarriage, and the question of Jewish self-hatred.

The New Traditionalists in Contemporary Jewish American Literature

A number of more contemporary writers are also appropriate for day school students. Allegra Goodman (*Kaaterskill Falls*), Dara Horn (*In the Image*), and Tova Mirvis (*The Outside World*) have depicted Orthodox Jews approvingly and with a modern sensibility. Their novels demonstrate that traditional belief did not end in the early twentieth century, and their narratives will appeal to contemporary day school students put off by stories set in the 1930s.

With the proliferation of non-Orthodox Jewish high schools such as Milken Community Schools in Los Angeles, Gann Academy near Boston, Golda Och Academy in New Jersey, and the Abraham Joshua Heschel School in Manhattan, the number of day school students who are Jewishly literate but not Orthodox has increased. Such students, while sharing many similarities with Orthodox day school students, invariably have different perspectives on the role of Jewish life in literature. Mamet, who is traditional but not Orthodox, may be an appropriate writer to assign to students at pluralistic day schools. Horn's *In the Image* examines the tensions between the secular and the traditional. The protagonist, Leora, while recovering from the death of a close friend, observes the Sabbath in a traditional yet non-Orthodox manner and demonstrates a positive Jewish identity, which can be observed in her relationships and romantic encounters. As the novel weaves through different time periods, Horn's exquisite references to Hebrew and Yiddish literature are a testament to her own study of these subjects. Horn's novels are an excellent resource for day school teachers seeking to integrate Jewish studies with the teaching of a literary text.

For too long, literary criticism has taken it to be self-evident that Jewish American literature charts a straight path from immigrant, religious, and parochial narrowness to enlightened, secular, American freedom. Yet popular Jewish American writers from Lewisohn, Fineman, and Wouk to Goodman, Mirvis, and Horn demonstrate that Jewish American readers continue to identify deeply with cultural and ritual tradition. The inclusion of these writers in day school curricula will surely be helpful to the next generation of writers—and readers—to emerge from Hebrew day schools.

Note

1. Lambert may have failed to make the connection because, historically, a much higher percentage of Jewish students attended day schools in Canada than in the United States and because two of Canada's most famous Jewish writers, Mordecai Richler and Leonard Cohen, attended such schools. See also Schoenfeld.

Works Cited

Aleichem, Sholem. *Tevye the Dairyman and the Railroad Stories.* Translated by Hillel Halkin, Schocken Books, 1987.
Cahan, Abraham. *The Rise of David Levinsky.* Harper & Brothers, 1917.
Fiddler on the Roof. Directed by Norman Jewison, United Artists, 1971.
Fineman, Irving. *Hear, Ye Sons.* Longmans, Green, 1933.

————. "The Image of the Jew in Our Fiction." *Tradition: A Journal of Orthodox Jewish Thought*, vol. 9, no. 4, 1966, pp. 19–47.

Gold, Michael. *Jews without Money.* Horace Liveright, 1930.

Goodman, Allegra. *Kaaterskill Falls.* Dial Press, 1998.

Harap, Louis. *Creative Awakening: The Jewish Presence in Twentieth-Century American Literature, 1900–1940s.* Greenwood Press, 1987.

Horn, Dara. *In the Image.* W. W. Norton, 2002.

Kaufmann, Myron S. *Remember Me to God.* J. P. Lippincott, 1957.

Lambert, Josh. "Finding a Place for Contemporary Jewish Literature in Jewish Day Schools." *Jewish Book Council*, 2 Feb. 2015, www.jewishbookcouncil.org/_blog/The_ProsenPeople/post/contemporary-jewish-literature-jewish-day-schools.

————. "Since 2000." *The Cambridge History of Jewish American Literature*, edited by Hana Wirth-Nesher, Cambridge UP, 2016, 622–42.

Lewisohn, Ludwig. *The Island Within.* Harper and Brothers, 1928.

————. *Up Stream: An American Chronicle.* Boni and Liveright, 1922.

Mailer, Norman. *The Naked and the Dead.* Rinehart, 1948.

Malamud, Bernard. *The Assistant.* Farrar, Straus and Giroux, 1957.

Mamet, David. *The Wicked Son.* Schocken Books, 2006.

Mirvis, Tovah. *The Outside World.* Vintage Books, 2004.

Roth, Henry. *Call It Sleep.* Avon Library, 1934.

Roth, Philip. *The Counterlife.* Farrar, Straus and Giroux, 1986.

————. *Letting Go.* Random House, 1962.

Schoenfeld, Stuart. "The Jewish Religion in North America: Canadian and American Comparisons." *The Canadian Journal of Sociology / Cahiers canadiens de sociologie*, vol. 3, no. 2, 1978, pp. 209–31. *JSTOR*, www.jstor.org/stable/3340279.

Strauss, Renee. "'I Am a Jew Gladly,' Ludwig Lewisohn Writes His New Credo." *The Sentinel*, 16 Mar. 1928, p. 10. *Historical Jewish Press*, http://www.jpress.nli.org.il/Olive/APA/NLI/SharedView.Article.aspx?href=CGS%2F1928%2F03%2F16&id=Ar01001&sk=324FD035.

Wisse, Ruth. "Wouk Reclaims Jewish Family Turf." *Montreal Gazette*, 13 Apr. 1985, B8. *Google News*, news.google.com/newspapers?nid=1946&dat=19850413&id=LyAyAAAAIBAJ&sjid=t6UFAAAAIBAJ&pg=1235,896562.

Wouk, Herman. *Inside, Outside.* Little Brown, 1985.

————. *War and Remembrance.* Little Brown, 1978.

Kathryn Hellerstein

Teaching Jewish American Literature with an Anthology

Every syllabus is an anthology. When selecting materials for a class to read throughout a semester, a teacher assembles a collection that will engage students with the central questions and issues of the course topic. The selected texts substantiate the theses that the teacher hopes to share with the students. The anthology a teacher uses can determine the breadth and depth of the course. For my course on Jewish American literature, I use *Jewish American Literature: A Norton Anthology*, which Jules Chametzky, John Felstiner, Hilene Flanzbaum, and I edited between 1996 and 2000. This volume was the first and is at present the only comprehensive anthology of Jewish American literature, and it is still in print. The anthology covers the range of Jewish history in North America, from 1654 through 2001, and includes texts translated from Yiddish, Hebrew, German, Dutch, Ladino, and Spanish. The anthology's selections include—along with poetry, fiction, and drama—letters, diaries, editorials, sermons, political speeches, songs, jokes, graphic novels, and translations. The chronological thrust of the collection, from colonial America through the period of major eastern European Jewish immigration, World War II, postwar America, and the late twentieth century, presents a narrative about how American Jews have continuously written and published

in the vernaculars of the United States. Three sections on genre—
"Jewish Humor," "The Golden Age of the Broadway Song," and "Jews
Translating Jews"—interrupt this narrative in an effort to expand the
categories of literature and culture and redefine generic boundaries, as
well as to disrupt the historical organization of the anthology. By including such a variety of genres and works in translation, this anthology presents an expanded canon and a new conception of teaching Jewish American
literature.

Before this anthology appeared, a typical syllabus for a Jewish American literature course might have covered literature from the 1881 eastern
European Jewish immigration through the 1980s, with a focus on male
novelists Abraham Cahan, Saul Bellow, Bernard Malamud, Philip Roth,
and perhaps on one or two women writers, such as Anzia Yezierska or Cynthia Ozick. Now, thanks to the anthology, courses can include a wider
range of Jewish American literature. For teachers building such courses,
the anthology offers the economy of a single book for students to purchase;
primary texts located within a critical apparatus of introductions, head-
notes, footnotes, and bibliographies; and a selection of relatively short
texts that can serve as a gateway to other materials.

The challenge in writing a syllabus, though, is how to anthologize
from the anthology. My course Jewish American Literature begins with
questions the anthology addresses: "What makes Jewish American literature
Jewish? What makes it American?" Such questions about religious, ethnic, and national literature open the discussion of how cultural identity
and ethnicity have shaped literature as Jewish writers have "immigrated"
from Yiddish, Hebrew, and other languages to American English (Hellerstein). While the first two parts of the course encompass the waves of arrival, a period of nearly three hundred years, 1656–1924, replicating the
first two chronological divisions of the anthology, parts 3 and 4 cover
1924–2001 and focus separately on prose and poetry. Despite the fact
that I coedited this anthology, I needed, for pedagogical and intellectual
purposes, to redefine the anthology's terms for my syllabus. Furthermore, while the syllabus selects from the anthology's primary texts and
apparatuses, it also supplements the anthology's offerings with readings,
videos, and other sources.

For example, consider the introductory class session, "What Is Jewish?
American? Literature?" The readings for this class include two selections
from the anthology: Grace Paley's short story "In This Country, but in
Another Language, My Aunt Refuses to Marry the Men Everyone Wants

Her To" and a sampling from "A Scattering of Contemporary and Perennial Jewish Jokes." But the conversation commences with a handout of the Polish Yiddish writer I. L. Peretz's "The Golem." Irving Howe's translation of this classic European Yiddish short story establishes at the outset that Jewish literature is multilingual and crosses borders, and that mid-twentieth-century Jewish American literature contains a deep knowledge of its own polyglot nature. Through a reading and discussion of Peretz's short story, a modern, political retelling of the sixteenth-century legend of the golem that miraculously rescued the Jews of Prague, students discover that the translated story is about how Jewish writers translate and transform tradition.

Translation itself is a topic that recurs throughout the course, not just as the means by which students gain access to works written in Yiddish, Hebrew, German, Dutch, Ladino, or Spanish, but as a force of cultural change and social adaptation for Jewish writers and their characters in America. This theme manifests itself in Paley's "In This Country," which exemplifies the need for translation between generations, genders, and the cultures of immigrants and their American-born children. We end the introductory class by reading aloud two or three Jewish American jokes in "A Scattering." These jokes introduce the topic of stereotypes and bring into focus the problems of the translation of Jewish life to the New World.

I organize part 1 of the course, encompassing six class sessions, to generate discussion about how genre (including translation), gender, religion, nationalism, and a sense of audience (public or private, American or Jewish American) help define the beginnings of Jewish American literature. We begin by reading the anthology's substantial collection of early Jewish American communications: political petitions, newspaper editorials, sermons, communal prayers, political addresses, and private letters and diaries, thus expanding the scope of literature. We then turn to Jewish belles lettres in English, examining two early works by American Jews written in conventional literary forms—drama and fiction. Mordecai Manuel Noah, a flamboyant politician and journalist in the early nineteenth century, was an early promoter of American theater and literature. His 1808 play *The Fortress of Sorrento* may have been the first drama published in America by a Jew. Its theme of political justice resonates with the other works the class has read so far, but the text's European origins and lack of explicit Jewish content provoke questions about what is Jewish and what is American writing. In contrast, an excerpt from the forgotten physician-writer Nathan Mayer's 1858 serialized novel *The*

Fatal Secret! or, Plots and Counterplots: A Novel of the Sixteenth Century explicitly presents Jewish history, culture, and practice, bringing to life the hope for religious freedom in America to the victims of the Portuguese Inquisition. The students come to see that Mayer's novel functions as a kind of prequel to the first reading in the anthology, a 1656 letter to Peter Stuyvesant, the governor of New Netherlands, from Abraham de Lucena and other Sephardic merchants who had fled the Portuguese colony of Recife when the Inquisition extended to Brazil. Noah's play and Mayer's novel prompt the class to consider which aspects of style and substance define a work of Jewish American literature.

In a class session on Jewish women poets, we discuss three poets publishing within a decade of each other in the mid-nineteenth century. Penina Moïse, the first Jewish American author to publish a collection of poems in the United States, wrote political, humorous, and satirical poems, short fiction, and journalism in Charleston, South Carolina. She was best known for her hymns, which contributed to the Americanization of the Reform Jewish liturgy. The syllabus includes two of Moïse's poems: "Miriam," a reinterpretation of Moses and Aaron's sister in Exodus, and "Hymn," which echoes the Protestant *Book of Common Prayer*. To contrast the collective voice in Moïse's devotional poems, we read three free-verse poems by the wildly unconventional poet and actor Adah Isaacs Menken. Menken's Jewish origins were debatable, yet she studied Hebrew and was "the first poet and the only woman poet before the twentieth century to follow the revolution in prosody started by [Walt] Whitman's *Leaves of Grass* (1855)" (Eiselein 24). Class discussion focuses on Menken's radical prayer poem "Hear, O Israel" and her interpretation of the Apocrypha's Jewish heroine in "Judith." Another poem called "Miriam," published in Isaac Mayer Wise's *American Israelite* in 1858 by an anonymous author, arguably a woman, provides a secular interpretation of the *Song of Songs* and the biblical character Miriam. Discussing these poems allows students to question how Jewish women writing in America changed both Judaism and poetry by incorporating traditional Jewish sources, and emphasizing biblical women, in the literary texts they created for Jewish American readers.

In the final class sessions in part 1 of the course, we examine poems by Emma Lazarus, the only one of these early figures to enter the twentieth-century American literary canon. Best known today for her sonnet "The New Colossus," inscribed on the base of the Statue of Liberty, Lazarus was, from girlhood, an ambitious American poet and translator of Jewish poets, including the medieval Spanish Hebrew poet Judah Halevi and the nineteenth-century German poet Heinrich Heine, and a student of Ralph Waldo Emerson's, who mentored her, and an acquaintance of Robert Browning's. Lazarus wrote her first poem on an explicitly Jewish subject, "In the Jewish Synagogue at Newport," in 1867, when she was eighteen, as a rebuttal to Henry Wadsworth Longfellow's "The Jewish Cemetery at Newport," a philo-Semitic proclamation on the death of Judaism in Christian America. Comparing these two poems (the Longfellow poem is a handout), the students consider the implications of this public literary dialogue initiated by a young Jewish woman with the most famous American poet at that time. We then turn to several of Lazarus's sonnets from the 1880s, including "The New Colossus," "1492," "Echoes," "The New Ezekiel," and "Venus of the Louvre," discussion of which foregrounds how Lazarus adapted this classical European form to make American, Jewish, and feminist themes part of the mainstream.

Before the publication of the anthology, part 2 of the course, on the great immigration of eastern European Jews, would have been less visible in Jewish American literature courses. In this part we explore the multilingual nature of immigrant life and literature in America. Thus, the class examines Cahan's English-language short story "A Ghetto Wedding" alongside both the "Bintl Briv," the advice column he wrote for the Yiddish newspaper *The Jewish Daily Forward*, and "The Yankee Talmud," written in Hebrew by two satirists who skewered immigrant life (Kotlier; Rosenzweig). To teach the process of Americanization, I place stories by the often-taught Mary Antin and Anzia Yezierska alongside works by the Yiddish writer Avrom Reysen and a forgotten Baltimore novelist, Sidney Nyberg. Together, these English and Yiddish narratives illuminate the changing power relations of Jewish men and women, including parents and children, as American culture destabilized the old social order.

A substantial section of part 2 focuses on Yiddish fiction and poetry in translation, which, following the publication of the anthology, have become more visible as an integral part of Jewish American literary expression. The anthology offers a selection of Yiddish short stories in translation that, having been written in the United States, reflect both on the life left behind in eastern Europe and on the linguistic and cultural negotiations required of immigrants and their children. While the anthology includes stories from the 1910s by Lamed Shapiro, Fradl Shtok ("Shorn Head"), Moyshe Nadir, and Yente Serdatsky, it also includes

Kadya Molodowsky's "The Lost Shabes," published in postwar America, thus challenging the stereotype that Yiddish writing flourished only during the early decades of the twentieth century.

Three classes present a compressed history of Yiddish poetry in America. The first class begins with the labor poets Morris Rosenfeld and David Edelstadt, whose hugely popular poems of the 1890s were political and written in a collective voice. In contrast, the rebellious younger generation in New York, Di Yunge ("The Young Ones"), represented by Joseph Rolnik and Mani Leyb, wrote aesthetic poems in the 1910s and 1920s, while I. J. Schwartz broke with Di Yunge to write a book-length narrative poem about the American South. The greatest of these poets, Moyshe-Leyb Halpern, combined the political bent of Rosenfeld with Di Yunge aesthetics to form his own perverse and powerful poetic individualism. Grouping poems for comparison can help students explore how generations of writers created an American Yiddish literary tradition.[1]

Continuing the discussion of literary tradition, the class looks next at the introspectivist poets Jacob Glatstein and A. Leyeles, who in the 1920s formulated a Yiddish modernist ideology, reflecting the American modernism of T. S. Eliot, Ezra Pound, and William Carlos Williams. The readings include translations of poems by Glatstein and by Leyeles. Glatstein's "1919" and Leyeles's "New York" both evoke fragmentation in urban life and in the Jewish psyche, while Glatstein's 1938 "Good Night, World" renounces the modern world, although the poem was written six months before Kristallnacht, and Leyeles's 1947 "The God of Israel" excoriates European society for its indifference to the destruction of European Jewry by the Nazis.[2] Reading the kaleidoscopic introspectivist poems thus deepens the class discussion of history and aesthetics.

We conclude the section on Yiddish poetry by considering gender and sex and the tradition of women writing in Yiddish. From the sixteenth century onward, women published Yiddish devotional poems, and women immigrants to America wrote poetry that subverted that tradition. Celia Dropkin, Anna Margolin, Shtok, and Malka Heifetz Tussman, who immigrated in the 1910s, published, among Di Yunge and the introspectivists, poems echoing both prayer and modernism. Their poems raise questions about women's religious, sexual, and cultural roles in Judaism and in America. Reading Dropkin's "The Circus Lady," Margolin's "I Was Once a Boy," and Shtok's "Sonnet" elicits class discussion of Jewish norms of gender and sexuality in relation to artistic creativity. Tussman's 1972 "Thunder My Brother" dramatizes a rebellion against the Jewish laws that silence women's voices. Kadya Molodowsky, who immigrated in 1935, published "Alphabet Letters" in 1937, satirizing assimilation, while the later "Letters from the Ghetto" and "God of Mercy" call for God to avenge those who perished in the Holocaust.

After units on fiction and memoirs about the Depression and by or about children of immigrants and Holocaust survivors, including work by Henry Roth, Bernard Malamud, Saul Bellow, Philip Roth, and Elie Wiesel, the syllabus returns to Yiddish. We first approach the problem of how American literature represents the Holocaust through the loss of Yiddish. Isaac Bashevis Singer's World War II–era short story "Gimpel the Fool," translated by Saul Bellow in 1953, recasts the shtetl's schlemiel in positive terms of survival and continuity. Cynthia Ozick's 1969 novella "Envy; or, Yiddish in America" depicts the problems and urgency of translation through the rivalry between an obscure Yiddish poet and a Yiddish novelist (modeled on Singer) who has become famous through his translator. Paley's 1972 "A Conversation with My Father" calls into question the whole endeavor of Jews telling stories and writing fiction in America. Two audio recordings supplement the texts: one of Singer delivering his 1978 Nobel Prize banquet speech, in Yiddish, and one of Paley reading "The Loudest Voice" ("VT Edition"). Students then look for echoes of Yiddish in recent stories by Tova Reich and Max Apple in the anthology.

The last eight classes of the course are spent on poetry. Three of these classes focus on poems whose subjects are Jewish and American languages and on poems that rewrite passages from the Hebrew Bible or recast the Hebrew liturgy.[3] In two classes we consider how the Holocaust is imagined in English-language poems written in the United States after World War II.[4] For contrast, students read poems by European Jews who survived the Holocaust, translated from Yiddish, Hebrew, Italian, and German into English by Jewish American poets.[5] These readings lead students to consider whether, and if so how, translators make these poems American. By juxtaposing these varied works—for instance, poems by Charles Reznikoff and Avrom Sutzkever, or by Adrienne Rich and Kadya Molodowsky, or by Robert Pinsky and Irena Klepfisz—we see the cultures and languages that Jews in America have lost and gained.

In my course, students have often expressed surprise at discovering the writers of the early period and the Yiddish writers, whose works prompt them to make connections between politics, social history, and literature. By studying these two less-taught groups of authors, the students find a context in which to place the standard figures in the course, such as

Wiesel, Philip Roth, and Bellow, whom students are more likely to have heard of, if not actually read, in high school.

With its range of genres, periods, and works in translation, the anthology provides materials for any number of other course topics or themes. A teacher could choose works to focus the course explicitly or implicitly on sex and gender, on historical moments, on literary movements, or on specific genres, such as poetry, memoir, or the short story, and could include only works written in English or also those in translation. For example, one could write a syllabus on women poets from Penina Moïse to Emma Lazarus and from Celia Dropkin to Muriel Rukeyser, Adrienne Rich, and Jacqueline Osherow.[6] Another syllabus could enable students to study how notions of American and Jewish education intersect.[7] A course could focus on literary movements, such as realism, modernism, and postmodernism, as well as the Yiddish and Hebrew poets' political and modernist movements. One could design a course on responses to anti-Semitism, from Haym Salomon's "Letter from 'a Jew Broker,'" to Chaim Grade's "My Quarrel with Hersh Rasseyner," Elie Wiesel's chapters from *Night*, Cynthia Ozick's "The Shawl," and Art Spiegelman's *Maus II*. Teachers could devise other courses on humor, irony, and satire; on Judaism and Jewishness, the juncture of religion and ethnicity; or on Jews in the city, the suburbs, and the countryside.

While the course I teach using *Jewish American Literature: A Norton Anthology* touches on many of these themes, it finds its coherence in the questions about language and cultural identity that most compel me and that the works on my syllabus evoke. Other teachers composing syllabi from this anthology will create their own collections of relevant works by first identifying the questions that most excite and enthrall them.

Notes

1. Teachers can group Rosenfeld's sentimental "My Little Son" with Halpern's "My Only Son," a parody of Rosenfeld's famous lyrics; or Rosenfeld's "Walt Whitman," Edelstadt's "My Testament," Rolnik's "Poets" and "The First Cigarette," Leyb's "I Am," and both translations (by Hollander, and by Hellerstein and Harshav) of Halpern's "Memento Mori."

2. The readings also include Glatstein's "We the Wordproletariat" and "The Joy of the Yiddish Word" and Leyeles's "Fabius Lind's Days."

3. For poems on Jewish and American languages, see Reznikoff, "Building Boom," "From 'A Short History,'" "From 'Early History,'" and "Russia"; and Zukovsky, "From 'A-8,'" "From 'A-12,'" and "From 'Poem Beginning "The."'" For poems that rewrite passages from the Hebrew Bible, see Nemerov, "Lot's

Wife," "Nicodemus," and "A Song"; Kaufman, "His Wife"; Hollander, "Adam's Task" and "Ziz"; and Pinsky, "Visions." For poems that recast the Hebrew liturgy, see Ginsberg, "Footnote" and "From 'Kaddish'"; Rich, "Yom Kippur"; Hollander, "Ninth"; and Piercy, "The Ram's Horn."

4. See Rothenberg, "Cokboy" and "Dibbukim"; Feldman, "Pripet Marshes" and "Psalm"; Levine, "On a Drawing," "Sources," "Sweetness," and "Zaydee"; Grossman; Osherow, "Brief Encounter," "Ch'vil Schreibn," and "Ponar"; Hecht, "Book" and "Room"; and Klepfisz, "Bashert" and "Fradel Shtok."

5. See Sutzkever; Gilboa; Kovner; Levi; and Celan.

6. See Rich, "From 'Eastern War,'" "From 'Sources,'" and "Trying"; Rukeyser, "Boy," "From *Letter*," "More of a Corpse," and "Paper Anniversary."

7. See, for instance, Gratz; Leeser; Antin; Gold; H. Roth; Odets; D. Schwartz; Simon; Olsen; P. Roth, "Eli, the Fanatic"; Bellow; and Goodman.

Works Cited

Antin, Mary. "The Lie." Chametzky, pp. 191–206.
Apple, Max. "The Eighth Day." Chametzky, pp. 1074–81.
Bellow, Saul. "Something to Remember Me By." Chametzky, pp. 749–70.
Brahinsky, Mani Leyb (Mani Leyb). "I Am." Translated by John Hollander. Chametzky, pp. 219–20.
Cahan, Abraham. "A Bintl Briv." Chametzky, pp. 298–308.
———. "A Ghetto Wedding." Chametzky, pp. 123–34.
Celan, Paul. "Deathfugue." Translated by John Felstiner. Chametzky, pp. 1166–67.
Chametzky, Jules, et al., editors. *Jewish American Literature: A Norton Anthology*. W. W. Norton, 2001.
Dropkin, Celia. "The Circus Lady." Translated by Kathryn Hellerstein. Chametzky, p. 260.
Edelstadt, David. "My Testament." Translated by Aaron Kramer. Chametzky, p. 139.
Eiselein, Gregory. Introduction. *Infelicia and Other Writings*, by Adah Isaacs Menken, edited by Eiselein, Broadview Literary Texts, 2002, pp. 15–35.
Feldman, Irving. "The Pripet Marshes." Chametzky, pp. 848–50.
———. "Psalm." Chametzky, pp. 850–51.
Gilboa, Amir. "Isaac." Translated by Shirley Kaufman. Chametzky, pp. 1163–64.
Ginsberg, Allen. "Footnote to Howl." Chametzky, pp. 834–35.
———. "From 'Kaddish: II.'" Chametzky, pp. 835–46.
Glanz, Aaron (A. Leyeles). "Fabius Lind's Days." Translated by Benjamin Harshav and Barbara Harshav. Chametzky, pp. 353–54.
———. "The God of Israel." Translated by Benjamin Harshav and Barbara Harshav. Chametzky, pp. 355–56.
———. "New York." Translated by Benjamin Harshav and Barbara Harshav. Chametzky, p. 356.
Glatstein, Jacob. "Good Night, World." Translated by Benjamin Harshav and Barbara Harshav. Chametzky, pp. 373–74.

———. "The Joy of the Yiddish Word." Translated by Benjamin Harshav and Barbara Harshav. Chametzky, p. 377.

———. "1919." Translated by Kathryn Hellerstein and Benjamin Harshav. Chametzky, p. 371.

———. "We the Wordproletariat." Translated by Benjamin Harshav and Barbara Harshav. Chametzky, pp. 372–73.

Gold, Michael. "From *Jews without Money*: 'Fifty Cents a Night.'" Chametzky, pp. 357–62.

Goodman, Allegra. "The Four Questions." Chametzky, pp. 1134–48.

Grade, Chaim. "My Quarrel with Hersh Rasseyner." Translated by Milton Himmelfarb. Chametzky, pp. 649–70.

Gratz, Rebecca. "From *Letters of Rebecca Gratz*." Chametzky, pp. 46–54.

Grossman, Allen. "Poland of Death (IV)." Chametzky, pp. 1042–45.

Halevi, Judah. "Longing for Jerusalem." Translated by Emma Lazarus. Chametzky, p. 1156.

Halpern, Moyshe-Leyb. "Memento Mori." Translated by Kathryn Hellerstein and Benjamin Harshav. Chametzky, p. 246.

———. "Memento Mori." Translated by John Hollander. Chametzky, pp. 246–47.

———. "My Only Son." Translated by Kathryn Hellerstein and Benjamin Harshav. Chametzky, pp. 252–53.

Hecht, Anthony. "The Book of Yolek." Chametzky, pp. 807–08.

———. "The Room." Chametzky, pp. 805–06.

Heine, Heinrich. "I know not what spell is o'er me." Translated by Emma Lazarus. Chametzky, p. 1157.

Hellerstein, Kathryn. "Syllabus for Jewish American Literature (Topics in Jewish American Literature)." GRMN263-401, University of Pennsylvania, Spring 2019.

Hollander, John. "Adam's Task." Chametzky, pp. 913–14.

———. "The Ninth of Ab." Chametzky, pp. 912–13.

———. "The Ziz." Chametzky, pp. 914–15.

Kaufman, Shirley. "His Wife." Chametzky, pp. 808–09.

Klepfisz, Irena. "Bashert." Chametzky, pp. 1081–83.

———. "Fradel Shtok." Chametzky, pp. 1083–85.

Kotlier, Abraham. "From the Tractate 'The Ways of the New Land.'" "The Yankee Talmud." Translated by David Stern. Chametzky, p. 297.

Kovner, Abba. "#28 My Little Sister." Translated by Shirley Kaufman. Chametzky, p. 1164.

Lazarus, Emma. "Echoes." Chametzky, pp. 105–06.

———. "1492." Chametzky, p. 104.

———. "In the Jewish Synagogue at Newport." Chametzky, pp. 103–04.

———. "The New Colossus." Chametzky, p. 106.

———. "The New Ezekiel." Chametzky, p. 105.

———. "Venus of the Louvre." Chametzky, pp. 106–07.

Lebensboym, Roza (Anna Margolin). "I Was Once a Boy" Translated by Kathryn Hellerstein. Chametzky, p. 265.

Leeser, Isaac. "From 'Discourses on the Jewish Religion: Discourse XXIV: The Dangers and Defenses of Judaism.'" Chametzky, pp. 75–82.

Levi, Primo. "Shema." Translated by Ruth Feldman. Chametzky, p. 1165.

Levine, Philip. "On a Drawing by Flavio." Chametzky, pp. 853–54.

———. "Sources." Chametzky, pp. 854–55.

———. "The Sweetness of Bobby Hefka." Chametzky, pp. 855–56.

———. "Zaydee." Chametzky, pp. 852–53.

Leyb, Mani. *See* Brahinsky, Mani Leyb.

Leyeles, A. *See* Glanz, Aaron.

Longfellow, Henry Wadsworth. "The Jewish Cemetery at Newport." *Poetry Foundation*, www.poetryfoundation.org/poems/44634/the-jewish-cemetery -at-newport.

Malamud, Bernard. "The Magic Barrel." Chametzky, pp. 736–47.

Margolin, Anna. *See* Lebensboym, Roza.

Mayer, Nathan. "From *The Fatal Secret! or, Plots and Counterplots: A Novel of the Sixteenth Century*: 'Chapter XLVI: The Escape.'" Chametzky, pp. 95–99.

Menken, Adah Isaacs. "Hear, O Israel." Chametzky, pp. 91–94.

———. "Judith." Chametzky, pp. 88–89.

"Miriam." Chametzky, pp. 100–01.

Moïse, Penina. "Hymn." Chametzky, pp. 72–73.

———. "Miriam." Chametzky, pp. 70–71.

Molodowsky, Kadya. "Alphabet Letters." Translated by Kathryn Hellerstein. Chametzky, pp. 604–05.

———. "God of Mercy." Translated by Irving Howe. Chametzky, p. 606.

———. "Letters from the Ghetto." Translated by Kathryn Hellerstein. Chametzky, p. 605.

———. "The Lost Shabes." Translated by Irena Klepfisz. Chametzky, pp. 607–08.

Nadir, Moyshe. *See* Reiss, Isaac.

Nemerov, Howard. "Lot's Wife." Chametzky, p. 791.

———. "Nicodemus." Chametzky, pp. 792–93.

———. "A Song of Degrees." Chametzky, p. 792.

Noah, Mordecai Manuel. *The Fortress of Sorrento*. Chametzky, pp. 54–69.

Odets, Clifford. *Awake and Sing!* Chametzky, pp. 452–96.

Olsen, Tillie. "Tell Me a Riddle." Chametzky, pp. 689–715.

Osherow, Jacqueline. "Brief Encounter with a Hero, Name Unknown." Chametzky, p. 1131.

———. "Ch'vil Schreibn a Poem auf Yiddish." Chametzky, pp. 1132–33.

———. "Ponar." Chametzky, pp. 1129–30.

Ozick, Cynthia. "Envy; or, Yiddish in America." Chametzky, pp. 858–96.

———. "The Shawl." Chametzky, pp. 896–99.

Paley, Grace. "A Conversation with My Father." Chametzky, pp. 799–803.

———. "In This Country, but in Another Language, My Aunt Refuses to Marry the Men Everyone Wants Her To." Chametzky, pp. 803–04.

Peretz, Isaac Leybush. "The Golem." Translated by Irving Howe. *A Treasury of Yiddish Stories*, edited by Irving Howe and Eliezer Greenberg, Schocken Books, 1973, pp. 245–46.

Piercy, Marge. "The Ram's Horn Sounding." Chametzky, pp. 1057–59.

Pinsky, Robert. "Visions of Daniel." Chametzky, pp. 1069–71.

Reich, Tova. "The Lost Girl." Chametzky, pp. 1046–55.

Reiss, Isaac (Moyshe Nadir). "The Man Who Slept through the End of the World." Translated by Irving Howe. Chametzky, pp. 230–32.

Reysen, Avrom. "Equality of the Sexes." Chametzky, pp. 145–49.

Reznikoff, Charles. "Building Boom." Chametzky, pp. 363–64.

———. "From 'A Short History of Israel, Notes and Glosses XI.'" Chametzky, pp. 367–68.

———. "From 'Early History of a Writer 15.'" Chametzky, pp. 368–69.

———. "Russia: *Anno* 1905." Chametzky, pp. 364–67.

Rich, Adrienne. "From 'Eastern War Time 10.'" Chametzky, p. 999.

———. "From 'Sources VII.'" Chametzky, pp. 998–99.

———. "Trying to Talk with a Man." Chametzky, pp. 994–95.

———. "Yom Kippur, 1984." Chametzky, pp. 996–98.

Rolnik, Joseph. "The First Cigarette." Translated by Irving Feldman. Chametzky, p. 164.

———. "Poets." Translated by Irving Feldman. Chametzky, p. 163.

Rosenfeld, Morris. "My Little Son." Translated by Aaron Kramer. Chametzky, pp. 135–36.

———. "Walt Whitman." Translated by Aaron Kramer. Chametzky, pp. 136–37.

Rosenzweig, Gershon. "From the Tractate 'America.'" "The Yankee Talmud." Translated by David Stern. Chametzky, pp. 296–97.

Roth, Henry. "From *Call It Sleep*: From 'Book I: The Cellar.'" Chametzky, pp. 414–23.

Roth, Philip. "Eli, the Fanatic." Chametzky, pp. 918–45.

Rothenberg, Jerome. "Cokboy: Part One." Chametzky, pp. 1038–41.

———. "Dibbukim (Dibbiks)." Chametzky, pp. 1036–37.

Rukeyser, Muriel. "Boy with His Hair Cut Short." Chametzky, pp. 535–36.

———. "From *Letter to the Front*: 7. [To be a Jew in the twentieth century]." Chametzky, p. 538.

———. "More of a Corpse Than a Woman." Chametzky, p. 536.

———. "Paper Anniversary." Chametzky, pp. 536–38.

Salomon, Haym. " Letter from 'a Jew Broker.'" Chametzky, pp. 32–36.

"A Scattering of Contemporary and Perennial Jewish Jokes." Chametzky, pp. 323–25.

Schwartz, Delmore. "In Dreams Begin Responsibilities." Chametzky, pp. 540–45.

Schwartz, I. J. "From *Kentucky*." Chametzky, pp. 225–29.

Serdatsky, Yente. "Unchanged." Translated by Frieda Forman and Ethel Raicus. Chametzky, pp. 150–54.

Shapiro, Lamed. "White Challah." Translated by Norbert Guterman. Chametzky, pp. 154–62.

Shtok, Fradl. "The Shorn Head." Translated by Irena Klepfisz. Chametzky, pp. 290–94.

———. "Sonnet." Translated by Kathryn Hellerstein. Chametzky, pp. 294–95.

Simon, Kate. "From *Bronx Primitive: Portraits of a Childhood*: '5. The Movies and Other Schools.'" Chametzky, pp. 682–87.

Singer, Isaac Bashevis. "Gimpel the Fool." Translated by Saul Bellow. Chametzky, pp. 612–23.

———. "Isaac Bashevis Singer's Yiddish Speech at a Dinner Celebrating His Nobel Prize in Stockholm 1978." *YouTube*, uploaded by kalabusha, 1 Apr. 2011, www.youtube.com/watch?v=4d8yeL0oEwU.

Spiegelman, Art. "From *Maus II, A Survivor's Tale: And Here My Troubles Began*." Chametzky, pp. 1095–104.

Sutzkever, Avraham. "A Load of Shoes." Translated by C. K. Williams. Chametzky, pp. 1162–63.

Tussman, Malka Heifetz. "Thunder My Brother." Translated by Kathryn Hellerstein. Chametzky, p. 600.

"VT Edition: Grace Paley Reads 'The Loudest Voice.'" *VPR Archive*, Vermont Public Radio, 10 Dec. 2009, vprarchive.vpr.net/vpr-news/vt-edition-grace -paley-reads-the-loudest-voice.

Wiesel, Elie. "From *Night*: 'Chapter 3.'" Chametzky, pp. 901–05.

———. "From *Night*: 'Chapter 9.'" Chametzky, pp. 905–06.

Yezierska, Anzia. "Children of Loneliness." Chametzky, pp. 234–44.

Zukovsky, Louis. "From 'A-8.'" Chametzky, p. 408.

———. "From 'A-12.'" Chametzky, pp. 408–10.

———. "From 'Poem Beginning "The."'" Chametzky, pp. 405–08.

Lucas Wilson

Dismantling Christian Readings of Jewish American Literature in the Christian College: A. M. Klein's *The Second Scroll*

The challenges of teaching Jewish American literature at a Christian college often differ from those at most nonsectarian universities. Not only do Christian students at such colleges tend to read Christian themes into Jewish texts, but often there are few, if any, Jewish students in the classroom. From 2015 to 2016 I taught in the English department at Lipscomb University, a private institution affiliated with the Church of Christ, where the majority of students are white and Christian, a significant minority are Latinx and Christian or are Muslim, and few if any are Jewish. Correspondingly, most students at the institution have a limited knowledge of Judaism and its varied expressions. When teaching Jewish literature, I therefore found it necessary to introduce my students to modern Jewish history, culture, and religious practices.

In my Representations of the Holocaust course, I introduced the literature of Holocaust survivors (e.g., Elie Wiesel's *Night* and Primo Levi's *Survival in Auschwitz*) as well as other literary responses to the Holocaust (e.g., A. M. Klein's *The Second Scroll* and W. H. Auden's "Refugee Blues") and the literature of children of survivors (e.g., Art Spiegelman's *Maus I* and *Maus II* and Sonia Pilcer's *The Holocaust Kid*). Considering the student demographics at Lipscomb, I also discussed with the class the ways in which Christianity has historically viewed Judaism and Jews. To prompt discussion, I had students read the first two chapters of John Roth and Richard Rubenstein's *Approaches to Auschwitz*, which provided them with a crucial overview of how Christian theology laid the theoretical foundation of modern anti-Judaism and anti-Semitism, which ultimately led to the Holocaust. I did so, at least in part, to demonstrate how Christianized readings of Jewish literature often draw upon anti-Semitic thinking. *Approaches to Auschwitz* helped shift students' evangelical views of Jews and Judaism, and as a result, students began noting in class how some of the preconceived notions they had learned while growing up borrowed heavily from the extensive cache of negative Christian constructions of Judaism and Jews. This process of disrupting students' preconceptions and providing historical background prepared students to begin considering Jewish literature as a set of un-Christianized, unappropriated texts.

Many Jewish texts, especially those written after the Holocaust, such as Klein's 1959 novel *The Second Scroll*,[1] offer a profound critique of Christianity, though many of my students had not known of these critiques before taking my course. The novel draws heavily upon biblical imagery and themes—both Jewish and Christian—and students were quick to recognize such allusions; however, their initial ideas about Klein's text often revealed more about their own Christian beliefs than about the text itself, and they recurrently struggled to read the text without interpreting it as a celebration or foreshadowing of Christianity.

My aim was to show students that evangelical readings of Jewish literature render the reader complicit in the historical suppression and colonization of Jewish voices.[2] Such suppression and colonization lead to the privileging of Christian narratives over their Jewish counterparts. Students demonstrated this impulse early in the course when exploring the scene in *Night* of the child hanging from the gallows. They read the child as a christological figure—an evangelized reading that Wiesel, reputedly, emphatically rejected—thereby demonstrating a tendency to eclipse Jews' lived realities with their own beliefs. When reading *The Second Scroll*, my class investigated how the novel inverts Christian scriptural allusions in order to critically examine Christianity as an institution that mobilized hatred against Jews for centuries; additionally, we explored how the text reappropriates Christian biblical references in order to affirm both Judaism and divine providence after the Holocaust.

The Second Scroll presents the character Melech Davidson as a Jewish Messiah. After surviving the Holocaust, Melech goes on a spiritual journey—first rejecting providence and then later affirming God's benevolence—as does his nephew, the narrator. The novel's critique of Christianity is far-reaching. For instance, the Monsignor, one of Melech's contacts in Rome who seeks Melech's conversion, is described as "a fisher of men" (34), which according to Roger Hyman "is representative of the pre-Holocaust value system inherent in European Christian attitudes to Jews which made the Holocaust possible in the first place" (113). Additionally, Melech reads the Sistine Chapel's paintings of scenes from the Hebrew Bible and the Christian New Testament in reverse chronological order, a correction of Christian triumphalism that leads "not only to a rejection of Christianity but to its indictment" (Steinberg 39).

At first, my students mistook Melech for a Messiah like Jesus, since the text subversively attributes christological characteristics to Melech even though he rejects Christianity and affirms Judaism. Indeed, as one critic argues, the novel parallels "the life of Jesus, [and] to that extent he [Klein] claims to have written another New Testament, a gospel" (James 201). Others refer to Melech as a "God-figure" (Hyman 73) and the symbol of "the Messiah concept" (Steinberg 41). Even Klein himself, in a letter explaining the parallels between Melech and Jesus to his Christian friend A. J. M. Smith, states: "As if by lucky accident, everything fell into a pattern, seemed to repeat the stations of your Messiah, seemed to make up a seconding of a testament already seconded" ("Some Letters" 13). In class I note the symbolism of Melech Davidson's name, connotative of kingship (*melech* means "king") through the lineage of King David, while also highlighting Melech's many messianic attributes.

Additional parallels between Melech and Jesus include Melech's "walking on water" (97); his lifelong singleness (25); his time spent with and talking to children (25); his preference for "the minority" (48); his abdication of comfort and safety to feel "the full weight of the yoke of exile" with Jewish outcasts (49); his relationship with "the beggars . . . the crippled, the dumb, the blind" who "have faith in him" (62); his recurrent conflict with government authorities; and his bringing together the chosen people in the promised land (85–86). Several of my students, noting these parallels, concluded that, since Melech is a Jesus archetype, the text must be sympathetic to Christianity.

These parallels are not, however, a celebration of Christianity but a reclamation of the Jewish notion of the Messiah, which has been co-opted by Christianity for two millennia. Melech as Messiah functions as a rejection of Christ the Messiah in favor of a Jewish "'anointed' political, spiritual and moral liberator" who seeks to restore "a universal order of peace, harmony and equality" (Hyman 138). When I placed these parallels in conversation with the narrative's larger project of constructing a "Second Scroll" (Greenstein 42–43)—a post-Holocaust testament of God's providence that comes to replace and reject the Christian scriptures—students were better able to think through the novel's emphatic critique.

In the novel, the Monsignor gestures toward a new conception of the Messiah when he says that Melech would return to Rome and "there would be a showing forth, an epiphany" (37). The Monsignor's declaration is rife with irony, since "epiphany" comes from late Greek *epiphaneia*—meaning "manifestation" or, in the Christian New Testament, "advent or manifestation of Christ"—and "Christ" is derived from *christos*, Greek for "anointed" and equivalent to the Hebrew *mashiach*, or "Messiah." The epiphany of which he speaks refers not to Christ manifesting or revealing himself to Melech but to Melech as an anointed Jewish embodiment of the messianic concept. Such diction reinforces Melech as Messiah, replacing Christ as Messiah. The text reclaims the Jewish Messiah in the service of affirming Judaism after the Holocaust, an event whose theoretical foundation was laid by Christian theology. The novel's vigorous critique of Christianity provoked my students to condemn anti-Semitism and various other iterations of hatred and called them to act like Melech, who fights for the outcast and stands up for the other.

My students learned how reading Jewish literature through an evangelical lens can displace Jewish themes, symbols, and theologies and distort the text's presentation of Jewishness. Students came to appreciate that this impulse to evangelize Jewish literature emerges from "Christianity's conventional wisdom about Judaism [which] still remains too often stuck in a New Testament interpretation that sees Judaism as eclipsed, superseded by Christian 'truth'" (Roth 265). Reading Holocaust literature from this perspective offers students in Christian colleges necessary tutelage in empathy, listening, and inclusion—which makes for more sensitive students, citizens, and people of faith.

Notes

1. Although *The Second Scroll* is not typically included in Holocaust literature courses, I included it in my course because of the Holocaust's centrality to its narrative. As Roger Hyman puts it, without the historical referent of the Holocaust, the novel "would have little meaning, or . . . meaning would be severely limited" (39); indeed, the entire plot pivots on the dialectic "between the historical triumph of Zionism and the historical disaster of the Holocaust" (54).

2. Of course, such Christianized readings are not exclusive to students in Christian colleges, and accordingly, my approach to teaching in the Christian-college context can be applied to nonreligious institutions as well. Presenting *The Second Scroll*'s critique of Christianity to students at non-Christian colleges offers insight into the Western tradition writ large, given Christianity's constitutive position in the West. The text's critique sheds light on how traces of Christian supersessionism and anti-Semitism permeate Western thinking and how exploring the major root causes for these phenomena may assist in resisting and dismantling anti-Semitism in secular contexts today.

Works Cited

Auden, W. H. "Refugee Blues." *W. H. Auden: Selected Poems*, edited by Edward Mendelson, Vintage, 2007, pp. 83–84.

Greenstein, Michael. "History in *The Second Scroll*." *Canadian Literature*, vol. 76, 1978, pp. 37–46.

Hyman, Roger. *Aught from Naught: A. M. Klein's* The Second Scroll. U of Victoria P, 1999.

James, William Closson. "Two Montreal Theodicies: Hugh MacLennan's *The Watch That Ends the Night* and A. M. Klein's *The Second Scroll*." *Literature and Theology*, vol. 7, no. 2, 1993, pp. 198–206.

Klein, A. M. *The Second Scroll*. McClelland and Stewart, 1994.

———. "Some Letters of A. M. Klein to A. J. M. Smith, 1941–1951." *The A. M. Klein Symposium*, edited by Seymour Mayne, U of Ottawa P, 1975.

Levi, Primo. *Survival in Auschwitz*. Touchstone, 1995.

Pilcer, Sonia. *The Holocaust Kid*. Persea Books, 2001.

Roth, John K. "Wiesel's Contribution to a Christian Understanding of Judaism." *Elie Wiesel: Jewish, Literary, and Moral Perspectives*, edited by Steven T. Katz and Alan Rosen, Indiana UP, 2013, pp. 264–76.

Roth, John K., and Richard L. Rubenstein. *Approaches to Auschwitz: The Holocaust and Its Legacy*. Westminster John Knox Press, 2003.

Spiegelman, Art. *Maus I: A Survivor's Tale: My Father Bleeds History*. Alfred A. Knopf, 1986.

———. *Maus II: A Survivor's Tale: And Here My Troubles Began*. Alfred A. Knopf, 1992.

Steinberg, M. W. "A Twentieth Century Pentateuch: A. M. Klein's *The Second Scroll*." *Canadian Literature*, vol. 2, 1959, pp. 37–46.

Wiesel, Elie. *Night*. Translated by Marion Wiesel, Farrar, Straus and Giroux, 2006.

Lori Hope Lefkovitz

The Sense of *Bashert*: Contingency in Dara Horn's *The World to Come* and Nicole Krauss's *History of Love*

> *Ben could not know then, for instance, that his sister would come to him now, years later, to tell him that she and Leonid were going to have a baby, that he would surprise himself by dreaming of the child who would be given his mother's or father's name—and in this yes or no lay the entire future, the entire world.*
>
> —Dara Horn, *The World to Come*

> *He couldn't have known it, but among the original run of* The History of Love, . . . *at least one copy was destined to change a life— more than one life.*
>
> —Nicole Krauss, *The History of Love*

The butterfly effect is strong in Jewish literature. The historical experience of Jews as a peripatetic, global people who carried a textual tradition on their backs, transmitted devotedly across time and place while accruing a miscellany of folkways, often manifests in contemporary Jewish American fictions as explorations into the relations between here and now and some other there and then. A new generation of accomplished Jewish storytellers have written novels whose intricate plots dramatize contingency—the accidental or fated dependence of later events on earlier ones. These novels

hint that the lives of young Jewish American characters have been determined by the choices and mixed fortunes of their ancestors and the
strangers with whom they became entangled, as if proposing to readers
that meaning is discernible only from an infinitely wide, cosmic point of
view. Texts and translations embedded in these works metaphorize problems of Jewish diasporic identity, suggesting that what can be known is
conjectural: memory fades, secrets die with their keepers, and documents
are lost, destroyed, or plagiarized. History turns on a dime. Storytelling,
an antidote to the vagaries of chance, makes connections visible, building
bridges between the contemporary American landscape of the characters
in these works and pre-Holocaust Europe, which constitutes part of the
characters' felt identities.

When my students have discussed contemporary Jewish novels, exemplified here by Dara Horn's *The World to Come* and Nicole Krauss's *The
History of Love*, in my course Modern and Contemporary Jewish Literature, they observe that the Jewish characters move in a nonlinear system
in which small causes have large effects. The modest hero of his or her own
story, but situated in the vastness of time and space, the individual means
nothing and everything. The novels illustrate the Hasidic dictum, attributed to the Polish rabbi Simcha Bunim of Peshischa, that each person must
carry in one pocket the sentence, "I am but dust and ashes," and in the
other, "For my sake, the world was created." The trick is to simultaneously
hold both truths. The second sentence derives from a talmudic equation
of each person with the world, such that anyone who kills a person has
destroyed a world, and anyone who saves a person saves a world (*Mishnah*,
Sanhedrin 4:5).

When Ben Ziskind, a bookish schoolchild and a protagonist of *The
World to Come*, swallows his pride and encourages his bullying nemesis,
Leonid, to call Ben's twin sister, he becomes the prime mover for the
eventual conception of his nephew Daniel, whose prenatal experience in
paradise (where Daniel's soul is lovingly schooled by the ancestors whose
biographies are embedded in Horn's novel) is recounted in the fantastic
closing chapter. This departure from realism unmoors the novel from time
and place and secures the morals of this story: we are who we are because
of those who have been, and everything is at stake in any single choice.

In class, we talk about historical phenomena referred to in the two
novels, such as Jewish socialism, the project of twinning bar mitzvahs for
American and Soviet Jewish boys, and the Soviet Jewry movement, as well
as textual sources. The novels are suffused with a sense of *bashert*, a Yiddish

word that means something like "destiny," that can refer to a soulmate ("one's *bashert*"), and that answers any "why" question, whether tragic or comic ("it was *bashert*"). Students see that contingency, which they recognize to be a universal philosophical concern, has Jewish formulations.

In *The World to Come*, Horn invents a relationship between two historical figures who in fact taught briefly at the same time in a remote Jewish orphanage in Russia: the famous artist Marc Chagall and the brilliant but less well-known Yiddish writer Pinkhas Kahanovitch, who wrote under the pen name Der Nister ("The Hidden One"). In Horn's fiction, when Kahanovitch asks Chagall what one of his paintings means, and Chagall answers, to Kahanovitch's frustration, "Blue," Chagall ripostes the question, "What does your daughter mean?" My students and I pause over this exchange to consider what kinds of answers we might expect when we ask what a work of art "means," and what kind of challenge Chagall's rejoinder poses when he analogizes the meaning of a painting to the meaning of a person.

Chagall also asks what Boris, a traumatized (fictional) orphan in their charge, "means." Later, in a heartbreaking letter to God that Horn invents, Der Nister asks what his adored daughter Hodel, a historical person who died tragically young and malnourished, meant. Hodel's meaning cannot derive, as Der Nister had hoped, from the Jewish customs of memorializing her father and naming a child in his memory. Boris, on another fictional trajectory, will suffer a miserable end at the hands of the Soviet police, though he at least will have left behind a daughter who ultimately grows up in America, marries Daniel, and bears the twins, Benjamin and Sara Ziskind, who are the protagonists of the novel *The World to Come*.

Before her death, the twins' mother writes and illustrates popular children's books, translations from the Yiddish of actual stories by Der Nister, which in the novel she publishes under her own name, having been unsuccessful at publishing them as translations. Horn reproduces several of these fables in full, accomplishing what her character had hoped to do (cf. Horn, "What We Have Lost"): that is, to gift a new generation of readers with great Yiddish literature, many of whose authors were rewarded for their work with state-sponsored murder. By looking at the stories within the story and at Chagall's art, students receive a compelling history lesson, a lesson in art and politics, and access to a body of literary texts that would not ordinarily find their way into a curriculum on American or even Jewish American literature.

Discussing the embedded Der Nister stories, I ask my students if the stories' meanings shift depending on context. Alongside Horn's novel, we read stories by Der Nister's contemporaries, such as David Bergelson's "At Night" and Isaac Babel's "The Story of My Dovecot," both available in Ilan Stavan's thoughtfully assembled collection *The Oxford Book of Jewish Short Stories*. Another illuminating intertext, and favorite with students, is Nathan Englander's "The Twenty-Seventh Man," which imagines the rounding up and final conversations of Jewish writers on Stalin's list for the firing squad. One of the writers (the only one who is unknown) recites a story, recreated by Englander, to the others before they all die, raising the question of what it means to exist. Englander creates a special case to dramatize that we can never recover the art and literature that were destroyed by the violence of history before they reached their audience. Like Horn, Englander demands that we consider the purpose of storytelling and the relation between Jewish history and art.

Widely acclaimed, *The History of Love* similarly problematizes existence and illustrates, in the manner of Charles Dickens's *Bleak House*, an unpredictable web of human connections, principally between an old man and Holocaust survivor, Leopold Gursky, and a fifteen-year-old American girl, Alma Singer. Alma is named after "every girl" in a novel central to her parents' courtship, a novel that Gursky wrote in Yiddish a lifetime ago in Poland for his lifelong beloved, Alma Mereminski. Gursky does not know that his manuscript, "The History of Love," survived and was translated into Spanish by his childhood friend Zvi Litvinoff, who, presuming that Gursky was murdered, published the work under his own name.

Krauss's *The History of Love* has four alternating narrators: Gursky; the American Alma; Alma's younger brother, nicknamed Bird; and an omniscient narrator, whom Philippe Codde argues may also be Gursky ("On the Problematic Omniscient Narrator"). As in William Faulkner's *The Sound and the Fury* or Robert Browning's *The Ring and the Book*, the multiple narratives in Krauss's novel invite students to think about relativism and limited perspectives. The puzzles in this story can be delightfully dizzying, as exemplified in this description of Litvinoff holding the book that is and isn't his: "The printed book in his hands was a copy of a copy of a copy of the original, which no longer existed, except in his head" (111).

Gursky is an endearing, tragicomic figure, who, dislocated by World War II, absents himself from the lives of his beloved Alma Mereminski and their son, who becomes a world-famous writer, Isaac Moritz. Gursky otherwise goes out of his way to be seen, posing nude for a drawing class or spilling his coffee at Starbucks. When discussing Gursky with the class, I introduce Saul Bellow's essay "On Jewish Storytelling" and his famous dictum that Jewish literature is characterized by "laughter and trembling" (15). We also theorize about ethnic literature using Hana Wirth-Nesher's essay "Defining the Indefinable: What Is Jewish Literature?" Krauss prompts this question about the relevance of authorial ethnicity when a reviewer quoted in Isaac Moritz's obituary protests: "to call him a Jewish writer . . . is to miss entirely the point of his humanity, which resisted all categorization" (78).

Alma Singer embodies the transnationalism of Jewish identity, and in one funny moment, her mother draws "sixteen *different* pie charts, each of them accurate!" (196), describing Alma's composition—part Polish, Czech, Hungarian, Russian, German, and English—based on her grandparents' countries of origin. Alma, a budding survivalist (a symbol for the particular Jewish historical experience) and naturalist (a symbol for universal experience), reacts to her mother's charts by protesting: "I'M AMERICAN!" While the mother shrugs, saying, "[S]uit yourself," Bird mutters a rejoinder whose sentiment is often felt by Diaspora Jews: "No, you're not. You're Jewish" (197).

Bird is a smart, eccentric, and idiosyncratically religious child reminiscent of Philip Roth's Ozzie Freedman in "The Conversion of the Jews," a celebrated story that raises questions of Jewish particularism in an American context. (Roth's story also works well on the course syllabus.) Bird believes himself to be one of the *lamed vovniks*, the thirty-six righteous people alive at any given moment for whose sake God does not destroy the world. Bird exemplifies the problem of how to act righteously given the limits of what is knowable. With partial information and a child's logic, he wonders: "If I am a lamed vovnik how do I find Alma's father whose name was Leopold Gursky and also Zvi Litvinoff and also Mr. Mereminski and also Mr. Moritz?" (217). Compounded errors lead to a mystified Gursky receiving a copy of his own book in translation—actually, a translation of a translation—a symbol for the translational experience of Jewish American identity and for the hall of mirrors that lives within every self.

I ask students in what way this novel is "a history of love." We talk about the war's interruption of the original love story, the reverberations of premature deaths, and plagiarism as identity theft. Students list instances of irony, misidentification, and doubling: the two or three Almas, doubled fathers and sons, authors confused for one another (through malice or by accident), authors as parents, and translators as surrogate or adoptive parents. We discuss how imagination resurrects the dead—for instance, Alma and Bird's strategy for revivifying their father through stories, some of which Alma invents to give her brother an idealized father—and the surprising revelation that one of the novel's characters is imaginary. Students discuss how they feel about an appealing character being a figment of another character's imagination. But are not all characters figments of the imagination? Finally, we talk about how the child Alma materializes for Gursky at the end, when he cannot be sure of the difference between a wished-for person and a real person. They share a park bench, which becomes the circle of life for old and young, girl and man, intimate strangers, whose existences are mutually redemptive.

Reflecting on the novel, my students talk about loss and the ways that the future redeems the past. A belief in such redemption seems to me basic to the Jewish worldview. Why do we name people for other people? Do the fictions within the fiction serve therapeutic purposes? How do stories help us know one another? I want students to understand that in the face of ordinary loss (a dead parent) or extraordinary loss (genocide), sharing stories expresses love and may be the best we can do.

Often read as examples of third-generation Holocaust fiction, Horn's and Krauss's novels prompt my students to think about their own family histories. While most of them enjoy some measure of privilege—if only by virtue of studying at a major university in the United States—many have had bequeathed to them stories of trauma: war, slavery, poverty, or more private losses. Many students come from families that came from somewhere else, and the question of who they are in relation to these other places and the people who once lived there, often under vastly different circumstances, is meaningful to them.

The previous generation of renowned Jewish American writers, including Bellow, Bernard Malamud, Cynthia Ozick, Grace Paley, and Philip Roth, consistently provoked questions of what constitutes their Jewishness (see Dickstein) and the extent to which they form a meaningful cohort. Today, we are seeing the flowering of another generation of luminous Jewish writers whose fiction engages with Judaism and the Jewish historical experience. Because this literature explores how art bridges the divides between worlds, cultures, generations, and life and death, it appeals to students compelled by inherited trauma and identities as second- and third-generation Americans (see Lang).

A syllabus of contemporary Jewish American literature that represents children's imaginative responses to the reverberating effects of the Holocaust, as Horn's and Krauss's works do, might also include novels such as Michael Chabon's *The Amazing Adventures of Kavalier and Clay*, Jonathan Safran Foer's *Everything Is Illuminated*, Aryeh Lev Stollman's *The Far Euphrates*, or Anne Michaels's *Fugitive Pieces* and memoirs such as Daniel Mendelsohn's *The Lost*, Judy Batalion's *White Walls*, or Sarah Wildman's *Paper Love*, as well as excerpts from the many critical and psychological studies that deal with what Marianne Hirsch calls "postmemory" and the neuroscientist Rachel Yehuda calls "inherited trauma."

Crowded with Jewish textual and historical references, this literature contains grandly existential ideas that appeal to students from all backgrounds. The protagonists in these stories are lonely but well-loved young people who, enduring personal loss, want to discover their own power and relative value in the context of history. They need to understand the chaos of European dislocations to account for their own privileged existence in North America. Jewish lore, as Horn reminds us in *The World to Come*, imagines that the bridge to paradise, on which the Messiah will walk, is made of paper. In a Hasidic metaphor and a popular Hebrew song, the world is likened to a narrow bridge, and humanity is enjoined not to be afraid. The paper bridge is what we cross when we escort students to other worlds by introducing them to America's ethnic literatures.

Works Cited

Babel, Isaac. "The Story of My Dovecot." *The Oxford Book of Jewish Short Stories*, edited by Ilan Stavans, Oxford UP, 1998, pp. 125–34.

Batalion, Judy. *White Walls: A Memoir about Motherhood, Daughterhood, and the Mess in Between*. New American Library, 2016.

Bellow, Saul. "On Jewish Storytelling." Wirth-Nesher, *What*, pp. 15–20.

Bergelson, David. "At Night." *The Oxford Book of Jewish Short Stories*, edited by Ilan Stavans, Oxford UP, 1998, pp. 89–91.

Chabon, Michael. *The Amazing Adventures of Kavalier and Clay*. Random House, 2000.

———. "On the Problematic Omniscient Narrator in Nicole Krauss's *History of Love*." *The Explicator*, vol. 69, no. 1, June 2011, pp. 48–50.

Dickstein, Morris. "The Complex Fate of the Jewish-American Writer." *The Nation*, 4 Oct. 2001, www.thenation.com/article/complex-fate-jewish -american-writer-0/.

Englander, Nathan. "The Twenty-Seventh Man." *For the Relief of Unbearable Urges*, Vintage Books / Random House, 1999.

Foer, Jonathan Safran. *Everything Is Illuminated*. Harper Perennial, 2002.

Hirsch, Marianne. *The Generation of Postmemory: Writing and Visual Culture after the Holocaust.* Columbia UP, 2012.

Horn, Dara. "What We Have Lost." *The Forward,* 11 July 2008, pp. 13, 15.

———. *The World to Come.* W. W. Norton, 2006.

Krauss, Nicole. *The History of Love.* W. W. Norton, 2005.

Lang, Jessica. "*The History of Love,* the Contemporary Reader, and the Transmission of Holocaust Memory." *Journal of Modern Literature,* vol. 33, no. 1, Fall 2009, pp. 43–56.

Mendelsohn, Daniel. *The Lost: A Search for Six of Six Million.* Harper Perennial, 2006.

Michaels, Anne. *Fugitive Pieces.* Vintage Books / Random House, 1996.

The Mishnah. Edited and translated by Jacob Neusner, Yale UP, 1991.

Roth, Philip. "The Conversion of the Jews." *The Oxford Book of Jewish Short Stories,* edited by Ilan Stavans, Oxford UP, 1998, pp. 312–24.

Stavans, Ilan, editor. *The Oxford Book of Jewish Short Stories.* Oxford UP, 1998.

Stollman, Aryeh Lev. *The Far Euphrates.* Riverhead Books, 1997.

Wildman, Sarah. *Paper Love: Searching for the Girl My Grandfather Left Behind.* Riverhead Books, 2014.

Wirth-Nesher, Hana. "Defining the Indefinable: What Is Jewish Literature?" Wirth-Nesher, *What,* pp. 3–12.

———, editor. *What Is Jewish Literature?* The Jewish Publication Society, 1994.

Yehuda, Rachel, et al. "Holocaust Exposure Induced Intergenerational Effects on FKBP5 Methylation." *Biological Psychiatry: A Journal of Psychiatric Neuroscience and Therapeutics,* vol. 80, no. 5, 1 Sept. 2016, pp. 372–80.

Part II

Comparative Teaching Approaches

Dean Franco

Jewish American Literature and the Multicultural Canon

Pluralism

For much of the twentieth century, Jewish American leaders advocated for democracy based on cultural pluralism, a social theory developed by Horace Kallen in 1915 (*Culture*, 35). In his work, Kallen, a pragmatist philosopher who trained with William James, parries criticisms from American nativists and assimilationists by arguing that there is no central American identity that needs conserving or that immigrants might adopt. Rather, for Kallen and like-minded advocates of pluralism, America is a constellation of beliefs and practices, including democracy, individualism, meritocracy, and representative rule. Key to what he calls "Americanism" is the distinction between the private sphere, where a variety of cultures can thrive in domestic, sectarian, or parochial spaces, and the public sphere, where those cultures enter into polity (*Culture* 36).

From the end of the nineteenth century to the mid–twentieth century, Jewish writers and poets produced a literature commensurate with this political vision and consonant with the fundamental American values of liberalism, public equity, public education, and capitalism. Kallen's "American idea" was examined by the Jewish writers Abraham Cahan,

Anzia Yezierska, Mary Antin, Henry Roth, and Delmore Schwartz, among others, in the early twentieth century, and when Saul Bellow opened his National Book Award–winning 1953 novel *The Adventures of Augie March* with the line, "I am an American, Chicago born," it was vernacular evidence of the triumph of pluralism. In Bellow's novel, the general "American" has to be qualified by the locale, "Chicago," as well as by Augie's prominent if initially unstated Jewishness.

However, while cultural pluralism afforded the acceptance of Jews in America, it was increasingly regarded by African American civil rights advocates as more of a crutch for the status quo than a remedy for racial injustice. The famous and often-cited breakdown of the black-Jewish alliance may be understood as a fracture along the lines of political strategy: pluralism, with its emphasis on public and private spheres, its emphasis on religion over race, and its faith in civil liberties based on individual rights, was a failure in the view of black, Chicano, and Native American civil rights advocates, who increasingly advocated for rights as well as remedies, and recognition as well as reparation (Greenberg 16). Multicultural politics and practice grew out of a radical rights movement that sought to erase pluralism's putative division between public and private spheres and to establish a public right of cultural belonging, which the movement viewed as a necessary remedy for racism and as a practice of recognition that would enable full parity.

Though many Jewish intellectuals and community leaders were caught off guard by the multicultural turn, some of the most prominent Jewish literature from this period—the late 1960s through the early 1970s—illustrates or comments on the failure of Jewish commitments to liberal, cultural pluralism and on the subsequent split between Jews and other ethnic groups over policies of rights and recognition. Bernard Malamud's *The Tenants* and Saul Bellow's *Mr. Sammler's Planet* depict complex scenes of black and Jewish identification and enmity, while Philip Roth's *Portnoy's Complaint* satirizes the liberal politics of opportunity that so many Jews found attractive. Meanwhile, Cynthia Ozick's early fiction, including the stories "Bloodshed," "Envy," and "The Pagan Rabbi," reflects on Jewish cultural separatism.

Perhaps no novel better depicts the convergence and separation of Jewish and other ethnic groups' political strategies than Lore Segal's *Her First American*, published in 1985, at the height of the debate about multiculturalism. Segal's autobiographical novel begins in the 1950s, when Ilka Weissnix, a refugee who escaped Nazi Germany through the *Kindertransport* ("children's transport"), strikes up a tragic romance with Carter

Bayoux, a sophisticated, older black journalist modeled on the great sociologist Horace Cayton. In the early years of their relationship, the mismatched pair explore the commensurability of their experiences, including race-based oppression, geographical displacement, and a growing enthusiasm for the establishment of national homelands—decolonized African nations for him, Israel for her. But by the novel's end, set in the 1960s, black radicals have co-opted Carter's life for a cultural-nationalist narrative, and Ilka has been written out of his story.

From the 1980s to the present, Jewish writers have remained interested in Jewish cultural difference, including what Michael Rothberg has called "multidirectional memory," the intersections of cultural memory that occur when ethnic groups look to other groups' histories for comparative understandings of their own (6–7). Representative works include Irena Klepfisz's collection of essays on Yiddish language and culture, *Dreams of an Insomniac: Jewish Feminist Essays, Speeches, and Diatribes*; Philip Roth's novel about race and political culture, *The Human Stain*; Michael Chabon's novel *The Yiddish Policemen's Union*; and Nicole Krauss's novel of intersecting Chilean and Jewish histories, *Great House*.

Teaching Jewish American Literature in a Multicultural Context

Teaching Jewish American literature in a multicultural context requires a methodology that is comparative but not static, and chronological but not teleological, and that uses theory less to excavate the meaning of a text and more to explore how the text engages national and even international conceptions of nation, race, and religion in localized and specific ways. Rather than teach the different ethnic literatures in blocks—a few weeks on Jews, a few weeks on African Americans, etc.—I stage comparisons of two and sometimes three texts around a given topic, movement, or location in American life, and thereby summon relevant questions about race and culture. I arrange this course roughly chronologically, but only insofar as doing so permits synchronic comparisons. The syllabus includes distinct units clustering theory and literature, in which the theoretical texts prompt questions and provide an analytical lexicon that the literature invariably extends and exceeds. Such units might include Migration Nation, Pluralism (and the New Pluralism), and Race and Recognition.

The course might begin with "Fictions of the Trans-American Imaginary," an essay by Paula M. L. Moya and Ramón Saldívar that surveys several critical engagements with imaginary conceptions of American national space, especially conceptions from the nineteenth century. From there, we might consider Emma Lazarus's poem "The New Colossus," with its now-famous American creed, "[G]ive me your tired, your poor, / Your huddled masses yearning to breathe free," a statement of welcome whose value is in the formulation itself. Students instantly recognize these lines, even when they don't know their origin, and are often surprised to learn that Lazarus was a well-educated Sephardic Jewish woman from a long-established, prosperous merchant family. Lazarus's use of the sonnet form suggests how the poem was written to be instantly familiar, even quotable upon delivery. But it is helpful for students to learn that "The New Colossus" was one of many literary claims about how the United States should respond to shifts in the nation's racial demographics, including those caused by the arrival of immigrants, the northward migration of African Americans, the colonization and dispersal of Native Americans, and the country's recent colonization of the Southwest and the Mexicans living there. Two years after Lazarus wrote her poem, María Amparo Ruiz de Burton published *The Squatter and the Don*, a novel about white settlers' usurpation of Mexican land in California, and ten years later Charles Chesnutt published the first of his "conjure tales," documenting the political economy of plantation life after the Civil War in a highly developed, ironic style. Taken together, these works by Lazarus, Ruiz de Burton, and Chesnutt represent a nation with dramatic population shifts, emerging or transforming practices of racism, and new arguments for a plurality of cultures. When read alone, Lazarus's late poems about Jewish immigration to the United States, including "In Exile," "The New Year," and "The New Colosuss," suggest a plausible congruence between Jewish settlement and the myth of America as a modern promised land, but when we read her work in conjunction with Ruiz de Burton's and Chesnutt's work, we recognize her poetry as one of several attempts to imagine the place of minority cultures in the future space of the nation.

My students discover a more dramatic instance of how formal differences reveal different accounts of national belonging when they compare two proximate novels, Nella Larsen's 1929 *Passing* and Henry Roth's 1934 *Call It Sleep*. *Passing* is written in an understated manner and uses textual ambiguity and linguistic play to confound certitudes about race: all of the characters obsess over race, but by the novel's end it would be hard for a reader to say just what constitutes blackness or whiteness, as each vanishes upon inspection, until the violent episode involving law enforcement at the conclusion. In contrast to Larsen's work, Roth's novel is crowded with neighborhoods, ethnicities, and linguistic idioms. But just as *Passing* deconstructs the black-white binary, though for different reasons, *Call It Sleep* never lands on any fixed or even typical way of being Jewish. Indeed, Roth's use of Christian symbolism suggests that religious patrimony is less important for determining who his protagonist will grow up to be than the heap of mythic material scattered about New York, including a desanctified Statue of Liberty, that is the refuse of other nations, available for repurposing by Jews and anyone else in the country. My students read these two texts alongside Judith Butler's essay on *Passing*, "Passing, Queering: Nella Larsen's Psychoanalytic Challenge," and Matthew Frye Jacobson's discussion of Jewish whiteness in *Whiteness of a Different Color.*

Reading this literature synchronically with students enables them to compare the different worlds imagined by writers working in the same time period and thus complicates our understanding of cultural pluralism, itself a theoretical antecedent to multiculturalism. As a classroom exercise, I pull up a map of New York and ask students to plot the localities of the two novels. Although Larsen's Harlem and Roth's Lower East Side are mere miles apart, they do not share the same "diegetic space," to use Eric Hayot's term, and this realization prompts comparative questions not about ethnic identities but about whole worlds of experience as perceived by each author (13). I ask my students the simple question, Can you imagine a character from one novel walking into the other novel? They cannot, although an exceptional moment in *Call It Sleep* may prove the rule, when the young protagonist, David, accompanies his greenhorn aunt Bertha to the Metropolitan Museum of Art. Bewildered by the art and the other visitors, the immigrant pair feel humiliated and somehow victimized by their overwhelming exposure to a version of New York that had been entirely out of sight for them and the reader. They only escape the museum by following a pair of museumgoers who seem to know their way around. Larsen's sophisticated, fair-skinned Clare and Irene could easily be around the corner in another gallery, perhaps passing, or simply letting others assume what they want about their race, as happens in Larsen's novel. Certainly Roth's characters would never know the difference. If *Call It Sleep* yields no singular model of Jewishness in its pages, reading it alongside another text from the same period and place reveals how both works are about navigating the American codes of race and identity.

Despite their many differences, *Passing* and *Call It Sleep* both end by
navigating the threshold between public and private spaces that characterizes so much thinking about cultural pluralism. In *Passing*, a racially
fluid party is disrupted when the white supremacist husband of a woman
who has been passing bursts in, insisting on his wife's and others' fidelity
to the color line. His wife's subsequent defenestration marks the border-
line between private and public spaces that had divided the novel's racial
imaginary thus far, and her death seems to suggest the impossibility of
reconciliation. *Call It Sleep* also concludes with a convergence of public
and private, when the injured David is carried into his home by a crowd of
concerned locals, who represent the pluralist public descending upon the
previously private space of his Jewish family. Unlike *Passing*, whose ending both foresees and forecloses a postracial imaginary, *Call It Sleep* puts
its faith in the public sphere and the polis for the formation of a new kind
of Jew and American. Reading *Call It Sleep* with *Passing* reveals that black
and Jewish writers similarly investigated the common bases of American
polity, and Jewish writers and their characters could make claims on mainstream American culture precisely through their mastery of the codes of
whiteness (Franco).

Pluralism turns out to be an evergreen concept, since nearly every generation after Kallen has invented what it would call "the new pluralism."
By the late 1950s, many social theorists were insisting that religion was
the most salient form of difference in American life, though by the early
1970s, the return of white ethnicity—and thus the would-be evasion or
obviation of whiteness as a stand-alone identity—captivated many social
theorists, who perceived yet another new pluralism (Herberg 85; see Hungerford xix, xx). This transition is evident in Ozick's 1976 stories "Bloodshed," about the tension between a secular, ethnic Jew and his Hasidic
cousin, and "Envy; or, Yiddish in America," which concludes with an un-
bidden phone conversation between a Yiddish poet and an anti-Semitic
interlocutor, during which the participants and the narrator let fly a constellation of slurs. In the twenty-first century, social theorists working on
pluralism have predictably returned to religion, though instead of relying
on the distinctions Kallen made between public and private spheres, writers like Judith Butler ("Is Judaism"), Michael Warner, and William Connolly, whose works I rotate into the syllabus at this point, recognize that
there are several simultaneous publics and constructs of religion cooper-
ating, and that there is a dynamic, even fluid, exchange of sectarian practices within the public sphere.

I assign chapters from Connolly's work of political theory *Pluralism* to expand the class's thinking about diversity, especially as the course ventures into post-1960s literature about rights and recognition. Connolly raises two questions that serve as useful prompts for students in a comparative, multicultural literature course: "To what extent does a cultural presumption of the normal individual or the preexisting subject precede and confine conventional pluralism? What conceptions of identity (and difference) are taken for granted in pluralist celebrations of 'diversity?'" (xiii). Following Connolly, we can do better than simply treat individual texts as static representations of ethnic experience; instead we can read them as representations and enactments of the larger contexts wherein ethnicity is formed and mediated. To apply such a reading, students might compare Allegra Goodman's novel *Kaaterskill Falls*, about a Jewish community of varying degrees of religiosity and apostasy, with Tomás Rivera's novel . . . *And the Earth Did Not Devour Him*, whose protagonist wrestles with his Mexican migrant community's Catholic fatalism while still attempting to sustain his ties to the community. Goodman's novel is Victorian-themed and realist, and Rivera's is experimental and minimalist, but each depicts a structurally similar context wherein a tightly organized sectarian community is confounded by the tension between privately held religious beliefs and public labor.

Students might also read Segal's *Her First American*, which is similarly mediated by a dynamic pluralism, with Gish Jen's *Mona in the Promised Land*. Segal's novel charts Ilka's discovery of the several contexts framing her relationship with Carter. When Ilka and Carter are alone together, they freely explore the resonances of Jewish and African American histories and experiences, though when in public, Ilka is advised by another character, "Jews not permitted here," a line that at first strikes her as anti-Semitic but that she eventually understands to mean that in the American public imaginary, Jewishness is eclipsed by black and white (210). Similar moments occur in *Mona in the Promised Land*, in which the daughter of Chinese immigrants converts to Judaism, to the puzzlement of both her black and white friends. They nickname her "Changowitz," which patches over the racial divides with humor, but the novel subtly demonstrates that what W. E. B. Du Bois deemed the "color line" between black and white constitutes a tightrope walk for other racial and ethnic groups (Du Bois 5). Students might compare both Segal's and Jen's novels with Percival Everett's novel *Watershed*, about an African American geologist who wishes to minimize the politics of race in his life but becomes involved in a land dispute between white ranchers and a local Indian tribe. Both groups interpolate him because of his race, and he learns that race, property rights, and even religion—all of which he has sought to avoid thinking about as an adult—are inscribed with different values on each side of the dispute.

It turns out that one of the effects of teaching Jewish American literature in a multicultural context is the complication of the term *multicultural* itself. Although this essay does not aim to swap pluralism in for multiculturalism, it makes evident that attention to the pluralist concerns for a dynamic exchange between public and private spheres, and to the protean slippage of religion into (and back out of) categories of race and ethnicity, allows for a complex study across different groupings of literature. Of course, Jewish American literature's rich account of Jewish and American cultures warrants its inclusion in a multicultural curriculum on its own merits; with the trailing theory of pluralism, the comparisons practically teach themselves.

Works Cited

Antin, Mary. *The Promised Land*. Penguin Classics, 2012.

Bellow, Saul. *The Adventures of Augie March*. Penguin Books, 1981.

———. *Mr. Sammler's Planet*. Viking Press, 1970.

Butler, Judith. "Is Judaism Zionism?" *The Power of Religion in the Public Sphere*, by Butler et al., edited by Eduardo Mendieta and Jonathan VanAntwerpen, Columbia UP, 2013, 70–91.

———. "Passing, Queering: Nella Larsen's Psychoanalytic Challenge." *Bodies That Matter: On the Discursive Limits of Sex*, by Butler, Routledge, 1993, 167–86.

Cahan, Abraham. Yekl *and "The Imported Bridegroom" and Other Stories of Yiddish New York*. Dover Publications, 1970.

Chabon, Michael. *The Yiddish Policemen's Union*. HarperCollins, 2007.

Chesnutt, Charles W. *The Conjure Stories*. Norton Critical Edition, W. W. Norton, 2011.

Connolly, William. *Pluralism*. Duke UP, 2005.

Du Bois, W. E. B. *The Souls of Black Folk*. W. W. Norton, 1999.

Everett, Percival. *Watershed*. Graywolf Press, 1996.

Franco, Dean. *Race, Rights, and Recognition: Jewish American Literature since 1969*. Cornell UP, 2012.

Goodman, Allegra. *Kaaterskill Falls*. Dial Press, 1998.

Greenberg, Cheryl. *Troubling the Waters: Black-Jewish Relations in the American Century*. Princeton UP, 2010.

Hayot, Eric. *On Literary Worlds*. Oxford UP, 2012.

Herberg, Will. *Protestant, Catholic, Jew: An Essay in American Religious Sociology*. Doubleday, 1960.

Hungerford, Amy. *Postmodern Belief: American Literature and Religion since 1960*. Princeton UP, 2010.

Jacobson, Matthew Frye. *Whiteness of a Different Color: European Immigrants and the Alchemy of Race*. Harvard UP, 1999.

Jen, Gish. *Mona in the Promised Land*. Vintage Books, 1997.

Kallen, Horace. *Culture and Democracy in the United States*. Transaction Publishers, 1998.

Klepfisz, Irene. *Dreams of an Insomniac: Jewish Feminist Essays, Speeches, and Diatribes*. Eighth Mountain Press, 1990.

Krauss, Nicole. *Great House*. W. W. Norton, 2010.

Larsen, Nella. *Passing*. 1929. Penguin Books, 2003.

Lazarus, Emma. "The New Colossus." 1883. *Selected Poems and Other Writings*, edited by Gregory Eiselein, Broadview Books, 2002, p. 233.

Malamud, Bernard. *The Tenants*. 1971. Farrar, Straus and Giroux, 2003.

Moya, Paula M. L., and Ramón Saldívar. "Fictions of the Trans-American Imaginary." *MFS: Modern Fiction Studies*, vol. 49, no. 1, 2003, pp. 1--18.

Ozick, Cynthia. "Bloodshed." *"Bloodshed" and Three Novellas*, by Ozick, Syracuse UP, 1995, pp. 53–72.

———. "Envy; or, Yiddish in America." Ozick, *"The Pagan Rabbi,"* pp. 39–100.

———. *"The Pagan Rabbi" and Other Stories*. Alfred A. Knopf, 1971.

———. "The Pagan Rabbi." Ozick, *"The Pagan Rabbi,"* pp. 1–38.

Rivera, Tomás. . . . *And the Earth Did Not Devour Him*. 1971. Arte Público, 1992.

Roth, Henry. *Call It Sleep*. 1934. Picador, 1991.

Roth, Philip. *The Human Stain*. Houghton Mifflin, 2000.

———. *Portnoy's Complaint*. 1969. Vintage Books, 1994.

Rothberg, Michael. *Multidirectional Memory: Remembering the Holocaust in the Age of Decolonization*. Stanford UP, 2009.

Ruiz de Burton, María Amparo. 1885. *The Squatter and the Don*. Arte Público, 1997.

Schwartz, Delmore. *"In Dreams Begin Responsibilities" and Other Stories*. New Directions Publishing, 1978.

Segal, Lore. *Her First American*. The New Press, 1985.

Warner, Michael. *Publics and Counterpublics*. Zone Books, 2002.

Yezierska, Anzia. *Hungry Hearts and Other Stories*. Persea Books, 1985.

Meri-Jane Rochelson and Donna Aza Weir-Soley

Team-Teaching Jewish and Caribbean Immigration Literature to Diverse Students in a State University

Although the majority of students at Florida International University (FIU) commute locally from South Florida, the university may be considered international because of its gateway location, its emphasis on international studies, and its campuses in other parts of the world. In addition, FIU's commuter population is composed largely of immigrants and children of immigrants from the Caribbean, South and Central America, and, in smaller numbers, Europe, Asia, and Africa. English majors at FIU are required to take a course in multicultural literature, options for which in the past included our separately taught courses on the literatures of Jewish and Caribbean immigration, but in 2004 we created the single, team-taught course Migrant Stories: Jewish and Caribbean, Caribbean and Jewish. This successful and rewarding course explored similarities among immigrant groups and modeled intellectual collaboration and principles of mutuality and respect.

Scheduling the team-taught course involved careful planning.[1] We taught alternating classes, in which Donna Aza Weir-Soley focused on Caribbean literature and Meri-Jane Rochelson on Jewish literature, and we scheduled one class each in which we taught a book from the other's half of the syllabus. We both taught *Days of Awe*, a novel that bridges the two cultures. We also sat in on every class we did not teach, and participated sparingly. We wanted to make clear to the students that one could teach as well as study a book from a cultural background not one's own, and that we were learning from each other's materials and methods.

We intended the course to combine rigorous content and personal engagement, so we taught using lectures and discussion. Lectures by both instructors provided background and drew on scholarship by historians of immigration as well as by literary critics. To familiarize students with the history and culture of the Caribbean, Weir-Soley called upon work by Caribbean writers and scholars. To assist with unfamiliar Jewish content, Rochelson posted on our supplemental *Blackboard* platform Web sites such as *Judaism 101* (www.jewfaq.org), a basic online encyclopedia that offers an Orthodox perspective but also explores differences among the various Jewish religious movements, and *My Jewish Learning*, a collection of articles on many aspects of Jewish life.

Common Ground and Difference in Immigrant Experience

Migrant Stories explored issues common to all immigrant groups: economic insecurity; discrimination; generational conflicts over changing mores, language use, and parent-child role reversals; disparities of gender, sexuality, class, and power in old and new cultures; and uncertainty about how much assimilation to a new culture is desirable or even possible. Our syllabus combined the syllabi of our previously separate courses and was roughly chronological, starting with the Jewish experience, moving into the Caribbean, and ending with Achy Obejas's *Days of Awe*. Obejas's novel combines both literary heritages and added Sephardic focus to a Jewish reading list that, because of the chronological structure, otherwise emphasized the Ashkenazi great wave of immigration.[2] Our syllabus also included texts written outside the United States. We began with Israel Zangwill's *Children of the Ghetto*, a British Victorian novel that introduced issues concerning immigrant experience that reappeared throughout the semester and covered Jewish life and ritual in a level of detail that other course texts did not.

Introducing students to Jews and Judaism was part of our course. FIU has a substantial Jewish student population, but only a small percentage take Jewish studies classes. In fact, the enrollment of Jewish students in this course did not differ significantly from enrollment in our other

British or American literature courses. Our students were predominantly Latinx, although a significant number were of African descent, and most had roots in the Caribbean and Latin America. Out of forty-five students in two classes, only five identified as Jewish. Many of our students may not have initially understood the value Judaism places on ritual and moral behaviors, in contrast to beliefs, or the distinction between the ethnic and religious components of Jewishness. Indeed, thorny questions of whether Jews are a nation, a people, or a religious group led to lively class discussions, especially since we were looking at the experiences of Jewish immigrants in and from many nations, including the United Kingdom, the United States, Cuba, Spain, and the Russian Empire.

We continued the part of the course on Jewish literature by reading the first chapters of Mary Antin's *The Promised Land*, including her descriptions of childhood in Russia and her early school years in Boston. We then read either Abraham Cahan's *The Rise of David Levinsky* or several of Cahan's short stories from Yekl *and "The Imported Bridegroom."* The stories include a variety of immigrant perspectives, including those of workers, and depict the disillusionment immigrants sometimes felt. The first part of the syllabus ended with Anzia Yezierska's *Bread Givers*, set just a few decades later.

The part of the course on Caribbean literature looked at the immigration of Caribbean people to places as diverse as London, the Dominican Republic, and New York. Weir-Soley discussed the critical reception history of the literary texts assigned to the class and taught students about postcolonial, black feminist, and other theoretical approaches relevant to examining those texts. Spirited conversations on history, race, gender, sexuality, culture, and politics characterized small and large group discussions, even as we analyzed books written at widely different times. For example, we discussed how Jews were racialized as nonwhite for much of the nineteenth century, and we also looked at issues of gender and sexuality in early-twentieth-century works by Cahan and Yezierska as well as in later fiction by Samuel Selvon and Paule Marshall.

Reading Marshall's *Brown Girl, Brownstones*, Julia Alvarez's *How the García Girls Lost Their Accents*, and Edwidge Danticat's *The Farming of Bones* helped students understand the complexities of colonialism, slavery, neocolonialism, dictatorships, poverty, and other historical, political, and economic conditions that forced Caribbean nationals to migrate to countries that were not always welcoming to them. Prior to taking the course, some students had not thought about the reasons for the linguistic and cultural diversity of the region we call the Caribbean. In the course we explored whether there is one Caribbean or several, and what linkages can be made among hispanophone, anglophone, and francophone Caribbean texts, cultures, and historiographies.

In addition to learning more about the Caribbean region, students learned to make linkages between Jewish and Caribbean immigration to the United Kingdom and the United States in different time periods and with different sociopolitical outcomes. For example, students compared racism and anti-Semitism in *Brown Girl, Brownstones* and *The Rise of David Levinsky*. Selvon's *Lonely Londoners* offered insight into the experiences of Caribbean immigrants to London during World War II, when they arrived as colonial subjects who either fought for the United Kingdom or shored up its war-depleted workforce. Students were surprised to discover that anglophone Caribbean citizens were British subjects and did not need visas to enter the United Kingdom during the colonial period. However, Caribbean immigrants faced discrimination and exclusion for a longer period of time than did British Jews, for whom economic success came relatively quickly, as seen in *Children of the Ghetto*. In large measure, this disparity was because Jews came to be seen as white.[3] We discussed race as a social construct, in which some minorities are accepted by the dominant ethnic group as white, and others are identified as black, to maintain hierarchies. Students saw the effects of American as well as British racism on Caribbean immigrants and the ways in which race acts as a barrier to acculturation and economic mobility.[4]

Engaging Difference in Pedagogical Collaborations

Differences in age, race, ethnicity, culture, gender, sexual orientation, personality, and teaching experience inform pedagogical styles. In 2004, when we first taught the course together, we were at different stages in our careers. Weir-Soley was a relatively new assistant professor and Rochelson had been teaching at FIU for twenty years. Weir-Soley identified ethnically as an Afro-Caribbean immigrant, while Rochelson identified as Jewish American, the daughter and granddaughter of immigrants. We also differed, at points, in pedagogical style. Rather than allow these differences to impede collaborations in the classroom, we accepted and used them as a necessary and fruitful part of cross-cultural collaboration. We saw each other as individuals and colleagues whose goal was to participate with students in a knowledge community also informed by historical, cultural, and literary differences and commonalities. Our classrooms, therefore, became microcosms of our communities. As Audre Lorde said in "The Master's Tools Will Never Dismantle the Master's House": "Difference must not be merely tolerated, but seen as a fund of necessary polarities between which our creativity can spark . . . a dialectic" (111).

Impact of the Course

Since our first collaboration in 2004, we have met former students who expressed what a life-changing experience the class was for them. Many former students who identify as white stated that they would never have developed an interest in African American or Caribbean literature had it not been for the course. Others said that the comparisons between Jewish literature and literature written by writers of African descent gave them a greater appreciation of what both groups shared as well as the ways in which they were different. Indeed, in a class discussion on generational conflict in *Bread Givers*, a student articulated what we had hoped would be one of the insights of the course: "I never realized Jews were so much like Haitians."

In 2004 we were aware of new congressional proposals to curtail immigration, but the threat they represented seemed far in the future; similarly, historical restrictions on nonwhite immigration to the United States, enshrined by the 1924 Johnson-Reed Act, seemed to be well in the past. In our course, we wanted to alert our students to this history and to future possibilities, but more centrally we wanted to show them the connections in experience among immigrant groups and to help them better understand those connections between groups in their own communities. Today the threats against immigration and asylum are real, and any course on immigration literature needs to be taught against that looming background.

The majority of students of African descent who attend FIU today are Haitian American. In a political context in which Haitians are not allowed the same right to refugee status as Cubans, even though they have fled dictatorships, natural disasters, and economic hardships, Haitian students are very much aware of their marginalized status in the United States. They have told us what a great impact the course had on them and how important it was for them to see Haitian American literature in particular, and Caribbean literature in general, analyzed side by side with Jewish literature. Jewish Americans were no longer marginalized in the America these students knew, so it was important for them to understand that it had not always been that way. Haitians have established themselves in the literary culture and the economy of the United States, but not much has changed for them politically. Under Donald Trump's presidency, Haitians have, in fact, experienced devastating setbacks. As of this writing, Haitians face the insecurity of their Temporary Protected Status, which means that they are vulnerable to deportation. At the same time, refugees from around the world clamor for the security that the United States once seemed to promise, while the Trump administration has created devastating conditions and human rights abuses at the southern border.

Today, it is more important than ever that we continue to make critical and historical links in our classrooms that show the United States as a nation of diverse peoples, most of whom came from elsewhere. We need to show both how far some groups have come and how far some still have to go before we can have the truly democratic society in our country that we strive to model in the classroom.

Notes

1. So that we would each get credit for teaching a full course, we offered two sections of the course at the same time and place, one section assigned to each of us. Students could register for either one. We each graded half of each set of reading responses, ensuring that students would get feedback from both of us throughout the semester. Midterm and final exams carried equal weight, so we each graded one exam, either the midterm or the final, for each student. We each reviewed half of the student papers and then traded; we then went over the grades we had assigned and recorded separately. Finding that we had similar grading standards was an unexpected plus.

2. When Rochelson taught a freestanding class in Jewish immigration literature, she started with Emma Lazarus's "The New Colossus" and Israel Zangwill's *The Melting-Pot,* focusing on immigration to North America. She omitted Zangwill's *Children of the Ghetto* but taught both Abraham Cahan's stories and *The Rise of David Levinsky* and stories by Anzia Yezierska in *How I Found America,* as well as *Days of Awe.* She taught Eva Hoffman's post-Holocaust *Lost in Translation* and Dalia Sofer's *Septembers of Shiraz,* adding to the diversity of histories and cultures represented. Weir-Soley's freestanding courses that featured immigrants focused on women writers from the Caribbean, Latin America, Mexico, and Asia. In the team-taught course, we established a gender balance and a sharper focus on Jewish and Caribbean writers.

3. A number of recent theorists have discussed how Jews in twentieth-century America became identified as white. Karen Brodkin's *How Jews Became White Folks* is worth a look, though it has some limitations.

4. In addition to the primary sources on our syllabus, we drew upon and referred to other primary as well as secondary sources throughout the course. Among these are works by Burch; Diner; Gartner, "Great Jewish Migration" and

Jewish Immigrant; Glissant and Dash; Hall; James; Kincaid; Pressman; and Zaborowska.

Works Cited

Alvarez, Julia. *How the García Girls Lost Their Accents.* Workman, 1991.
Antin, Mary. *The Promised Land.* 1912. Modern Library Paperback, Random House, 2001.
Brodkin, Karen. *How Jews Became White Folks and What That Says about Race in America.* Rutgers UP, 1999.
Burch, C. Beth. "Mary Antin's *The Promised Land* and the Unspoken Failure of Assimilation." *The Changing Mosaic: From Cahan to Malamud, Roth and Ozick*, special issue of *Studies in American Jewish Literature*, vol. 12, 1993, pp. 36–41
Cahan, Abraham. *The Rise of David Levinsky.* 1917. Penguin Books, 1993.
———. *Yekl and "The Imported Bridegroom" and Other Stories of Yiddish New York.* Dover Publications, 1970.
Danticat, Edwidge. *The Farming of Bones.* Soho Press, 1998.
Diner, Hasia. *Jewish Americans: The Immigrant Experience.* Hugh Lauter Levin Associates, 2002.
Gartner, Lloyd P. "The Great Jewish Migration, 1881–1914: Myths and Realities." 1984. Kaplan Centre Papers, U of Cape Town, South Africa.
———. *The Jewish Immigrant in England, 1870–1914.* Wayne State UP, 1960. 2nd ed., Vallentine Mitchell Publishers, 2001.
Glissant, Edouard, and Michael Dash. *Caribbean Discourse.* UP of Virginia, 1989.
Hall, Stuart. "The Formation of a Diasporic Intellectual: An Interview with Stuart Hall." By Kuan-hsing Chen. *Stuart Hall: Critical Dialogues in Cultural Studies*, edited by David Morley and Chen, Routledge, 1996, pp. 492–502.
Hoffman, Eva. *Lost in Translation: A Life in a New Language.* Penguin Books, 1989.
James, C. L. R. *The Black Jacobins.* Secker and Warburg, 1938.
Kincaid, Jamaica. *A Small Place.* Farrar, Straus and Giroux, 1988.
Lazarus, Emma. "The New Colossus." 1883. *Poetry Foundation*, https://www.poetryfoundation.org/poems/46550/the-new-colossus.
Lorde, Audre. "The Master's Tools Will Never Dismantle the Master's House." *Sister Outsider: Essays and Speeches by Audre Lorde*, Crossing Press, 1984, pp. 110–13.
Marshall, Paule. *Brown Girl, Brownstones.* Feminist Press, 1959.
Obejas, Achy. *Days of Awe.* Ballantine Books, 2001.
Pressman, Richard S. "Abraham Cahan, Capitalist: David Levinsky, Socialist." *The Changing Mosaic: From Cahan to Malamud, Roth and Ozick*, special issue of *Studies in American Jewish Literature*, vol. 12, 1993, pp. 2–17.
Selvon, Samuel. *The Lonely Londoners.* 1956. Longman, 1987. Longman Caribbean Writers Series.
Sofer, Dalia. *The Septembers of Shiraz.* Harper Perennial, 2008.

Yezierska, Anzia. *Bread Givers.* 1925. 3rd ed., Persea Books, 2003.

———. *How I Found America: Collected Stories of Anzia Yezierska.* Persea Books, 1991.

Zaborowska, Magdalena J. "Americanization of a 'Queer Fellow': Performing Jewishness and Sexuality in Abraham Cahan's *The Rise of David Levinsky.*" *American Studies in Scandinavia,* vol. 29, no. 1, 1997, pp. 18–27.

Zangwill, Israel. *Children of the Ghetto: A Study of a Peculiar People.* 1892. Edited by Meri-Jane Rochelson, Wayne State UP, 1998.

———. *The Melting-Pot.* Edited by Meri-Jane Rochelson, Broadview Press, 2018. Broadview Editions.

Sarah Phillips Casteel

Teaching Black-Jewish Literary Relations in Transnational Perspective

Black-Jewish relations in the United States are by now a well-established topic of research in a number of humanities and social science disciplines. The topic's popularity is such that, according to one critic, it has spawned a veritable "industry" of cultural production and scholarship (Itzkovitz, "Race" 3). For instructors and students, the black-Jewish relations framework also holds considerable appeal, as it allows for a classroom exploration of ethnicity beyond a black-white binary and for an engagement with the histories of two ethnic minorities that have become mutually entangled in American political and social life. Moreover, investigating the connections between these two minorities invites a broader consideration of issues of contemporary relevance, such as interethnic contact and interracial identity as well as assimilation, cultural appropriation, and the social construction of race.

Much like the scholarship, the teaching of black-Jewish relations tends to be organized around the narrative of an uneasy alliance between the two groups that is fatally threatened by a sense of competition and diverging interests. According to the standard account, the black-Jewish alliance was forged in the early twentieth century, reached its height in the civil rights era, began to unravel during the same period, and finally came undone in the early 1990s, its demise marked by the Crown Heights riots and the Nation of Islam's publication of *The Secret Relationship between Blacks and Jews*.[1] Drawing on this account, courses on blacks and Jews often couch the interethnic dynamic in terms of cooperation and conflict, or identification and estrangement, and generally confine themselves to a focus on the United States in the twentieth century.

What may be gained, however, by extending our classroom consideration of blacks and Jews beyond the borders of the United States? This essay discusses how the teaching of black-Jewish literary relations may be beneficially reframed in hemispheric American terms and argues that the topic lends itself to a transnational treatment. Moreover, the hemispheric approach outlined here is not only geographically but also temporally expansive, uncovering a deeper history of black-Jewish encounters in the colonial Americas. To illustrate this approach, I draw on my experience designing a graduate seminar entitled Blacks and Jews: Comparative Diasporas in Transnational Perspective. Informed by emerging historical research on the Jewish Atlantic as well as recent theorizations of global Holocaust memory, the course considers not only prominent texts from the United States but also lesser-known Caribbean engagements with Jewish historical experience. Adopting a comparative-diasporas approach that draws inspiration from what Paul Gilroy calls "the intercultural history of the diaspora concept" (211), the syllabus brings diverse ethnic minority and postcolonial literary traditions into dialogue. I offer the course as an example of how, through the lens of black-Jewish relations, instructors can unsettle the methodological nationalism that has shaped the teaching of literature and open up the study of ethnic literatures in the United States to a larger literary and historical field. This transnational reframing responds to literary studies' recent reorientation toward transnational and comparative paradigms such as hemispheric American studies and world literature while remaining attentive to national and regional contexts of literary production.

Blacks and Jews: Comparative Diasporas in Transnational Perspective has two central goals. The first is to introduce students to the fraught history of twentieth-century black-Jewish relations in the United States as they have been portrayed in literature and performance. The second is to encourage students to situate these portrayals within a broader hemispheric American context of black-Jewish encounter. In particular, I want students to consider how Caribbean literary engagements with Jewishness recast the master narrative of an uneasy alliance and the assumptions about competitive victimhood that underpin that narrative. As I have argued elsewhere

(Casteel, *Calypso Jews*), Caribbean and Caribbean diaspora critics and writers make persistent reference to Jewish history. Gilroy, for example, takes pains to acknowledge a debt to Jewish thinkers at the end of *The Black Atlantic*, while the Guadeloupean novelist Maryse Condé and the St. Kitts–born British novelist Caryl Phillips explore connections between Jewish and African diasporic experiences of persecution and displacement. Why does Jewishness emerge as a key reference point for some Caribbean writers? How do they approach the vexed question of the role of Jews in the Atlantic slave trade? How does the Holocaust figure in the literature of Caribbean decolonization? Incorporating Caribbean perspectives into the course not only sheds new light on familiar issues but also raises questions that expand and complicate students' understanding of both black and Jewish experience in the Americas.

The first half of the course surveys defining moments in the cultural and literary history of black-Jewish relations in the United States. After a session in which we discuss the racial status of early-twentieth-century Jewishness and the practice of Jewish blackface in the film *The Jazz Singer*, in the second week of the course we examine Alice Walker's feminist presentation in *Meridian* of interracial relations within the civil rights movement. We then address Bernard Malamud's *The Tenants* and the battle it stages between two writer figures, one African American and the other Jewish American, against the backdrop of the emergence of the black power movement. Next, we consider the theme of interethnic impersonation in the late twentieth century through two works: the film version of Anna Deavere Smith's one-woman show *Fires in the Mirror*, which rehearses contestations surrounding the 1991 Crown Heights riots, and Philip Roth's *The Human Stain*, which reimagines the novel of racial passing. To round out this first half of the course, we read Rebecca Walker's interracial memoir *Black, White and Jewish* alongside Katya Gibel Azoulay's ethnography *Black, Jewish, and Interracial*.[2]

The session on interracial memoir helps students make the transition to the Caribbean-focused second half of the course, in which identity is presented as creolized and, therefore, as incompatible with the binary formulations that tend to structure discussions of identity in the United States. Having familiarized students with key narratives of black-Jewish relations in the United States in the first half of the course, I now defamiliarize those narratives by turning to Caribbean settings. We begin by considering how Jewishness is variously invoked in Caribbean intellectual history. Our readings for this session range from the early pan-Africanist work of Edward Wilmot Blyden, to the anticolonial writings of Aimé Césaire and Frantz Fanon, to the more recent theoretical interventions of Gilroy. Moving from theory to fiction, we then turn to Condé's neoslave narrative *I, Tituba, Black Witch of Salem*. Students are often drawn to Condé's novel for its imaginative reconstruction of the life of the slave Tituba, one of the first to be accused in the Salem witch trials. For the purposes of this class, our focus is on Condé's inclusion in her novel of a Jewish merchant, whose purchase and eventual liberation of Tituba invites a discussion of controversies and spurious claims surrounding Jewish involvement in Atlantic slavery.

While Condé alludes to the settlement of Sephardic Jews in the Caribbean after their expulsion from the Iberian Peninsula in the 1490s, other Caribbean writers address a more recent Jewish historical trauma: the Holocaust. Accordingly, we next turn to the work of two Caribbean writers who invoke the figure of Anne Frank. We examine the striking cross-cultural juxtapositions that Phillips introduces both in his essays "Anne Frank's Amsterdam" and "In the Ghetto" and in his novel *The Nature of Blood*, which intertwines the story of Othello with that of a Holocaust survivor. Finally, we consider the radicalizing impact of Frank's diary and its film adaptation on the Jamaican heroine of Michelle Cliff's *Abeng*. Although not without tensions and ambivalences, these Caribbean texts diverge from some of the works that describe black-Jewish relations in the United States by advancing a predominantly sympathetic and identificatory, rather than competitive, reading of Jewishness. Moreover, they evidence a rising interest in Jewishness in late twentieth-century Caribbean writing that runs counter to the standard narrative of alliance and decline that has shaped discussions in the United States. These differences reflect the Caribbean's distinctive history of black-Jewish contact as well as the impact of the Holocaust on Caribbean intellectuals who came of age during World War II and in the early postwar decades.

Other recent Caribbean and African diasporic texts that illustrate this rising interest in Jewishness include the St. Lucian poet Derek Walcott's *Tiepolo's Hound*, a verse biography of the Sephardic Caribbean painter Camille Pissarro (which could be paired with the American writer Alice Hoffman's *The Marriage of Opposites*); the Guyanese British writer David Dabydeen's postmodern slavery novels *A Harlot's Progress* and *Johnson's Dictionary*; the Surinamese writer Cynthia McLeod's Jewish plantation novel *The Cost of Sugar*; the Cuban American writer Achy Obejas's *Days of Awe*; the Haitian writers Myriam Chancy's *The Loneliness of Angels* and

Louis-Philippe Dalembert's *Avant que les ombres s'effacent*; and the African Canadian writer Lawrence Hill's *The Book of Negroes*.[3]

This alternative canon of black-Jewish literary relations can serve as a resource for instructors who seek to expand the boundaries of their teaching beyond the framework of the United States and to engage students who are interested in postcolonial and world literatures. Jewish settlement in the Caribbean spanned a period of more than three hundred years, beginning in the seventeenth century and peaking in the latter half of the eighteenth century. Few islands were untouched by a Jewish presence; significant Jewish communities established themselves in Barbados, Jamaica, Curaçao, Suriname, and elsewhere. Indeed, in some parts of the colonial Caribbean, Jews made up as much as one third of the European population (Schorsch 58–59). Recentering pedagogical discussions of black-Jewish relations on the Caribbean thus establishes a more expansive geography of Jewish American experience, bringing to light transnational networks of exchange that developed between Jewish communities in the Caribbean, North America, and Europe. By including in their syllabi Caribbean texts that register this deep and multilayered history of black-Jewish encounters in the Americas, instructors can bridge the gap between ethnic American and postcolonial studies.

Moreover, Caribbean texts such as *I, Tituba* and *Tiepolo's Hound*, which recall the resettlement of Sephardic Jews in the Caribbean, offer instructors an opportunity to explore Sephardic Jewishness with their students. Caribbean literary Sephardism—the invocation of Sephardic historical experience in Caribbean literature—attests to the resonance of the Iberian expulsion for African diaspora writers concerned with concealed identities and questions of cultural resilience in the aftermath of the Middle Passage. In their texts, 1492 refers to both Columbus's so-called discovery of the New World and the expulsion of Sephardic Jews from Spain and Portugal. The year 1492 emerges as a key node of cross-cultural identification that conjoins African diasporic, Jewish, and Indigenous histories of dispossession even as it introduces a more complex understanding of Jews as participants in the colonial project. Contemporary Caribbean writing, which tends to recognize the ambivalent status of Jews in the colonial Americas as "both victims and agents of empire" (Israel 1), can help students nuance narratives of Jewish victimhood by attuning them to Jews' shifting relation to structures of power and whiteness.

Caribbean writing not only reveals the double resonance of 1492 but also attests to the transcultural, global dimensions of Holocaust memory.

In this regard, instructors can benefit from the recent colonial turn in Holocaust studies. In particular, Michael Rothberg's model of "multidirectional memory," in which Holocaust memory enables the memorialization of other historical traumas (Rothberg 3), illuminates the Caribbean context in which, in the absence of a public discourse about slavery, some Caribbean writers turned to the Holocaust as a "surrogate issue" (Philip 84) through which to explore the legacies of the Middle Passage. Together with the historical influx of Holocaust refugees into the Caribbean, the phenomenon of multidirectional memory helps account for the appearance of a number of Caribbean Holocaust narratives in the 1980s and 1990s. In the classroom, instructors can use fictional and autobiographical texts by Phillips, Cliff, NourbeSe Philip, and other writers to illustrate how Holocaust memory has been reanimated in colonial and African diasporic settings. Such texts can prompt a classroom discussion about competitive and multidirectional forms of cultural memory—about the tensions as well as the possibilities generated by the global circulation of Holocaust icons.

An interdisciplinary approach can further enhance courses that reframe black-Jewish relations in transnational terms. In particular, music, a medium that has a unique capacity to dynamically layer diverse cultural influences, can be introduced to further illustrate the reciprocity of black and Jewish intellectual traditions. In the opening session of my course, for example, we listen to tracks by Matisyahu and Bob Marley. Matisyahu's fusion of reggae music with Jewish themes could simply be read as a form of Jewish blackface and cultural appropriation. But playing Marley's "Redemption Song" alongside Matisyahu's Marley-inspired "What I'm Fighting For" highlights Rastafarianism's own borrowings from Jewish narrative traditions and suggests a more complex, recursive form of intercultural influence that challenges discourses of authenticity and purity.[4] Alongside these musical examples, I introduce Smith's uncanny ventriloquism of black and Jewish figures in her play *Fires in the Mirror*, which raises vital questions about racialization and the performativity of identity. Finally, I draw on the visual and material culture of the Jewish Caribbean to help orient students with respect to an unfamiliar history. Wyatt Gallery's photographs of the beautiful sand-floored synagogues and Jewish cemeteries of the Caribbean provide context for the literary works that refer to this history, while the lithographs, drawings, and paintings of the nineteenth-century Sephardic Caribbean artists Isaac Mendes Belisario and Camille Pissarro serve as visual intertexts for the Sephardic-themed course readings (Barringer et al.; Brettell and Zukowski).

I have outlined here one method of reframing a course on black-Jewish literary relations in transnational terms. Caribbean literary engagements with Jewishness attest to the flexibility of the black-Jewish framework and its susceptibility to a transnational, hemispheric treatment. Other transnational framings might address black-Jewish literary relations in European settings such as Britain and France, or engage a wider North American context by including Canadian texts. North Africa and Israel are other possible foci. Regardless of the choice of locale, instructors will want to emphasize how the historical, political, and cultural specificities of each regional and national setting have shaped the development of African and Jewish diasporic communities and their interethnic relation. By the same token, given the migratory trajectories of African and Jewish diasporic histories, and the diverse sites in which these trajectories have overlapped, a transnational treatment of black-Jewish literary relations is both pertinent and productive and can provide a new means of engaging students with Jewish studies.

Notes

1. Some critics have complicated this account. Daniel Itzkovitz, for example, questions the investment of Jews in a narrative of alliance and rupture as well as their tendency to idealize the civil rights partnership ("Notes"). Major statements such as Eric Sundquist's *Strangers in the Land* incorporate this kind of nuance but nonetheless endorse "the prevailing historical interpretation that black-Jewish relations suffered serious erosion over the last half of the twentieth century" (Sundquist 4), resulting in what Sundquist characterizes as a "political and cultural divorce" (5).

2. James McBride's *The Color of Water* is another good option for instructors who wish to include an interracial black-Jewish memoir on their syllabi.

3. See Sarah Phillips Casteel, *Calypso Jews* and "David Dabydeen's Hogarth," for detailed discussions of these texts.

4. Other musical instances of this recursive relation range from Johnny Mathis's "Kol Nidre" and Billie Holiday's "My Yiddishe Momme" to the Jewish Canadian hip-hop klezmer artist Socalled's "You Are Never Alone." (The music video for Socalled's song, available at www.socalledmusic.com, is also worth screening for students.) The Mathis and Holiday tracks are included in the Idelsohn Society for Musical Preservation's *Black Sabbath: The Secret Musical History of Black-Jewish Relations.*

Works Cited

Azoulay, Katya Gibel. *Black, Jewish, and Interracial: It's Not the Color of Your Skin, but the Race of Your Kin, and Other Myths of Identity.* Duke UP, 1997.

Barringer, T. J., et al. *Art and Emancipation in Jamaica: Isaac Mendes Belisario and His World.* Yale Center for British Art, 2007.

Blyden, Edward W. "The Jewish Question." *Black Spokesman: Selected Writings of Edward Wilmot Blyden,* edited by Hollis R. Lynch, Frank Cass, 1971, pp. 209–14.

Brettell, Richard R., and Karen Zukowski. *Camille Pissarro in the Caribbean, 1850–1855: Drawings from the Collection at Olana.* Introduction by Joachim Pissarro, Hebrew Congregation of St. Thomas, 1996.

Casteel, Sarah Phillips. *Calypso Jews: Jewishness in the Caribbean Literary Imagination.* Columbia UP, 2016.

———. "David Dabydeen's Hogarth: Blacks, Jews and Postcolonial Ekphrasis." *The Cambridge Journal of Postcolonial Literary Inquiry,* vol. 3, no. 1, Jan. 2016, pp. 117–33.

Césaire, Aimé. *Discourse on Colonialism.* Translated by Joan Pinkham, Monthly Review Press, 1972.

Chancy, Myriam. *The Loneliness of Angels.* Peepal Tree Press, 2010.

Cliff, Michelle. *Abeng.* 1984. Plume, 1995.

Condé, Maryse. *I, Tituba, Black Witch of Salem.* 1986. Translated by Richard Philcox, Random House, 1992.

Dabydeen, David. *A Harlot's Progress.* Vintage Books, 2000.

———. *Johnson's Dictionary.* Peepal Tree Press, 2013.

Dalembert, Louis-Philippe. *Avant que les ombres s'effacent.* Sabine Wespieser, 2017.

The Diary of Anne Frank. Directed by George Stevens, George Stevens Productions, 1959.

Fanon, Frantz. *Black Skin, White Masks.* 1967. Translated by Charles Lamm Markmann, Grove Press, 2008.

Frank, Anne. *The Diary of A Young Girl.* 1953. Pocket Books, 1958.

Gallery, Wyatt. *Jewish Treasures of the Caribbean.* Schiffer Publishing, 2016.

Gilroy, Paul. *The Black Atlantic: Modernity and Double Consciousness.* 1993. Harvard UP, 1996.

Hill, Lawrence. *The Book of Negroes.* HarperCollins, 2007.

Hoffman, Alice. *The Marriage of Opposites.* Simon and Schuster, 2015.

Holiday, Billie. "My Yiddishe Momme." *Black Sabbath: The Secret Musical History of Black-Jewish Relations,* Idelsohn Society for Musical Preservation, 2010.

Israel, Jonathan. *Diasporas within a Diaspora: Jews, Crypto-Jews, and the World of Maritime Empires (1540–1740).* Brill, 2002.

Itzkovitz, Daniel. "Notes from the Black-Jewish Monologue." *Transition,* vol. 105, 2011, pp. 3–20.

———. "Race and Jews in America: An Introduction." *Shofar,* vol. 23, no. 4, Summer 2005, pp. 1–8.

The Jazz Singer. Directed by Alan Crosland, music by Al Jolson, Warner Bros., 1927

Malamud, Bernard. *The Tenants.* Farrar, Straus and Giroux, 1971.

Marley, Bob. "Redemption Song." *Uprising,* Tuff Gong Studios, 1980.

Mathis, Johnny. "Kol Nidre." *Black Sabbath: The Secret Musical History of Black-Jewish Relations*, Idelsohn Society for Musical Preservation, 2010.

Matisyahu. "What I'm Fighting For." *Youth*, Epic/Sony, 2006.

McBride, James. *The Color of Water: A Black Man's Tribute to His White Mother*. Riverhead Books, 1996.

McLeod, Cynthia. *The Cost of Sugar*. 1987. Translated by Gerald R. Mettam, Waterfront Press, 2010.

Obejas, Achy. *Days of Awe*. Ballantine Books, 2001.

Philip, M. NourbeSe. *Showing Grit: Showboating North of the 44th Parallel*. Poui Publications, 1993.

Phillips, Caryl. "Anne Frank's Amsterdam." *The European Tribe*, by Phillips, Faber and Faber, 1987, pp. 66–71.

———. "In the Ghetto." *The European Tribe*, by Phillips, Faber and Faber, 1987, pp. 52–55.

———. *The Nature of Blood*. Vintage Books, 1997.

Roth, Philip. *The Human Stain*. Vintage Books, 2000.

Rothberg, Michael. *Multidirectional Memory: Remembering the Holocaust in the Age of Decolonization*. Stanford UP, 2009.

Schorsch, Jonathan. *Jews and Blacks in the Early Modern World*. Cambridge UP, 2004.

The Secret Relationship between Blacks and Jews: Volume One. Nation of Islam, 1991.

Smith, Anna Deavere, writer and performer. *Fires in the Mirror: Crown Heights, Brooklyn and Other Identities*. Directed by George C. Wolfe, American Playhouse, 1993.

Socalled. "You Are Never Alone." *Ghetto Blaster*, JDub Records, 2007.

Sundquist, Eric J. *Strangers in the Land: Blacks, Jews, Post-Holocaust America*. Harvard UP, 2005.

Walcott, Derek. *Tiepolo's Hound*. Farrar, Straus and Giroux, 2000.

Walker, Alice. *Meridian*. Harcourt, 1976.

Walker, Rebecca. *Black, White and Jewish*. Riverhead Books, 2001.

Jodi Eichler-Levine

Teaching Jewish American Children's and Young Adult Literature

Teaching Jewish American literature for children and young adults at the seams of many kinds of overlapping difference entails highlighting two genres that are often overlooked in the academy. Children's literature was once shunned by critics as insufficiently serious, and Jewish children's literature was alternately seen as too "ethnic" to be a part of the canon and too "white" to be included in multicultural literature (Levitt 7). Even students may be puzzled by Jewish children's literature, finding it too religious, not religious enough, too particular, or too universal, in a space at the intersection of religion and ethnicity.

This essay introduces the teaching of Jewish children's literature and pays particular attention to the juxtapositions of gender, religion, and ethnicity within it. Two facts about my teaching are relevant. The first is that, for the most part, my classes in Jewish children's literature are not offered in literature departments: I have always been employed in departments of religious studies (my doctoral field), though my courses are prolifically cross-listed. The second is that I have taught at two different institutions: first, at the University of Wisconsin, Oshkosh, a regional state university, and second, at Lehigh University, a small private research university in Pennsylvania. A focus on the intersectional nature of gender, ethnicity, religion, and other aspects of identity informs my teaching and links the study of Jewish American children's literature to a host of other fields.[1]

What Is Jewish Children's Literature?

Jewish children's literature is not a coherent category. On the one hand, American Jews have been publishing titles aimed at children since the nineteenth century, including Rabbi Isaac Leeser's 1863 *Catechism for Jewish Children* and biographies and biblical stories from the Jewish Publication Society (Sarna). On the other hand, the current debate over what constitutes "Jewish children's literature" parallels the debates over other ethnic literature categories. Does the author or the illustrator need to be Jewish? What is Jewish content? How does one distinguish books for young people from books for adults? The place of Jewish identity at the crossroads of race, ethnicity, and religion further complicates this picture. Many students expect my courses to be filled with holiday stories; they are surprised when I include Judy Blume's *Are You There God? It's Me, Margaret*, and they have rarely heard of creative takes on biblical texts like Julius Lester's *Pharaoh's Daughter*.

Teaching Jewish children's literature entails defining the genre for students in order to deconstruct it. Students are usually unfamiliar with the early- and mid-twentieth-century classics of Jewish children's literature, from Sadie Weilerstein's 1935 *The Adventures of K'tonton* to Sydney Taylor's 1951 *All-of-a-Kind Family*. The genre can be broadly defined as including books by or about Jews. I teach novels, chapter books, picture books, and poetry from the full length of Jewish American history, though I do focus on works from the twentieth and early twenty-first centuries. These works may be published by either the remaining imprints that specialize in the genre (e.g., Kar-Ben) or by more general publishers. In recent years, PJ Library, a project of the Harold Grinspoon Foundation, has dramatically altered the scene for Jewish children's literature by distributing large numbers of free books to Jewish children and thus exercising power over both new publications and publishers' backlists; the effects of this are just beginning to be studied (Gross 2017).

Teachers can open up the topic for students by situating Jewish children's literature within children's literature more generally. Assigning short pieces from either *Keywords for Children's Literature* (Nel and Paul) or *The Oxford Handbook of Children's Literature* (Mickenberg and Vallone) can help, as can in-class exercises. One of my favorite exercises, which I often assign during the first week of the semester, is a group tagging exercise. First, students spend ten minutes brainstorming every children's or young adult book they can remember. Then they are asked to review their lists and tally how many books include representations of religion, ethnic or racial diversity, LGBTQ+ characters, variance in ability, class issues, and so on. The results, which I write on the board, prompt discussion and typically reveal a rather white and Christian picture of children's literature. The exercise also reveals category confusions, as students debate what counts as religion in a children's book—which, of course, raises the question of what we mean when we say "religion."[2]

Teaching across the Gaps

I usually teach Jewish children's literature comparatively with other youth literatures. Doing so helps students connect to a genre that might seem either exotic or dully familiar. Crucially, the act of comparison helps them move from a descriptive or reactive mode to a higher-level mode of thinking. To compare multiple items is to notice, and thus to potentially dismantle, their structures. The religious studies scholar Jonathan Z. Smith famously observed that "in comparison a magic dwells"; although he was critical of flat comparisons, he noted that "[c]omparison requires the postulation of difference as the grounds of its being interesting (rather than tautological) and a methodical manipulation of difference, a playing across the 'gap' in the service of some useful end" (35).

Those gaps are fertile intellectual ground. At the University of Wisconsin, Oshkosh, I developed a comparative course titled Religion, Children's Books, Difference as part of a university-wide general education reform. The course was designed for a class of twenty-five first-semester students. The curricular goals were to introduce students to the liberal arts and to engage with the theme of intercultural knowledge. The syllabus included Jewish children's books such as Taylor's *All-of-a-Kind Family* and Sandy Eisenberg Sasso's *Abuelita's Secret Matzahs*, as well as books on other traditions, such as Jacqueline Woodson's *Feathers*, Naomi Shihab Nye's *Habibi*, Sanjay Patel's *Little Book of Hindu Deities*, Lester's *The Old African*, and, one year, selections from the American Girl series (Greene, *Meet Rebecca* and *Candlelight*; Porter), which includes both Jewish and Christian examples.

By placing *All-of-a-Kind Family* near the beginning of the syllabus, I was able to show students what one piece of ethnic American literature looked like in the 1950s, as a historical starting point. *All-of-a-Kind Family*, the first book in the All-of-a-Kind series, is semiautobiographical; it describes the experience of a Jewish family with five daughters living on the Lower East Side of New York City in 1914. Assigning some of June Cummins's critical essays on the novel provided historical context on the Cold War atmosphere that influenced many of Taylor's editorial choices; I also included biographical background on Taylor and a tool for analyzing the overlaps of ethnicity, gender, religion, and citizenship in children's literature. Other helpful ancillary materials included Hasia Diner's *Lower East Side Memories* and passages from Jacob Riis's *How the Other Half Lives*. Diner's work introduces the idea of nostalgia and how different communities imagine their origins. Using Riis's study as a primary text helped students see the coconstruction of ethnicity and gender in rhetoric about immigrant communities. I also had them strategically examine user reviews of the book from *Amazon* as examples of reader-response criticism.

The vast majority of my students in Northeast Wisconsin were not Jewish, and many had never met a Jewish person or heard of most Jewish holidays; for these students, *All-of-a-Kind Family* was an accessible text for introducing Jewish ritual and history. I have concerns, however, that the text places Judaism in a sepia-toned vision of the past rather than in the present, and more broadly, that the "all-white world" of children's literature is reflected in the mostly "Ashke-normative" world of Jewish children's literature (Larrick). That said, correctives for this problem exist. One particularly useful text in this regard is Sasso's *Abuelita's Secret Matzahs*. This 2005 picture book is invaluable for presenting a perspective on Jewish diversity and for highlighting the fact that one's religious identity is not always an either-or proposition. *Abuelita* tells the story of Jacobo, who visits his Catholic *abuelita* ("grandma") in New Mexico and starts to notice the similarities between her practices and those of her Jewish neighbors. Eventually, she reveals her secret: she is the descendant of *conversos*, Spanish Jews who converted to Catholicism at the time of the Inquisition but may have retained Jewish customs, such as abstaining from pork or lighting candles on Friday nights. The text closes on an ambivalent note: when Jacobo asks, "Who am I, Abuelita? Am I a Catholic, or a Jew?" she answers, "As you grow up, *mijito*, that will be for you to decide."

Comparative approaches prod students to frame more abstract connections between different literatures. In this course, the theme of bridges emerged powerfully. Woodson's *Feathers* tells what happens in a de facto segregated 1971 elementary school classroom of black students when a new, white student appears one day and says his name is Jesus. This short novel features bridges across the highway that so dramatically divides neighborhoods in terms of race and class, and bridges of understanding between Sean, who is deaf, and the hearing girls who make fun of him. In sign language, Sean asks his sister, Fanny: "I mean, like imagine if there was a bridge from every single window in the world to some whole new place. That would be crazy, wouldn't it? It would mean we could all just step out of our worlds into these whole new ones" (16–17).

This dialogue distills the power of the humanities in the classroom. In my course, students were asked to understand and bridge cultural difference, as part of the university's general education reform, but Woodson's bridge metaphor helped me push them to question what a bridge is, how it functions, and how geography can both influence culture directly and serve as a useful metaphor for conceptualizing it. Overall, this course benefited from its fluidity and my excitement in introducing first-year students to the study of literature and religion in a critical vein. The challenge of the course, in retrospect, was that it had too broad a scope. Even with many religious traditions and subgroups within those traditions excluded—for example, different regional groups of Jews— I fear the class glided too easily along the surface of some themes, since we had so much ground to cover. When using a comparative approach to teaching Jewish children's literature, I now narrow the field by covering fewer traditions and by emphasizing the afterlives of the book of Exodus.

Promised Lands and Memory

My teaching is deeply informed by a number of theoretical perspectives, which I sometimes introduce to students through reading assignments but at other times simply describe in class. One perspective that I find particularly helpful in a comparative setting is what Michael Rothberg calls multidirectional memory (5). Rothberg argues that we can read across different communities' experiences of discrimination, trauma, and other stresses without descending into a comparison of who has suffered most; suffering, in his framing, is not scarce "real estate" (2). Discussing this approach in the classroom helps students avoid the simplistic question of who suffered the most and prompts them to think generatively instead.

Rothberg's perspective has been particularly useful for my course *Promised Lands: Jewish and African American Children's Literature*, which I first taught in fall 2016 at Lehigh. The course brings my research interest in those two groups, and their overlaps—since some Jews, like the author Julius Lester, are also African American—into the classroom. We begin the semester by studying the picture book *As Good as Anybody*, which tells the stories of Martin Luther King, Jr., and Abraham Joshua Heschel in parallel, then joins them, and brings to light the stakes of complicated political alliances (Michelson). Using Exodus as a foundation, we then proceed through three major thematic units: Biblical Afterlives (in which we read *Pharaoh's Daughter* and work by Carole Boston Weatherford on Harriet Tubman as Moses); Semiautobiographical Stories (in which we read Woodson's *Brown Girl Dreaming*, *All-of-a-Kind Family*, and Patricia Polacco's *Chicken Sunday*); and Engaging Historical Traumas (in which we read Laurie Halse Anderson's *Chains*, Jane Yolen's *The Devil's Arithmetic*, Karen Hesse's *Witness*, and Marilyn Nelson's *A Wreath for Emmett Till*). We finish the course with stories from African American folklore, adapted by Virginia Hamilton, that also feature themes of suffering, resilience, and intergenerational connection.

My first semester teaching this course coincided with the 2016 presidential election in the United States, which prompted many frank and emotional discussions among my twelve students. The course was cross-listed in the Departments of English and Religion Studies and the programs in Africana studies and Jewish studies. The students self-identified as Jewish (as well as Ashkenazi and Sephardic), African American or black, Latinx, white, and mixed; they were Christian, Jewish, Christian and Jewish, or unaffiliated.

In ways I had not consciously intended, poetry emerged as a running thread throughout the term. During the week that we read *Brown Girl Dreaming*—a series of poems about Woodson's childhood experiences in South Carolina and in Brooklyn—Terrence Crutcher was killed by police in Tulsa, Oklahoma, and Keith Lamont Scott was killed by police in Charlotte, North Carolina, sparking further national protests and an on-campus forum at Lehigh on the Black Lives Matter movement. Feeling shaken by the week's news and unsure of how to proceed, I brought copies of Audre Lorde's essay "Poetry Is Not a Luxury" to class. Lorde posits that poetry "forms the quality of the light within which we predicate our hopes and dreams toward survival and change," and that poetry is "the way we help give name to the nameless so it can be thought" (37), making a case for the social necessity of poetry in a painful world.

In class we acknowledged that we all probably had different reactions to the week's events, and that it would be illuminating to spend some time toward the end of the class period looking at Lorde's text and considering what it meant for our literary endeavors. Students took turns reading paragraphs of the essay aloud in a round robin. It was difficult for the class to find a balance between catharsis and analysis, but the session was palpably charged; students commented on it in their weekly journals and in some of their end-of-semester reflections.

Two days after the 2016 election, we read Hesse's *Witness*, which uses poetry to imagine life in a 1920s Vermont town where the Ku Klux Klan comes in and harasses the town's minorities, including one African American family and one Jewish one. *Witness*, which is told in the voices of the town members, struck a deep chord with my students in the light of the nativist discourse voiced during that election season. It also formed an interesting bookend with the start of the semester. Earlier in the term, students initially read *As Good as Anybody* in the celebratory manner in which it was intended; I found myself pushing them to also think critically about how black-Jewish alliances have been romanticized, particularly by Ashkenazi Jews. But in November, as I watched them form various alliances of their own in classroom conversations and extracurricular activities, I found myself questioning my own critique. *Witness*—which is a darker book, geared toward older readers—resonated with my students as their political experiences were being, in Lorde's words, "first made into language, then into idea, then into more tangible action" (37). Multidirectionally—as Rothberg means it, noncompetitively—they were not erasing difference; in fact, they enunciated their embodied experiences ever more clearly as they described walking around campus throughout the political cycle, during which racist incidents occurred in the region and on campus. They were, however, also clearly drawing strength from the resilience of the novel's characters.

In the wake of the 2016 election, my students and I often found ourselves engaging with one another emotionally as we reckoned with Black Lives Matter and waded through an account of the Ku Klux Klan. Comparison is a vulnerable act, leading us across chasms of cultural difference in search of glimpses of recognition or understanding. I often struggle with its perils. My experiences in two difference states and many classrooms, though, suggest that even if comparison is not magic, the teaching of Jewish children's literature benefits from a pedagogy that is generously comparative and engaged—and that offers a hint of emotional risk.

Teaching Jewish children's and young adult literature opens students up to seeing profound complexity in a genre that they often conceive of as straightforward or simplistic when they first enter the college classroom. While children's literature is not inherently either more or less affective than other genres, the discourse around it is laden with emotion, evocations of innocence, and debates over the role of ideology and didacticism in literature. The unique cadences and imagery of picture books, novels in verse, and young adult literature's interior monologues all provoke deep levels of reflexivity and emotional intimacy from college students—perhaps because this is the first time they are approaching such works with adult eyes. This is a prime moment to invite them into a genre that is not merely instrumental but also, in the words of Ruth Bottigheimer, "an important system of its own" (190). This system is growing ever more capacious, despite its often troubled history, and now includes a wider variety of ethnic and religious voices. Into this mix, Jewish literary voices add a rich timbre: one that is best heard in counterpoint with other American ethnic and religious literatures.

Notes

1. At the University of Wisconsin, Oshkosh, I also regularly offered a class called Gendering Jewish Children's Literature.

2. My chief observation, after years of leading this exercise in class, is that students will engage in interesting debates about whether ascribing race to animal characters is appropriate, and if it is, how to do it. Speciesist as it may seem, I sometimes create a separate "animals" list.

Works Cited

Anderson, Laurie Halse. *Chains*. Atheneum, 2010.

Blume, Judy. *Are You There God? It's Me, Margaret*. 1970. Random House, 2011.

Bottigheimer, Ruth. "An Important System of Its Own: Defining Children's Literature." *Princeton University Library Chronicle*, vol. 59, no. 2, 1998, 190–210.

Cummins, June. "Becoming An 'All of a Kind American': Sydney Taylor and Strategies of Assimilation." *The Lion and the Unicorn*, vol. 27, no. 3, 2003, 324–43.

Diner, Hasia. *Lower East Side Memories: A Jewish Place in America*. Princeton UP, 2000.

Greene, Jacqueline Dembar. *Candlelight for Rebecca*. Illustrated by Robert Hunt, American Girl, 2009.

———. *Meet Rebecca: An American Girl*. Illustrated by Robert Hunt, American Girl, 2009.

Gross, Rachel B. "People of the Picture Book: PJ Library and American Jewish Religion." *Religion and Popular Culture in America*, edited by Bruce David Forbes and Jeffrey H. Mahan, 3rd ed., U of California P, 2017, pp. 177–94.

Hamilton, Virginia. *The People Could Fly: American Black Folktales.* Illustrated by Leo Dillon and Diane Dillon, Alfred A. Knopf, 1993.

Hesse, Karen. *Witness.* Scholastic, 2001.

Larrick, Nancy. "The All-White World of Children's Books." *The Saturday Review,* 11 Sept. 1965, pp. 63–65.

Leeser, Isaac. *Catechism for Jewish Children: Designed as a Religious Manual for Home and School.* Sherman, 1863.

Lester, Julius. *The Old African.* Illustrated by Julius Pinkney. Dial Books, 2005.

———. *Pharaoh's Daughter: A Novel of Ancient Egypt.* Houghton Mifflin Harcourt, 2000.

Levitt, Laura. *Jews and Feminism: The Ambivalent Search for Home.* Routledge, 1997.

Lorde, Audre. "Poetry Is Not a Luxury." *Sister Outsider: Essays and Speeches by Audre Lorde.* Crossing Press, 1984, pp. 36–39.

Michelson, Richard. *As Good as Anybody: Martin Luther King, Jr., and Abraham Joshua Heschel's March toward Freedom.* Illustrated by Raul Colón, Knopf, 2008.

Mickenberg, Julie, and Lynne Vallone, editors. *The Oxford Handbook of Children's Literature.* Oxford UP, 2012.

Nel, Philip, and Kissa Paul, editors. *Keywords for Children's Literature.* New York UP, 2011.

Nelson, Marilyn. *A Wreath for Emmett Till.* Illustrated by Philippe Lardy, Houghton Mifflin, 2005.

Nye, Naomi Shihab. *Habibi.* Simon Pulse, 1999.

Patel, Sanjay. *The Little Book of Hindu Deities.* Penguin Books, 2006.

Polacco, Patricia. *Chicken Sunday.* Reprint, Puffin Books, 1998.

Porter, Connie. *Addy's Surprise.* Illustrated by Dahl Taylor, American Girl, 1993.

Riis, Jacob. A. *How the Other Half Lives: Studies among the Tenements of New York.* Bedford / St. Martin's Press, 1890.

Rothberg, Michael. *Multidirectional Memory: Remembering the Holocaust in the Age of Decolonization.* Stanford UP, 2009.

Sarna, Jonathan D. *JPS: The Americanization of Jewish Culture, 1888–1988.* The Jewish Publication Society, 1989.

Sasso, Sandy Eisenberg. *Abuelita's Secret Matzahs.* Illustrated by Diana Breyer, Clerisy Press, 2005.

Smith, Jonathan Z. *Imagining Religion, from Babylon to Jonestown.* Chicago UP, 1982.

Taylor, Sydney. *All-of-a-Kind Family.* Dell Yearling, 1989.

Weatherford, Carole Boston. *Moses: When Harriet Tubman Led Her People to Freedom.* Illustrated by Kadir Nelson, Hyperion, 2006.

Weilerstein, Sadie. *The Adventures of K'tonton.* Bloch Publishing, 1935.

Woodson, Jacqueline. *Brown Girl Dreaming.* Nancy Paulsen Books, 2014.

———. *Feathers.* Reprint, Speak, 2009.

Yolen, Jane. *The Devil's Arithmetic.* Puffin Books, 1990.

Sasha Senderovich

Teaching with Things: The Clutter of Russian Jewish American Literature

Clutter pervades a good deal of the creative work by the sizeable—and growing—cohort of Soviet-born writers who have begun to enter the Jewish American literary scene since the beginning of the twenty-first century.[1] Literary fiction, memoirs, and autobiographically inspired narratives by Anya Ulinich, Gary Shteyngart, and others overflow with stuff. Discrete objects become conduits for stories of migration and of encounters with new cultural contexts. Lugged in immigrants' suitcases, carried through ports of transit, and displayed and bandied about to impress unwitting hosts upon reaching termini, these items are wonderful focal points when teaching this fresh literary output written in the acquired English of its émigré authors (Boym, *Future* 327–36; Idov). In courses on Jewish American literature and the Russian Jewish experience, the clutter of these texts is an aid for teaching students how literary works can challenge seemingly established historical narratives—in this case, narratives about the place of immigrant Jews from the Soviet Union in the landscape of the Jewish experience in North America during and after the Cold War.

Both general readers and students may tend to view literary texts about the immigrant experience in terms of the binaries that deceptively appear at the surface level. The dichotomies of home/exile, old/new, native/foreign, and familiar/strange offer a blueprint for reading literary texts about the immigrant experience and highlight differences between the origin points and points of arrival that immigrant writers explore in their work. For students, such binaries provide a shorthand for understanding the subject—as binaries in the learning process tend to do more generally. This understanding, however, conventionally frames the immigrant story as one of successful arrival and embrace of American and Jewish American values.

Unquestioned dichotomies, when used as a mechanism for comprehending course material, obscure the opportunities that literary texts offer to challenge established communal narratives. To the reader first sizing up these sets of opposites, the immigrant experience is likely to appear unidirectional: in this case, a movement from political oppression in the Soviet Union to freedom in the West, from the perceived inability to be meaningfully Jewish to open engagement with an understanding of Jewish identity in North America that tends to center on Judaism as a religious affiliation. This dichotomous understanding of Soviet Jewish immigration mirrors narratives about the influx of Jews from the USSR commonly told in Jewish American communities, narratives that view Soviet Jews primarily as beneficiaries of American Jews' involvement in the Soviet Jewry movement. Russian Jews were perceived to have been saved through the activism of the people they would come to reside among upon arrival in the West (Beckerman; Kelner).

Creative works by Russian Jewish émigré authors supply a range of provocative correctives to this narrative. They are populated with sets of ideologically charged objects that might appear, at first glance, to confirm simplistic understandings of the Russian Jews' immigrant experience, including, for example, the supposed paucity of markers of Jewish identity in their lives—a consequence of what Zvi Gitelman has termed, after Clifford Geertz, "thin culture" (Gitelman 22, 22–23). However, the exercise of examining these items closely can introduce nuances into the generalized and one-sided narrative that has taken hold in the last few decades in Jewish communities in the West. In this essay, I look at depictions of immigrant wares that—once introduced into the cultural landscape outside the Soviet Union—have come to encapsulate the miscommunication and miscomprehension between Russian Jews and Jews in North America.

In her graphic novel *Lena Finkle's Magic Barrel*, Ulinich deploys two different styles of drawing. On the one hand, she creates nuanced and detailed images in the parts of the book that narrate her eponymous protagonist's life as an adult. On the other hand, more simplistic draw-ings in the style of caricature dominate the chapters about the protago-nist's childhood and teenage years in Moscow and her early years as an immigrant in Arizona. In the first set of caricature frames at the book's beginning, Lena Finkle's mother shows off her daughter's "gold medal" to a Jewish American couple visiting the newly arrived Soviet Jewish family. A rare and coveted award for completing Soviet secondary educa-tion with top grades, the object is a sign of distinction for her daughter and, implicitly, for the family as a whole, and Lena's mother wants it to make an impression on the Jewish American sponsors, whose recommen-dation will determine the family's immigration status. But upon seeing the medal, the visitors appear befuddled by the visage of Vladimir Lenin that happens to be stamped on the medal's obverse (2–3).

Ulinich draws the Lenin medal, which is not actually made of gold, inside a small decorative case with a transparent glass lid. Styled as a caricature, the picture humorously recalls the image of Lenin inside the glass-topped sarcophagus in his Red Square mausoleum in Moscow; Ulinich thus gives this iconic image, circulated widely inside and outside the Soviet Union, a satirical makeover. She employs a similar logic of caricature in drawing the Jewish American visitors in Hasidic garb, a costume that nonobservant Jewish immigrants from the Soviet Union would likely associate with non-Russian Jews, no matter their level of reli-gious practice. The labels "Moscow 1991" and "Arizona 1991" above these two neighboring frames in this panel further emphasize the contrast and the degree of miscommunication between the American Jews and the Rus-sian Jews.

In this encounter, American Jews appear bewildered that the people they fought to liberate from the Soviet regime would show off an object marked by the image of the regime's founder. At the same time, the Soviet Jewish immigrants fail to convey that their story of recognized scholastic achievement within the Soviet system is one of the markers of a specifically Soviet Jewish identity. The story of how a gold medal came to be viewed as a Jewish object in the specific circumstances that Soviet Jews faced is also never told.

In a later chapter of the book, Ulinich further develops the narrative of miscommunication between Russian and American Jews. Another object is introduced into the story: a menorah belonging to a Jewish American woman, who uses it to educate the young Russian immigrant cleaning her house about expected ways of being Jewish. If the Lenin medal depicted earlier represents the first half of a contrast between atheist Soviet culture and Jewish culture, the menorah represents the other half. The menorah signifies the ritual life that, in the established Jewish American narrative, is supposed to replace markers of Soviet ideology in the lives of these Soviet Jews as they transition from Moscow to Arizona and from what is Soviet to what is American. In drawing this encounter in caricature, Ulinich cleverly undermines this conventional narrative, showing—with the help of charged and carefully planted objects—that the acceptable unidirectional narrative may not reflect the reality of the Soviet Jewish experience. While the Lenin medal and the menorah appear at some distance from each other in the text, students can learn to link and connect these objects: the Lenin medal is one of a host of idiosyncratic markers of Soviet Jewishness that do not necessarily become displaced by markers of Jewish identity that are more familiar in North America.

Another Lenin image, a statue of the Soviet Union's founder in Leningrad, plays an important narrative role in Shteyngart's memoir, *Little Failure*. It, too, has a double: a Catholic pendant with an image of the Madonna and child, which Shteyngart picked up during his family's transit through Rome on their way to America (see also Bezmozgis, *The Free World*; Boym, "A Soviet Drop-Out's Journey"). Unlike the Lenin-menorah pairing in Ulinich's book—a pairing that intentionally amplifies, through caricature, the predictable attributes of a Russian Jewish and Jewish American encounter—Shteyngart's binary of the Lenin statue and the Madonna pendant challenges the reader to look beyond the two objects' initial appearances.

Stationed near the apartment building where little Gary's family lived until they emigrated, the Lenin statue looms large in the boy's imagination and in the memoir. One chapter is structured around the statue and the idiosyncratic image of Lenin it created for the impressionable boy. The chapter refers to Lenin as a beloved relation of sorts: "His full name is Vladimir Ilyich Lenin, and I love him" (45). This proclamation is made in an earnest child's voice, but the satirical undertones of an adult writer conveying his childhood thoughts also peek through. Cleverly inserted between separate chapters focused on Shteyngart's mother and father, respectively, the Lenin chapter reproduces a cultural trope of Soviet children's literature in which the Soviet Union's founder is "Grandpa Lenin" and thus, implicitly, a member of little Gary's family. The statue widely known in Leningrad as "dancing" Lenin, with "his coat sexily unfurling in the wind," provides a comforting and also entertaining presence for the boy who suffers from panic-laced asthma attacks (47). While an English-language reader might assume that the statue communicates Soviet ideology, for Gary it is also a site of filial bonding with his father, as the pair play hide-and-seek around Lenin's granite legs.

Most importantly, Shteyngart turns the statue of Lenin into the generative locus of his creativity. The statue purportedly inspires the first novel by Shteyngart, "commissioned" by his grandmother and written when he was five. He describes the novel—now lost—as being a version of the Swedish writer Selma Lagerlöf's story about a young boy's travels with a flock of geese, but mixed with the ideological narratives and Lenin imagery that surrounded Gary in his early life. His decision to become a writer in this environment seems inevitable: "who wouldn't under the circumstances?" Shteyngart queries rhetorically (55). Lenin in this context becomes the kind of superhero that a sickly Soviet boy needs to stimulate his imagination and to rescue him from the reality of his own helplessness.

Upon Gary's departure from Leningrad, the memory of the Lenin statue marks the disappearance of the familiar and the boy's longing for it. "Do you dream of me?" Shteyngart queries, addressing the statue in warm and familiar terms, suggesting that the object, which little Gary has domesticated into his imagination, might grieve the boy's departure (63). A series of objects—all of them temporary replacements for the statue—accompany little Gary during his family's transit through Vienna and Rome: they include the Moscow Olympic Games pin that Gary wears on his shirt on the plane out of Russia and a candy wrapper imprinted with Mozart's portrait, which is gifted to him upon the family's arrival in Austria. In Rome, however, one object outlasts all the others: "a little golden medal depicting Raphael's *Madonna del Granduca*" that the boy buys in a church gift shop while touring the city with his grandmother. Confused by the unfamiliar surroundings, Gary keeps locking himself in the bathroom and crying: "alone, I let the tears drop out of me with complete hot abandon as I kiss and kiss the beatific Virgin, whispering 'Santa Maria, Santa Maria, Santa Maria'" (90). The pendant is so central to the story of Shteyngart's journey that an entire chapter—following the sequence of chapters about Gary's father, Lenin's statue, and Gary's mother—is named after this putative new family member: "My Madonnachka."

For students who have just read *Little Failure* as a story of Russian Jewish immigration to America, the suggestion of pairing the Lenin statue and a Catholic pendant depicting the Virgin and child might, at first, appear confusing. However, when students read past the surface expectations of the text, they perceive a more complex relation between these objects. The unease that little Gary experiences while en route to America exacerbates the anxiety with which he was raised in the Soviet Union—anxiety determined by the fact of his being "born a Jewish person," as Shteyngart's mother reportedly puts it. Mrs. Shteyngart's comment draws additional family stories into the narrative: the movement of older family members from the Pale of Settlement into big cities, the murder of relatives during the Holocaust, the anti-Semitism experienced by little Gary's parents in the postwar Soviet Union, and so on. In this context, the statue of Lenin, domesticated into the boy's imagination, alleviates Gary's Soviet Jewish anxiety, and later, to the asthmatic, sickly, and dislodged Jewish child, the Catholic pendant provides as much comfort as the statue did before the family's departure: "Haloed Baby Jesus is so porky here, so content with his extra, protecting layer of flesh. . . . What a lucky boy Jesus is" (90).

On the surface, the pairing of the Lenin statue and Catholic pendant suggests the opposition of Soviet iconography with Christian-inflected belief. Like Ulinich's Lenin-menorah pairing, however, Shteyngart's objects anchor the Soviet Jewish story that floats through his memoir in bits and pieces that can be gathered only through the exercise of close reading. Objects that appear in other literary works written by émigré Russian Jewish authors in English present possibilities for similar and somewhat simpler pedagogical exercises: those objects include a Star of David pendant forcibly placed on a Russian Jewish immigrant child by a Jewish American host who wants the new arrival to have a recognizable Jewish appearance (Ulinich, *Petropolis* 153–60); and a similar piece of ethnically and religiously marked jewelry that Russian Jewish immigrant parents force their child to wear because they assume their Jewish American hosts will want to see such a clearly articulated and thus easily relatable attribute of Jewish identity (Bezmozgis, "Roman Berman, Massage Therapist" 31). The profusion of objects akin to Ulinich's and Shteyngart's Lenins (and the objects they are paired with) offers a useful set of pedagogical tools for those studying the literature of the Russian Jewish immigrant experience. The narrative turns that these objects induce challenge students to delve deeper into these rich creative works.

Note

1. See, for example, Furman; Katsnelson; Levantovskaya; Senderovich, "Scenes" and "Soviet Jews"; Wanner, *Out of Russia* and "Russian Jews."

Works Cited

Beckerman, Gal. *When They Come for Us, We'll Be Gone: The Epic Struggle to Save Soviet Jewry.* Houghton Mifflin Harcourt, 2010.

Bezmozgis, David. *The Free World.* Farrar, Straus and Giroux, 2011.

———. "Roman Berman, Massage Therapist." *"Natasha" and Other Stories,* Farrar, Straus and Giroux, 2004, pp. 19–36.

Boym, Svetlana. *The Future of Nostalgia.* Basic Books, 2001.

———. "A Soviet Drop-Out's Journey to Freedom." *Tablet Magazine,* 3 July 2014, www.tabletmag.com/jewish-arts-and-culture/books/176945 /camp-tale.

Furman, Yelena. "Hybrid Selves, Hybrid Texts: Embracing the Hyphen in Russian-American Fiction." *Slavic and East European Journal,* vol. 55, no. 1, 2011, pp. 19–37.

Gitelman, Zvi Y. *Jewish Identities in Postcommunist Russia and Ukraine: An Uncertain Ethnicity.* Cambridge UP, 2012.

Idov, Michael, editor. *Made in Russia: Unsung Icons of Soviet Design.* Rizzoli, 2011.

Katsnelson, Anna. "Introduction to the New Wave of Russian Jewish American Culture." *East European Jewish Affairs,* special issue of *The New Wave of Russian Jewish American Culture,* edited by Katsnelson, vol. 46, no. 3, Fall-Winter 2016, pp. 241–44.

Kelner, Shaul. "Ritualized Protest and Redemptive Politics: Cultural Consequences of the American Mobilization to Free Soviet Jewry." *Jewish Social Studies,* vol. 14, no. 3, Spring-Summer 2008, pp. 1–37.

Levantovskaya, Margarita. "Homes without a Homeland: Finding Diasporic Intimacy in Contemporary Russian-Jewish American Fiction." *Comparative Literature,* vol. 69, no. 4, Winter 2017, pp. 394–412.

Senderovich, Sasha. "Scenes of Encounter: The 'Soviet Jew' in Fiction by Russian Jewish Writers in America." *Prooftexts,* vol. 35, no. 1, Winter 2015, pp. 98–132.

———. "Soviet Jews, Re-Imagined: Anglophone Emigre Jewish Writers from the USSR." *The Edinburgh Companion to Modern Jewish Fiction,* edited by David Brauner and Axel Staehler, Edinburgh UP, 2015, pp. 90–104.

Shteyngart, Gary. *Little Failure: A Memoir.* Random House, 2014.

Ulinich, Anya. *Lena Finkle's Magic Barrel: A Graphic Novel.* Penguin Books, 2014.

———. *Petropolis: A Novel.* Penguin Books, 2007.

Wanner, Adrian. *Out of Russia: Fictions of a New Translingual Diaspora.* Northwestern UP, 2011.

———. "Russian Jews as American Writers: A New Paradigm for Jewish Multiculturalism?" *MELUS,* vol. 37, no. 2, Summer 2012, pp. 157–176.

Nadia Fayidh Mohammed

Teaching a Jewish and Arab American Literary Collaboration in Iraq

Effective and engaged teaching practices are those that recognise the importance of making real world connections between the subject material taught, and the students' experiences, through "engaged" teaching and working to encourage the student to become reflexive and critical thinking societal participants.

—Maheshvari Naidu, "Engaged Pedagogy and Performative Teaching: Examples from Teaching Practice"

In contemporary Iraq, universities need a new curriculum for English literature to replace the one taught under the censorship of Saddam Hussein's Baathist regime. Given the new political and social awareness of Iraqis, this new curriculum needs to address issues of identity and diversity and to promote self-expression and multiculturalism. A revised, multicultural curriculum can promote an awareness of the consequences of violence and war among young Iraqis, who have been drawn to different armed groups since 2003. In this context the poetry book *Diaspo/Renga*, the product of a literary collaboration between the Jewish American author Marilyn Hacker and the Palestinian American author Deema K. Shehabi, is an ideal text to include in a course on multiethnic literature with a focus on women's voices and on bridging cultural gaps and addressing misunderstandings.

Diaspo/Renga is a good choice because of the multiethnic identities of the authors, its use of *renga* (a Japanese genre of collaborative poetry), and the poems themselves, which address the current conflict between the Jewish and Arab communities. The curriculum for English as a foreign language (EFL) in Iraq now includes this work, and the fact that *Diaspo/Renga* is taught against the country's current political and social upheavals adds meaning to the poems. Hacker and Shehabi's collaboration suggests the possibility of dialogue and coexistence. The poems are taught not just to educate Iraqi students about multiethnic literature and women writers but to broaden students' horizons concerning their own situation. Written in haikus, the poems discuss a wide range of themes that might speak to these students, who face the crumbling of a homogeneous Iraqi identity and its replacement with several fragmented identities.

The sessions I describe in this essay were part of an EFL class titled Multiethnic Literature and Multicultural Writing, which I taught during the 2014–15 academic year in fulfillment of the literature and literary criticism module for fourth-year students in the Department of English at the University of Mustansereyah in Baghdad.[1]

Engaged Pedagogy: Teaching Culture, Literature, and English as a Foreign Language

The philosophy I used to teach *Diaspo/Renga* is inspired by bell hooks's "engaged pedagogy" (13–22), which affirms the connections between education and life and between the public and private spheres. This essay presents how an engaged pedagogy can be applied to teaching *Diaspo/Renga* with an emphasis on the themes of otherness and multiculturalism. To achieve my teaching goal, I needed to move away from traditional pedagogies.

Departments of English in Iraq offer undergraduate courses that allow students to fulfill their required literature modules; these modules are covered in six terms. Starting in the second year, students study three modules of English literature: poetry, drama, and fiction. The literary texts chosen for these modules are often classics of English literature from the fifteenth to the twentieth century, which lack the cultural diversity and topical relevance needed to engage contemporary students in the Middle East. Particularly in the EFL classroom, as students fail to relate to the texts they read, they may perceive these texts as an unnecessary burden on language learning. Although English classics do have value in EFL classes, students are unlikely to gain cultural understanding only by reading texts that they cannot relate to their own experience. As literature modules are obligatory for EFL students in Iraq, learners often find themselves forced to read with the sole purpose of passing the module, without being actively involved in the process of learning. From an engaged pedagogy perspective, this state of affairs undermines the process of learning. In engaged pedagogy, a literary text should invite readers to engage with the experiences featured in the narrative. According to hooks, education is a "practice of freedom," where "anyone can learn" (14).

Since the United States' invasion of Iraq in 2003, Iraqis have developed a new awareness of their diverse ethnosectarian identities, which had been suppressed for decades by the former regime in favor of Arab nationalism. The expression of identity was never considered in the academic critical discourse in Iraq, where the former regime had established a collective identity for the people as homogeneous Muslims who were Iraqis by birth, Arabs by ethnicity. Other identities were not given space for self-expression or even exploration. For instance, many Iraqi Kurds, born and raised outside the Kurdistan region, do not speak their native language and are unfamiliar with their ethnic history and cultural heritage. Other ethnic groups were totally invisible, having been forced to assimilate to the dominant Arab culture.

Given the emerging awareness of Iraq's cultural and religious diversity, Iraqi academia needs to address the country's multiculturalism and to give space for self-expression. In Iraqi EFL classes it has become possible to address the subject of cultural and racial diversity by selecting more contemporary texts. Teachers of American literature have found that assigning texts from the canon of multiethnic American literature gives English learners the opportunity to explore the writers' experiences of racial and ethnic identities, self-expression, and diversity and homogeneity.

Diaspo/Renga:
Jewish and Arab Literary Collaboration

I taught *Diaspo/Renga* in my class on multiethnic American literature for a number of reasons. First, the work introduces students to an unfamiliar genre and shows the influence of other literary traditions on American poetry. Second, the poems are written in contemporary English, which corresponded to my students' language competency. Third, the identities of the poets can generate discussions about the ongoing conflict between Palestine and Israel. Hacker is a Jewish American expatriate living in France, and Shehabi is a Palestinian American who was born in Kuwait and later immigrated to the United States. Fourth, the themes and content of the poems resonate with the reality of young Iraqis.

Hacker is the first Jewish writer to be taught in EFL classrooms in Iraq. Because of the conflict with Israel, Arabs have allowed a pan-Arab nationalist agenda to repress Jewish culture and religion in the Middle East. Iraq's Jewish community was forced to leave during one of the darkest episodes of modern Iraqi history.[2] After 2003, many Iraqi Jews expressed their intention to return to Iraq, but the country was not ready to accept a community that has been demonized for decades, including in textbooks and academic discourse. Having been denied access to the work of British and American Jewish writers when I was a student, I decided to introduce the work of a Jewish writer in my class.

In her work, Hacker explores questions of identity, particularly how the self is fashioned through discourses of sexuality, gender, class, and ethnicity. Hayan Charara, in *Inclined to Speak*, describes Shehabi as a "new" Arab American who "challenge[s] notions about women in America [and about] Arab and Arab American culture" (xxix). In *Diaspo/Renga* both poets address imperialism, displacement, and war, themes that resonate with young Iraqis who grew up with these concepts as a reality.

Given that the two poets are known for their feminist writings, the collection presents another challenging theme to Iraqi students. In a traditional EFL literature class, Iraqi students read the work of only two female authors, Jane Austen and Emily Brontë. Though both authors wrote works that present strong female characters and discuss women's issues, students in EFL classes are not introduced to feminism as a critical approach. Such an approach would allow them to consider how literature reinforces or undermines the economic, political, social, and psychological oppression of women.

To help my students to engage with *Diaspo/Renga*, therefore, I familiarized them with strands of the feminist tradition. I gave a brief outline of the three waves of feminism and the women's movement in the twentieth century, highlighting women's struggle for political representation and economic equality. Then we discussed intersectional feminism and how ethnicity, religion, and class have influenced women's movements. Since we were in a country torn by war, we also discussed the impact of war and displacement on women and their well-being.

Diaspo/Renga:
Jewishness, Gender, and Otherness

Students of English in Iraq encounter Jewish characters in only two literary works: *The Merchant of Venice* and *Oliver Twist*. Secondary school students read these texts in simplified versions that present Shylock and Fagin as villains whose primary intent is to hurt the innocent. In both texts, the Jewish characters are stereotyped and silenced, further demonizing and dehumanizing the Jewish community in the minds of young Iraqis. Adult education does not include work by Jewish writers or literary works that humanize the Jewish community. In modern Iraq, the Jew is the other, often stereotyped as stingy, evil, and racist. Misreadings of history and misinformed religious teachings have created what seems an irreconcilable rift between Arabs (Muslim and Christian) and Jews. Missing from Iraqi classrooms is the narrative about how Jewish communities, who lived for centuries across the Arab world, found themselves displaced from their homelands to live in either the newly created state of Israel or in the Diaspora.

In my multiethnic American literature class, students read poems by a Jewish poet who is recognized as an admirer of Arabic language, literature, and culture. When I introduced students to Hacker's work in the collection, I instructed them to read through several of her poems. Using a Venn diagram, students were asked to describe the different references to Jewish characters in the poems and to make a character sketch for the speaker's persona. Students collaborated in drawing one or more diagrams. While most students agreed that the speaker is a student or translator of Arabic poetry, they disagreed about the gender of the speaker. A majority rejected the notion that a female poet can write in a male voice, which more or less reflects the gender expectations dictated by an Iraqi patriarchy that ranks women writers as inferior to fictional male characters. When students learned that the speaker is the poet herself, reflecting on her own experiences, they were asked to read a poem in which the speaker engages in a conversation with a doctor "from Cairo" about cultural differences and similarities (110). In the poem, the speaker tells her interlocutor that cheek kissing is a common greeting in her culture in Cairo, and it is also common practice within the Jewish community. The poem draws on the similar customs of the speaker and the Arab doctor, and reading it motivated students to learn more about Jewish culture.

To help students engage with the theme of the poem, I introduced a Venn diagram on the board (fig. 1). Then students filled in the spaces

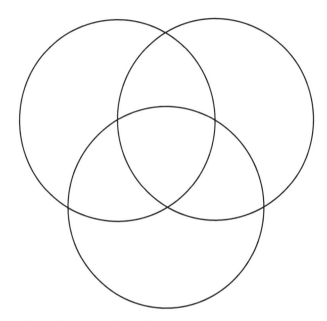

Figure I. Venn diagram by the author.

shared by the three circles. This activity helped them locate more shared and distinctive cultural features of Arab and Jewish communities.

Afterward I drew a bigger diagram on the board, with a circle for each poet (fig. 2). In the circles I provided examples of the characters that populate *Diaspo/Renga*. Students were asked to draw similar diagrams showing ideas and images common to Hacker's and Shehabi's poems. This activity not only motivated the students to think critically but also provoked them to trace the cultural dialogue between the characters in the collection. While students were filling in the diagrams on the board, they asked about characters that have been given no ethnic background or gender. The child Nadjma, for example, lives in Paris, and her name is Arabic, but it is not clear whether she is an Arab. Speculation about the characters' ethnic identities was only possible because the students were now aware of the similarities between Jewish and Arab cultures.

After students explored the stories in the poems, I gave them another diagram and asked them to fill it in with themes featured in the poems (fig. 3). Students were then asked to select possible topics for their essays about *Diaspo/Renga*. These exercises helped them not only engage with the text but also draw from their own experiences and share stories that resonated with the poems' themes.

Marilyn Hacker   Deema K. Shehabi

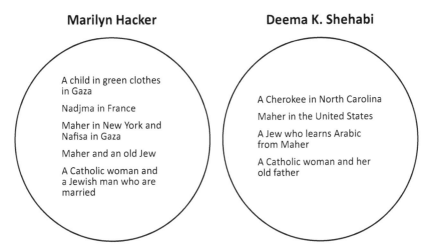

A child in green clothes in Gaza

Nadjma in France

Maher in New York and Nafisa in Gaza

Maher and an old Jew

A Catholic woman and a Jewish man who are married

A Cherokee in North Carolina

Maher in the United States

A Jew who learns Arabic from Maher

A Catholic woman and her old father

Figure 2. Characters in *Diaspo/Renga*. Diagram by the author.

Marilyn Hacker   Deema K. Shehabi

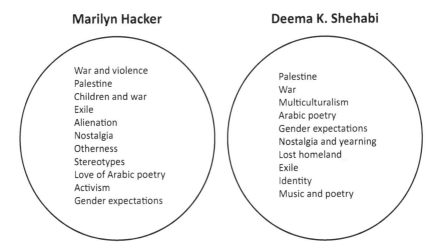

War and violence
Palestine
Children and war
Exile
Alienation
Nostalgia
Otherness
Stereotypes
Love of Arabic poetry
Activism
Gender expectations

Palestine
War
Multiculturalism
Arabic poetry
Gender expectations
Nostalgia and yearning
Lost homeland
Exile
Identity
Music and poetry

Figure 3. Themes in *Diaspo/Renga*. Diagram by the author.

In one *renga*, Hacker and Shehabi explore the impact of marrying outside one's community. Two poems summarize the struggle of a Catholic woman who is now "safer in exile," and married to a Jewish man, but is thinking of her father, who may die without seeing her. The safety provided by exile is blemished by her longing for her family in the homeland. The two poems resonated with Iraqi students who had witnessed or heard similar stories since 2003. Interfaith or inter-sect marriages, common in Iraq before 2003, are now taboo, so students gave these poems special attention. Students were asked to write alternative narratives where, separately, the woman and the man are Muslim, in order to explore the consequences when Muslim Iraqi women and men break social norms. Before writing their alternative narratives, students engaged in heated discussion over the subject of religious and social patriarchies and gender expectations.

Studying *Diaspo/Renga* introduced students to multiethnic American literature as well as concepts of racial discrimination, otherness, and gender expectations. Students recognized the need to revolutionize academic discourse in Iraqi universities and to participate actively in learning. Because of my teaching philosophy, based on engaged pedagogy, students came to realize the importance of being personally engaged in the experience featured in the literary work. In reflecting on the impact of reading this poetry collection, the product of Arab-Jewish collaboration, students became aware of the dominant cultural practice of stereotyping Jews. They also became more conscious of the discrimination that is deeply entrenched in Iraqi society, where identity and cultural diversity are given limited, if any, space for self-expression.

Literature appeared to be effective in shaping the moral and social attitudes of my students. In the Arab world, we need to know more about Jewish literature as well as multiethnic literature more broadly to teach the rising generation to embrace diversity. Given the ongoing Arab-Israeli conflict, which prompts Arabs to hold negative attitudes about Jews everywhere, our universities need to include the work of Jewish writers in their curricula, especially work that discusses and negotiates Arab-Jewish relations and the common history and culture of both peoples. Finally, this course worked well in Iraq because professors enjoyed, at the time, relative freedom to decide what to teach, and because Iraqi society after 2003 has been open to considering ethnic and religious diversity. This course can work equally well in other Arab countries where ethnic and religious minorities are looking for means of self-expression, such as countries in North Africa and the Levant.

Notes

1. In the Iraqi system, modules are requirements for learning about certain subjects; there are no optional modules. Each year students study a set number of modules, which they are required to pass with a grade of no less than 50 percent on the final exams in order to move to the next year.

2. For further information, see Shiblak.

Works Cited

Charara, Hayan, editor. *Inclined to Speak: Anthology of Contemporary Arabic Poetry.* U of Arkansas P, 2008.

Hacker, Marilyn, and Deema K. Shehabi. *Diaspo/Renga.* Holland Park Press, 2014.

hooks, bell. *Teaching to Transgress: Education as the Practice of Freedom.* Routledge, 1994.

Shiblak, Abbas. *Iraqi Jews: A History of Mass Exodus.* Saqi Books, 2005.

Part III

Multilingual and Transnational Approaches

Justin Cammy

Unsettling the Linguistic and Geographical Borders of Jewish American Literature: Régine Robin's *La Québécoite*

The editors of *The Cambridge History of Canadian Literature* suggest that Canada's literary history "has always been a fractured discourse, notoriously difficult to define . . . [given] the conceptual challenges posed by changing meanings of 'Canadian' as an identity category and by periodic reformulations of Canada as an imagined community" (Howells and Kröller 2). As was the case in the United States, by the end of the twentieth century Canadian literary history broadened significantly "as formerly marginalized voices and suppressed histories assum[ed] their proper place within a restructured and increasingly diversified literary tradition" (4). Such observations reinforce the importance of examining how border crossings, cross-cultural exchange, literary multilingualism, translation, debates about indigenousness, and transnational identities have simultaneously challenged and expanded our understanding of national literary traditions.

The field of Jewish American literature should no longer be limited geographically to the political borders of the United States and dominated by English-language texts. My undergraduate survey course on Jewish American literature therefore includes several weeks on Yiddish and Hebrew writers.[1] The exploration of their overlapping and competing global literary networks broadens the field's conceptual, linguistic, and geographic limits. Further, I incorporate a transcontinental approach that is inclusive of works originally published in English, French, Spanish, and Portuguese beyond the United States.[2] This approach prompted my inclusion on the syllabus of Régine Robin's French-language, postmodern novel *La Québécoite* (*The Wanderer*). Robin's experimental novel proves pedagogically valuable because it offers students an alternative model for thinking through the tangled relations between local, national, and transnational identities and the literary traditions that inform them.

The question of Canadianness has long vexed interpreters of Canadian identity. Though Canadians are eager to define themselves in the negative—as definitively not American—they have had more difficulty forging a coherent national identity. Those who attempt to craft a metanarrative of Canadianness often point to Canada as the product of two founding nations, French-speaking Catholics and English-speaking Protestants. However, Hugh MacLennan's classic novel *Two Solitudes* suggests Canada is better understood through the irreconcilable divide between these two groups. Multiculturalism and a greater sensitivity to Canadian diversity further complicated the founding myth of Canadian binationalism by prompting a belated acknowledgment of the rights of Canada's First Nations in the Constitution Act of 1982. The limitations of the American melting-pot model also informed attempts to define Canada alternatively as a mosaic, in which cultural communities retain their distinctiveness but when pieced together form a colorful portrait. Though the model of the cultural mosaic is theoretically less coercive toward minority cultures than that of the melting pot, neither paradigm has gone uncontested.[3]

Underlying tensions between Protestant and Catholic, English and French, and colonial and native populations produced a dilemma for immigrants, especially Jews, whose language and religion did not fit into the dominant paradigms of Canadian identity. Jews learned that, in the Canadian context, language contains an array of ethnonational assumptions. Nowhere was this more complicated than in Montreal, a multilingual island within North America's only majority French-speaking province. The wave of Yiddish-speaking, eastern European Jewish immigrants who began arriving in the late nineteenth century found themselves a double minority, alienated from both the French-speaking majority and the city's Anglo-Protestant establishment. When they gravitated to English as part of their acculturation rather than to French, their position as Montreal's "third solitude" (see Greenstein, *Third Solitudes*) was solidified, reflected first in the liminal location of immigrant Jewish neighborhoods between English-speaking West and French-speaking East Montreal, and then in their move to suburban, majority-Jewish areas on the periphery of more established, non-Jewish neighborhoods. In Mordecai Richler's *The Street*, a fictional treatment of the author's childhood in Montreal's downtown Jewish ghetto, Richler goes so far as to suggest that for his family "Canada was not a choice, but an accident," while "the real America" was across the border (17). In my course, students are prompted to consider what Richler was trying to suggest with this phrase, and what its implications are for appreciating the gravitational force of the American mythos.

I begin the class discussion of *La Québécoite* by noting that the classical English-French binary of Canadian literature operates in tension with the multilingual and transnational fluidity of Jewish literature. In Montreal, writers worked in Yiddish, English, and French and found themselves on the periphery of not one but two non-Jewish national literatures.[4] Although Jewish Montreal writers like A. M. Klein, Irving Layton, Leonard Cohen, and Richler broadened the ethnic borders of Canadian literature, they were excluded from the emerging countercanon of Quebecois literature because they wrote in English, despite the fact that each writer published significant works that interpreted the cultural landscape of Quebec, and especially of Montreal, its largest city.[5] The city's Yiddish writers, whose literary networks extended abroad, were also excluded.[6] Here I draw students into a comparative discussion of Yiddish literary history, observing that Yiddish writers in interwar Poland faced similar challenges when they were excluded from consideration as Polish writers, because their decision to write in Yiddish marked them as other, even though Poland was at the imaginative center of their writing.

Next the class analyzes Robin's afterword to the English translation of *La Québécoite*, in which she observes that nationalist guardians of Quebecois literature invented a new term, *neo-Quebecois*, to designate French writing by immigrant writers, thus marking it (and the writers) as a "problem" ("Writing" 175). We pause on Robin's insistence that as a Jewish novelist in Quebec who writes in French (the language of the local majority but of still a minority of Canadian Jews) she occupies a threshold position, "neither fully within nor fully without" (182). Students come to recognize that as Robin's protagonist wanders through different neighborhoods and communities, she moves between multiple, even competing, identities that challenge narrow, exclusionary nationalist paradigms: "What exactly do you feel you are—American, Canadian, Québécois, Jewish,

French? . . . WE WOULD NEVER BECOME TRULY QUÉBÉCOIS. On the other side of the linguistic barrier. . . . A Yiddishophone imagination . . ." (*Wanderer* 23–24).[7] Disentangling overlapping identities that challenge how literary canons are formed and refashioned provides students an opportunity to adjust their earlier thinking about what constitutes "American" in Jewish American literature.

Régine Robin (born Rivka Ajzersztejn in Paris in 1939 to Polish Jewish parents) arrived in Montreal in 1977, a moment of nationalist hope and unrest due to the recent election of the first government in Quebec committed to independence from Canada. Robin emerged as one of the leading figures of *écritures migrantes* ("migrant writings"; see Berrouët-Oriol and Fournier), a transcultural mode of writing that calls attention to the experience of living within and between overlapping worlds through challenging and deconstructing established ethnonational literary canons. One of her techniques involves the reproduction in fiction of vernacular texts. I ask my students to bring examples of such texts in the novel to class, and then I challenge them to discuss how the inclusion of lists of local store and bank names, the previous night's hockey scores, a page from the newspaper television guide, and local menus is not only an experiment in postmodern play but also a way to appreciate the narratives of belonging or exclusion these texts contain. For instance, I call to their attention the novel's reading of a subway map that shows Lionel Groulx as a major downtown Montreal metro station. The novel reflects on the fact that the Catholic priest and historian after whom the stop is named was sympathetic to a variant of Quebecois nativism that included anti-Semitism. In this way, the novel teaches readers that relations of power and marginalization are inscribed in everyday texts and landscapes.

I then contrast the novel's fascination with the minutiae of daily life in Montreal with its incorporation of Yiddish and Russian Jewish stories set in eastern Europe. Robin not only quotes these stories directly, bringing the French Canadian reader into the heart of Yiddish literary culture, but also meditates on Yiddish itself, as when she visually reproduces it on the page. My students appreciate how this stylistic decision aggressively and visually incorporates the migrant writer's languages and memories into French Canadian literature, thereby broadening its imaginative scope: "On the slopes of Galicia the moon still traces א, ב, ג, and ד; in the gardens of Ukraine, the stems of the sunflowers still form ש, ק and ל; but no longer is there anyone to decode them, to grasp their meaning, their savour" (70–71). This passage allows us to discuss theoretical questions of Yiddish postvernacularity and the way Robin appropriates it as a kind of "graphic image that is a whole landscape" (113).[8] In the same vein, I invite students to ponder how the novel seems to simultaneously advocate for inhabiting language as a homeland while feeling "in exile in one's own language" (76). Such an approach allows us to engage conceptual issues raised earlier in the semester regarding "Yiddishland," the fantasy of a transnational, diasporic homeland experienced in language and culture (Shandler).

By turning our attention to the novel's extensive quotations from Jewish literary sources,[9] I invite students to think about how such texts embedded in a French novel set in Montreal must prove as strange and destabilizing to the Quebecois reader as the novel's aforementioned examples of local vernacular texts are for new immigrants to the city. Robin's strategy here is to ensure that no reader is ever in control of the entire narrative. Nonetheless, this compulsive exercise in citation and translation from Jewish sources self-consciously Judaizes Montreal as a cultural space. I here suggest to students that Robin may be less interested in becoming Quebecois than in creating her own experience of Quebec that redefines and expands its potential meaning to be more inclusive of all its inhabitants and their varied histories.

Students come to appreciate how the novel's division into three sections allows Robin to imagine three potential lives for her protagonist that are conditioned by the character's lived experience and relationships in distinct urban neighborhoods, suggesting that national or civic identities are both formed and disrupted at the more granular level of the local street. Each neighborhood has its own subculture: the Anglo- and Jewish-inflected suburb of Snowdon; Outremont, home to Montreal's Quebecois political elite; and the downtown area around Atwater market, where the protagonist hangs out with activists who remind her of the communists she knew in her youth back in Paris. As we follow her from one neighborhood to the next, the text also plays with the archetype of the wandering Jew in empowering new ways, here as cosmopolitan flaneur. We discuss how the meaning of the novel inevitably shifts in translation when its original title, *La Québécoite* (an ironic neologism that suggests one who is in Quebec but culturally silenced by it), is rendered in English as *The Wanderer*. In each neighborhood the novel demonstrates the challenge of decoding the semiotics of language, space, and belonging. These journeys suggest that the only way to write an authentic novel of Montreal is to make it interlingual and intercultural.

I also invite my students to think of *La Québécoite* as a text interested in challenging the formation of national canons by constructing its own postnational and transnational countercanons. My students are then better able to appreciate how the same literary texts may serve multiple, even competing readerships in radically different ways. By way of example, I point out that the professor in the novel teaches the same early Soviet Yiddish writers to students at Montreal's English-language McGill University and to their French Canadian peers across town at L'Université de Montréal. At McGill, the many Jewish students in the class resist the Soviet Yiddish writers' articulation of a revolutionary Jewishness because it does not easily map onto their own experience of Montreal Jewry as a double minority, one with a strong sense of Jewish tradition, ethnic solidarity and commitment to Zionism's realization of a Jewish nation-state. By contrast, the French Canadian students in the novel are fascinated by Soviet Yiddish writers' attempts to liberate themselves from religious tradition and reconstruct themselves through language, a process that mirrors the students' efforts to free themselves from the shadow of the church and to negotiate the tension between nationalist yearnings for independence and a more cosmopolitan sense of themselves as part of a transnational *Francophonie*, or French-speaking community. Robin's abundant borrowings from other texts open up an entire canon of Yiddish writers in French translation and reveal the ways in which they claimed eastern European space as their own, despite their minority status. The translation of Soviet Yiddish texts for a Quebecois readership thus introduces Yiddish literature as a model for minority cultures interested in thinking about cultural self-assertion beyond the parameters of the nation-state.

The act of conjuring lost Jewish spaces within a novel about Quebec also becomes a form of dialogic exchange in which immigrant writer and native reader meditate on each other's condition. Here, Robin suggests that the Jews and the Quebecois have more in common than they might realize, given the degree to which their fear of being swallowed up by larger cultures is a defining condition of their collective identities. My students and I pause to theorize together about what Robin might mean when she writes about "immigrant words in suspense between two HISTORIES." We discuss how liminality here exists as an alternative to linguistic assimilation, which she reads as the betrayal of "go[ing] over to the other side" (*Wanderer* 124). For instance, when the novel's protagonist translates the prose of modernist Yiddish master Dovid Bergelson for her students, she is especially moved by one of his stories about a man's return to his native village after World War I. When the man speaks to a young girl in Yiddish about his wartime experiences, she immediately translates his words into Russian. In response to her inquiry regarding the accuracy of her translation, he counters: "What can I say? The suffering was in Yiddish" (123). This passage reveals that the element of collective memory contained in language is not easily translatable, and that the stakes of translation are high, especially when the power dynamics of the exchange are between a minority and majority language and culture.

If the successful Jewish immigrant depicted in early-twentieth-century American literature readily gives himself over to the social and economic opportunities that come with linguistic assimilation, then Robin's *La Québécoite* offers a countermodel of cultural and linguistic exchange and mutual respect.[10] This model is a product of both Robin's alienation from Quebec society, which keeps reminding Robin that she can never really share in Quebecois history or identity because she is an immigrant and a Jew, and her sense of exclusion from Montreal's English-speaking, conservative Jewish establishment, which sees her as a French writer with unreliable political sympathies. I suggest that Robin's inclusion of quotations from Yiddish and other Jewish texts in a French novel of Quebec emphasizes in-betweenness, translation, multilingualism and border crossing as a way to challenge the cultural and linguistic borders of ethnonationalism. Students come to appreciate how and why the novel celebrates the syncretic possibilities of urban encounters where different groups and languages intermingle.

The class's analysis of *La Québécoite* concludes with consideration of three intertexts that appear in the heart of the novel, each of which highlights the complications and dangers of the nativist discourse that informed the political context of the novel's composition. The first is a section from a schoolbook about early French colonial history, which presents Catholic missionaries as the first martyrs for the cause of Quebec, murdered by the Iroquois they attempted to convert. My students appreciate how Robin's analysis of this schoolbook exposes the writing of colonial history as a fictional enterprise in which indigenousness is at first an object of curiosity and opportunity, then something to be feared and eradicated, and only later something to be appropriated. The next text we consider is decidedly less heady: a menu Robin reproduces from Ben's delicatessen, which includes the story of the business's growth from a pushcart where a Jewish immigrant sold sandwiches to workers to a restaurant that exports the unique flavors of Montreal cuisine to Hollywood. We discuss how the menu is itself a classic immigrant story, depicting Ben's success as a model for the ways in which the immigrant presence enhances the flavor of the host community rather than threatens it. Finally, we consider the novel's inclusion of the full manifesto of the Front de libération du Québéc ("Quebec Liberation Front"), with its call to "Make Your Revolution" (*Wanderer* 101). If the narrator's husband (who is Quebecois) is inspired by "the intense emotion that had gripped him when he heard [the manifesto] read" (96), then to the narrator's immigrant ear its jingoism is an ominous sign of the subsequent violence that would be perpetrated by the FLQ in the name of nationalism:

> The fear of homogeneity
> of unanimity
> of the Us that excludes all others
> of the pure.   (107)

Our reading of these three texts allows me to demonstrate how the novel sets up a conversation between colonial history, vernacular texts, and political literature that collectively performs Robin's fictional mantra to "note all the differences" (86, 91).

By discussing how *La Québécoite* navigates the tensions between languages and home to problematize and complicate identity, students appreciate how Robin's immigrant counternarratives serve as conspicuous interventions into exclusivist master narratives. In this way, memories of Jewish eastern Europe are not only recovered for the novel's Jewish readers but also form the genesis of a more dialogic and transcultural literature of Canada and Quebec, one that requires "no literary passports or visas" ("Writing" 178).

Notes

1. I include Benjamin Harshav and Barbara Harshav's *American Yiddish Poetry*, an essay by Isaac Bashevis Singer ("Problems of Yiddish Prose in America"), and selections about the Hebrew literary encounter with Native America from Mintz's *Sanctuary in the Wilderness*, pp. 367–89. I have recently included Israeli novels that imagine America as an alternative Jewish homeland, such as Nava Semel's *Isra Isle*, about Mordecai Manuel Noah's nineteenth-century effort to establish a refuge for Jews on Grand Island in New York, and contemporary American works that are interested in Yiddish not only as a bridge to the past but also as a means of exploring the pleasures of Jewish interlingualism, such as Dara Horn's *The World to Come* and Peter Manseau's *Songs for the Butcher's Daughter*.

2. These include, from Canada, A. M. Klein's *The Second Scroll*, Mordecai Richler's *The Apprenticeship of Duddy Kravitz*, and Chava Rosenfarb's *Survivors*;

from Brazil, Moacyr Scliar's *The Centaur in the Garden*; from Argentina, Alberto Gerchunoff's *The Jewish Gauchos of the Pampas*; and Achy Obejas's interlingual and transnational Cuban-American novel *Days of Awe*.

3. Quebecois nationalists have criticized Canadian multicultural policy as a neocolonial strategy to contain their aspirations for independence, and Canada's First Nations have viewed it as a distraction from the historical mistreatment of native peoples.

4. Montreal's Yiddish literary community included such voices as J. I. Segal, Sholem Shtern, and Ida Maze, joined after the Holocaust by Melekh Ravitsh, Rokhl Korn, Chava Rosenfarb, and Yehuda Elberg. Other Jewish writers working in French, like Robin, include Monique Bosco, Naïm Kattan, and Michel Solomon.

5. For overviews of Canadian Jewish writing, see Brenner, "Canadian Jews"; Greenstein, "Introduction"; and Margolis, "Across the Border."

6. For more on Yiddish Montreal, see Margolis, *Jewish Roots*. For more on Montreal as a multilingual literary center, see Simon, *Translating Montreal*.

7. Robin's word "Yiddishophone" is a pun on the term *allophone*, used in Quebec to refer to someone whose mother tongue is neither English nor French, and who therefore complicates Canada's established binational and bilingual dualities.

8. Yiddish postvernacularity refers to the phenomenon in which Yiddish as a means of spoken communication becomes secondary to Yiddish as part of a symbolic system of representation, cultural performance, and metasignification. See Shandler 4.

9. The list is too long to cite fully but includes excerpts from the Russian Jewish writer Isaac Babel's *Red Cavalry*; work by Soviet Yiddish poets Moyshe Kulbak, Peretz Markish, and Dovid Hofshteyn; poems by the American Yiddish modernist poet Yankev Glatshteyn; retellings of Jewish folklore; and work by the German Israeli philosopher Gershom Scholem, as well as references to the medieval mystical tract *The Zohar*.

10. For a theoretical statement of Robin's approach to mediating ethnic particularism and assimilation, see her essay "Sortir de l'ethnicité."

Works Cited

Berrouët-Oriol, Robert. "L'effet d'exil." *Vice Versa*, no. 17, Dec. 1986-Jan. 1987, pp. 20–21.

Berrouët-Oriol, Robert, and Robert Fournier. "L'Émergence des écritures migrantes et métisses au Québec." *Québec Studies*, vol. 14, 1992, pp. 7–22.

Brenner, Rachel Feldhay. "Canadian Jews and Their Story: The Making of Canadian Jewish Literature." *Prooftexts*, vol. 18, no. 3, Sept. 1998, pp. 283–97.

Gerchunoff, Alberto. *Jewish Gauchos of the Pampas*. Translated by Prudencio de Pereda, U of New Mexico P, 1988. Translation of *Los gauchos judíos*, Talleres Gráficos Joaquín Sesé, 1910.

Greenstein, Michael. "Introduction: Sambation to Saskatchewan." *Contemporary Jewish Writing in Canada: An Anthology*, edited by Greenstein, U of Nebraska P, 2004, pp. xi–l.

———. *Third Solitudes: Tradition and Discontinuity in Jewish-Canadian Literature.* McGill-Queens UP, 1989.

Harshav, Benjamin, and Barbara Harshav. *American Yiddish Poetry: A Bilingual Anthology.* U of California P, 1996.

Horn, Dara. *The World to Come.* W.W. Norton, 2006.

Howells, Coral Ann, and Eva-Marie Kröller. Introduction. *The Cambridge History of Canadian Literature,* edited by Howells and Kröller, Cambridge UP, 2009, pp. 1–6.

Klein, A. M. *The Second Scroll.* Alfred A. Knopf, 1951.

MacLennan, Hugh. *Two Solitudes.* Duell, Sloan and Pearce, 1945.

Manseau, Peter. *Songs for the Butcher's Daughter.* Free Press, 2008.

Margolis, Rebecca. "Across the Border: Canadian Jewish Writing." *The Cambridge History of Jewish American Literature,* edited by Hana Wirth-Nesher, Cambridge UP, 2015, pp. 432–46.

———. *Jewish Roots, Canadian Soil: Yiddish Culture in Montreal, 1905–1945.* McGill-Queens UP, 2011.

Mintz, Alan. *Sanctuary in the Wilderness: A Critical Introduction to American Hebrew Poetry.* Syracuse UP, 2011.

Obejas, Achy. *Days of Awe.* Ballantine Books, 2001.

Richler, Mordecai. *The Apprenticeship of Duddy Kravitz.* Little Brown, 1959.

———. *The Street.* McClelland and Stewart, 1969.

Robin, Régine. *La Québécoite: Roman.* Québec/Amérique, 1983.

———. "Sortir de l'ethnicité." *Métamorphoses de l'utopie,* edited by Fulvio Caccia and Jean-Michel Lacroix, Presses Sorbonne Nouvelle, 1992, pp. 25–41.

———. *The Wanderer.* Translated by Phyllis Aronoff, Alter Ego, 1997.

———. "The Writing of an Allophone from France: Afterword to *The Wanderer* Fifteen Years Later." Robin, *Wanderer,* pp. 173–82.

Rosenfarb, Chava. *Survivors: Seven Short Stories.* Cormorant Books, 2004.

Scliar, Moacyr. *The Centaur in the Garden.* Translated by Margaret Neves. U of Wisconsin P, 2003. Translation of *O Centauro no jardim,* Editora Nova Fronteira, 1980.

Semel, Nava. *Isra Isle.* Mandel Vilar Press, 2016.

Shandler, Jeffrey. *Adventures in Yiddishland: Postvernacular Language and Culture.* U of California P, 2006.

Simon, Sherry. *Translating Montreal: Episodes in the Life of a Divided City.* McGill-Queens UP, 2006.

Singer, Isaac Bashevis. "Problems of Yiddish Prose in America." *Prooftexts,* vol. 9, no. 1, Jan. 1989, pp. 5–12.

Ilan Stavans

Jews beyond America:
The One and the Many

The classroom is a place where curiosity must prevail and where we should imagine ourselves in alternative ways. In classrooms narrowness must collapse of its own accord, and language and culture must be pushed to their limits in their interaction with the environment. In short, nothing in the classroom should be considered sacred, immobile, or settled. I write all of this in reaction to the frequent parochialism of the Jewish American studies classroom. In English, the proper noun *America* is taken as a synonym for *the United States*. Yet in other tongues it describes a vast continent that goes from Alaska to Patagonia. Similarly, the word *Jewish* denotes an individual who belongs not to a specific country but to a religious, political, and cultural tradition with multiple homes across space and time.

For too long, the teaching of Jewish American culture in the classroom has been centered on the United States and narrowly defined. While the United States may be where the class meets, it should not be taken as its destination. The Jewish American studies classroom should be the place where immigration is studied not only nationally but panoramically. After all, Jewish life is shaped first and foremost by change. Change is the one constant, and it requires adaptability and renewal. And immigration is always about change: to travel from one context to another is to become someone else.

Traveling enables Jews to be at once insiders and outsiders, to see things from within as well as from a distance, and to be simultaneously objective and subjective. The classroom must replicate that versatility, encouraging students to look at a particular artifact (such as a painting, a novel, or a popular movie) not for its consumer value—for example, what students expect to get, in practical terms as they navigate life after college—but for the circumstances that gestated it. Those circumstances invariably include national and linguistic attributes.

When one looks at Jewish American culture on its own, the result is often insular. It favors American exceptionalism, the belief that the United States is home to the most privileged Jewish diasporic community, where in fact that community is just another example of the historical journey of Jews from biblical times to the future, as imperfect as any other community. It represents not the end of Jewish history but only another chapter of it. All this is a sign of parochialism. It represents a refusal to see it from a larger stand, not a particular but as a universal stance.

This is the antiparochial and antiteleological argument I make in Jews beyond America, an interdisciplinary course I have taught several times. The course uses elements from history, anthropology, political science, linguistics, religion, economics, and cultural studies, and it draws on diverse sources. The material for the most part is organized chronologically to follow the historical forces driving Jewishness across civilizations. While the primary language of the course is English (again, the locus of the course is the United States, plus for research purposes I use English as the de facto lingua franca), students are asked to immerse themselves in other languages, either Jewish (Yiddish, Ladino, Judeo-Arabic, and so on) or non-Jewish (German, French, Spanish, Italian, Portuguese, etc.), so they can explore the linguistic diversity of Jewish and non-Jewish texts.

My objective is to allow the students to scrutinize what Jews did in other diasporic settings. For instance, I look at the exilic period in Babylon and the quest for nationhood in Canaan, both depicted in the Bible. Or I consider how the Babylonian Talmud was composed in response to the pressures for Jews to acculturate in Mesopotamia, where they had settled after the destruction of the Second Temple. Or I investigate La Convivencia ("The Coexistence"), the period in which adherents of the three major Abrahamic religions cohabited on the Iberian Peninsula. Or I explore the Haskalah ("Enlightenment") in Germany. Or I look at the emergence of Yiddish civilization in the Pale of Settlement. Or I study the development of nationalism, anarchism, Zionism, and other isms in the second half of the nineteenth century. Or I assess the Holocaust as the major defining event in modern Jewish life.

Artifacts in the syllabus may include, but are not limited to, portions of Genesis, a passage from the Dead Sea Scrolls, the midrash "The Oven of Akhnai" from the Talmudic tractate *Bava metzia*, a series of verses by Spanish poets such as Samuel ha-Nagid and Solomon ibn Gabirol from *The Penguin Book of Hebrew Verse*, edited by T. Carmi, a section from Maimonides's *Commentary on the Mishna*, the first part of Spinoza's *Ethics*, titled "Concerning God: Definitions, Axioms, Propositions," and the converso writings in *The Poem of Queen Esther* by João Pinto Delgado. The course materials may also feature the *Self-Portrait at 63* by Rembrandt or a stained-glass window like *Tribe of Levi* by Marc Chagall, an essay by Moses Mendelsson, two chapters from Sholem Aleichem's *Tevye the Dairyman* ("Tevye Strikes It Rich" and "Tevye Blows a Small Fortune"), several of Martin Buber's Hasidic tales, Theodor Herzl's *The Jewish State*, an essay on anarchism by Emma Goldman in the anthology *How Yiddish Changed America and How America Changed Yiddish*, a disquisition on Hebrew by Eliezer ben Yehuda as related in *Resurrecting Hebrew*, Paul Celan's "Death Fugue," Emma Lazarus's "The New Colossus," A. M. Klein's *The Second Scroll*, a fragment from Mary Antin's *The Promised Land*, Art Spiegelman's *Maus I* and *II*, Isaac Bashevis Singer's "Gimpel the Fool," Moacyr Scliar's *The Centaur in the Garden*, Maurice Sendak's *Where the Wild Things Are*, Woody Allen's film *Zelig*, a segment from David Grossman's novel *To the End of the Land*, the *New World Haggadah*, an episode like "The Letting Go" of the TV show *Transparent*, and hybridized music such as Jewish salsa in Benjamin Lapidus's *Herencia Judía*.

In selecting course materials, I respond to two impulses. The first is to present a diverse sample. Each item ought to be representative, embodying crucial elements that speak to the place and time in which it was created. For example, when teaching *Tevye the Dairyman*, I highlight the way Sholem Aleichem explores the economic, social, political, cultural, and religious issues at stake for mid-nineteenth-century Jews in the Pale of Settlement. I do the same with *Transparent* in regards to American Jews in the second decade of the twenty-first century. By pairing the two works, I invite students to compare Jewish responses to these respective milieus. That comparison allows students to draw insightful conclusions, not only in regards to the distant past, but also in terms of how the immediate past, which for the students is perceived as their present, needs to be looked at with a historical lens.

As for the second impulse, an added benefit of this comparison is that the texts were produced in different cultures. Rather than give my students two texts from the same cultural ecosystem, say a novel from the Pale of Settlement published in 1868 and another published in 1935, or one from the United States in 1917 and another in 1997, I have them look at material across habitats. This allows the class to analyze a culture from a distance—in Spinoza's expression, sub specie aeternitatis—which helps them see their own milieu with a degree of objectivity.

Since the journey of Jews across diasporas is invariably about commingling with the local mainstream culture as well as with other minorities, I always make an effort to include on the syllabus non-Jewish disquisitions about Jews. It is important for us to look at Jewish life and production from the viewpoints of those who respond to it, as well as those who create it, because in my course I place an emphasis on how Jews react to the social environment in which they live and on how that environment changes them. The view from the outside is allowed in.

Hence, portions of the course, generally intermingled in the appropriate chronological location, feature the Gospel according to Matthew, Shakespeare's *The Merchant of Venice*, Jean-Paul Sartre's *Anti-Semite and Jew*, Jorge Luis Borges's essay "The Argentine Writer and Tradition," and anti-Israel jihadist propaganda. I use two catch-words as a teaching tool whose semantic meanings clearly overlap: one is *translation*, the other *interpretation*. Translation is understood not only as a strategy used by Jews to decode the autochthonous culture of a society in which they settle but also as a mechanism through which that culture is reimagined by the Jews for their internal consumption. Interpretation is the device that allows Jews to make meaning of whatever they experience in the given society. Through translation and interpretation, they build an understanding of their reality that complies with the requirements of daily life and allows them to experience an inner sense of freedom and self-determination.

I apply the concepts of translation and interpretation to two twentieth-century works. Celan's "Death Fugue" uses music to investigate the way Jews in German concentration camps went to their deaths with an internal strength that responded to their total subjugation. Scliar's *The Centaur in the Garden* is an imaginative response to the difficulty of existing as a Jew and a Brazilian in the 1930s in Rio Grande do Sul, where the protagonist, Guedali Tartakowsky, is born a literal half-and-half: part animal, part human. Celan's poem explores questions of life and death. Scliar's novel offers an escapist response through humor to the questions of assimilation.

In my course, I am careful to reject triumphalism. Everything in the course is seen as being in transit. No place or epoch is presented as the end of suffering. Jewish diasporic communities are seen as temporary stations, each with its own lifespan. My goal is to allow the students to simultaneously see the small and large pictures and to look at Jews as one people among many, enduring the vicissitudes that accompany exile. What has kept Jews together? Why do they persevere? Would it be easier to simply give in to the inclement demands of a particular environment? The answers to these questions enable students to take a global outlook.

A couple of examples will illustrate. While analyzing *The Merchant of Venice*, and specifically in a close reading of the soliloquy "Hath not a Jew eyes? Hath not a Jew hands, organs, dimensions, senses, affections, passions?" (*MV* 3.1.1364), I invite the class to think of Shylock not as the template for an anti-Semitic stereotype but as Shakespeare's alter ego. I propose that throughout the play the Jewish merchant is a pariah in the way that artists might also be. I ask them to consider the possibility that Shylock might be the character in the play with whom Shakespeare as an artist identifies the most. Next I introduce "The Argentine Writer and Tradition," in which Borges insinuates that the Jews survive in one host society after another because they perceive themselves simultaneously as cultural insiders and outsiders. This mechanism, according to Borges, allows them to be local and global at the same time. This argument is attractive to students in the course because it helps them see Jewish culture as untied, connecting Jews to specific environments but also to a larger historical arc.

No doubt controversially in Jews beyond America, I see the state of Israel after 1948 as another part of the Diaspora and not as an end to the Diaspora. I include a poem by Yehuda Amichai, such as "The Diameter of the Bomb," or the opening chapter of Grossman's *The Yellow Wind* (5–17) on Israeli-Palestinian relations and ask the students to look at these works as yet another manifestation of a particular context: in this case, Jewish life in a Jewish nation that includes minorities whose status is not unlike that of Jews in diasporic communities elsewhere.

This perspective works well with a diverse student body. Only half to two-thirds of my students are Jewish, and two-thirds were born in the United States. This diversity is part of what makes the course exciting. Of course, I want the students to come from different parts of the planet, to speak different languages, and to be the products of heterogeneous cultural traditions. The less uniform the population, the more valuable the result. I encourage the classroom to become the locale—edgy, inquisitive, and pregnant with meanings—where insights arise in response to cross-fertilization. With the intellectual tools acquired during this intellectual journey, students can draw their own larger conclusions. I don't always know what these are likely to be because each student is another world.

One pedagogical benefit of Jews beyond America is that by the end of the semester all of us, teacher and students alike, think of the Jewish and Jewish American literary canons in an elastic way. Rather than looking at these texts as belonging to particular nations, we recognize spatial and temporal borders as artificial conceits. What makes Isaac Babel and Philip Roth part of the same Jewish literary tradition? It is obviously not language or a specific passport. Distilling what writers like these have in common is the task of the class.

Let me add a final word about self-interest. I teach Jews beyond America not only because I'm tired of the nearsightedness of Jewish American life that is projected into the Jewish American studies classroom. My rationale is equally egotistic. I want the experience to teach me about what it means to survive as a Jew. I want it to make me less nearsighted, less parochial. This generally happens throughout the course. By the end of it, after numerous close readings, after intense and fruitful discussions, what I happily draw from the course is that a new generation of students is eager to understand Jewish life not confined in a specific environment but in toto.

Works Cited

Aleichem, Sholem. "Tevye Blows a Small Fortune." Tevye the Dairyman *and* The Railroad Stories, translated by Hillel Halkin, Penguin Classics, 1996, pp. 21–35.

———. "Tevye Strikes It Rich." Tevye the Dairyman *and* The Railroad Stories, translated by Hillel Halkin, Penguin Classics, 1996, pp. 3–20.

Allen, Woody, director. *Zelig*. Warner Bros., 1983.

Amichai, Yehuda. "The Diameter of the Bomb." Translated by Chana Bloch, *The Selected Poetry of Yehuda Amichai*, U of California P, 1996. *Chana Bloch*, www.chanabloch.com/amichai.html.

Antin, Mary. *The Promised Land*. Penguin Classics, 2012.

Borges, Jorge Luis. "The Argentine Writer and Tradition." *Selected Non-fictions*, edited by Eliot Weinberger, translated by Esther Allen et al., Viking, 1999, pp. 213–16.

Carmi, T., editor. *The Penguin Book of Hebrew Verse*. New York: Penguin Classics, 2006.

Celan, Paul. "Death Fugue." Translated by Jerome Rothenberg. *Academy of America Poets*, poets.org/poem/death-fugue.

Chagall, Marc. *Tribe of Levi*. 1961. *Wikimedia Commons*, commons.wikimedia.org/wiki/File:Hadassah_Chagall_Windows-_Tribe_of_Levi.jpg.

Goldman, Emma. "Against Marriage as Private Possession." *How Yiddish Changed America and How America Changed Yiddish*, edited by Ilan Stavans and Josh Lambert, Restless Books, 2019, pp. 66–69.

Gospel according to Matthew. *The Bible*, Authorized King James Version, Oxford World's Classics, 2008, pp. 3–44

Grossman, David. *To the End of the Land*. Translated by Haim Watzman, Vintage Books, 2011.

———. *The Yellow Wind*. Translated by Haim Watzman, Picador, 2002.

Herzl, Theodore. *The Jewish State*. Dover Publications, 1989.

Klein, A. M. *The Second Scroll*. Introduction by Sydney Feshbach, Marlboro Press, 1985.

Lapidus, Benjamin. *Herencia Judía*, Tresero Productions, 2008, benjaminlapidus.com/music/.

Lazarus, Emma. "The New Colossus." *Emma Lazarus: Selected Poems*, Library of America, 2005.

"The Letting Go." *Transparent*, created by Jill Soloway, season 1, episode 2. Amazon Video, 2014.

Maimonides. "Commentary on the Mishna." *Everyman's Talmud: The Major Teachings of the Rabbinic Sages*, edited by Abraham Cohen, Shocken Books, 1995.

"The Oven of Akhnai." *Tractate* Bava Metzia. 1989. *The Talmud: The Steinsaltz Edition*, edited by Adin Steinsaltz, vol. 1, part 1, Random House, 1989.

Pinto Delgado, João. *The Poem of Queen Esther*. Translated by David R. Slavitt, Oxford UP, 1999.

Rembrandt. *Self-Portrait at 63*. 1669. National Portrait Gallery, London, www.nationalgallery.org.uk/paintings/rembrandt-self-portrait-at-the-age-of-63.

Sartre, Jean-Paul. *Anti-Semite and Jew*. Translation by George J. Becker, Schocken Books, 1976.

Scliar, Moacyr. *The Centaur in the Garden*. Translated by Margaret A. Neves, introduction by Ilan Stavans, U of Wisconsin P, 2003.

Sendak, Maurice. *Where the Wild Things Are*. HarperCollins, 2016.

Shakespeare, William. *The Merchant of Venice*. *The Norton Shakespeare*, edited by Stephen Greenblatt et al., 3rd ed., W. W. Norton, 2016, pp. 1327–94.

Singer, Isaac Bashevis. "Gimpel the Fool." *"Gimpel the Fool" to "The Letter Writer,"* Library of America, 2004, pp. 3–14. Vol. 1 of *Collected Stories*, edited by Ilan Stavans.

Spiegelman, Art. *Maus I: A Survivor's Tale: My Father Bleeds History*. Pantheon Books, 1986.

———. *Maus II: A Survivor's Tale: And Here My Troubles Began*. Pantheon Books, 1992.

Spinoza, Baruch. "Concerning God: Definitions, Axioms, Propositions." *Ethics*, translated by Edwin Curley, introduction by Stuart Hampshire, Penguin Classics, 2005, pp. 2–37.

Stavans, Ilan. *Resurrecting Hebrew*. New York: Schocken / Next Book, 2008.

———. *New World Haggadah*. Gaon Books, 2017.

Naomi B. Sokoloff

American Poetry, Jewish Prayer, World Literature

Undergraduate students at North American colleges are less likely to sign up for a course on Jewish poetry—or a course on Jewish American life and culture—than to sign up for a course that asks broad cross-cultural questions, such as, What is prayer? Why do people pray, and what does prayer look like in different religious traditions (Judaism, Christianity, Islam, and others)? Can age-old prayers continue to inspire faith or serve contemporary sensibilities? Teaching modern poems that respond to and reinterpret prayer can address those questions and guide students toward comparative literary studies in a world literature context. Moreover, co-teaching and cross-listing courses (in, for instance, comparative religion or Near East studies, or to address diversity requirements) can enhance interdisciplinary inquiry while boosting enrollment and student enthusiasm. In this essay I offer some thoughts on aspects of this approach to teaching that pertain to Jewish literature.[1]

By examining poems that draw on elements of Jewish liturgy, students can learn how recent literary works reconsider foundational texts of Judaism. In addition, reading the work of American poets together with the work of poets from Europe, Israel, and elsewhere can help students achieve one of the principal aims of world literature: to acquire a "broad perspective for discussing thematic affinities and patterns of literary imagination beyond the gaps of languages and cultures" (Zhang 71). Indeed, Jewish literature, transnational and multilingual as it is, may fit well into curricular frameworks that emphasize translation studies and the global circulation of culture.[2] Furthermore, while American literature has often been excluded from world literature, some scholars have advocated restoring it to international frameworks. With that aim in mind, teachers may find that consideration of religions serves as an especially good point of departure for world literature syllabus design; as Wai Chee Dimock has noted, because of their longevity and diffusion, religious texts "have done much to integrate the globe" (307).

Since the 1990s, major anthologies of world literature have included some biblical texts, but little attention has gone to rabbinic literature or Jewish prayer. Classic Jewish sources certainly merit more attention than this. Examining connections between Jewish American poetry and ancient sources can open students' eyes to the great traditions of Judaic writing while also yielding new perspectives on and innovative interpretations of Jewish thought. At the same time, more knowledge of Jewish literature can lead to increased student understanding of what constitutes American poetry. While liturgy has never been a central focus of Jewish American poets,[3] acknowledging allusions to prayer in American writing may allow teachers to shift the spotlight to fascinating texts that might otherwise be overlooked in literature courses. In addition, poems about prayer deserve consideration, as they bring multisensory dimensions into literary study. Prayer entails oral recitation, as well as written texts, and often has musical components. Its performative elements—embodied expression, symbolic motions, and the spatial orientation of both—can make texts come alive. Videos, musical adaptations of poems, and visual or material displays can inject welcome vitality into the classroom. Furthermore, since the awarding of the 2016 Nobel Prize in Literature to the songwriter Bob Dylan, debates about the place of oral genres in world literature have taken on greater prominence; instructors can introduce these debates to students by teaching about prayer and poetry. The rest of this essay deals with suggested texts.

For instructors seeking background information on Jewish prayer, a number of excellent resources are now available. The outstanding book series *My People's Prayer Book*, edited by Lawrence A. Hoffman, covers the history of major liturgical texts and explores translation issues, observance practices, religious law, gender questions, and mystical interpretations of prayer in accessible yet rigorous commentaries. Other useful guides to Jewish prayer and synagogue customs include Hoffman's *The Way into Jewish Prayer*, Alan Mintz's "Prayer and the Prayerbook," and Hayim Halevy Donin's *To Pray as a Jew*.[4] Teaching texts in translation has become an accepted part of world literature pedagogy, as working with translations may open up interpretation rather than shut it down. For instance, looking at a number of translated versions of a prayer—even with students who have no previous knowledge of the original language—creates an opportunity to discuss semantic range. This makes it possible to point out ways in which individual Hebrew or Aramaic words do not map exactly onto English vocabulary. Such an approach assumes that "translation is never a simple transfer of information but a dynamic process of interpretive recontextualization" (Damrosch, "Introduction" 16).[5]

Genres, texts, or themes that invite particular scrutiny include the *Shema* (Judaism's basic declaration of monotheistic belief), *piyyut* (a type of liturgical poem), psalms, and Sabbath ritual. The *Shema* has received thoughtful treatment from many modern poets. For example, Marcia Falk's reworking of this text in English and in Hebrew foregrounds the challenges of translating and adapting prayer and demonstrates that Americans may compose poetry in various languages—not only English. Similarly, American Sign Language renditions of the *Shema* raise compelling questions about translation, such as how the opening words of the traditional text, "Hear, O Israel," have and have not spoken to those who are hearing-impaired.[6] These texts make for productive comparison, too, with Primo Levi's poem "Shema" (published originally in Italian in 1947) and with contemporary Hebrew poems by Israeli poets, such as Eliaz Cohen's "Hear O Lord."[7] Turning to *piyyut*, instructors might consider teaching "Unetaneh Tokef," the High Holiday text that inspired Leonard Cohen's haunting song "Who by Fire, Who by Water." Cohen's lyrics, in turn, can be read in conjunction with Falk's version of "Unetaneh Tokef," since both offer variations on themes of fate and forgiveness and engage closely with wording from the prayer book.[8] In contrast, other American writers move far away from traditional wordings as they reflect on prayer in their work. Notably, George Oppen's "Psalm" at first sight bears little resemblance to synagogue hymns. Deeper reading, though, reveals an emphasis on mindfulness and a celebration of creation very much in keeping with the Hallel (Psalms 145–50 from Hebrew scripture). Oppen's poem gains further resonance when read side by side with Hebrew poet Admiel Kosman's "Psalm of the Day." As for the Sabbath, quite a few poems delve into obser-

vances related to the day of rest. Among them, "Der mames shabbosim /
My Mother's Sabbath Days," composed by Irena Klepfisz in a mixture of
English and Yiddish, invites reading in tandem with another example of
American Yiddish writing: Malka Heifetz Tussman's "Forgotten."[9]

One of the best-known Jewish prayers in the United States is the
Mourner's Kaddish. Writers have referred to it quite often in fiction and
poetry. However, as Hana Wirth-Nesher has argued (123), the Kaddish
in such texts figures primarily as a vestige of ethnic identity and not as a
religious text. Accordingly, two poems that do engage more deeply with
the Kaddish command special attention. One, composed in English, is the
American poet Adrienne Rich's "Tattered Kaddish." The other, presenting a mix of Hebrew and Aramaic, is "Kaddish yetomah" ("A Woman's
Mourner's Kaddish"), by the Israeli poet Hava Pinhas-Cohen.

To pursue interpretation of this material, students must first learn
some things about the prayer-book version of the Mourner's Kaddish: The
prayer does not mention death or the deceased but rather affirms God's
glory. The Kaddish requires a minyan (a group of ten adult Jews), and a
cluster of rules stipulate who recites the Kaddish and for whom. Significantly, women do not say Kaddish in some denominations; in others,
they do. Mourners recite the Kaddish over the course of a year; custom
differs in the case of suicide. Equipped with this information, students
can benefit from discussion of how this prayer has traveled and the ways
it is gendered and modified by cultural taboos. For instance, it emerged
from an ancient milieu, and its closeness to the Lord's Prayer indicates
how Judaism and Christianity grew out of similar historical contexts
(each prayer sanctifies God's name and heralds the coming of God's kingdom). The customs surrounding the Kaddish were shaped in medieval
Europe, in part under the influence of Christian beliefs; the prayer arrived in America and other locales through modern migrations; and in
the twentieth century, especially in the Diaspora, recitation of the Kaddish entered into women's religious observance—in defiance of long-
standing Orthodox custom.

Rich, in "Tattered Kaddish," defies Jewish law by honoring suicides
and offering "praise to them." She uses her text explicitly as a memorial,
whereas the Mourner's Kaddish does not openly lament loss. Nonetheless,
by creating an evocative, liturgical-sounding series of couplets that all
begin "praise to life," Rich expresses a sentiment in keeping with Judaism. She insistently celebrates life, and so even as the poem secularizes
its material (by never mentioning God), it stays within the spirit of the

Kaddish. Similarly, Rich aligns herself with the communal aspect of the traditional prayer through repeated use of the word "we."

At the same time, Rich's poem also acknowledges the struggle of mourners to cope with bereavement. The quasi-liturgical list of praises, the orderly arrangement of semiparallel lines, is preceded by a perplexing opening—one that conveys the chaotic feelings of those who are left behind.

> Taurean reaper of the wild apple field
> messenger from earthmire gleaning
> transcripts of fog

A pivotal word in this first stanza is "earthmire"—an invented term that suggests muddy perplexity. "Mire" means "bog," "mud," or, metaphorically, a troublesome, intractable situation. Here, as mud calls to mind earthiness or perhaps burial, the first line of the poem provides some context to explain what is troubling: the word "reaper" recalls the grim reaper, "Taurean" refers to an astrological figure related to springtime, and the mention of an apple field disconcerts, since apples ripen for harvest only later in the year. Accordingly, the reader senses that at issue is an untimely death, a reaping that comes too early. The mention of "earthmire" in line 2 therefore gestures toward unresolved grief, a condition of feeling bogged down in emotions difficult to articulate. Adding to this picture, the word "gleaning" implies a kind of impoverished harvest. It is a word often connected in English to "meaning," but the sole meaning to be gleaned here comes from "transcripts of fog"—unclear records or something elusive, made of mist. Only subsequently, out of this murkiness and nebulous imagery, does Rich's poem finally emerge with a sense of order, affirming faith in the way things are and accepting an imperfect or fallen world.[10] Rich thus departs from the traditional Kaddish, but by maintaining the collective voice, using the imperative, and deploying repetitions that echo prayer, she acknowledges and wrestles with liturgical impulses. Her efforts make "Tattered Kaddish" unusual in the context of Jewish American literature, which rarely uses the mourner's prayer to deal with theological questions.

Pinhas-Cohen's poem, in contrast to Rich's, engages directly with the language of traditional prayer.[11] The central portion of this text presents a female mourner's inner thoughts, as words from the Kaddish appear in a separate column of print. The layout indicates that, while others are reciting the Kaddish, the mourner struggles with her feelings of isolation and exclusion from public ritual. The poem in this way questions gender roles in Judaism, and it also rebels against tradition by focusing on the mourner's subjective experience. Pinhas-Cohen emphasizes not the sanctification of God's name but an individual's internal turmoil. Moreover, while the poem refers to God in the third person, as does the traditional Kaddish, the woman in Pinhas-Cohen's poem addresses her dead husband through the use of the second person. He remains the center of her attention. In tension with the traditional prayer, the images through which the mourner conveys her grief echo the Kaddish yet deviate from it. A long string of verbs—"pull and direct and guide and drag and carry"—indicate that she hopes God will direct her soul upward toward a vision of her late husband. In this line the poem recalls the traditional idea that reciting Kaddish will help the soul of the departed rise to heaven, but the poet recasts and subverts the trope of ascent by applying it to the mourner's situation.

Rich's "Tattered Kaddish" and Pinhas-Cohen's "Kaddish yetoma" honor the Kaddish by engaging with it earnestly—albeit differently. Each calls attention to certain aspects of the original prayer and not others. While Rich focuses on suicide, Pinhas-Cohen more emphatically dramatizes gender issues. Pinhas-Cohen's imagery draws deliberately on classic sources; Rich's revolves around neologism. Both poets speak for those marginalized in Orthodox tradition, and both struggle with the question, To what extent does public prayer provide community at a moment of great loss and sorrow? Both poems generate further considerations when read together with other poetic responses to the mourner's prayer: notably, Allen Ginsberg's "Kaddish" as well as a poem called "Kaddish" by another well-known American poet, Charles Reznikoff, and the Israeli pop song "Traffic Jam of Miracles," by Kobi Oz.

Teaching poems and prayers in comparative contexts, therefore, can help students pay heed to textual detail and also move from specific texts back to overarching concepts and the kind of big-picture thinking that an undergraduate education, at its best, can provide. The poems by Rich and Pinhas-Cohen discussed here pose a variety of far-reaching questions: What is the role of women in highly gendered cultures? Does the individual find meaning by relying on or rebelling against strictures of traditional religious practice? How do texts travel through space, time, and languages? Far from limiting instructors to parochial or narrowly specialized matters, teaching poems that grapple with Jewish prayer can address universal issues deserving of wide audiences, while directing students toward distinctively Jewish aspects of Jewish American literature.

In the context of courses that also present Islamic, Christian, or other traditions along with Jewish texts, these materials take on even more meaning.

Notes

1. I have tested this approach at the University of Washington in a course I taught with Samad Alavi titled Prayer and Poetry: Judaic and Islamic Traditions.

2. For a discussion of Jewish literature in relation to multiple models of world literature, see Levy and Schachter.

3. For an excellent overview of Jewish American poetry, see Shreiber, *Singing*.

4. Print sources for the poems discussed in this essay can be found in the works-cited list; however, an Internet search will also yield access to most of the poems.

5. Damrosch makes special reference here to the work of Lawrence Venuti.

6. An illuminating explanation accompanies Rabbi Darby Jared Leigh's American Sign Language version of the *Shema*.

7. For a more extensive discussion, see Sokoloff.

8. Zierler provides insightful commentary.

9. These are but a few examples of potential readings for students. Modern Hebrew poetry, exuberantly rich in allusion to prayer, offers many possibilities— including such masterful works as Yehuda Amichai's "Elim mitchalfim, hatefilot nisharot le'ad" ("Gods Change, Prayers Are Here to Stay").

10. Rich defined the speaker of "Tattered Kaddish" as a feminine figure from the Kabbalah, adding a gendered aspect to the poem (Shreiber, "Kaddish").

11. Jacobson provides helpful commentary on this poem (170–71) and on other Hebrew poetry that alludes to prayer.

Works Cited

Amichai, Yehuda. "Elim mitchalfim, hatefilot nisharot le'ad." *Patuach sagur patuach*, by Amichai, Schocken Books, 1998, pp. 5–19.

———. "Gods Change, Prayers Are Here to Stay." *Open Closed Open: Poems*, by Amichai, translated by Chana Bloch and Chana Kronfeld, Harcourt, 2000, pp. 39–48.

Cohen, Eliaz. "Hear O Lord" [Shema Ado-nai]. *Hear O Lord: Poems from the Disturbances of 2000–2009*, by Cohen, translated by Larry Barak, Toby Press, 2010, pp. 15–16.

Cohen, Leonard. "Who by Water, Who by Fire?" *New Skin for the Old Ceremony*, Columbia Studios, 1974.

Damrosch, David. "Introduction: All the World in the Time." Damrosch, *Teaching World Literature*, pp. 1–11.

———, editor. *Teaching World Literature*. Modern Language Association of America, 2009.

Dimock, Wai Chee. "American Literature and Islamic Time." Damrosch, *Teaching World Literature*, pp. 306–16.

Donin, Hayim Halevy. *To Pray as a Jew: A Guide to the Prayer Book and the Synagogue Service*. Basic Books, 1980.

Falk, Marcia. "*Sh'ma*: Communal Declaration of Faith." *The Book of Blessings: New Jewish Prayers for Daily Life, the Sabbath, and the New Moon Festival*, by Falk, HarperCollins, 1996, pp. 170–73.

———. "Unetaneh Tokef." *The Days Between: Blessings, Poems, and Directions of the Heart for the Jewish High Holiday Season*, by Falk, Brandeis UP, 2014, 26–35.

Ginsberg, Allen. "Kaddish." *"Kaddish" and Other Poems, 1958–1960*, City Lights Books, 1961, pp. 7–36.

Hoffman, Lawrence A. *My People's Prayerbook: Traditional Prayers, Modern Commentaries*. Jewish Lights Publishing, 1997–2007. 10 vols.

———. *The Way into Jewish Prayer*. Jewish Lights Publishing, 2000.

Jacobson, David C. *Creator, Are You Listening? Israeli Poets on God and Prayer*. Indiana UP, 2007.

Klepfisz, Irena. "Der mames shabbosim / My Mother's Sabbath Days." *A Few Words in the Mother Tongue: Poems Selected and New (1971–1990)*, by Klepfisz, Eighth Mountain Press, 1990, pp. 230–31.

Kosman, Admiel. "Psalm of the Day" [Shir shel yom]. Translated by David C. Jacobson. Jacobson, p. 191.

Leigh, Darby Jared. "Ritualwell.org: Shema in ASL." *YouTube*, uploaded by ritualwell, 26 Sept. 2011, www.youtube.com/watch?v=MDUU4vy2tmM.

Levi, Primo. "Shema." Translated by Ruth Feldman and Brian Swann. *Poem-Hunter.com*, www.poemhunter.com/poem/shema/. Accessed 7 Aug. 2017.

Levy, Lital, and Allison Schachter. "A Non-universal Global: On Jewish Writing and World Literature." *Prooftexts*, vol. 36, nos. 1–2, 2017, pp. 1–26. *Literature Online*, doi:10.2979.

Mintz, Alan. "Prayer and the Prayerbook." *Back to the Sources: Reading the Classic Jewish Texts*, edited by Barry W. Holtz, Summit Books, 1984, pp. 403–29.

Oppen, George. "Psalm." *New Collected Poems*, by Oppen, edited by Michael Davidson, New Directions, 2008, p. 99.

Oz, Kobi. "Traffic Jam of Miracles." *YouTube*, uploaded by psalms4perplexed, 8 Apr. 2010, www.youtube.com/watch?v=3sE-KHnkGOc.

Pinhas-Cohen, Hava. "A Woman's Mourner's Kaddish" [Kaddish yetomah]. Translated by David C. Jacobson. Jacobson, pp. 169–70.

Reznikoff, Charles. "Kaddish." *By the Waters of Manhattan*. New Directions, 1962, pp. 52–53.

Rich, Adrienne. "Tattered Kaddish." *Adrienne Rich's Poetry and Prose: Poems, Prose, Reviews and Criticism*, edited by Barbara Charlesworth Gelpi and Albert Gelpi, W. W. Norton, 1993, p. 159.

Shreiber, Maeera. "Kaddish: Jewish American Elegy Post-1945." *The Oxford Handbook of the Elegy*, edited by Karen Weisman, Oxford UP, 2010, pp. 397–412.

———. *Singing in a Strange Land: A Jewish American Poetics*. Stanford UP, 2007.

Sokoloff, Naomi. "Reading the Shema: Jewish Literature as World Literature." *New Directions in Jewish American and Holocaust Literatures: Reading and*

Teaching, edited by Victoria Aarons and Holli Levitsky, State U of New York P, 2019.

Tussman, Malka Heifetz. "Forgotten" [Fargessen]. Translated by Kathryn Hellerstein. *American Yiddish Poetry*, edited by Benjamin Harshav and Barbara Harshav, U of California P, 1986, pp. 616–17.

Wirth-Nesher, Hana. "Magnified and Sanctified: Liturgy in Contemporary Jewish American Literature." *Ideology and Jewish Identity in Israeli and American Literature*, edited by Emily Miller Budick, State U of New York P, 2001, pp. 115–30.

Zhang Longxi. "What Is Literature? Reading across Cultures." Damrosch, *Teaching World Literature*, pp. 61–72.

Zierler, Wendy. "Who by Fire: Contemporary Personal and Literary Reflections." *Who by Fire, Who by Water: Un'taneh Tokef*, edited by Lawrence A. Hoffman, Jewish Lights Publishing, 2010, pp. 131–36.

Hana Wirth-Nesher

Beyond English: Language, Sound, and Voice in Jewish American Literature

Dis a choych?
> —Abraham Cahan, "The Imported Bridegroom"

Y'hei sh'mei raboh m'vorakh l'olam ul'olmei ol'mayoh. May His great Name be blessed forever and ever.
> —Philip Roth, *Nemesis*

Living as a Jew has always meant inhabiting more than one language. The Jewish American experience is no exception, not only for immigrants and their children, but also for native-born American Jews whose everyday life may take place exclusively in English. For generations, Jews in America have retained traces of other languages in their speech and writing whether they actually know these languages or not. What traces remain, how they are represented and received, and what is at stake in going beyond English are questions that serve as productive points of entry for discussing Jewish American literary works. In this essay, I will focus on two dominant modes of multilingual writing that have resonated in the classroom: the importing of foreign words and phrases across a wide spectrum of texts, from religious liturgy to everyday idioms, and the transcribing of speech as accented.

When it comes to inserting words, we might ask ourselves why any author would call attention to the foreign in writing that aims to convey American experience. As my students are quick to point out, some words simply aren't translatable, because their meaning is derived from the particular cultural and historical experience from which they emerge. The first chapter of Mary Antin's *The Promised Land*, which I often assign in Jewish American literature courses for its ecstatic embrace of America, illustrates this writing strategy. In her famous autobiography, Antin begins her narrative with a description of Czarist Russia, likening her escape from the Old World to the children of Israel's escape from bondage in Egypt, and hence treating America as the new promised land. Right at the start she inserts "pogrom," a Russian word meaning "devastation," which entered Yiddish to distinguish a specific type of violence against Jews. Antin offers the following definition:

> The Gentiles made Passover a time of horror for the Jews. Somebody would start up that lie about murdering Christian children, and the stupid peasants would get mad about it, and fill themselves with vodka, and set out to kill the Jews. They attacked them with knives and clubs and scythes and axes, killed them or tortured them, and burned their houses. This was called a "pogrom." (10)

Just as this word signals a collective trauma that was the prime mover for the two most significant migrations of Ashkenazi Jews to America and Palestine in the late nineteenth and early twentieth centuries, the word "converso" recurs in works by Jewish American authors inspired by Sephardic history, such as Victor Perera's memoir *The Cross and the Pear Tree* and Achy Obejas's novel *Days of Awe*. The term's English equivalent, "convert," does not convey the history of Jews who converted to Catholicism under physical and mental duress during the Spanish Inquisition, secretly retained their Jewish faith and practice, and were considered to be potential traitors to their new faith because of their Jewish blood. When an American couple touring Spain in Henry Roth's story "The Surveyor" is apprehended by the police for using surveying instruments without a permit "for purposes they refused to disclose," the state attorney who interrogates them rightly suspects that they were attempting to pinpoint the precise location for laying a wreath in Seville. "This is the *quemadero*," says the attorney, "where criminals were burned to death." "This is where I laid the wreath" (148), replies one of the Americans to the Spaniard, who has by now deduced the reason for this unusual act: "Because this was the same *quemadero* where heretics found guilty by the Inquisition were burned—among others, relapsed *conversos*, those Catholics who secretly clung to their old Judaic faith." In the American's words, "I honored them because no one in Spain honors them" (149). After the attorney discloses that he, too, is the descendant of conversos, they retreat to a café to toast their shared lineage, raising their glasses to both *"salud"* and *"l'chaim."* The story concludes with the American's discovery on his way back to his hotel that he has left his wreath at the café. It is an apt ending for a tale fixated on remembering what has been repressed, whether it is the Spaniard's grandfather's practice of lighting candles on Friday nights or the intention of the Jewish Americans to pay respects to the martyrs of the Inquisition. The two strands of the story are reminders that 1492 was, in Emma Lazarus's famous words, a "two-faced year," in which the Jews were expelled from Spain by the same monarchs who dispatched Christopher Columbus on a voyage that would eventually result in the Americas becoming a haven for persecuted Jews.

The presence of foreign words maps the author's or character's origins and emphasizes Jewish history, recent and distant. Whereas "pogrom" refers to acts perpetrated against Jews, "converso" refers to acts performed by Jews to survive, yet both non-English words tap into Jewish collective memory prior to the migration to the Americas. Of course, imported words from another language aren't always associated with traumatic events. When a talking crow alights on a windowsill in New York City in Bernard Malamud's comic fantasy "The Jewbird," Malamud describes him as "dovening," before he elaborates, "He prayed without Book or tallith, but with passion" (322). Since the word "prayed" might conjure up the Christian practice of folding hands and singing hymns, Malamud evokes eastern European Orthodox Judaism's practice of rocking the body and mumbling in prayer to convey the old-world ethos that accompanies this crow's intrusion into this assimilating New York family.

Furthermore, authors treat untranslatables in diverse ways. On the one hand, they may choose to be exclusive, dividing their readership by preserving the foreign word in the text without any explanation, a common practice for minority authors in recent years, while on the other hand they may choose to be inclusive by offering detailed definitions either in the text or in a glossary. In Boris Fishman's *A Replacement Life*, for example, the author insists on the refusal to translate as an ethical act. The protagonist, Slava, is a struggling Jewish American journalist. When his grandmother, a Holocaust survivor, dies at the beginning of this novel, his resourceful grandfather, Yevgeny, who spent the war years in the Soviet Union, asks Slava to compose her biography as if it were Yevgeny's and so complete an application for German restitution, which arrived too late for her to submit. Caught between the ethics of his adopted country, where forging the application would be considered fraudulent, and his grandfather's rationale that having one's entire family murdered is just cause for restitution by the murderers, Slava takes on this project yet struggles with the ethical question it poses. On the last page of the novel, when he stands at his grandmother's gravesite, Slava notices a flower that was common in the meadows around Minsk, "a greenish stem with a space helmet of white puff bobs." Here are the final words of *A Replacement Life*:

> Slava can summon the name of the flower only in Russian, and in the moment before he scatters the down across what remains of his grandmother, he knows . . . that he will never look up the English translation. The white wisps settle like summertime snow. *Oduvanchik*. (316)

The Russian word has the final word—untranslatable and irreplaceable, like his grandmother, whose life cannot stand in for others. The best tribute to her, therefore, in this English-language book is a Russian word, albeit one compromised and hybridized by being transliterated from the Cyrillic to the Latin alphabet.

In contrast to Fishman's refusal to translate, many authors have compiled glossaries of foreign terms for their readers. In some cases, the words are specific to Jewish culture and have no English equivalent, such as "shlemazl," defined as "a person with continued bad luck," in Henry Roth's *A Star Shines over Mt. Morris Park* (288). Reading glossary entries in class makes for lively discussion, as they are intriguing for what they reveal about the attitudes of their authors toward their old and new cultures. Antin's fierce devotion to her new homeland and her aspiration to pass as an American create a distance between Antin and the words that she defines, evident in her entry for "hallah," which she defines as a "wheaten loaf of peculiar shape used in the Sabbath ceremonial" (293). Although a hallah is simply a braided bread, Antin's description of it as peculiar seems to be her projection of how a gentile might regard an item of Jewish religious practice. Through such eyes, even a braided bread could appear strange.

A century later, Michael Chabon compiled an innovative glossary for his murder mystery, *The Yiddish Policemen's Union*, in which familiar Yiddish words are redefined as slang in the postwar town of Sitka, Alaska. For example, a "shoyfer," literally a ram's horn sounded during the High Holidays, becomes the brand name of a cell-phone company (417); "shammes," the sexton of a synagogue, refers to a police detective (416); and a "noz," literally a nose, is a cop (416). This curious and comical use of Yiddish is part of an alternative history created for the novel, which depicts a community of Yiddish-speaking Holocaust survivors whose land lease in Alaska is about to expire, and who have no other refuge because Israel was defeated in its war of independence. This glossary and the cleverly bleak dialogue of Sitka inhabitants blend Yiddish, the language of a community nearly annihilated in the Holocaust, with the witty doom of film noir: Chabon expresses nostalgia for a lost Yiddish world by recreating movie dialogue from a bygone era. Similarly, the glossary in *The Road to Fez* acts as a commentary on the vanished world that the author, Ruth Knafo Setton, depicts. In this spiritual journey of a young woman to the site of her family's roots, her choice of foreign words exemplifies the multifaceted makeup of the Moroccan Jewish community, which has negotiated French colonial rule and Arab Islamic culture; for example, she includes "Fes," the French spelling of the city of Fez, and "Maghreb" (229), a geographic term that means "west" from the perspective of Arab Muslims.

While students may find reading about alternative and vanished worlds a fascinating introduction to multilingual writing, it is essential for teachers to also point out the traces of other languages that make their way into literature and continue to be vibrant in contemporary Jewish American religious or spiritual practice. Jewish Americans who may not be bilingual still encounter foreignness, paradoxically in their most familiar Jewish practices and rites of passage, and often import elements of this foreignness into their writings. One of the most prevalent of these texts is the Mourners' Prayer, or Kaddish, whose incantatory opening line, "Yiskadal v'yiskadash," surfaces again and again, from Allen Ginsberg's poem "Kaddish" to Philip Roth's last novel, *Nemesis*. Set in Newark in the early 1950s, Roth's novel vividly captures the polio epidemic, as panic-stricken parents and teachers bury one pupil after another. In contrast to authors who invoke the Kaddish as a touchstone of Jewish authenticity, Roth maintains a nonbeliever's outrage at the recitation of this doxology for a deity indifferent to unrelenting child mortality. When his main character hears this prayer in its original Aramaic, he protests "praising God's almightiness, praising extravagantly, unstintingly, the very God who allowed everything, including children, to be destroyed by death" (74).

Languages other than English leave their traces in Jewish American writing not only through the words themselves but also through sound. Garret Stewart has persuasively argued that reading is not a silent activity; we actually do hear the text in our minds. It is appropriate, therefore, to ask if readers hear a Jewish accent even when reading in English, and if so, what does that mean? Henry James did notice, and did scorn, the Jewish accent that he heard in Lower East Side cafés, which he called "torture chambers of the living idiom" (139). Jewish immigrants during the first half of the twentieth century found themselves in a hostile environment linguistically, and they responded with frenetic attempts to improve their English. Abraham Cahan had one of his characters bemoan the fate of non-English speakers: "that I was not born in America was something like a physical defect which, alas! no surgeon in the world was capable of removing" (291). In *The Rise of David Levinsky*, Cahan joins other writers in dramatizing this fierce ambition to speak what white, Protestant America regarded as Standard English. Anzia Yezierska's *Bread Givers* portrays a young immigrant woman who attains status as an English teacher intent on improving the lives of her immigrant pupils by drilling them in English pronunciation. It is not surprising that she finds Prince Charming in the form of the principal, who corrects her own diction. Antin, who immigrated to the United States at the age of twelve, was so embarrassed by her accented English that when she recounts her own mispronunciation in her autobiography, she swerves into the third person. Despite her compulsive practice of diction routines to overcome any trace of Yiddish in her speech, she admits that "I learned at least to think in English without an accent" (282).[1]

Authors who submit to the dictates of standardized English will tend to maintain boundaries between flawed and ideal speech in their works. When Flora's father in "The Imported Bridegroom" asks a passerby if the building he is pointing to is "a choych," Cahan mocks him not only for the way that he pronounces the word but mainly for his blindness in not recognizing that the building is a library, a temple of culture whose purpose is to Americanize immigrants and educate the masses (Yekl 152). In Israel Zangwill's popular play *The Melting Pot*, his characters speak with accents (Yiddish, Russian, French, Irish, and German) that are transcribed phonetically in the script, with the exception of his immigrant hero and heroine, who surmount old-world prejudices and therefore require miraculously purified English.

During the latter half of the twentieth century, as Jewish American writers felt more secure as Americans, they celebrated their voices by boldly portraying difference. Just as Antin waves the flag of American canonical literature with her echoes of Ralph Waldo Emerson and Walt Whitman, Grace Paley waves a flag of proud resistance to the control of American language and culture by white, Protestant Americans. In her story "The Loudest Voice," Paley overturns the stereotype of Jewish voices as loud and uncultivated by giving her child character, Shirley Abramowitz, the most coveted role in the school's Christmas pageant, the voice of Jesus. While her parents speak in Yiddish-inflected, transposed syntax, "In the grave it will be quiet" (55), and her gentile teachers speak in stereotypically affected style, "You're absolutely a pleasure to work with, my dear, dear child" (59), Shirley recites the Nativity story as if she were Jesus reminiscing about his origins, "I remember the house where I was born" (61), and predicting his own glory, "I shall have life eternal" (62). Her booming Jewish voice prevails in an ironic success story of American meritocracy.

In recent years, the accented speech of Holocaust survivors, first in taped testimonies and then in literary works, has become a mark of authenticity, as if the languages in which they experienced their physical and emotional pain have been inscribed on their bodies, an inscription that requires recognition. Among the authors who have made accents an integral part of their artistry is Cynthia Ozick in *The Shawl*, Art Spiegelman in *Maus I* and *II*, and Lore Segal in *Her First American.*

There are no objective measures to determine whether a word is foreign or how it is accented. Such labels depend on shifting linguistic, cultural, and social norms. In fact, what makes a word sound foreign may not always be an external linguistic source but may instead be the efforts of a character or author distancing herself from the word itself. This is dramatized powerfully in one of Hortense Calisher's stories, where a Jew separates herself from other Jews, whom she regards as her social inferiors, and instead seeks acceptance from gentile Americans. In "Old Stock," Mrs. Elkin and her daughter Hester join other Jews for a summer retreat in the Catskills despite their sinking income, for "they were still of a status which made it unthinkable that they would not leave New York for some part of the season" (142). However, Mrs. Elkin avoids contact with "those people," Jews whose speech and manners she considers to be crude. Instead, she regularly visits Miss Onderdonk, a year-round Catskills resident whose descent from DeWitt Clinton designates her as genuine American "old stock." During one visit, Onderdonk complains that visitors, "all ninnied out for town" to look for antiques, "holler at me as if I'm the foreign one. . . . I told Elizabeth Smith [the owner of the boarding house where Mrs. Elkins and her daughter are staying] she'd rue the day she ever started taking in Jews" (151). Hester envisions the word "Jews" soaring in an arc toward her mother's face. "I thought you knew, Miss Onderdonk," said her mother, "that we were—Hebrews" (152). Opting for the "ultimate refinement" by substituting "Hebrews" for "Jews," Mrs. Elkin places her family in an ancient, noble lineage shared by the Puritan founding fathers, just as Henry Wadsworth Longfellow referred to "the Hebrews in their Graves" in his poem "The Jewish Cemetery in Newport." Jews, on the other hand, as implied by Miss Onderdonk, are a despised racial other contaminating Christian white America. But the child, Hester, like the child of her namesake in *The Scarlet Letter*, wants her mother to utter the truth. "Say it, Hester prayed. . . . Please say it, Mother. *Say 'Jew.'* . . . She heard the word in her own mind . . . like the ram's horn at Yom Kippur" (152). Sensing her daughter's plea, Mrs. Elkin nearly reclaims the word she has treated as foreign to her very being by conceding the adjective, but not the noun, "Mr. Elkin and I are Jewish." Although Miss Onderdonk admits that "the girl here has the look," she insists that Mrs. Elkin "ain't no Jew," because "[g]ood blood shows, any day" (152). In this story, "Jew" is a foreign word in sense and sound for both a gentile American and a Jewish American. The former reclaims ownership of her country from what she perceives as "Jew" foreigners, and the latter, who takes pride in being a descendant of Richmond, Virginia, "Hebrews," reluctantly admits to an identity whose word she cannot even bring herself to utter.

When we excavate the linguistic layers of Jewish American writing, we discover not only foreign words and sounds but also the letters of the Hebrew alphabet, which have accompanied Jews over time and across continents. These letters constitute the languages of Hebrew, Yiddish, and Ladino, among other Judaic hybrid tongues, and they have also served as signifiers of Jewish civilization. Some writers invoke Hebrew by transliterating it into the Latin alphabet, as Philip Roth does to the Aramaic Kaddish in *Nemesis*, and others actually reproduce Hebrew letters on the page or stage, including Art Spiegelman in *Maus I* and *II*, Aryeh Lev Stollman in *The Far Euphrates*, and Tony Kushner in *Angels in America*. Whether these Hebrew letters hearken back to kabbalistic accounts of the creation of the world, or represent shop windows in a Jewish marketplace, they serve as reminders that Jewish experience, even as far west as America, has its linguistic roots in the East.

I have found that a multilingual point of entry for reading Jewish American literature in a heterogeneous classroom will inevitably lead to broader questions about how we identify what is foreign and what is familiar in other writings by minority authors, how we map the worlds that are invoked in literature even when they lie within America's geographic boundaries, who identifies as an outsider or insider reader, and how concepts of Standard English have changed over time. What once signaled Jewish difference may by now have been absorbed into mainstream American culture. What once was a source of embarrassment may have become a source of inspiration.

Note

1. For extensive discussions of Cahan's and Antin's representations of language in their works and for a broader discussion of multilingualism in Jewish American writing, see Wirth-Nesher.

Works Cited

Antin, Mary. *The Promised Land*. 1912. Penguin Books, 1997.

Cahan, Abraham. *The Rise of David Levinsky*. 1917. Penguin Books, 1993.

———. Yekl *and "The Imported Bridegroom" and Other Stories of Yiddish New York*. Dover Publications, 1970.

Calisher, Hortense. "Old Stock." *America and I: Short Stories by American Jewish Women Writers*, edited by Joyce Antler, Beacon Press, 1990, pp. 142–55.

Chabon, Michael. *The Yiddish Policemen's Union*. Harper Perennial, 2008.

Fishman, Boris. *A Replacement Life: A Novel*. HarperCollins, 2014.

James, Henry. "The Fate of the Language." *The American Scene*. 1906. Indiana UP, 1968, pp. 139–40.

Knafo Setton, Ruth. *The Road to Fez: A Novel*. Counterpoint, 2000.

Kushner, Tony. *Angels in America*. Theater Communications Group, 1992–93.

Lazarus, Emma. "1492." *The Poems of Emma Lazarus, Volume II: Jewish Poems and Translations*, edited by Susan L. Rattiner, Dover Publications, 2015, pp. 22–23.

Longfellow, Henry Wadsworth. "The Jewish Cemetery in Newport." *Poems and Other Writings*, by Longfellow, Library of America, 2000, pp. 335–36.

Malamud, Bernard. "The Jewbird." *The Complete Stories*, by Malamud, edited by Robert Giroux, Farrar, Straus and Giroux, 1997, pp. 322–31.

Obejas, Achy. *Days of Awe*. Ballantine Books, 2001.

Ozick, Cynthia. *The Shawl*. Random House, 1990.

Paley, Grace. "The Loudest Voice." *The Little Disturbances of Man*. 1959. By Paley, New American Library, 1973, pp. 53–64.

Perera, Victor. *The Cross and the Pear Tree: A Sephardic Journey.* Alfred A. Knopf, 1995.

Roth, Henry. *A Star Shines over Mt. Morris Park,* St. Martin's Press, 1994. Vol. 1 of *Mercy of a Rude Stream.*

———. "The Surveyor." *Shifting Landscape: A Composite, 1925–1987,* by Roth, Jewish Publication Society, 1987, pp. 134–54.

Roth, Philip. *Nemesis.* Houghton Mifflin Harcourt, 2010.

Segal, Lore. *Her First American.* The New Press, 1985.

Spiegelman, Art. *Maus I: A Survivor's Tale: My Father Bleeds History.* Pantheon Books, 1986.

———. *Maus II: A Survivor's Tale: And Here My Troubles Began.* Pantheon Books, 1991.

Stewart, Garrett. *Reading Voices: Literature and the Phonotext.* U of California P, 1990.

Stollman, Aryeh Lev. *The Far Euphrates.* Riverhead Books, 1997.

Wirth-Nesher, Hana. *Call It English: The Languages of Jewish American Literature.* Princeton UP, 2006.

Yezierska, Anzia. *Bread Givers.* Doubleday Page, 1925.

Zangwill, Israel. *The Melting-Pot.* Macmillan, 1909.

Joanna Meadvin and Katharine G. Trostel

Postvernacular Ladino: Chameleon Languages and Translation Studies

Framing the Course

The study of Jewish literature, intricately connected to the study of Jewish languages, raises vital questions for Jewish and non-Jewish students who enter the university classroom with a range of relations to their mother tongues (including English). In our globalized era in which languages around the world are in danger of extinction, many young people grapple with varying degrees of estrangement from their native tongues. In the class that we teach, students engage with Ladino literature as a case study that sheds light on the plight of and possibilities for all heritage languages.[1] The study of Ladino literature, written in the language that Sephardic Jews carried with them into exile from Spain in the fifteenth century, brings to the surface questions of displacement, historical memory, belonging, and linguistic encounter—themes relevant for the twenty-first-century classroom.

Our course begins with Jeffrey Shandler's claim that Ladino, like Yiddish, has become "postvernacular," meaning it has reached a life stage in which its symbolic value outweighs its practical value because of its limited everyday use. Shandler argues that

> [p]ost-vernacular engagements with language inevitably engender differ-
> ent kinds of cultural practices from those of the native speaker . . .
> prompting possibilities of language use other than the vernacular model
> of full fluency as an indigenous mother tongue. Thus, post-vernacularity
> has important implications for the interrelation of language, culture, and
> identity. (23)

Shandler's characterization of postvernacularity is of particular interest at the University of California, Santa Cruz, a Hispanic-serving institution where our introduction of Ladino offers students the opportunity
to review Spanish's status as a global language—a language of expulsions
and conquests, and a language that forms multiple hybrids as it comes into
contact with other languages across the globe.[2] In our course, students
begin to recognize how Ladino is marked by encounters with other languages. Mexican Jewish author Myriam Moscona has compared Ladino
to a chameleon that picks up the "colors" of the vernacular speech around
it. She notes in the introduction to her entirely Ladino poetry collection,
Ansina, "El juego consiste en mezclar ambos tiempos sin atender la pureza
que tan poco me preocupa" ("The game consists in mixing both times
without paying attention to purity, which I'm really not concerned with";
11). The study of hybrid texts that play with the intersection of Spanish
and Ladino complicates students' notions that languages, histories, or
identities can ever be "pure" or self-contained systems.

This class guides students to examine identity through the lens of a
language minor to both national and Jewish literary canons. Minor-language
literature registers a process of loss, leaves behind an impression or memory, and works through the challenge of understanding identities in flux.
How do you write a book in a language that is not your own? The work of
Moscona and the work of the Argentine Jewish author Juan Gelman attempt to answer this question and serve as touchstone texts. Both of these
authors have embraced Ladino as a postvernacular language, without any
illusions of recuperating it for daily speech, "salvo dejar una memoria" ("except for leaving a memory"; "Janum"). Writing in Ladino allows Moscona
and Gelman to position themselves in relation to issues of national belonging and to their hybrid identities as Jewish Latin Americans.

Confronting Language:
Entering the Field of Translation Studies

On the first day of class, students work in pairs to translate two Spanish
quotations, whether they know the language or not, from Jewish Latin

American authors who also write in Ladino. The first quotation is from Gelman, who writes:

> Soy de origen judío, pero no sefardí, y supongo que eso tuvo algo que ver con el asunto . . . como si buscar el sustrato de ese castellano, sustrato a su vez del nuestro, hubiera sido mi obsesión. Como si la soledad extrema del exilio me empujara a buscar raíces en la lengua, las más profundas y exiliadas de la lengua. (7)[3]

> I'm of Jewish origin, but I'm not Sephardic, and I guess this had something to do with it . . . as if searching for the substratum of this Spanish, which is, in turn, the substratum of our own Spanish, had been my obsession. As if the extreme isolation of exile had pushed me to search for my roots in the language, the most profound and exiled roots of the language.

The second, from Moscona, reflects similar sentiments and deploys similar language:

> Bajo el castellano actual, existe otra lengua secreta, de la que pocos han oído siquiera hablar. ¿Qué resulta más importante? ¿La infancia de mi lengua o la lengua de mi infancia? (Moscona, "Myriam")

> Under contemporary Spanish there is another, secret language, which few people have even heard of. What's more important? The infancy of my language or the language of my infancy?

Stumbling—or flying—students immediately plunge into the discomfort, strangeness, and intimacy that is the act of translation. They grapple with the twists and turns of a language, Spanish, that may or may not feel like it is theirs. Gelman makes a somewhat roundabout claim on Ladino—which he calls Sefardí—by way of his Jewishness and his connection to Argentine Spanish. Translating his quote, students begin to interrogate the connections between language, history, and identity. In translating Moscona's identification of "another, secret language" that exists underneath Spanish, they explore what it means to call a language one's own.

Students learn that Gelman grew up speaking Spanish, Yiddish, and Russian. When he claims a connection to Ladino through his Jewishness, he reinforces biological and historical linguistic determinism; as a Jew, he may be said to have rights to Ladino. However, Gelman also disrupts such determinism when he admits to being an Ashkenazi, rather than a Sephardic, Jew. In contrast, Moscona, born in Mexico City to Bulgarian Jewish immigrants, was raised in a household where Ladino was spoken. However, it was not her native language.[4] As students debate whether Moscona has a greater claim to Ladino than Gelman, they begin to interrogate their own relations to the various languages to which they have access. They discuss Gelman's attraction to Ladino in the context of his bilingual Ladino-Spanish poetry collection *Dibaxu* ("Underneath"), which he wrote while living in exile from Jorge Rafael Videla's military dictatorship in Argentina. The dictatorship murdered his son and daughter-in-law and stole his granddaughter. Students explore the resonances of the Ladino word "dibaxu"—whose usage is similar to Moscona's use of the Spanish "bajo" ("underneath") to describe the Ladino language— Ladino underneath Spanish, history underneath the present, children underneath the earth.

Course Arc and Suggested Texts

The course briefly traces the history of minor Jewish languages beyond Ladino, exposing students to notions of linguistic hybridity and impurity, as well as introducing them to the concept that linguistic dominance is always linked to power. In this portion of the class, students encounter critical texts in translation theory. Reading work by Kwame Anthony Appiah, Roman Jakobson, Jacques Derrida, Walter Benjamin, Eugene Nida, Gideon Toury, John McWhorter, Naomi Seidman, Gloria Anzaldúa, and Wai Chee Dimock helps them to recognize that languages are ever shifting and impure—that the border between languages is not only artificial but always a reflection of politics and power. Early on, we encourage students to reflect upon the act of translation as a powerful means of thinking about language itself. Further, we encourage them to think of themselves as translators, as actors and thinkers at the borders of languages. Readings and discussion quickly focus on the relation between Ladino and Spanish and lead to a conversation about the role of language in nation formation in the context of the Americas. Students read a number of short stories written by Sephardic immigrants to Argentina, Guatemala, and Mexico. The course highlights the recent Ladino anthology *Por mi boka*, edited by Moscona and Jacobo Sefamí, a collection that demonstrates historical breadth and that also includes contemporary pieces.[5] However, the majority of the class is devoted to contemporary works by, among others, the Argentine writer Denise León, the Guatemalan writer Victor Perera, and the Mexican writer Rosa Nissán.

The two weeks each devoted to Moscona's Spanish and Ladino novel, *Tela de sevoya* ("Onion Skin"), and Gelman's *Dibaxu* are framed by the question, Why Ladino? Anzaldúa provides a rationale for this focus when she describes Chicano English, a hybrid language marked by its own history of subjugation, resistance, and resilience, as a "secret language . . . a homeland" (77). Moscona echoes Anzaldúa when she calls Ladino a "secret language" that moves beneath Spanish, reworking it into something unfamiliar (Moscona, "Myriam"). Examining these secret languages that live both inside and outside of the Spanish language reminds students that there was never a singular Spanish language; no matter what a dictatorship or a colonizing force may claim, there have only ever been Spanishes, each one "un lenguaje que corresponde a un modo de vivir" ("a language that fits a way of living"; Anzaldúa 77).

The extended encounter with Moscona's and Gelman's texts allows students to see that both authors employ Ladino as a means of claiming hybrid identities to work through trauma. The class is encouraged to ask how and why in the wake of twentieth-century traumas (including the abuses of dictatorships, the Holocaust, and the loss of community through migration and assimilation), Jewish Latin American writers—both Sephardic and Ashkenazi—turn to Ladino. These Ladino texts argue for the importance of Ladino itself, a secret linguistic home that complicates, undermines, and challenges the global Spanish of expulsions and conquests. The uncanny relation between Ladino and Spanish is a function of both place (Jews carried their language from Spain, to the Ottoman Empire, to the Americas) and time (Ladino is the language of medieval Spain, preserved in the diasporic community). Ladino echoes Spanish and other Jewish languages, helping to disrupt the story of a racially and linguistically pure nation. In this way, Ladino may allow its speakers to write histories out of step with the language of authoritarianism by reminding readers that racial and linguistic others have always been present.

Moscona's and Gelman's writings suggest an approach to teaching Jewish literature that highlights the themes of multilingualism, transnationality, and hybridity and that helps students grapple with their American identities. As Moscona and Sefamí point out in the introduction to their anthology,

> Esa lengua se fue contagiando del turco, francés, hebreo, búlgaro, erbio, rumano, italiano, árabe, portugués. Sus giros poco a poco se impregnaron de esas hablas y cada vez con mayores variantes respeto del idioma original. Como una Babel adentro de otra, las variantes del ladino obedecen a las lenguas que se filtraron por los intersticios del

español hasta formar híbridos, giros, invenciones, pequeñas células que se reprodujeron para favorecer nuevos mestizajes de palabras. (12)

The language was contaminated over time by Turkish, French, Hebrew, Bulgarian, Serbian, Romanian, Italian, Arabic, Portuguese. Its turns of phrase, little by little, were impregnated by those tongues, each time with more variation in relation to the original language. Like one Babel inside another, the varieties of Ladino obey the languages that were filtered through the cracks of Spanish until they formed hybrids, turns of phrase, inventions, small cells that reproduced themselves in favor of new fusions of words.

Moscona and Sefamí's collection guides students toward the possibilities offered by linguistic and cultural impurity. Bringing a language so closely related to fifteenth-century Spanish into contemporary speech helps students articulate issues of hybridity, language, and trauma in their own lives.[6]

In *Dibaxu*, Gelman describes his engagement with Ladino as a quest for the "profound and exilic roots of the Spanish language" (7). In this spirit, we assign a final project to students, asking them to interrogate the connections between their own languages, histories, and identities by writing a creative piece in a language other than English. Rather than being a stumbling block, the range of linguistic tools and competencies that our students bring to the class presents an opportunity. Some students work with forgotten or pieced-together heritage languages and translation engines, while other students may mix and code-switch between the languages at their disposal. Students who define themselves as "English-only" speakers interrogate notions of linguistic belonging, otherness, and boundaries by translating a piece from one English register to another. The project encourages students to expand their definition of what it means to be bi- or multilingual; to step away from notions of mastery, authenticity, and ownership; and to explore the possibilities opened by engagement with the borders between languages.

The final project also asks students to consider the possibilities engendered by the idea that to some users a language can be a living, breathing vehicle for communication, while to others it is postvernacular. Such a language's "instrumental value as a vehicle for communicating information, opinions, feelings, ideas—is narrowing in scope. At the same time its secondary, or meta-level of signification—the symbolic value that is invested in the language apart from the semantic value of any given utterance in it—is expanding" (Shandler 4). Through the creative language project, students explore their postvernacular relation to Spanish (and other languages), even as the language itself may continue to be robustly vernacular. During this project, some students will register the loss of—and also celebrate their relation to—a language that lingers. As Shandler points out, language loss is not a problem only Jews face—the loss of minor languages (and for our students, increasing disconnection from major heritage languages) is a global phenomenon. Students ask: How do we confront this trend in general? One possible answer is that literature can tackle this problem from a unique position. Fiction creates a world view that is preserved in language. Through literature, language can leave behind an impression or a memory.

Moscona and Sefamí write, "Hoy en día es común llamar 'ladino' a esa lengua que permanece como una capa oculta, abajo, en el envés del español contemporáneo" ("Nowadays, it's common to call that language that remains like a hidden layer, below, on the underside of contemporary Spanish, 'Ladino'"; 13). By the end of the course, students have an appreciation for the rich and productive conflicts embraced by contemporary Ladino literature. However, perhaps more importantly, they have reexamined their own relations to the languages they speak. Students perform a balancing act as they struggle to conform to the demands of the English-language university environment and also to preserve and celebrate their own particular identities and languages. While this struggle often includes experiences of loss, our course searches for the power that can be found in taking an outsider's perspective. Ultimately, we encourage our students to be alert to the secret languages hiding in the languages they speak.

Notes

All translations in the essay are ours.

1. Jeffrey Shandler suggests that the case of Yiddish has larger implications for thinking through issues of language and language loss in a global context. He asks, "When language no longer seems inevitable, rooted, indigenous, but appears instead to be fading, moribund, or even dead, what are the implications for its attendant culture?" (26).

2. About thirty percent of the sixteen thousand undergraduates at the University of California, Santa Cruz, identify as Latino, while ten percent identify as Jewish.

3. From the author's gloss to *Dibaxu*—written between 1983 and 1985 while the author was in exile in Mexico City.

4. And most of her semiautobiographical novel, *Tela de sevoya*, deals with her struggle to recuperate this lost heritage language—an effort complicated by the fact that there are very few native speakers still alive.

5. We additionally recommend that teachers use Bryan Kirschen's *Judeo-Spanish and the Making of Community*—a collection of essays that stem from the ucLADINO Judeo-Spanish Symposia and that trace the history of Ladino-speaking communities from the fifteenth century to the present day, exploring historical and geographic diversity. Of interest is Tracy K. Harris's *Death of a Language: The History of Judeo-Spanish*—a sociolinguistic study that outlines the development of Ladino from 1492 to the present day and that includes interviews with members of contemporary Ladino-speaking communities in the United States and in Israel. We also suggest the work of Olga Borovaya, whose scholarship traces the history of Ladino print culture.

6. Students may be interested to learn that Ladino shares characteristics with the Spanish spoken in rural parts of Mexico, particularly by indigenous communities, whose dialect preserves many of the same elements of fifteenth-century Spanish that sets Ladino apart from contemporary Spanish. Consider, for instance, words such as *ansina*, *muncho*, and *mezmo*. Moscona reflects upon this overlapping language use in an interview with *De iletradoperocuerdo*: "Esas expresiones, consideradas barbarismos en mi país (y hasta el día de hoy emplean los indios), no son sino palabras de ese castellano que trajeron los primeros pobladores a América y que en las zonas rurales menos favorecidas permanecieron, hasta el día de hoy, congeladas" ("These expressions, considered barbaric in my country (and used by Indians even today), are nothing less than words from the Spanish that the first inhabitants of America brought with them and that remained frozen in neglected rural areas to this very day"; "Janum").

Works Cited

Anzaldúa, Gloria. *Borderlands / La frontera: The New Mestiza*. Aunt Lute Books, 2007.

Appiah, Kwame Anthony. "Thick Translation." Venuti, pp. 389–401.

Benjamin, Walter. "The Task of the Translator: An Introduction to the Translation of Baudelaire's *Tableaux Parisiens*." Translated by Harry Zohn. Venuti, pp. 75–82.

Borovaya, Olga. *Modern Ladino Culture: Press, Belles Lettres, and Theater in the Late Ottoman Empire*. Indiana UP, 2012. Indiana Series in Sephardi and Mizrahi Studies.

Derrida, Jacques. "What Is a 'Relevant' Translation?" Venuti, pp. 423–46.

Dimock, Wai Chee. "African, Caribbean, American: Black English as Creole Tongue." *Shades of the Planet: American Literature as World Literature*, edited by Dimock and Lawrence Buell, Princeton UP, 2007, pp. 274–300.

Gelman, Juan. *Dibaxu*. Seix Barral, 1994.

Harris, Tracy K. *Death of a Language: The History of Judeo-Spanish*. U of Delaware P, 1994.

Jakobson, Roman. "On Linguistic Aspects of Translation." Venuti, pp. 138–44.

"Janum: Charlando con Myriam Moscona." *De iletradoperocuerdo*, 19 Dec. 2015, iletradoperocuerdo.com/2015/12/19/janum-charlando-con-myriam-moscona.

Kirschen, Bryan. *Judeo-Spanish and the Making of Community.* Cambridge Scholars Publishing, 2015.

León, Denise. *Poemas de Estambul.* Alción Editora, 2008.

McWhorter, John. *The Power of Babel: A Natural History of Language.* Harper Perennial, 2003.

Moscona, Myriam. *Ansina.* Vaso Roto Ediciones, 2013.

———. "Myriam Moscona: 'Los hombres olvidamos, pero las lenguas, no.'" Interview by Pedro Vallín. *Lavanguardia.com*, 25 June 2014, www.lavanguardia .com/cultura/20140625/54410371915/myriam-moscona-hombres-olvidamos -lenguas.html.

———. *Tela de sevoya.* Lumen, 2013.

Moscona, Myriam, and Jacobo Sefamí, editors. *Por mi boka: Textos de la diáspora sefardí en ladino (y versiones en español contemporáneo).* Lumen, 2013.

Nida, Eugene. "Principles of Correspondence." Venuti, pp. 153–67.

Nissán, Rosa. *Like a Bride and Like a Mother.* Translated by Dick Gerdes, edited by Ilan Stavans, U of New Mexico P, 2002.

Perera, Victor. *The Cross and the Pear Tree: A Sephardic Journey.* U of California P, 1996.

Seidman, Naomi. "Introduction: Translator as Double Agent." *Faithful Renderings: Jewish-Christian Difference and the Politics of Translation,* by Seidman, U of Chicago P, 2006, pp. 1–36.

Shandler, Jeffrey. *Adventures in Yiddishland: Postvernacular Language and Culture.* U of California P, 2005.

Toury, Gideon. "The Nature and Role of Norms in Translation." Venuti, pp. 205–18.

Venuti, Lawrence, editor. *The Translation Studies Reader.* 2nd ed., Routledge, 2004.

Dalia Kandiyoti

Sephardic Writing of the United States in a Comparative, Trans-American, and Transatlantic Frame

Literature about Sephardic history and culture is sometimes presented as inherently cosmopolitan, comparative, and transnational (Stavans, "Introduction" xxxi). This is perhaps one reason it does not figure as prominently as it should in national or ethnoracial conceptions of Jewish American literature or literature of the United States. While few narratives of Sephardic and Mizrahi American experiences are easily contained in conventional spatial, temporal, ethnic, or national framings, Sephardic writing is nourished in specific ways by contact with other cultures and literatures. This essay explores how contemporary Sephardic writing can be taught in trans-American and comparative contexts in courses on Jewish American literature and on literature in the United States. Although there are many routes one could take when teaching recent Sephardic and Mizrahi literature in the United States, the focus here will be on fictional works about Iberian Sephardim, with reference to trans-American, Latinx, and Arab American texts, all of which have created imaginaries about little-discussed entangled histories and afterlives of the Spanish Empire in the Atlantic and the Americas.

Several works that introduce instructors and students to Sephardic writing in the Americas are relevant to comparative study with Latinx and trans-American literature, Diane Matza's and Ilan Stavans's anthologies being two of them. Chapters from Aviva Ben-Ur's *Sephardic Jews in America* can provide background on the variety of Judeo-Spanish cultures and insight into the Hispanism that arose during the interwar years. This Hispanism, associated closely with Meir Benardete, the Sephardic American scholar (see Ben-Ur), emphasizes the Judeo-Spanish culture of Muslim Spain (Al-Andalus), Christian Spain, and their diasporic communities, though it minimizes the Middle Eastern and North African influences on Sephardic culture after the expulsions from Spain in 1492 and Portugal in 1496. The particular Sephardism, meaning the investment in Sephardic history and identity, that was conceived by intellectuals in the United States whom Ben-Ur has studied has something in common with the embattled Hispanic or Latinx identities of those from predominantly Spanish-speaking Americas. The process of latinization and hispanicization also frequently makes minorities invisible (e.g., indigenous and Afro-Latinx people), for whom the mainstream Hispanic or Latinx labels can be far from inclusive, and "pure" Castilian Spanish is a hegemonic language.

For descendants of Ottoman, Balkan, and other Sephardic communities as well as for many Latin Americans, Christian Spain is blurry in its remoteness and remains a contradictory point of origin because of its twin legacies as a cultural fount and a source of terror. Yet it looms large as a preponderant national myth or as an ancestral homeland. Many Sephardic Jews and most Latinx in the United States have more in common through the Spanish languages that they speak or that their ancestors spoke than through their shared Spanish origin. The linguistic commonalities constitute one of the reasons to teach Sephardic and Latinx texts together in literature classes in the United States.

Many of the contemporary Sephardic authors writing about Ottoman and Turkish migrations to the United States, some of whom have identified as Hispanic or Latinx Jews, use familial Jewish Spanish in their English-language texts in ways similar to other Latinx authors' use of bilingualism.[1] These Sephardic authors insert Jewish Spanish into English to exhibit the dailiness of the language and its affective import, to visually demonstrate linguistic mixing in North American diasporic communities, to mark their estrangement from monolingual mainstream culture in the United States, and to reproduce and reinvent their multilingualism, including the mixtures of Spanglish and Judeo-Spanish. There may also be an element of self-exoticism in the code-switching in such works. However, unlike these works by Sephardic authors, non-Sephardic Latinx texts tend to emphasize language stigmatization. Gloria Anzaldúa's "How to Tame a Wild Tongue," a poetic, hybrid-genre essay about the linguistic exclusion and oppression suffered by Chicanx in the Southwest, should serve as a primer. Sephardic writing about Jewish migration from the Ottoman Empire often depicts families whose primary language was Spanish but who also had to speak the many local languages in the Ottoman world; these works offer a further contrast to the monolingual context in the United States.

Narratives about Sephardic Jews in Latin America present a fuller set of confluences with literature about non-Jewish Latinx experiences than do narratives about Jewish Ottoman immigrants to the United States. Works by authors in the United States who identify as both Sephardic and Latinx, such as Cuban-born Ruth Behar and Victor Perera, a Guatemalan American, are exemplary in their engagement with trans-American and transatlantic Sephardic history, Latin American culture, and the process by which Latinx peoples become diasporic. The memoirs and fiction of these writers can be fruitfully taught in conjunction with the work of other Cuban American and Central American authors who are also multidisciplinary cultural producers. Behar's and Perera's written oeuvres span multiple genres, including novel, memoir, journalism, and scholarship. As invested as they are in exploring and expanding Sephardic culture, they are also trans-American authors in that their work bridges separations between nations and peoples in the Americas. Behar's 1995 anthology *Bridges to Cuba* (followed by the 2008 *The Portable Island*) was a key cultural endeavor in the closing of the political and cultural gap between Cuba and the United States, and between Cuban Americans and Cubans, appearing at a time when a thaw in relations between the countries was possible but fraught with peril. Perera's interest in boundary-defying Sephardic culture coexisted with his commitment to documenting the plight and the cultural richness of the Lacandon Maya. In a book he wrote about this group, with whom he lived at different times, he connected the presumably remote worlds of indigenous, Sephardic, and other Latin and North American cultures, even finding links between kabbalistic and Mayan ideas (Perera and Bruce, *The Last Lords*).

The memoir work of Perera and Behar in books and essays also follows the many strands of transatlantic and trans-American histories that inform their lives and passions. *The Cross and the Pear Tree*, by Perera, involves a quest for the author's roots in Iberia and provides a dizzyingly multisited historiography of his ancestry, and his *Rites: A Guatemalan*

Boyhood chronicles an unusual Sephardic coming of age in Guatemala City. Behar's creative memoir *Traveling Heavy* can be taught in comparison with other Cuban memoirs, but it can also be compared with fiction because of the literary quality of Behar's writing, which shares with Cuban American literature (e.g., Cristina García's *Dreaming in Cuban* and Ana Menéndez's *In Cuba I Was a German Shepherd*) the themes of exile, nostalgia, return, and belonging. Teaching these Cuban diasporic texts together can also generate fruitful class discussions about the choice of genre (autobiography, fiction, and creative nonfiction) in telling diasporic stories as well as about the rhetoric of intimacy, vulnerability, and belonging. Behar's narrative also tracks the migrations of Jews from Iberia to the Ottoman Empire to the Caribbean and to the United States, which expands and complicates the diaspora/homeland binary presented in much Latinx fiction, including Cuban writing in the United States.

Afro-Cuban and Afro–Puerto Rican perspectives (e.g., Coco Fusco's and Piri Thomas's) also provide valuable insight into the complications of home and the racialization of Latinx (Jiménez Ramón and Flores) and Hispanic identities, and Melanie Kaye/Kantrowitz's work is a useful study of Jews of color, a topic that should be part of teaching Sephardic writing. Further, when instructors teach Behar's work in the context of the large body of Cuban American and Latinx writing rather than solely in a Jewish American context, they shift the hegemonic narrative that the Jewish American story is one of (largely eastern) European Jewish migration to the Americas. This narrative can reinforce ideas about the presumably monolithic process through which Jews in the United States become white, which Latinx Jews (like others) may experience only partially, if at all, by virtue of their association with the racialized non-Jewish Latinx population. Sociological studies have shown that Latinx Jews identify significantly with the non-Jewish Latinx population (Limonic 157–94), and it is important for teachers to convey that Sephardic Latinx and Hispanic writing has literary, cultural, and historical connections to the writing of diasporic groups in the United States other than Jewish Americans.

Other Sephardic Latinx texts, in which ethnic and racial crossroads in Iberia and the Americas are sources of identity and storytelling, include those by and about crypto-Jews and their descendants in the Americas. Prominent Latinx authors Achy Obejas and Kathleen Alcalá have devoted a significant portion of their fictional oeuvre to investigating and fictionalizing their own and others' descent from conversos (converts from Judaism to Christianity) and crypto-Jews (conversos who maintain secret

Jewish practices or identities). A unit on Sephardic crypto-Jews in the
Americas can be introduced with a historical overview of the conversos
who left both Iberia and the urban centers of the Americas (e.g., Mexico
City or Lima), where, irrespective of whether they were sincere Christians,
they could have been persecuted on allegations of judaizing (Gitlitz 53–63).
Obejas's and Alcalá's novels can be contrasted for their styles, settings, and
ideas about secret identities, as well as for their configuration of Latinx and
Jewish conjunctures through crypto-Jewish history (Kandiyoti). While
Obejas's novel continuously shifts from one time period to another, Alcalá's is set in the late nineteenth century in northern Mexico, reputed at
the time to be a remote and relatively safe place where the persecuted could
escape scrutiny. Unlike conventional historical novels, Alcalá's is composed
of chapters with different narrators and perspectives that link through the
motifs of secrecy and double consciousness. *Days of Awe* recreates centuries of crypto-Jews in hiding in Cuba and the United States. Spain appears
as an object of longing for the first-person narrator's contemporary crypto-
Jewish father, but the lost Iberian homeland is primarily an unspoken
substitute for the lost Cuba. A multigenerational and transhistorical fiction about Sephardic crypto-Jews, *Days of Awe* is also very much a novel
of Cuban exile. But it dismantles the categories it is placed in, since other
Cuban American novels rarely include Sephardic or crypto-Jewish histories, and normative Sephardic writing about family and ancestry is infre-
quently about converts who do not necessarily return to Judaism. The
novel's more muted queer dimension contrasts with its foregrounding of
Cuban and crypto-Jewish themes.

Alcalá's work is also a category-defying example of borderlands, indigenous, and Chicanx literature, one that is inflected by Sephardic crypto-
Jewish themes and that challenges existing definitions of Jewish American writing. Teachers may assign scholarly approaches to trans-American
cultural phenomena (e.g., by Paula M. Moya and Ramón Saldívar and by
José David Saldívar) alongside Alcalá's novel to emphasize the uncontain-
ability of literature and culture within available national and ethnoracial
categories.

All of these works cover several, overlapping diasporic and exilic contexts, with Spain frequently appearing as an origin, for better or worse.
Yet the Spain of the Moors and Iberian and North African Muslims in
the Americas appear more rarely in Latinx and Sephardic fiction. For this
reason, students will benefit from reading the above texts alongside Arab

American literature, particularly Moroccan American Laila Lalami's *The Moor's Account*. With this novel, Lalami not only makes a unique contribution to the Arab American canon but also participates in a practice common to literature of the Americas, particularly of Latin America and the Caribbean, of rewriting from critical contemporary perspectives the foundational texts of the conquest era (see López; Juan-Navarro and Young). Also like the many postcolonial authors recasting key Western texts through the points of view of their silenced subjects (as in Jean Rhys's *The Wide Sargasso Sea*) or to subvert the texts' meanings to reveal discursive violence (as in Aimé Césaire's *A Tempest*), Lalami seizes on the significant yet brief mentions of "the Moor" as a member of the conquering party in the Spanish conquistador Álvar Núñez Cabeza de Vaca's influential *Chronicle of the Narváez Expedition*, which recounts his infamous expedition to Florida and New Spain in search of gold and other riches in the 1520s and 1530s (Cabeza de Vaca). But precious little has been discovered about the so-called Moor, Mustafa al-Zamori, most likely one of the first Muslims in the Americas, who was converted by the Spaniards and given the diminutive nickname "Estevanico." Lalami's counterdiscursive historical novel invents a past for al-Zamori. In this imagined first-person account, the appropriate genre for the conquest period, al-Zamori recounts his experiences in Morocco, in Spain, and, at greater length, in the Americas as a slave forced to be a conqueror; the real al-Zamori was probably murdered by the Zuni people in what is now New Mexico. Assigning the excerpts from Cabeza de Vaca's *Chronicle* that are reproduced in reconfigured form in Lalami's novel helps students access this remote period and consider the extent to which the Moroccan American author has rewritten the original narrative. By reading the chapter in Anouar Majid's *We Are All Moors* in which Lalami first encountered a reference to al-Zamori, students can contextualize the concept of the Moor and its overlaps with and distinctions from blackness in the Americas (see also Gomez). Teaching Lalami's text with Obejas's and Alcalá's is fruitful, as they are all historical novels concerned with the impact of Spain on Jewish and Muslim lives and with the ravages of empire in the Atlantic world, where forced conversion and racism were instruments of oppression transported from Iberia and not invented in the Americas (Shohat, "Genealogies" 15).

The complexity of religious conversion as depicted in *The Moor's Account* and Cabeza de Vaca's *Chronicle* echoes the explorations of crypto-Jewishness in Obejas's and Alcalá's novels. It is the original, racialized religions and not conversion through which the identities of the Jewish and Muslim converts are designated, and all three novels offer analogies to contemporary experiences of migration, passing (and not passing), hiding, and assimilation into dominant cultures. Additionally, Lalami and Alcalá both stage likely but little-documented encounters between indigenous people and Sephardic and Muslim Iberian and Mediterranean people. They each imagine convergences of destinies and genealogies in the violent formations of the Americas in marronage-like experiences, which are in productive tension with the tropes of bondage, secrecy, and hiding that the narratives build on. In these texts, temporary situations of flight, deracination, and homelessness allow characters to experience cultural crossings that would have been forbidden to them under conditions of captivity.[2] Although Jewish-Muslim interactions are hardly present in the novels, reading the works together is also an acknowledgment of those obscured links and the common, if not identical, destinies of Jews, Muslims, and converts from both faiths under Iberian Christian rule. Assigning Ella Shohat's key conceptual texts on the links between Christopher Columbus and modern Palestine and on the "Sephardi-Moorish Atlantic" ("Taboo Memories," "Sephardi-Moorish Atlantic," and "Genealogies") can productively frame the reading together of Sephardic, Latinx, Moroccan, Arab American, and indigenous stories of the Americas, thus furthering students' understanding of these conjunctures, which are often overlooked in area studies and noncomparative ethnoracial studies (Kandiyoti and Franco; Shohat, "Taboo Memories"). Moreover, Sephardic, Jewish American, and Arab American literatures rarely recast the foundational stories of the Americas. These texts by Obejas, Alcalá, and Lalami are also in the company, then, of other writing from the United States that fictionalizes the recovery and adaptation of occluded histories, such as feminist works about historical foremothers and neo-slave narratives.

Teaching Sephardic literature in such comparative contexts makes an intervention not only into Jewish American studies but also into related fields such as Latinx, trans-American, and Arab American studies, in which Jewish, Muslim, and Latinx convergences or common destinies seldom appear. There are many ways to approach the connectivity that is so often a feature of literature about Sephardic worlds. This brief essay focuses only on Sephardic stories about the displacement of Iberian peoples in the Americas and about diasporic journeys across the hemisphere. These stories do, however, serve to underscore the trans-American and transatlantic aspects of writing from the United States about migration, and they compel us to read Jewish literature relationally.

Notes

1. Such authors include Ruth Behar, Gloria DeVidas Kirchheimer, Shalach Manot, Victor Perera, Edouard Roditi (*Delights* and *Thrice Chosen*), and Brenda Serotte, among others. See also Matza.

2. Fugitivity and marronage are concepts developed most prominently in African American thought. See, for example, Roberts; Saucier and Woods. On a related note, see Casteel 91–97 on Caribbean authors' inclusion of the *marrano* ("Jewish convert") in staging marronage.

Works Cited

Alcalá, Kathleen. *Spirits of the Ordinary: A Tale of Casas Grandes*. Chronicle Books, 1997.

Anzaldúa, Gloria. "How to Tame a Wild Tongue." *Borderlands / La frontera: The New Mestiza*, by Anzaldúa, Aunt Lute Books, pp. 53–64.

Behar, Ruth, editor. *Bridges to Cuba / Puentes a Cuba*. U of Michigan P, 1995.

———. *The Portable Island: Cubans at Home in the World*. Palgrave Macmillan, 2008.

———. *Traveling Heavy: A Memoir in between Journeys*. Duke UP, 2013.

Ben-Ur, Aviva. *Sephardic Jews in America: A Diasporic History*. New York UP, 2009.

Cabeza de Vaca, Álvar Núñez de. *Chronicle of the Narváez Expedition: A New Translation, Contexts, Criticism*. Edited by David L. Frye and Ilan Stavans, W. W. Norton, 2013.

Casteel, Sarah Phillips. *Calypso Jews: Jewishness in the Caribbean Literary Imagination*. Columbia UP, 2016.

Fusco, Coco. *English Is Broken Here: Notes on Cultural Fusion in the Americas*. New Press, 1995.

García, Cristina. *Dreaming in Cuban*. Alfred A. Knopf, 1992.

Gitlitz, David. *Secrecy and Deceit: The Religion of the Crypto-Jews*. UP of New Mexico, 2002.

Gomez, Michael. *Black Crescent: The Experience and Legacy of African Muslims in the Americas*. Cambridge UP, 2005.

Jiménez Ramón, Miriam, and Juan Flores, editors. *The Afro-Latin@ Reader: History and Culture in the United States*. Duke UP, 2010.

Juan-Navarro, Santiago, and Theodore Robert Young, editors. *A Twice-Told Tale: Reinventing the Encounter in Iberian / Iberian American Literature and Film*. UP of Delaware, 2001.

Kandiyoti, Dalia. *The Converso's Return: The Afterlives of Conversion in Contemporary Literature and Culture*. Stanford UP, forthcoming.

Kandiyoti, Dalia, and Dean Franco. "Guest Editors' Introduction: Jewish-Muslim Crossings in the United States and the Americas." *Studies in American Jewish Literature*, vol. 35, no.1, 2016, pp. 2–12.

Kaye/Kantrowitz, Melanie. *The Colors of Jews: Racial Politics and Radical Diasporism*. Indiana UP, 2007.

Kirchheimer, Gloria DeVidas. *Goodbye, Evil Eye: Stories*. Holmes and Meier, 2000.

Lalami, Laila. *The Moor's Account*. Pantheon Books, 2014.

Limonic, Laura. *Kugel and Frijoles: Latino Jews in the United States*. Wayne State UP, 2019.

López, Kimberlé. *Latin American Novels of the Conquest: Reinventing the New World*. U of Missouri P, 2002.

Majid, Anouar. *We Are All Moors*. U of Minnesota P, 2009.

Manot, Shalach. *His Hundred Years: A Tale*. Albion Andalus, 2016.

Matza, Diane. *Sephardic-American Voices: Two Hundred Years of a Literary Legacy*. Brandeis UP, 1997.

Menéndez, Ana. *In Cuba I Was a German Shepherd*. Grove Press, 2001.

Moya, Paula M., and Ramón Saldívar. "Fictions of the Trans-American Imaginary." *Modern Fiction Studies*, vol. 49, no. 1, 2003, pp. 1–18.

Obejas, Achy. *Days of Awe*. Ballantine Books, 2001.

Perera, Victor. *The Cross and the Pear Tree*. Alfred A. Knopf, 1995.

———. *Rites: A Guatemalan Boyhood*. Harcourt, 1986.

Perera, Victor, and Robert D. Bruce. *The Last Lords of Palenque: The Lacandon Mayas of the Mexican Rainforest*. Little, Brown, 1982.

Roberts, Neil. *Freedom as Marronage*. U of Chicago P, 2015.

Roditi, Edouard. *The Delights of Turkey: Twenty Tales*. New Directions Publishing, 1977.

———. *Thrice Chosen*. Black Sparrow Press, 1981.

Saldívar, José David. *Trans-Americanity: Subaltern Modernities, Global Coloniality, and the Cultures of Greater Mexico*. Duke UP, 2012.

Saucier, P. Khalil, and Tryon P. Woods. *On Marronage: Ethical Confrontations with Antiblackness*. Africa World Press, 2015.

Serotte, Brenda. *The Fortune Teller's Kiss*. U of Nebraska P, 2006.

Shohat, Ella. "Genealogies of Orientalism and Occidentalism: Sephardi Jews, Muslims, and the Americas." *Studies in American Jewish Literature*, vol. 35, no. 1, 2016, pp. 13–32.

———. "The Sephardi-Moorish Atlantic: Between Orientalism and Occidentalism." *Between the Middle East and the Americas: The Cultural Politics of Diaspora*, edited by Evelyn Alsultany and Shohat, U of Michigan P, 2013, pp. 42–63.

———. "Taboo Memories, Diasporic Visions: Columbus, Palestine, and the Jews." *Taboo Memories, Diasporic Voices*, by Shohat, Duke UP, 2006, pp. 201–32.

Stavans, Ilan. "Introduction: Unity and Dispersion." Stavans, pp. xv–xxxii.

———, editor. *The Schocken Book of Modern Sephardic Literature*. Schocken Books, 2005.

Thomas, Piri. *Down These Mean Streets*. Alfred A. Knopf, 1967.

Part IV

Gender and Sexuality Approaches

Yaron Peleg

Writing New Kinds of Jews: A Course in Literary Genetics and Masculinity

The course described here examines one of the most significant developments in modern Jewish history: the decline of Jewish culture in eastern Europe and the subsequent emergence of two alternative Jewish cultural centers, in Israel and in the United States.

Between the 1880s and the 1920s, millions of Jews left eastern Europe and migrated across the globe, primarily to the United States and to Palestine, later Israel. The two communities became the largest and most significant centers of Jewish culture outside of Europe, especially after the Holocaust, and both continued to develop their old traditions in the new communities they established.

The course looks at this cultural legacy by tracing its evolution in literature in three stages. By reading short stories and novels written in eastern Europe, Israel, and the United States and originally published in Yiddish, Hebrew, and English, we look at the various ways Jews, primarily Jewish men, reconstructed their culture and themselves at the beginning of the twentieth century.

The course engages in "literary genetics"—the study of a source culture's literature to identify reflections of its development in the major daughter cultures it has inspired. The common heritage of Jewish immigrant communities in the United States and Palestine included religious and educational traditions, a language (Yiddish), a history as a religious and ethnic minority, and a geographic origin (the Pale of Settlement). Yet despite these many commonalities, the character of the communities Jewish migrants established overseas diverged widely depending on their destination. The Jews who immigrated to the United States assimilated into the American host culture but retained some of their old-world traditions in the process, as did other immigrant groups (e.g., Irish and Italians). The Jews who immigrated to Palestine engaged in a radical process of social engineering designed to completely change many of the traditions that had distinguished them as Jews in Europe.

One of the most interesting sociohistorical developments these literary genetics reveal concerns communal dynamics related to anti-Semitism. The establishment of a national Jewish community in Palestine and the growth of the Jewish community in the United States were greatly influenced by anti-Jewish sentiments in nineteenth-century Europe. Both communities were founded by Jews who sought a better future for themselves outside of an increasingly alienating Europe. The Jews who immigrated to Palestine wished to change the very nature of their community and turn it from a minority into a majority culture. The Jews who immigrated to the United States were much less communally ambitious and sought to improve their personal lot in a country they hoped would be more tolerant of them. While this is not a new insight, the course introduces it through the unusual angle of literature and focuses on one aspect of this complex history—masculinity—to explain and demonstrate it.

The study of masculinity as part of Jewish sexuality has been one of the most fruitful categories of inquiry into Jewish modernity in the last few decades, attracting the attention of such scholars as George Mosse, Sander Gilman, David Biale, and Daniel Boyarin, among others. Masculinity played an important part in the development of Zionism in the nineteenth century and has had an influence on Jewish American culture since then.

The course examines these cultural developments by looking at novels that were written in eastern Europe, in the United States, and in Israel over a period of about one hundred years that corresponds to the history described above. Since the period examined is long, the course focuses narrowly on Jewish masculinity as one of the central tropes in the study of modern Jewishness and as a dynamic field of inquiry within it. The course looks at traditional eastern European Jewish masculinity and the challenges it faced under modernism and then follows the effects of migration on masculinity in Israel and the United States.

The course uses literature as a cultural-historical tool to gauge some of the changes that the communities in question underwent. The reading is guided by various theoretical frameworks that include the history of sexuality (Foucault; Sedgwick; Biale; and Gilmore), studies in gender and nationalism (Mosse; Gilman, Armstrong; and Boyarin) as well as gender and Zionism (Dieckhoff; Bartal; Brenner and Reuveni; Pressner; and Almog), and various literary studies (Miron; Shaked; Alter; Wirth-Nesher; Franco; and Levinson). Based on these studies, the main thesis of the course is that one of the most nagging aspects of the so-called Jewish problem in nineteenth-century Europe was the anti-Semitic perception of Jews as weak and effeminate. The Jewish community in Palestine, which wanted to sever ties to its diasporic past, developed a revolutionary Jewish masculinity that, ironically, was modeled after the Western and Christian ideals of masculinity (such as physical strength, military prowess, a clear distinction from femininity, etc.) that had shaped European national ideals. The Jewish community in the United States developed differently. Rather than engage in social engineering, American Jews concentrated on personal advancement—and they were so successful that they eventually became paragons of the American dream. As an accidental result of this process, when American Jews gained financial, cultural, and political success, Jewish traits that had earlier on been denigrated lost many of their negative associations. One of these traits was the softer and kinder masculinity (read as weak and effeminate) associated with Jewish men in the United States.

The novels selected for the course focus on the lives of young Jewish men who are also the narrators of the stories. The novels use adolescence as a formative period in life to connect different historical periods and different geographic locations, and as a metaphor for the young Jewish literatures of Israel and the United States and for the communities they reflect.

The course begins with Sholem Aleichem's 1916 Yiddish novel *Motl, the Cantor's Son*, which represents eastern European Jewish society. It then looks at the concurrent development of Jewish literatures in Israel and the United States. Students read two Israeli novels, Moshe Shamir's 1951 work *With His Own Hands* and David Grossman's 1991 work *The Book of Intimate Grammar*, and two American novels, Henry Roth's 1934 work *Call It Sleep* and Phillip Roth's 1969 work *Portnoy's Complaint*.

Motl is an immigration novel that follows its preadolescent hero from eastern Europe to New York City. The work is deeply rooted in the traditions of the shtetl even as it moves its hero from the Old World to the new. The familiar, closely knit world of the Jewish communities in the Pale of Settlement is on full display in the novel, which faithfully evinces the importance of family and religious ritual. The hero of the novel is an orphaned youth who rejoices in the freedom that the absence of parents affords, although his surface happiness is deeply affected by the precariousness of Jewish life in the shtetl and, later, the vicissitudes of immigration. Since Motl is a boy, not a man, the novel engages with masculine imagery indirectly. However, the anxiety and vulnerability of the immigrants during their journey to the United States is emblematic of the precariousness of the diasporic Jewish condition, which was often gendered as feminine, and of the failure of Jewish men to make it more secure. At the same time, Motl's energy and mischief are early indicators of his latent masculinity, which may perhaps develop differently in America, especially since he does not have a father to mold it according to shtetl ideals.

The two Israeli novels and the two Jewish American novels that follow Sholem Aleichem's novel in the course develop different aspects of masculinity. The two Israeli novels reflect on the new beginnings of the Jewish pioneering community in Palestine and its rejection of the eastern European past, a rejection that often led to the development of alternative masculine models. The first novel, *With His Own Hands*, is the story of a young Israeli man, Elik, who, as the novel's first sentence famously proclaims, "was born from the sea." Elik is sent to an elite agricultural school to be groomed as a farmer who will till the land of Israel and make it bloom and prosper. But when Israel's war of independence breaks out during his last year at school, Elik volunteers to serve in the nation's embryonic army and dies for his country on the battlefield. The novel articulates two prominent archetypes of the new Jewish masculinity that Zionism developed and mythologized in the early part of the twentieth century, the farmer and the fighter.

The second novel, *The Book of Intimate Grammar*, continues the Israeli search for a new Jewish masculinity by commenting on the country's pioneering origins represented by Elik, as well as by critiquing them. The novel takes place on the eve of the 1967 War, which saw the apogee of the new Jewish masculinity developed by Zionism. Aaron, the novel's young protagonist, is inspired by that masculine ideal as well as intimidated by it and tries to resist it by refusing to grow up and be like his brawny father.

The two Jewish American novels chart a different developmental path for Jewish masculinity. The first one, *Call It Sleep*, is set in the Jewish immigrant community of New York's Lower East Side at the beginning of the twentieth century. The protagonist, David, is the young son of an immigrant Jewish family, who has a complicated relationship with his parents, an especially affectionate mother and a distant, sometimes abusive father. The boy is shaped by the pained relationship with his parents as well as by the Jewish religious education he receives in addition to his state schooling. Since David, like Motl, is still young, his masculinity is indirectly referred to through the sexually saturated environment of his home and street life, and especially through his infatuation with another boy, a Christian classmate. His attraction to another boy and his attachment to his mother represent his soft side, his so-called effeminate Jewish masculinity. At the same time, his harsh father, like the symbolic father he meets in the image of the Hebrew God in his religious schooling, represents another masculine model. The novel's exploration of masculine ideals and sexual stereotypes is thus very different from Shamir's *With His Own Hands*, presenting a far more fluid, open-ended, and natural approach than the strict ideological construct of aggressive masculinity we find in the Israeli novel.

Portnoy's Complaint can be read as a sequel to *Call It Sleep*, since Henry Roth's adolescent protagonist has now turned into a sexual cowboy. But although he is completely acculturated to America, he is still haunted by the ghosts of his Jewish past. Alexander Portnoy, the book's protagonist, seems overwhelmed by the openness and permissiveness of 1960s American culture. But while he avails himself liberally of its sexual opportunities, a faint awareness of a much more restrictive Jewish heritage riddles him with guilt and sends him to the psychiatrist's couch to try and diminish his anxiety. If *Call It Sleep* explored the effeminate side of Jewish masculinity through homosexual desire, *Portnoy* plays with another anti-Semitic stereotype, that of the Jew as hypersexual (and thus effeminate as well). At the same time, in its juxtaposition of libertinism and Jewish morality, *Portnoy's Complaint* is also a deliberation on modern sexuality, whose Jewish American context makes it useful for this course.

The course then follows the literary genetic trail of Jewish masculinities from eastern Europe to Israel and the United States. As indicated before, the masculine qualities evident in Motl, the protagonist of the course's first book, evolved differently in the two Jewish branches that split from eastern European Jewish culture. The Zionist, and later Israeli, branch sought to reject the eastern European Jewish past altogether and develop masculine traits that were allegedly absent from shtetl Jewishness, primarily a reconnection with the soil through the training of Jewish farmers. The growing conflict with the Arabs produced a more militant masculinity that eventually overshadowed the masculinity of the farmer and instead privileged the fighter. The second Israeli novel in the course, *The Book of Intimate Grammar*, grapples with that legacy and censures some of its militant excesses. While the novel does not revert to older models of Jewish masculinity, the image of Aaron as a child who refuses to grow up represents both his resistance to his hypermasculine father and a wish for new models that are as yet unarticulated.

The two Jewish American novels retain some of the ambiguities and effeminate aspects (homosexuality, hypersexuality) of the eastern European Jewish models of masculinity. Perhaps because of this, their young male protagonists transition to their new environment less abruptly than their Zionist counterparts; therefore, issues of masculinity continue to preoccupy them. In *Call It Sleep*, that preoccupation is expressed by the tension between David's infatuation with another boy and his attraction to older and less forgiving Jewish traditions. In *Portnoy's Complaint*, the crisis unfolds in the form of Alexander's hypersexual lifestyle, which becomes a metaphor for the protagonist's inability to mature, and which ill prepares him to meet the challenge of the more rigid Israeli masculinity. When Alexander visits Israel in the last part of the book, he is unable to perform sexually with a female soldier he finds intimidatingly masculine.

As a conclusion to the course, students are encouraged to think about present-day expressions of Jewish masculinity and their implications. Students consider the political consequences of the increased role of the military and militarism in Israeli society as well as the degree of Jewish integration into American culture and the ways the culture has incorporated Jewish values.

Works Cited

Aleichem, Sholem. *Letters of Menakhem-Mendl and Sheyne-Sheyndl* and *Motl, the Cantor's Son*. Yale UP, 2002.

Almog, Oz. *The Sabra: The Creation of the New Jew*. U of California P, 2000.

Alter, Robert. *Hebrew and Modernity*. Indiana UP, 1994.

Armstrong, Nancy. *Desire and Domestic Fiction: A Political History of the Novel*. Oxford UP, 1987.

Bartal, Yisrael. *The Jews of Eastern Europe, 1777–1881*. U of Pennsylvania P, 2005.

Biale, David. *Eros and the Jews*. U of California P, 1997.

Boyarin, Daniel. *Unheroic Conduct: The Rise of Heterosexuality and the Invention of the Jewish Man.* U of California P, 1997.

Brenner, Michael, and Gideon Reuveni, editors. *Emancipation through Muscles.* U of Nebraska P, 2006.

Dieckhoff, Alain. *The Invention of a Nation.* Hurst Publishers, 2003.

Foucault, Michel. *The History of Sexuality*, translated by Robert Hurley, Vintage, 1990. 2 vols.

Franco, Dean J. *Race, Rights, and Recognition: Jewish American Fiction since 1969.* Cornell UP, 2012.

Gilman, Sander L. *Jewish Self-Hatred: Anti-Semitism and the Hidden Language of the Jews.* Johns Hopkins UP, 1986.

Gilmore, David D. *Manhood in the Making.* Yale UP, 1990.

Grossman, David. *The Book of Intimate Grammar.* Vintage Books, 2010.

Levinson, Julian. *Exiles on Main Street: Jewish American Writers and American Literary Culture.* Indiana UP, 2008.

Miron, Dan. *A Traveler Disguised: The Rise of Modern Yiddish Fiction in the Nineteenth Century.* Syracuse UP, 1996.

Mosse, George L. *The Image of Man: The Creation of Modern Masculinity.* Oxford UP, 1996.

Pressner, Todd S. *Muscular Judaism.* Routledge, 2007.

Roth, Henry. *Call It Sleep.* Penguin Books, 1976.

Roth, Phillip. *Portnoy's Complaint.* Vintage Books, 1995.

Sedgwick, Eve Kosofsky. *Between Men: English Literature and Male Homosocial Desire.* Columbia UP, 1985.

Shaked, Gershon. *Modern Hebrew Fiction.* Indiana UP, 2000.

Shamir, Moshe. *With His Own Hands.* Israel UP, 1970.

Wirth-Nesher, Hana, editor. *New Essays on* Call It Sleep. Cambridge UP, 1996.

Corinne E. Blackmer

Gender, Genre, and Lesbian Identity in Four Modernist Jewish Texts

Canonical modernist Jewish texts provide a rich opportunity to demonstrate how genre informs discourses on gender, Jewishness, and lesbian identity. When approaching these texts through these lenses, students acquire insight into the diverse and sometimes competing perspectives of modernist Jewish authors. These texts and methods are suitable to an array of pedagogical contexts, including upper-division and graduate courses in Jewish American, women's, LGBTQ, and modernist literature. In my course on sexuality and ethics, students explore how the intertwined topics of sexual orientation, women and economics, religious custom and class, and intersectional struggles for LGBTQ rights inform the representation of gender, genre, Jewishness, and lesbianism in texts that span the twentieth century. These texts include Sholem Asch's tragic drama *God of Vengeance*, Sigmund Freud's case study "The Psychogenesis of a Case of Homosexuality in a Woman," Gertrude Stein's short story "Miss Furr and Miss Skeene," and Adrienne Rich's poem "Yom Kippur, 1984." These works are united in their diverse representations of lesbian identity, gender, and Jewishness. I teach them in a six-week thematic unit to provide students with an in-depth understanding of how Jewish lesbian identity has remained an important, continuous, and visible thread throughout the twentieth century.

Some of these authors take diametrically opposed viewpoints toward lesbian desire. While Asch's play presents an idealized vision of overt lesbian lovers tragically thwarted by male economic control over women, Freud's case study features the same issues of financial coercion while grounding female homosexuality as a pathological product of unresolved childhood conflict. Stein and Rich, both Jewish lesbian authors, provide distinctly positive views of lesbian identity in their work, but Stein's story provides a witty, personal view of linguistic history that culminates in the contemporary meaning of *gay* as "homosexual." Rich's poem presents a global perspective on the political struggles of queers, women, Jews, and blacks to survive and flourish.

This class module begins with *God of Vengeance*, which became an international succès de scandale and was translated from the original Yiddish into dozens of languages. The play heralds Jewish modernism and exemplifies the progressive character of modern secular Yiddish culture, while critiquing patriarchal Jewish culture and traditional gender roles. It represents the principal lesbian dramatis personae, Manke and Rivkele, in an open, unapologetic, and even idealized fashion.[1] Asch eschews coded contemporary allusions to queerness and the gender polarities of medical sexology, which perceived queer women as "men trapped in women's bodies."[2] The youthful lesbian protagonists are women-identified women who face the same economic and social prejudices as other women. Rivkele is a privileged Jewish daughter whose parents own a brothel but fetishize her virginity, because they believe her sexual innocence redeems their hypocrisy and abuse of Jewish law. For instance, they intend to marry her to an upper-class Yeshiva student, and for the occasion, they have a scribe write an expensive Torah scroll, paid for with the proceeds from trafficking in women. But Rivkele dreads her upcoming marriage and passionately loves Manke, a poor, young prostitute who works for Rivkele's father, Yekel, in the brothel located in the basement of their house. The two women escape but then suffer a forced return. The story ends when Yekel becomes violently insane after he suspects his daughter has lost her vaunted purity. He hits her with the "sacred" (31) Torah scroll, throws it to the ground, stomps on it, and then forces his daughter to descend downstairs to the brothel and into prostitution. *God of Vengeance* queries the relation of lesbianism to Jewish law and the economic status of women in early-twentieth-century eastern European Jewish culture.

The sins of the corrupt father are visited upon the innocent daughter in this play, and various assignments can deepen students' understanding of this revolutionary work. For instance, students can research biblical Jewish law on lesbian sexuality, where they will discover that there are no prohibitions against female homosexuality. Other assignments might also include the investigation of premodern mores that mandated procreation and defined women as the property of men. Women's status as property precluded the large-scale emergence of lesbianism until the end of the nineteenth century. To enhance comprehension of the underlying dynamics of this play and of Freud's case study—both of which depict the relation between economics and lesbian sexuality—students can read the gay historian John D'Emilio's groundbreaking essay "Capitalism and Gay Identity." He contends that the late-ninteenth-century rise of wage labor eviscerated families' economic dominance and empowered individuals, as can be seen in *God of Vengeance*, where Rivkele has the economic wherewithal to contemplate having a relationship with her lesbian lover beyond her family's control.

These economic developments, in turn, enabled the emergence of gay people with permanent, stable identities who joined ranks with other allegedly disreputable types (e.g., prostitutes, petty criminals, and performers) who were also divorcing themselves from the financial constraints of traditional families. Finally, this play is not technically Jewish American, inasmuch as it was originally set and performed in Europe, but it became notorious in the United States after its English-language Broadway production in 1922, which led to an obscenity trial.[3] And the play has been adapted to American settings by Donald Margulies[4] and reenvisioned as a hit Broadway show in Paula Vogel's *Indecent*,[5] which stresses the eroticism of the relationship between Manke and Rivkele. Thus, teaching the play affords opportunities for examining the relation between Jewish and Jewish American literature, as well as changing representations of lesbian identities throughout the twentieth and early twenty-first centuries. *God of Vengeance* explores how reducing human sexuality to business transactions—whether in prostitution or arranged heterosexual marriage—abuses both lesbians and Jewish ethics.

If Yekel abuses his daughter and her lover by prostituting them, then Freud in his case study largely fails to appreciate how his compromised financial dealings with the parents of his client (and her dealings with her parents) fatally undermine his treatment of his "beautiful and clever" young Jewish lesbian client (246). This case study tells a convoluted story replete with contradictory theorizations as Freud, the male Jewish analyst, attempts to diagnose his client, who he admits has no neurosis about her homosexuality. Because the text is difficult, teaching this case study works best by first providing students with a historical overview of Freudian theories of arrested development and lesbian masculine identification. The instructor should explain that Freud, unlike his medical sexologist predecessors, who perceived homosexuality as a congenital anomaly or degenerative taint, attempted, however imperfectly, to humanize homosexuals. However, Freud accepts payment from his client's father, who wants his daughter cured of homosexuality. Meanwhile, the client has a lover, a coquette who, like Manke in *God of Vengeance*, uses prostitution to support her life as a lesbian. In the course of the analysis, Freud concludes rather desperately that the young woman "remained homosexual out of defiance against her father" and to satisfy her "keenest desire" for "revenge" by parading her "homosexual love before him" (261). In the end, Freud decides to discontinue treatment and send her to a female psychoanalyst. His client reveals, moreover, that she intends to marry, but only to escape the tyranny of her father, and that she believes she can manage a husband and have lesbian affairs just as her ladylove does. In a reprise of the abusive father-daughter dynamic of *God of Vengeance,* and a rejection of the role that economics plays in definitions of female homosexuality, Freud ejects his client and contradicts his earlier theorizations, concluding that the case represents "congenital homosexuality" (264).

As a Jewish lesbian author who was well acquainted with Freudian theories of homosexuality, Gertrude Stein parodies them in "Miss Furr and Miss Skeene." Her close interaction with Freud makes this story a perfect pedagogical complement to Freud's case study, for the two authors have diametrically opposed views as to how gay identities emerge and develop. Whereas Freud roots gendered and sexual identities in historically groundbreaking but dubious theories of childhood experience, Stein grounds them in verifiable linguistic history—which tracks the processes whereby words acquire novel meanings to accommodate altered circumstances. The main protagonists of this story are not only the two dramatic characters, the couple Miss Furr and Miss Skeene, but also the signal word *gay*, which functions as both a noun and a predicate adjective. Through repetition of "gay," as well as of "traveling," "cultivating voices," "pleasant," and "regular," the narrator paints an exact verbal portrait of a couple who become happy ("gay") by becoming gay ("homosexual"; 563, 564). They enhance their artistic talents and knowledge about how to act as and transform into gay persons with advanced understanding of how to "cultivate their voices" and transmit gay cultural knowledge to other "gay ones" (567). Finally, in line with D'Emilio's argument about economic wherewithal and the development of stable gay identities, this story depicts two women who evidently have the means to live a permanent and independent gay life.

The story follows the shift in the received meaning of *gay* from "happy" or "pathological" to "gay person," while it narrates the dramatic history of the characters. The narrative tells the history of two women who, in the beginning, are not "gay" in their (heterosexual) marriages, which they leave. But whereas Manke and Rivkele in *God of Vengeance* fail in their efforts to escape heteropatriarchy, in this comic story the heroines succeed in building a "gay" life when they meet each other, which underscores the fact that they have the economic means required for an independent lesbian existence. They remain gay even after their romance ends, at the end of the story, over their differing tastes for travel and adventure. Indeed, Miss Skeene has become so expert at "gayness" that she instructs other gay people, "telling them again and again" the ways of "being gay" (568).

There are rich opportunities for instructors to prepare illuminating assignments around this story, whose wit students usually find delightful. Students can conduct a historical character study or a verbal portrait of the word *gay*. Such a portrait would begin with the word's twelfth-century origins as a term denoting "joyful," then continue through its eighteenth-century connotations of a life of erotic, heterosexual adventure, to its early-nineteenth-century meanings of "carefree" and "licentious," and finally, to its late-ninteenth-century loose identification with an underground homosexual community. Indeed, as Linda Wagner-Martin notes in *Favored Strangers: Gertrude Stein and Her Family*, Stein's short story "feature[s] the sly repetition of the word gay, used with [homo]sexual intent for one of the first times in linguistic history" (167). In brief, Stein solidifies the modern meaning of the term *gay* as referring to homosexuals and homosexuality. She also establishes the crucial idea of having a permanent, stable, and nonpathological gay identity through repeated use of the words "regularly" and "cultivating," in addition to the sense of joyous consonance produced by continuous use of internal rhyme. Finally, as in *God of Vengeance,* Stein liberates lesbianism and gayness from negative associations with masculinity and arrested psychosocial development and from identification as a congenital disorder, an act that the work of Freud and the early medical sexologists had adumbrated. Rather, in this story, to be gay (and joyous) means to develop a social space with gay people who, as the narrator notes, are "cultivating their voices and other things needing cultivating" (562).

Explicitly Jewish American in its themes and written decades after the works of Asch, Freud, and Stein, Rich's poem "Yom Kippur, 1984" extends the course's vision of queer identities to include blacks, women, Jews, and Arabs across Europe, America, and the Middle East. Lyric poems typically focus on romantic love, as well as on evocations of sublime beauty and nature that putatively transcend politics. However, Rich subverts these expectations to explore what her identities as a Jewish, lesbian, and feminist poet signify. Indeed, while Asch, Freud, and Stein examine the private lives of individual lesbians, Rich sees lesbian relationships more in their political than in their romantic dimensions. She focuses on the Jewish concept of *rachamim* ("compassionate love") as she considers the significance of Yom Kippur in 1984. That year witnessed both escalating violence in the Israeli-Palestinian conflict and the deliverance of famine-stricken Ethiopian Jews to Israel in Operation Moses.

On Yom Kippur, Jews seek atonement for sins against God and against other human beings. This occasion enables Rich to express her longing to unite Jews and Arabs, whom she characterizes as "lonely within their tribes" (996), and to end the persecution of women, blacks, queers, and Jews. The poem depicts these embattled minorities as having suffered through a history of violence and hate crimes, and Rich, in line with the ethical call of the yizkor, or "remembrance," prayer, memorializes their fates so that they will not disappear from history. Rich asks a series of rhetorical questions about affective states: the impulse to stick to one's own tribe for safety, even though obeying that impulse can be dangerous; the need for solitude in order to create; and the fear of encountering those who are different, represented in the poem by the "Stranger" (997), even though such encounters can be educational.

Instructors can help students understand the background and the existential issues at stake in this long lyric poem by discussing its generic innovations and by having students do research assignments on the multilayered allusions in this work—to everything from Robinson Jeffers's poem "Prelude" to historical crimes against blacks, queers, and women; Walt Whitman; the value accorded to the stranger in Jewish law; and the Israeli-Palestinian conflict. In addition, students can come to appreciate how Rich's minority identities do not connote something rarified or obscure but rather provide an enlarged perspective on some of the most significant global issues of the modern period: anti-Semitism, homophobia, sexism, racism, endemic conflict, and entrenched tribal loyalties and enmities.

The poem ends in an apocalyptic vision in which the "edges and centers" (998) and majorities and minorities become crushed together by the
destruction of the hierarchical order that has prevailed in human history.
In this chthonic confusion, Rich tentatively prophesies that the children of
those who currently suffer alienation, fear, and loneliness—including Arabs and Jews, heterosexuals and queers, and males and females—will look
back on our era through a consciousness no longer marked by violence
and hatred. The poet considers that the refugee, or Jewish, child and the
exiled, or Palestinian, child shall "re-open the blasted and forbidden
city" (998), which appears to refer to both the literal Jerusalem and a
Jerusalem "newborn and haunted" (998), where tribal politics no longer
dominate.

From a vision of how two lesbian lovers battle against patriarchal control, to an account of how lesbian identity is supposedly grounded in arrested development, to a linguistic history of the word *gay*, and, finally, to
a worldwide prophetic vision of how minorities are caught up in a historical narrative that erases them, these four canonical Jewish texts enrich
students' moral and intellectual understanding. These texts provide perspective on the changing interpretations of lesbian desire as well as its importance as a historical subject and a literary symbol of social, political, and
economic struggle.

Notes

1. See Faderman's classic treatment of romantic friendship between women
in *Surpassing the Love of Men*, as well as the idealization of lesbian relationships
before the opening decades of the twentieth century. *God of Vengeance* occupies
a unique liminal space, in which the idealization of love between women intersects with sexualized lesbian love.

2. See Herdt for an extended discussion of how conventional gender binaries
configured early conceptions of homosexuality.

3. Margulies sets the action in contemporary New York City.

4. Vogel, who is both Jewish and lesbian, in her research for the play, traced its
stage history from its debut in Warsaw to the Holocaust, when it was performed
as an act of artistic defiance in an attic in the Lodz ghetto of German-occupied
Poland.

5. See Pick for a definitive account of the theory of homosexuality as degenerative, based on genetics or heredity.

Works Cited

Asch, Sholem. *God of Vengeance.* Translated by Isaac Goldberg, preface by
    Abraham Cahan, Stratford Publishers, 1918.

D'Emilio, John. "Capitalism and Gay Identity." *Powers of Desire: The Politics of Sexuality,* edited by Ann Snitow et al., Monthly Review Press, 1983, 100–13.

Faderman, Lillian. *Surpassing the Love of Men: Romantic Friendship and Love between Women from the Renaissance to the Present.* Harper, 1998.

Freud, Sigmund. "The Psychogenesis of a Case of Homosexuality in a Woman." *Freud on Women: A Reader,* edited and with an introduction by Elisabeth Bruehl-Young, W. W. Norton, 1990, 241–66.

Herdt, Gilbert H. *Same Sex, Different Cultures: Exploring Gay and Lesbian Lives.* Basic Books, 1997.

Margulies, Donald. *God of Vengeance: Adapted from the Play by Sholem Asch.* Dramatists Play Service, 2003.

Pick, Daniel. *Faces of Degeneration: A European Disorder, c. 1848– c. 1918.* Cambridge UP, 1989.

Rich, Adrienne. "Yom Kippur, 1984." *Jewish American Literature: A Norton Anthology.* Edited by Jules Chametsky et al., W. W. Norton, 2001, 996–98.

Stein, Gertrude. "Miss Furr and Miss Skeene." *Stein: A Reader,* edited by Ulla E. Dydo, Northwestern UP, 1993, 254–59.

Vogel, Paula. *Indecent.* Dramatists Play Service, 2015.

Wagner-Martin, Linda. *Gertrude Stein and Her Family.* Rutgers UP, 1995.

Judith Lewin

Teaching Jewish American Women's Writing

Josh Lambert describes "a little experiment" that he performs in his Jewish literature classes: "I ask them to take out a piece of paper and a pen or pencil. . . . I say, 'Draw a Jew.' . . . One of my favorite questions to ask first is this: 'How many of you drew a woman?' (Usually, it's at most one or two. . . .)" Most students' inability to imagine a woman as a Jew is worth dwelling upon.[1] Why is it Jewish American women are invisible, inaudible, and insufficiently read? This essay proposes a curriculum that engages students in thinking broadly about Jewish American women authors and the issues and themes in their fiction. Previous pedagogical essays on Jewish American women's writing include two, in the fields of sociology and women's studies, on identities (see Friedman and Rosenberg; Sigalow), Sheila Jelen's essay in *Shofar* on Hebrew and Yiddish texts, and essays in *MELUS* volume 37, number 2 (Summer 2012), a special issue on Jewish American literary studies that includes women's literature but does not focus on gender. The aim of this essay, by contrast, is to introduce teachers of American literature to an array of texts written by Jewish American women that will engage the critical reading, thinking, and writing of college undergraduates.

Two questions immediately arise. First, how does one justify treating Jewish American women's writing in isolation in a course? Second, how does one contest student expectations about what kinds of narratives such a course would include? As Lambert demonstrated with his informal survey, Jewish women writers are invisible, as women, to Jewish literature and, as Jews, to women's literature. Yet scholars like Ann Shapiro call upon "Jewish feminists to make sure that [Jewish] women's literature is included in the Jewish American canon" (78). A pragmatic as well as ideological strategy for responding to the issue of treating women's literature in isolation is to turn the question itself into one the course problematizes. Ask students: How should we place Jewish American women writers within a female literary tradition or an American or Jewish one? How does the term *tradition* resonate for Jewish American women? How does Jewish religious or community membership influence women authors' representations of gender, nationality, class, sexual orientation, and ethnicity? What are the problems with and justifications for grouping these writings together? Rather than think of a course on Jewish American women's writing as isolating or reductive, instructors should focus on the advantages of an intersectional approach to these texts found in overlapping questions of Jewishness and gender and of racial, ethnic, queer, and religious feminist identities.[2]

Ideally, when teaching a course on Jewish American women's writing, one would explore received notions of who is a Jewish woman and what it means to be one by adopting stories about unexpected issues and through constant questioning of student preconceptions. Instructors and students must do the work of "unlearning" together in order to dislodge preconceptions (Tinberg and Weisberger 103), which, as Lambert's description of his class exercise demonstrates, students may possess even when they are unfamiliar with the writers whose work they will encounter. Preconceptions may derive from a lack of knowledge of Jewish women's lives or from a reductive knowledge that, in the words of Evelyn Torton Beck, "often focus[es] exclusively on the patriarchal aspects of the Jewish religion, fail[s] to mention feminist transformations of Judaism, and fail[s] to speak of the diversity [of] Jewish Women . . ." (187). This comment reinforces the need to introduce students to institutions such as the Hadassah-Brandeis Institute, which studies Jewish women and gender issues, the Jewish Women's Archive, and the Jewish Orthodox Feminist Alliance. This pedagogical strategy diversifies the conventional American narrative of eastern European Orthodox male immigration by including alternative stories by marginalized Jews.

The course I teach on Jewish American women's writing is aimed at undergraduate students who have taken either an introduction to literature, gender studies, or religious studies. The experience of leading this course has required that I assume no prior knowledge, pose the big theoretical questions immediately, and organize the course coherently. To explore the diverse fiction produced by Jewish American women within the constraints of a ten-week term, I teach four sections with about two novels in each (interspersed with a few short stories), and I limit myself to the long twentieth century. I update the syllabus between offerings of the course.[3]

Each time I offer the course, I invite preenrolled students to respond to a questionnaire that solicits information about their interests and preferences, and that includes a list of titles I am considering. In this way, I accomplish three things. First, the students invest in the ownership of the class. Second, I get a sense for the enrollees' interests before placing final book orders. Third, students are primed to think about how many texts there are to choose from, and how appealing they are. When novels within a certain rubric, such as those by Iranian American Jewish women (like Gina Nahai), are not selected by the majority of students to be read by the whole class, students who wished to read those works have the opportunity to do the reading themselves and present a comparative book report to the class. In such cases, presenters link their interpretations of the outside reading to a book the class has read together, which also helps them prepare comparative essays.

The course is divided into four units that survey the issues and themes prevalent in Jewish women's writing: Have We Arrived or Were We Already Here?; Historical Fiction / Fictions of History; Americans on/in Israel; and Jewish American Otherness / Other Jewish Americans.[4] Instructors may wish to include works from genres besides fiction (e.g., drama, poetry, memoir, or graphic novel) within these units or in a separate, generic one; they may also decide that literature about the Holocaust belongs in its own unit. The Holocaust pervades the Jewish imagination, however, and its shadow stretches over a great many postwar texts, so I tend to treat it obliquely.

The first novel in the unit Have We Arrived or Were We Already Here? explodes stereotypes. *Other Things Being Equal*, by the California writer

Emma Wolf, is set in 1880s San Francisco and focuses on intermarriage. Barbara Cantalupo's 2002 critical edition offers abundant surrounding materials to situate Wolf both in the Jewish community of nineteenth-century San Francisco and in the American publishing world of the period. Wolf's novel is a good place to start because it challenges preconceptions of a monolithic Jewish American culture. The novel is inhabited by Jews who are not Orthodox, eastern European, Yiddish-speaking, or impoverished, who do not live in New York, and who do not partake of any aspect of the expected narrative aside from debating Jewish-Christian intermarriage, a topic that remains timely. Although I include subsequent texts that do contain many conventional elements such as Yiddish-speaking, isolated, poor, and religious Jewish immigrants to New York, beginning the course with nineteenth-century Californian Jews interacting on equal footing with their Christian neighbors effectively shatters student assumptions. Therefore, in terms of the criteria for inclusion, Wolf's novel is unexpected and her culturally Jewish world balances out the Orthodox worlds in other texts to follow.[5]

This first unit of the course also features books set in other unexpected American cities: Boston and Cleveland. After Wolf's novel, instructors may assign a short memoir by Mary Antin (*From Plotzk to Boston*) or Antin's short story "Malinke's Atonement," about an eastern European Jewish small-town girl and her crisis of faith. When teaching these works and complementary short stories such as Anzia Yezierska's "The Fat of the Land" or Grace Paley's "The Loudest Voice," instructors may stress how the authors contrast Yiddish-inflected syntax and sound with the clear, unmarked American voice of the narrator. While these short works contribute to the conventional (expected) narrative this course design contests, there can be no basis for argument if students read nothing canonical. Balancing texts that are for and against tradition permits teachers to bring a meta-discussion into the classroom regarding contested Jewish histories that ignore many identity positions.

To complete unit 1, I follow Wolf's novel with Jo Sinclair's *The Changelings*, set in Cleveland in the 1950s. This novel implicitly thematizes queer issues while overtly depicting intermarriage, generational conflict, and the racial prejudice perpetrated by recent immigrants, both Jews and Italians, who want to become "real" Americans. I read Sinclair alongside two short stories that could serve as a module on Jewish American women's depictions of mid-century Jewish relations with African Americans:

"O Yes," by Tillie Olsen, and "Stations of the Cross," a historical fiction by Julie Orringer, both of which, along with Sinclair's novel, feature complex relationships between blacks and Jews. In their works, Sinclair, Olsen, and Orringer describe female characters who ask intersectional, ethical questions about racial, religious, and gender prejudice. Instructors can prompt class discussion by asking whether the non-African-American family in Olsen's story is necessarily Jewish or simply unmarked. What assumptions are in play? For Jewish American women writers, "tradition can no longer be assumed as a framework," to the extent that their fiction is populated by "protagonists [who] must define the terms of their Jewishness" (Burstein, "Jewish-American Women's Literature" 9, 10). These three texts set up a thematic thread that continues in other parts of the syllabus, as we shall see, inviting potential comparative discussions or assignments: Wolf, Sinclair, and Orringer on intermarriage; Sinclair, Olsen, Orringer, Dara Horn, and Achy Obejas on prejudice, horizontal oppression, and sexual orientation.

The subsequent course units, Fictions of History, Americans in/on Israel, and Jewish American Otherness / Other Jewish Americans, concentrate on issues such as the intersection of nationalities, ethnicities, and patriotisms; gendered relations toward traditional Judaism; Jewish heteronormativity; crypto-Judaism; and non-Ashkenazi American immigrants. Following Sinclair, Horn's third novel, *All Other Nights*, is a historical fiction about Jewish participation on both sides of the American Civil War. The text reinforces the fact that Jews inhabited America prior to the 1880s eastern European migration and continues a thematic link between Jews and African Americans by presenting Jewish slaveholders celebrating Passover and being waited on by black servants. Anita Diamant's *Day after Night*, about the British incarceration of Holocaust survivors who immigrated to Mandatory Palestine from 1945 to 1948, completes this section. The novels by Horn and Diamant are lesser known within each author's corpus and portray little-discussed historical events that will surprise readers. Having students read other, better-known fictions about history that present both religious and secular characters and inhabit multiple points of view may facilitate a research-oriented writing assignment. Such works include Diamant's *The Red Tent*, Horn's *In the Image*, Rebecca Goldstein's *Mazel*, and Allegra Goodman's *Kaaterskill Falls*.[6]

The unit Americans in/on Israel contains work by Ruchama King and Rachel Kadish, whose novels are set in religious and secular Israeli society, respectively. King's *Seven Blessings* is a text that presents various perspectives, that is generally positive in its depiction of religion, and that includes a Holocaust survivor as one of its characters, as does Kadish's secular *From a Sealed Room*, which discusses Gulf War trauma and features an American college student living abroad. Other effective novels featuring college students in Israel include Joan Leegant's politically complex *Wherever You Go* and Jessamyn Hope's *Safekeeping*, with its unique setting in a Marxist kibbutz.

The last unit, Jewish American Otherness / Other Jewish Americans, features work by the Cuban American writer Obejas and by the Iranian American writer Dalia Sofer. One of the prolific author Gina Nahai's novels (*Cry of the Peacock, Moonlight on the Avenue of Faith, Caspian Rain*, or *The Luminous Heart of Jonah S.*) could substitute for Sofer's *Septembers of Shiraz* on the syllabus; however, Obejas's *Days of Awe* is particularly valuable because it combines themes of immigrant dislocation and bisexuality with an effort to unearth the author's Jewishness. Other texts could include works by or about being Jewish by choice, such as Geraldine Brooks's *People of the Book*, which is also a historical fiction of Sephardim (Jews from Spain or western Europe). This unit may also include stories about Mizrahim, or Middle Eastern Jews (Nomi Eve's *Henna House*, about Yemen), Russian Jewish American immigrants (Anya Ulinich's *Petropolis*), or LGBTQ+ characters (Elana Dykewomon's *Beyond the Pale* or Lilian Nattel's *The River Midnight*). Of course where characters hail from and how they identify may intersect, as in the works by Sinclair and Obejas discussed above.[7] Gender-inflected issues to consider for class discussion throughout the term include heteronormative pressure, intermarriage, Jewish purity laws, menstruation, childbearing and infertility, modesty, family dynamics, women's education (sacred and secular), and women's traditional obligations (to bake the Sabbath bread, light the Sabbath candles, and observe ritual immersion) and exemptions (from praying with phylacteries, studying Talmud, reciting the mourner's prayer, and singing or praying aloud).[8]

A course that focuses exclusively on Jewish American women's writing can offer texts that provide nuanced rather than one-note depictions. Instructors may draw from a wide variety of complex, many-voiced narratives that reward classroom study and create a fulfilling course with intersectional perspectives that dislodges preconceptions and challenges expectations.

Notes

1. On Jewish women's invisibility see Peskowitz and Levitt, Boyarin and Boyarin, and Oksman.

2. *Intersectionality* originally referred to oppression based on gender, race, and class; the concept has broadened to include oppression based on ethnicity, sexuality, ability, and religion. Yet Jewish women's experience continues to be excluded, a problem that this essay and the course it describes seek to remedy. For Jewish intersectionality in practice, see Brettschneider and also Hahn Tapper. Extensive explanatory notes for Hahn Tapper are available for download at www .ucpress.edu/book/9780520281356/judaisms.

3. See Doyle and Zakrajsek for learner-centered teaching, especially chapters 5 and 6.

4. Readings for unit 1 include Wolf; either work by Antin (or Yezierska or Paley); Sinclair; Olsen; and Orringer. Readings for unit 2 include one work each by Horn; Diamant. Readings for unit 3 include Kadish; King. Readings for unit 4 include Obejas; Sofer.

5. Lori Harrison-Kahan promotes Wolf's novels as offering "alternatives to the ghetto genre" (5).

6. For criticism, see Meyers; Lewin; Zierler; and Shapiro.

7. On Obejas, see Kandiyoti; Socolovsky; and Wirth-Nesher. In relation to Sofer and Nahai, see Goldin and also Sarshar. On Brooks, see Kondali. In relation to Eve, see Druyan. On Ulinich, see Senderovich. On Nattel, see Burstein, "Recalling Home." On Sinclair, see Zierler.

8. For background on these issues, see Adler; Alpert; and Biale. To introduce traditional Jewish religious issues to students through fiction, use Anton; King; or Brafman, all of which clearly explicate gender issues related to Orthodoxy, and which help construct a syllabus that balances religious and secular texts.

Works Cited

Adler, Rachel. *Engendering Judaism: An Inclusive Theology and Ethics.* Jewish Publication Society, 1998.

Alpert, Rebecca. "Sex in Jewish Law and Culture." *Sexuality and the World's Religions,* edited by David W. Machacek and Melissa M. Wilcox, ABC-CLIO, 2003.

Antin, Mary. *From Plotzk to Boston.* 2003. Budge, 2009.

———. "Malinke's Atonement." 1911. *America and I: Short Stories by American Jewish Women Writers,* edited by Joyce Antler, Beacon Press, 1990, pp. 27–41.

Anton, Maggie. *Rashi's Daughters: Book One, Joheved.* 2005. Plume, 2007.

Biale, Rachel. *Women and Jewish Law.* 1984. Schocken Books, 1995.

Boyarin, Daniel, and Jonathan Boyarin, editors. *Jews and Other Differences.* 1997. U of Minnesota P, 2008.

Brafman, Michelle. *Washing the Dead.* Prospect Park Books, 2015.

Brettschneider, Marla. *Jewish Feminism and Intersectionality.* State U of New York P, 2016.

Brooks, Geraldine. *People of the Book*. Penguin Books, 2008.

Burstein, Janet. "Jewish-American Women's Literature: The Long Quarrel with God." *Studies in American Jewish Literature*, vol. 8, no. 1, Spring 1989, pp. 9–25. *JSTOR*, www.jstor.org/stable/41205700.

———. "Recalling Home: American Jewish Women Writers of the New Wave." *Contemporary Literature*, vol. 42, no. 4, Winter 2001, pp. 800–24. *JSTOR*, doi:10.2307/1209054.

Diamant, Anita. *Day after Night*. Scribner, 2010.

———. *The Red Tent*. 1997. Scribner, 2017.

Doyle, Terry, and Todd Zakrajsek. *Learner-Centered Teaching*. Stylus Publishing, 2011.

Druyan, Nitza, editor. *Yemenite Jewish Women*. Special issue of *Nashim: A Journal of Jewish Women's Studies and Gender Issues*, vol. 11, Spring 2006. *JSTOR*, www.jstor.org/stable/i40013892.

Dykewomon, Elana. *Beyond the Pale*. 1990. Digital edition, Open Road Media, 2013.

Eve, Nomi. *Henna House*. Scribner, 2015.

Friedman, Kathie, and Karen Rosenberg. "Performing Identities in the Classroom: Teaching Jewish Women's Studies." *Teaching Sociology*, vol. 35, no. 4, October 2007, pp. 315–33.

Goldin, Farideh Dayanim, editor. *Iranian Jewish Women*. Special issue of *Nashim*, vol. 18, Fall 2009. *JSTOR*, www.jstor.org/stable/10.2979/nas.2009.-.issue-18.

Goldstein, Rebecca. *Mazel*. U of Wisconsin P, 2002.

Goodman, Allegra. *Kaaterskill Falls*. Delta, 1998.

Hahn Tapper, Aaron. *Judaisms: A Twenty-First-Century Introduction to Jews and Jewish Identities*. U of California P, 2016.

Harrison-Kahan, Lori. "'A Grave Experiment': Emma Wolf's Marriage Plots and the Deghettoization of American Jewish Fiction." *American Jewish History*, vol. 101, no. 1, Jan. 2017, pp. 5–34. *ProjectMuse*, muse.jhu.edu .libproxy.union.edu/article/645160.

Harrison-Kahan, Lori, and Josh Lambert, editors. *The Future of Jewish American Literary Studies*. Special issue of *MELUS*, vol. 37, no. 2, Summer 2012. *ProjectMuse*, doi:10.1353/mel.2012.0028.

Hope, Jessamyn. *Safekeeping*. Fig Tree Books, 2015.

Horn, Dara. *All Other Nights*. W. W. Norton, 2010.

———. *In the Image*. 2002. W. W. Norton, 2003.

Jelen, Sheila. "Women and Jewish Literature." *Nashim*, vol.16, no. 2, Fall 2008, pp. 153–73. *Project Muse*, muse.jhu.edu/article/254182.

Kadish, Rachel. *From a Sealed Room*. Mariner Books, 2006.

Kandiyoti, Dalia. "Sephardism in Latina Literature." *Sephardism: Spanish Jewish History and Modern Literary Imagination*, edited by Yael Halevi-Wise, Stanford UP, 2012, pp. 235–55.

King, Ruchama. *Seven Blessings*. 2003. St. Martin's Griffin, 2004.

Kondali, Ksenija. "Deconstructing the Text and (Re)Constructing the Past: History and Identity in Geraldine Brooks' *People of the Book*." *ELOPE*, vol. 5, nos. 1–2, 2008, pp. 125–38. *Open Journal Systems*, doi:10.4312/ elope.5.1-2.125-138.

Lambert, Josh. "Taking It on the Nose? A Fresh Look at Cartoon Jews and Anti-Semitism." *Haaretz*, 1 Aug. 2017, www.haaretz.com/life/books /.premium-1.803932.

Leegant, Joan. *Wherever You Go*. W. W. Norton, 2011.

Lewin, Judith. "Diving into the Wreck: Binding Oneself to Judaism in Contemporary Jewish Women's Fiction." *Shofar*, vol. 26, no. 3, Spring 2008, pp. 48–67. *ProjectMuse*, doi:10.1353/sho.0.0183.

Meyers, Helene. "Jewish Gender Trouble: Women Writing Men of Valor." *Tulsa Studies in Women's Literature*, vol. 25, no. 2, Fall 2006, pp. 323–34. *JSTOR*, www.jstor.org/stable/20455285.

Nahai, Gina. *Caspian Rain*. 2007. MacAdam/Cage, 2008.

———. *Cry of the Peacock*. 1991. Createspace, 2015.

———. *The Luminous Heart of Jonah S*. Akashic Books, 2014.

———. *Moonlight on the Avenue of Faith*. 1999. Createspace, 2015.

Nattel, Lilian. *The River Midnight*. Scribner, 1999.

Obejas, Achy. *Days of Awe*. Ballantine Books, 2002.

Oksman, Tahneer. *"How Come Boys Get to Keep Their Noses?" Women and Jewish American Identity in Contemporary Graphic Memoirs*. Columbia UP, 2016.

Olsen, Tillie. "O Yes." *"Tell Me a Riddle," "Requi I," and Other Works*. 1961. Bison Books, 2013, pp. 37–56.

Orringer, Julie. "Stations of the Cross." *How to Breathe Underwater: Stories*. Vintage, 2005, pp. 195–222.

Paley, Grace. "The Loudest Voice." 1956. *Collected Stories*. Farrar, Straus and Giroux, 1994, pp. 34–40.

Peskowitz, Miriam, and Laura Levitt, editors. *Judaism since Gender*. Routledge, 1997.

Sarshar, Houman, editor. *The Jews of Iran: The History, Religion and Culture of a Community in the Islamic World*. I. B. Tauris, 2014.

Senderovich, Sasha. "Scenes of Encounter: The 'Soviet Jew' in Fiction by Russian Jewish Writers in America." *Prooftexts*, vol. 25, no. 1, Winter 2015, pp. 98–132. *ProjectMuse*, muse.jhu.edu/article/633612.

Shapiro, Ann. "The Flight of Lilith: Modern Jewish American Feminist Literature." *Studies in American Jewish Literature*, vol. 29, 2010, pp. 68–79. *ProjectMuse*, doi:10.1353/ajl.2010.0018.

Sigalow, Emily. "Reflections on Teaching a Course on Jewish Identities." *Shofar*, vol. 32, no. 3, 2014, pp. 76–88. *ProjectMuse*, doi:10.1353/sho.2014.0041.

Sinclair, Jo [Ruth Seid]. *The Changelings*. 1955. Feminist Press, 1993.

Socolovsky, Maya. "Deconstructing a Secret History: Trace, Translation, and Crypto-Judaism in Achy Obejas's *Days of Awe*." *Contemporary Literature*, vol. 44, no. 2, Summer 2003, pp. 225–49. *JSTOR*, doi:10.2307/1209096.

Sofer, Dalia. *The Septembers of Shiraz*. Harper Perennial, 2008.

Tinberg, Howard, and Ronald Weisberger. *Teaching, Learning, and the Holocaust: An Integrative Approach*. Indiana UP, 2014.

Torton Beck, Evelyn. "The Politics of Jewish Invisibility in Women's Studies." *Transforming the Curriculum: Ethnic Studies and Women's Studies*, edited by Johnnella Butler and John C. Walter, State U of New York P, 1991.

Ulinich, Anya. *Petropolis*. Penguin Books, 2008.

Wirth-Nesher, Hana. "'Who Put the Shma in Shmattas?' Multilingual Jewish American Writing." *MELUS*, vol. 37, no. 2, Summer 2012, pp. 47–58. *ProjectMuse*, doi:10.1353/mel.2012.0028.

Wolf, Emma. *Other Things Being Equal*. 1892. Edited by Barbara Cantalupo, Wayne State UP, 2002.

Yezierska, Anzia. "The Fat of the Land." *Follow My Footprints: Changing Images of Women in American Jewish Fiction*, edited by Sylvia Barack Fishman, Brandeis UP, 1992, pp. 176–93.

Zierler, Wendy. "The Making and Re-making of Jewish-American Literary History." *Shofar*, vol. 27, no. 2, 2009, pp. 69–101. *ProjectMuse*, doi:10.1353/sho.0.0225.

Zohar Weiman-Kelman

Poetic Pedagogies: Teaching Irena Klepfisz in Israel/Palestine

In her poem "Fradel Shtok," the lesbian Jewish American poet Irena Klepfisz addresses the reader while using a first-person speaker to narrate the impact of the linguistic struggle of moving between languages:

> Think of it: *heym* and *home* the meaning
> the same of course exactly
> but the shift in vowel was the ocean
> in which I drowned.

The speaker of these lines is not Klepfisz herself, but rather the poet Fradel Shtok, as Klepfisz reveals by opening the poem with a biographical epigraph:

> Yiddish writer. B. 1890 in Skale, Galicia. Emigrated to New York in 1907. Became known when she introduced the sonnet form into Yiddish poetry, Author of *Erzeylungen* (*Stories*, 1919), a collection in Yiddish. Switched to English and published *For Musicians Only* (1927). Institutionalized and died in a sanitarium around 1930.

In this extremely condensed version of an entire life, Klepfisz gives us only the points that are important to an understanding of her poem, at the center of which stands Shtok's emigration and transition from Yiddish to

English. Naming Shtok a "Yiddish writer" despite her eventual "switch" to English implies the failure of this transition in Klepfisz's eyes, which Klepfisz links to her subsequent insanity and hospitalization. As the quote above shows, losing the language in which "home" is spoken is tantamount to losing home altogether. The poem's second epigraph, "language is the only homeland" (Czesław Miłosz), further cements this sentiment.

In 2013, back home in Israel/Palestine after seven years away, I got to teach this poem in a course at the University of Haifa.[1] The course I taught, Passing: Movements of Race and Gender in American Literature, aimed to introduce students to narratives of gender and race as social constructs. While the lessons were conducted in English (as is customary in English departments in Israeli universities), the students' first languages were mainly Hebrew and Arabic. The class, composed of twenty-five students, was extremely diverse. As typical for the Department of English at the University of Haifa, the majority of students were Palestinians with Israeli citizenship: Christians, Muslims, and Druze. Of the four Jewish students, three were Israeli-born, and one was a Russian immigrant; three were Ashkenazi, and one Mizrahi. All but one of the students were women, and only two or three were lesbian or identified as queer (though students shared their identities with me during office hours rather than in the classroom).

Of all the materials studied throughout the semester, the poetry of Klepfisz dealt most explicitly with Jewish content and was the first to address lesbian identity and desire. Moreover, her poetry was the only place where these two themes, the lesbian and the Jewish, appeared together. Beyond worrying how the predominantly heterosexual student body would read her lesbian content, and how the non-Jewish students would read the Jewish references in her work, my primary concern was what they would make of her use of language, or more specifically, her unique bilingual poetics, which interweave Yiddish and English.

The question of language is particularly charged in the context of the state of Israel. Though both Hebrew and Arabic are official languages (as of 2017, a political move to remove Arabic is underway), the dominant language and culture is Hebrew, and the Arabic-speaking students are subjected to this unequal cultural dynamic on a daily basis, inside the university and in most aspects of public life. For students, the teaching of English literature in English (Hebrew is the language of instruction for other subjects) offers a connection to another cultural and geographic center. This connection is perhaps more significant for marginalized students, as Ayelet Ben-Yishai points out (93), even if teaching in English is itself a product of a specific colonial and global history. In practice, the English department is able to create a unique alternative to dominant Hebrew culture. For this reason, I hesitated before bringing not only Jewish content but also another Jewish language into the English-language refuge of the department.

Out of this hesitation began the project that I continue to negotiate now that I have joined the Department of Foreign Literatures and Linguistics at Ben Gurion University: How might I teach Jewish American literature and Yiddish, the materials of my expertise and my passion, yet not infringe upon the alternative space born of this unique academic setting? How might I find a way to build upon and fortify this unique space? Luckily, Yiddish proved to be a productive tool for this pedagogical project, as it was similarly (if not equally) foreign to all the students, and it exposed them to a Jewish history outside the realms familiar to Jews and Arabs alike.

But bringing Klepfisz's work to class was about more than invoking an alternative Jewish language and history; it was also about introducing her lesbian-feminist politics and poetics. This is no small burden to lay on one poet, and yet her poetry enabled me to achieve both goals and more. This essay presents Klepfisz's writing through the teaching moments offered by three poems, "Fradel Shtok," with which I opened, and "Di tsung / The Tongue" and "Etlekhe verter oyf mame-loshn / A Few Words in the Mother Tongue," which I will go on to discuss. If the poem "Fradel Shtok" narrates the loss of language and home, the poem "Di tsung" moves between English and Yiddish on the primal level of sounds, vowels, and bodily gestures, while the poem "Etlekhe verter" moves between the two languages to create original bilingual Jewish lesbian poetry. Taken together, these poems amount to a queer bilingual poetic pedagogy. What I wish to highlight is not simply what Klepfisz's work allows me to teach, but what teaching her poems teaches me about her poetry, and about teaching Jewish American literature in Israel/Palestine.

The lens of linguistic struggle, as formulated in the poem "Fradel Shtok," has shaped my scholarly approach to reading Klepfisz's bilingual poetry. This struggle to find language is written into the content and form of the poem, expressing an effort so unbearable that it led to the silence of writers like Fradel Shtok. However, teaching this poetry, I notice that suddenly the same lines that previously held struggle now hold pedagogic potential; the struggle for each word of poetry becomes an initiation into the Yiddish language. This lesson begins as the most rudimentary introduction in the poem "Di tsung":

Zi shvaygt.

Di verter feln ir
she lacks the words
and all that she can force

is sound
unformed sound:

a
der klang
          the sound

o
dos vort
          the word

u
di tsung
          the tongue

o
dos loshn
          the language

e
di trern
          the tears.

In each line of the poem Klepfisz offers a "sound," or more specifically, a vowel, which could either be English or Yiddish, and then brings a full Yiddish word to illustrate the vowel before it: "*o*" as in "*vort*" (like *a* as in *apple*). As the vowels accumulate, the reader not only learns a lesson in Yiddish pronunciation but gains the basic vocabulary, in both Yiddish and English, for poetic proficiency—the sound, the word, the tongue, the language, the tears. In this lesson the speaker learns the words "she lacks" for writing or speaking, and the students learn the words they need for understanding a Yiddish poem.

"Etlekhe verter" raises the stakes of this pedagogical project, moving from the rudimentary construction (*a* as in *apple*) to the materials of a more advanced language primer or even a dictionary:

lemoshl: for example
di kurve the whore
a woman who acknowledges her passions

> *di yidene* the Jewess the Jewish woman
> ignorant overbearing
> let's face it: every woman is one
>
> *di yente* the gossip the busybody
> who knows what's what
> and is never caught off guard
>
> *di lezbianke* the one with
> a roommate though we never used
> the word
>
> *dos vaybl* the wife
> or the little woman

Pairing Yiddish words with what appear to be their English translations, this poem both invokes and undermines the dictionary function of offering a literal definition. The opening example, *"lemoshl,"* translated accurately as "for example," indicates a straightforward dictionary definition. The next pair, the word *"kurve"* and the English translation "whore," might seem to follow suit; however, the explanatory phrase that follows, "a woman who acknowledges her passions," is, of course, anything but the expected elucidation of "whore" in either Yiddish- or English-speaking circles.

For students new to Yiddish and to lesbian-feminist discourse alike, this poetic construction created a unique pedagogical process; the students, who were dependent on dictionaries to understand relatively simple English-language poetry, were here being taught to question the authority of the dictionary, as well as the discourse it represents. How might this be an empowering process, specifically one that arms students with new lesbian-feminist-Yiddish-poetic knowledge?

The key to the process lay in the movement between knowing and unknowing, familiarity and foreignness. In the initial encounter, the foreignness of Yiddish legitimated the students' dependence on a dictionary, despite the shame they might have regarding this dependence in the case of English. However, this dependence is soon replaced by a new sense of authority, because the poem demands that its readers identify the irony of linking the English translation of each word to a false interpretation. This consequently allows, and even forces, the students to question hegemonic meaning as a unified category, thereby returning the power of knowledge and naming into their own hands.

The verse translating the word *"lezbianke"* offers an especially important intervention. Recognizing the Yiddish word as a cognate for "lesbian" makes the Yiddish familiar rather than foreign. At the same time, "*lezbianke*," a word seldom, if ever, used in Yiddish, must remain unspoken in its English version, which is erased through the closeted or homophobic euphemism "roommate." Adding the qualification "though we never used the word," Klepfisz highlights both the presence and the unspeakableness of the lesbian dwelling in the term "roommate," and in the Yiddish word "*lezbianke*," which may be explicit but is equally unused.

If the homophobic irony is what stood out to me in earlier readings, when I taught the poem in Haifa the interplay between speech and silence made the lesbian story both more visible and more accessible. For the "roommate" arrangement would indeed be familiar to women living in a society with limited lesbian visibility. In this context, rather than erasing such relationships, Klepfisz's lines legitimate them. Klepfisz's poem thus outs a certain lesbian way of life, bringing it into speech. By including the silences within that speech, she addresses both the fact of lesbian existence and its contested discourse.

Significantly, recognizing queerness was difficult for both Jewish and Palestinian women taking the course, a fact that undermines the narrative that presents Jewish Israeli society as progressive and LGBT friendly, and Palestinian society as conservative and homophobic. The work of challenging this narrative parallels Klepfisz's attempt in "Etlekhe verter" to break down the binary of English as progressive and Yiddish as backward. This attempt is evident in the poem's use of Yiddish for the most explicit expression of lesbianism, and its use of English to express the silencing and erasure of lesbianism.

The poetic pedagogy culminates in the ending of "Etlekhe verter," which is entirely in Yiddish and describes a woman's dream about a woman. Rather than excluding non-Yiddish speakers, this poem, alongside the other two read here, equips the reader to understand its Yiddish, as well as its lesbian-feminist content. Over and against Shtok's loss of her native language, her mind, and even her freedom to the English-speaking world, in Klepfisz's poems it is Yiddish that triumphs, taking with it English-, Arabic-, and Hebrew-speaking readers.

We also read the work of Klepfisz's comrade Gloria Anzaldúa, whom Klepfisz credits as the inspiration for her turn to Yiddish. In the piece "how to tame a wild tongue," a section of her bilingual work *Borderlands / La frontera* (54), Anzaldúa cites Klepfisz's poetry as part of her own project of recuperating feminist and lesbian language. If the work of Klepfisz and Anzaldúa brought the bilingual aesthetics of the 1980s women's movement to class, I was surprised to find that whereas Klepfisz's Jewish language supplied students with a new vocabulary, Anzaldúa's work sparked intense tensions among the students. Anzaldúa's text led to the most direct discussion we had all semester of local language politics and the painful realities students were navigating. This discussion may have been provoked by the familiar echoes of colonialism in Anzaldúa's direct address, by the distance of her Mexican American context from our local context, or by both.

This heated debate made me reconsider my initial decision to teach the poems by Klepfisz that speak directly to the Israeli occupation of Palestinian territories, written following her activism in the United States and the time she spent in Israel and Palestine in the 1980s. Trying to maintain the space for discussion that had already been created in our learning environment, I chose not to include those poems that might have struck too close to home. My sense was that engaging with such familiar themes would foreclose the discussion prompted by Klepfisz's use of Yiddish and the alternative histories (outside of Zionism and heteronormativity) her work introduced. Even so, the students read about her Middle East poetry and activism in her essay "Di feder fun harts / The Pen of the Heart: Tsveyshprakhikayt / Bilingualism in Jewish American Poetry," where Klepfisz describes how someone refused to participate on a panel with her if she read her political works, while claiming to have a deep appreciation of her Holocaust poetry. To me, the attempt to separate any of Klepfisz's work from the realms of the political seems utterly unfeasible; her Holocaust poetry is a product of her radical mode of creation (challenging normative conventions of language, sexuality, and history), which is deeply political.

Still, I chose not to teach Klepfisz's Holocaust poetry, fearing it would be as divisive as I imagined her Middle East poems would be. My students, on the other hand, seemed to read all of her poetry relating to the Holocaust on their own, which led many of them to connect to the work in surprising ways. Teaching in the same department, my colleague Ben-Yishai was surprised to find her students turning to the Holocaust in the context of a course on the Indian Partition. Ben-Yishai suggests that their invocation of the Holocaust was based on a desire to avoid discussing the Nakba (the displacement and dispossession of the Palestinian people following the war of 1948), on the one hand, and the ready availability of Holocaust themes, on the other. Discussing the Holocaust offered her students an opportunity for agreement (about which side was evil) and allowed them to bypass questions of guilt and responsibility that discussing the local history would raise (82). As careful as I wanted to be, I was not looking to bypass these questions. Therefore, I used the connections my students made by way of the Holocaust to turn to other histories invoked by Klepfisz's poetry. For example, we explored how Zionist language politics before and after the Holocaust deeply affected the vitality of the Yiddish language. This discussion allowed the students to see Yiddish as a language associated with Jewish powerlessness and victimization, offering both Jewish and Palestinian students a glimpse into histories beyond the current political and linguistic realities in which they were living. In this way Yiddish could also invoke potential futures for the contested land we all called home.

Klepfisz's poetic pedagogies gave all of my students space to inhabit the painful gap between *"heym"* and home, as she describes in "Fradel Shtok." And yet between *bayt* and *bayt*, the word for "home" in both Hebrew and Arabic, there is not even the vowel shift that Klepfisz describes in her poem. Moreover, in both languages the word *bayt* has a poetic meaning, "verse" in Arabic and "stanza" in Hebrew. Teaching in Israel/ Palestine, sharing tools of literary scholarship and texts of Jewish American literature, instructors will find Klepfisz's poetry to be a shared home for linguistic struggle, lesbian-feminist dreams, and perhaps even queer hope for a future we can't yet speak.[2]

Notes

1. I use the term *Israel/Palestine* to designate the overlapping space of the state of Israel and the land of Palestine within the borders drawn following the 1948 Arab-Israeli War.

2. I am grateful for comments on this essay from my friend and mentor Ayelet Ben-Yishai and from my friend and student Raya Naamneh.

Works Cited

Anzaldúa, Gloria. *Borderlands / La frontera: The New Mestiza.* Aunt Lute Books, 1999.

Ben-Yishai, Ayelet. "Stories of Partition: Pedagogy, Politics, and the India-Israel Comparative Project." *Teoria Ubikoret,* vol. 44, 2015, pp. 77–96.

Klepfisz, Irena. "Di feder fun harts / The Pen of the Heart: Tsveyshprakhikayt / Bilingualism in Jewish American Poetry." *Jewish American Poetry: Reflections, Poems, Commentary,* edited by Jonathan Barron and Eric Murphy Selinger, UP of New England, 2000, pp. 320–47.

———. "Di tsung / The Tongue." Klepfisz, *Few Words,* p. 223.

———. "Etlekhe verter oyf mame-loshn / A Few Words in the Mother Tongue." Klepfisz, *Few Words,* pp. 225–27.

———. *A Few Words in the Mother Tongue: Poems Selected and New (1971–1990).* Eighth Mountain Press, 1990.

———. "Fradel Shtok." Klepfisz, *Few Words,* pp. 228–29.

Peter Antelyes

Jews, Gender, and Comix

Teachers of Jewish American literature have been quick to include popular culture materials in their courses. In comics and graphic novels in particular, they have found a compelling way to enrich and complicate how their classes engage the meanings of and intersections among the key terms *Jewish*, *American*, and *literature*. Most commonly one finds Art Spiegelman's *Maus* taught in such courses, and, less frequently, a brief history of the comics with an emphasis on the superhero genre of the late 1930s through *Superman* and *Batman*. While these are pertinent inclusions, this version of the role played by Jews and Jewishness in comics history leaves out a central facet of that history, namely the contributions of female Jewish writers and artists.

A good choice for introducing these materials is the graphic art of two exemplary figures from the 1970s, Aline Kominsky-Crumb and Diane Noomin, who were instrumental in the emergence of a uniquely Jewish form of women's comics. This essay will show how to contextualize these works at the crucial moment in American cultural history when second-wave and Jewish feminisms emerged and clashed. It will also explore ways to read the formal dimensions of comics within these and other Jewish American contexts. These comics are especially effective vehicles for placing women and women's concerns at the center of the multifaceted story of Jewish American literature. Through them, one can address a variety of issues: representations of Jewishness and gender, artistic efforts to make Jewish women visible (both through and beyond the stereotypes), the positioning of Jewish women within different feminisms, the links between Jewish Americanness and gender as sites of internalization and resistance, and the aesthetics of female Jewish American confessional and satirical autobiography.

To address the nature of the comics and their contributions, teachers and students must know something about a number of specific cultural contexts. Primary among those contexts is the Jewish milieu of the postwar Northeast, from its struggle with conformity in the 1950s to the blooming of that struggle into active resistance in the 1960s and 1970s. Kominsky-Crumb was born in 1948 in Long Beach, Long Island, and Noomin in 1947 in Brooklyn, and both grew up primarily in postwar suburbs with significant Jewish populations. Kominsky-Crumb recounts her impressions of life in Woodmere, Long Island, by describing the environment as "the crassest aspect of middle class, materialistic, New York suburban Jewish culture" ("Public Conversation" 128). Noomin strikes a similar note about Canarsie: "the epitome of a crass, nouveauy, bourgeoisie, suburban nightmare" (Interview 177), or, as she puts it elsewhere, "a modern shtetl" ("I Felt"). Both artists moved to San Francisco in the early 1970s, immersing themselves in that city's hippie culture, and began their comics careers.

Both artists focused on these cultural forces and transformations of the 1950s and 1960s, with their mix of hegemonic and antiauthoritarian elements: the rapid growth of the suburbs and commodity culture, the sexual revolution, the feminist and antiwar movements, and the growth of alternative economies of representation such as underground comix. These were also particularly fertile years in Jewish American cultural production, when Jewish artists engaged these developments and cultural tensions with heightened brashness.[1] Kominsky-Crumb and Noomin have cited many of these artists and their works as influences, and brief introductions to some of them can provide students with a sense of the animating transmedia context alluded to in their comics.

Among the most immediately pertinent cultural contexts for understanding the comics' treatment of Jewish women's experiences and identities are second-wave feminism and women's underground comix.[2] It was not just the feminist movement in general that shaped Kominsky-Crumb's and Noomin's art, but the specific relation and later tensions between second-wave feminism and Jewishness. Betty Friedan's seminal text *The Feminine Mystique* can provide students with glimpses of this link and these tensions. What this work makes evident is that while the second wave was not a Jewish movement per se, it was certainly inflected by Jewish American women's concerns (Antler; Diner et. al.; Horowitz, "Jewish Women" and "Rethinking Betty Friedan"; Hyman; and Prell). To read the book in these terms is to reconsider the criticism that the second wave was a univocal movement, both shaped and hindered by an obtuse, universalizing expression of privileged whiteness. Emerging also from the diasporic perspective of the Jewish insider/outsider, Friedan's book provides a critique of second-wave feminism that stands alongside, and in tension with, the book's more conventional perspective. The book doesn't simply deploy universalism to gain recognition by the wider culture but also criticizes that universalism as a site of exclusion and oppression. *The Feminine Mystique* expresses a profoundly ambivalent relation to the middle-class housewives who are its subject. At once identifying with and scornful of these women—in one remarkable chapter, it describes their state as that of those living in a "comfortable concentration camp" (256)—the book can be read as emerging from and taking part in a debate among Jewish American women about their roles in the multiple patriarchal social worlds they inhabited, from mainstream America to their own Jewish American community.

Strikingly, though, Jewish women's interests were essentially invisible in second-wave feminism (Beck), which operated under the universal idea of *woman*. A focus on Jewishness was dismissed on the grounds that it was irrelevant, that it was a provincializing distraction from the broader aims of the movement, and that it collided with the movement's allied political interests, including the Palestinian cause. In time many Jewish feminists turned to address their own interests and mine their own resources, whether by creating a uniquely Jewish feminism that shaped itself around a critique and modification of Judaic theology and ritual, or, as in the case of Kominsky-Crumb and Noomin, by speaking from a more secularly oriented Jewish viewpoint.[3] This split in the movement would be echoed in the politics of women's underground comix, where a comparable struggle for visibility and legitimacy would become manifest, only this time in a medium that was about visibility itself.

Reaction against the exclusionary properties of universalism also characterizes the growth of feminism in the world of underground comix, arising first between the male and female writers, and then within the women's community. The first generation of the underground comix movement maintained the wider culture's patriarchal bent, including a domination by male cartoonists who often used degrading images of women as a key instrument of their politics. The women were quick to respond. In 1970 the first feminist comix anthology was published. *It Aint Me Babe*, edited by Jewish artist Trina Robbins, included stories by many of the artists that would become central to the movement. Featuring satires of romance and "queen of the jungle" comics, stories about abortion and sexism in the workplace, and myths about goddesses and women warriors, it set the stage on which Kominsky-Crumb and Noomin later appeared.

That stage was San Francisco's Wimmen's Comix Collective, which had many Jewish women in key roles, including its leader, Robbins, who had published a comic about the Triangle Shirtwaist Fire in the Jewish feminist journal *Lilith* in 1972, and Sharon Rudahl, who wrote a number of comics on explicitly Jewish themes. Kominsky-Crumb joined the group before Noomin and published her first comic, "Goldie: A Neurotic Woman," in the initial issue of *Wimmen's Comix*. She then brought Noomin in for the third issue, which included Noomin's "The Agony and Ecstasy of a Shayna Madel." But while Kominsky-Crumb and Noomin, like Robbins and Rudahl, were comfortable with pursuing Jewish subjects, they differed on the extent to which an explicit focus on Jewishness was appropriate to a feminist agenda.

According to Noomin, she and Kominsky-Crumb felt that *Wimmen's Comix* "published a certain type of work—pseudo-feminist idealized goddess bullshit" (Noomin, Interview). Within such a context, their works' unique combination of Jewish, autobiographical, and de-idealizing elements were largely unwelcome. Kominsky-Crumb noted, for instance, that Robbins and Rudahl were "very down on autobiographical comics" in particular and found them insufficiently entertaining or "uplifting" (Kominsky-Crumb, Interview). But Noomin's and Kominsky-Crumb's comics were not just autobiographical; they were also, in Noomin's terms, "self-deprecating, ironic, crude, [and] in-your-face" (Noomin, Interview). In their discomfort with Noomin's and Kominsky-Crumb's approach, Robbins and Rudahl were not acting out of any explicit animus toward Jewish concerns; they both wrote positive and explicitly Jewish stories of their own, such as their jointly composed "Zog Nit Keyn Mol: The Partisans Song." For Robbins, though, her Jewish identity did "not much" affect her art: "mostly what influenced my work is that I'm a woman" ("Graphic Details"). These arguments within second-wave feminism were thus embodied in arguments about the appropriate visibility and representation of female Jewish identity. As with the second wave's antagonistic relation to a feminism that strove to explicitly address the needs of Jewish women, these differing views and their resulting tensions led to a split within the community. Kominsky-Crumb and Noomin left the collective in 1974 to publish their own comic, *Twisted Sisters*. From that point on, they were freer to explore their own perspectives in their work, which in turn led to new forms of expression by Jewish American women in autographics and comics more generally.

Turning to the comics in *Twisted Sister*, one notes first that if their forms were new, they were new in particular Jewish ways, which is to say that they drew on Jewish modes of diasporic textuality, from the modes of argumentation in talmudic commentary to the imaginative interventions of midrashic commentary, from double voicing to social satire. In this sense, they fit well in Jewish American literature courses, in which these modes are foregrounded. In these comics one finds familiar Jewish concerns, such as an emphasis on the body and embodiment, and particularly the messier facets of sexuality and desire. What was new about Kominsky-Crumb's and Noomin's works was the use of a hybrid form of text and image as the means of expression, representation, and commentary (though the architecture of the Talmud page offers a suggestive imaginative precursor). To appreciate what these comics have to offer, students will need a brief introduction to the close reading of comics, including panel and page design, image-text relations, and the politics of visual-verbal representation. They will also need a brief introduction to the characteristic visual and verbal strategies of underground comix, which torqued conventions to their own ends. Then the students will be able to link more adroitly the comics' features to Jewish American modes of writing and reading.[4]

One key text with which to introduce Kominsky-Crumb's work is the cover of the first issue of *Twisted Sisters* (fig. 1).[5] While the dominant image seems to contain no explicit Jewish content, a closer look reveals Jewish markers: the combination of anxiety and pleasure attending the figure's graphic and obsessive relation to bowel movements (Brauner); the depiction of both adulthood and infantilism in how the figure is positioned; and the aggressive yet unsettled satirical tone. It's not quite clear, for instance, if the figure is being mocked for her internalization of the

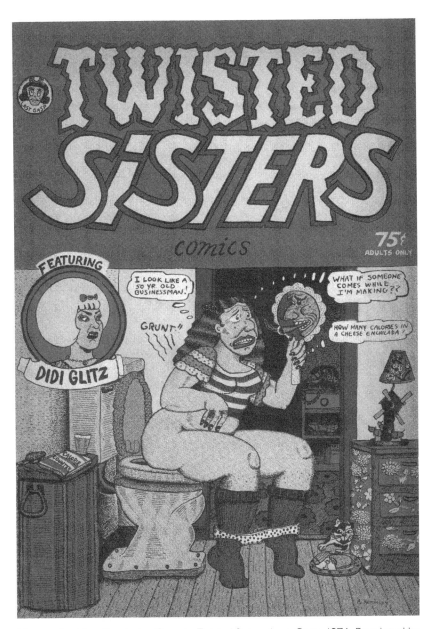

Figure I. Aline Kominsky-Crumb. *Twisted Sisters*, Last Gasp, 1976. Reprinted by permission of the author.

patriarchal point of view, or if the life of such a woman is merely being presented, or even embraced, in all its messiness. Such doubling of consciousness, an unstable mixture of othering and identification, is a characteristic of much Jewish American writing, including Friedan's *Feminine Mystique*. The elements that mark the figure as "antifeminine," such as her undignified position (and pose), her focus on "making," and her curly hair and big nose, are signals to readers who are aware of these tropes that this is very much a Jewish scene. It's an image behind which stand the transgressive provocations of Philip Roth's novels; the angry and yet also self-abusive comedic persona of Joan Rivers; the smaller-than-life characters Woody Allen plays in his films; the messy, anti-erotic body art of Judy Chicago; and the neurotic talk of Jules Feiffer comics. The *Twisted Sisters* cover, then, can be seen as a declaration of a new kind of Jewish American feminist comic. As Kominsky-Crumb slyly put it, "It's nice to read comics on the toilet" ("Aline Kominsky-Crumb Interview"). "Making," in this sense, indelibly links the work's Jewish approach to its claims on creative authority.

This treatment of the divided and changing self and the messy and vulgar body; the peculiar mix of broad satire and comic realism; the aesthetic of revulsion and its medium, the grotesque; the owning and disavowal of internalized sexism and anti-Semitism—all of these features were evident in Kominsky-Crumb's very first comic, "Goldie," which appeared in the first issue of *Wimmen's Comix* in 1972.[6] Other critics have provided illuminating readings of this comic (Chute; Oksman), so I'll only note a few examples pertinent to a Jewish American literature class.

"Goldie" is a five-page story that has often been credited as the first foray into women's autobiographical graphic narratives. It's about a young Jewish girl's fall from happiness and innocence into a puberty that brings ugliness, an insatiable sexual desire that merges guilt and pleasure and that recognizes no appropriate boundaries of direction or attachment, unhappy affairs with men, and, finally, a newfound independence. However positive the ending, though, the weight of the piece, and in particular its Jewishness, lies in the endlessly recursive nature of Goldie's fall, as is evident in the two panels that identify the causes of Goldie's "neurotic" formation (fig. 2). While the second panel visually and verbally declares that puberty brought "uglyness and guilt," the first and supposedly Edenic panel cleverly positions the book Goldie is reading at her spread legs, as if to suggest that neurosis, identity, sexuality, and art were bound together from the beginning.

Figure 2. Aline Kominsky-Crumb. "Goldie: A Neurotic Woman." *Wimmen's Comix*, no. 1, Last Gasp, 1972. Reprinted by permission of the author.

Ultimately, the most consistent visual signifier of these bound elements is the nose. "I always start with the nose," Kominsky-Crumb has said ("Public Conversation" 120; see also Kominsky-Crumb, "Nose Job"). The nose's role as a visual signifier is especially vivid in the two middle panels on the final page of "Goldie" (fig. 3). The nose stands at the center of the page and breaks the panel boundaries, encroaching on, and in some ways participating in, the vision of sexual excess in the prior panel. It's as if that nose is not just a marker for the Jewish body in general but more precisely the site of its sexuality: excessive, distorted, ugly, and transgressive. That transgressiveness is most visually apparent in the way the nose traverses the boundary, or "gutter" (the comics term for the crucial meaning-making space between the panels). As this boundary-breaking capacity suggests, the meaning of the nose is difficult to pin down. The nose can be read simultaneously as a sign of internalized self-hatred, an insidious coupling of sexism and anti-Semitism, an expression of pride in and possession of Jewish difference, and some indeterminate, boundary-defying space of identification. Grappling with this troubling mixture of meanings, with, in particular, the nose's offensiveness, is the very heart of the experience of reading Kominsky-Crumb's work, which provided a rich aesthetic vein for the development of Jewish American women's autographic writing.

If Kominsky-Crumb's work was archetypically Jewish American in this sense, though, it was not the only kind of critique emerging from that

Figure 3. Aline Kominsky-Crumb. "Goldie: A Neurotic Woman." *Wimmen's Comix*, no. I, Last Gasp, 1972. Reprinted by permission of the author.

perspective. Kominsky-Crumb's partner in *Twisted* Sisters, Diane Noomin, produced work that engaged its targets not by naturalizing but by de-essentializing them. This difference in the two writers' approaches is immediately evident in the treatment of their main characters. Kominsky-Crumb's main figure, "The Bunch," is emphatically autobiographical, and always striving toward direct expression and a sense of liberation through the recovery of the unmediated, the embodied, the natural ("natural" in this context meaning Jewish-neurotic). Noomin's main character, DiDi Glitz, is only remotely autobiographical, and her sources and modes of identification are inescapably mediated through preexisting images and stereotypes. This mediation is particularly vivid in the association of DiDi's identity and representation with performance. Noomin describes Didi as "[p]art alter ego, part satire and a way of discussing things with myself from an antithetical point of view" (qtd. in Leonard 93). This difference between the two writers' works can be partly explained by Noomin's biography. While both artists lived in and wrote about the Jewish suburbs, Noomin didn't settle in Canarsie until she was thirteen. Before that she lived mainly in an integrated working-class neighborhood in Long Island, where she was raised by communist parents, a story told in a two-page comic entitled "I Was a Red Diaper Baby" and included in her *Glitz-2-Go*. As a result, she had a somewhat more critically distanced relation to the suburbs, Jewish and otherwise.

Figure 4. Diane Noomin. "The Fabulous World of DiDi Glitz." *Glitz-2-Go*, Fantagraphics, 2011, p. 79. Reprinted by permission of Fantagraphics.

At her most radical, DiDi is essentially a drag figure, complete with an obvious blond wig. In one panel from "The Fabulous World of DiDi Glitz" (fig. 4), included in the first issue of *Twisted Sisters*, we see she's actually bald, missing the dark mane of "Jewish hair" (and the "Jewish nose" as well) that is the object of such obsession for The Bunch. Note the deconstruction and reconstruction of DiDi's self in the sequence, visually intensified by the absence of gutters and the clotting of visual detail. Note, too, the fact that the "real" DiDi is precisely the most performative. That the wig is blond links her to another figment of the Jewish American imagination during this period of second-wave feminism, Barbie, who is similarly multivalent as a vehicle of identifications and disidentifications: a stand-in for her Jewish female creator, an embodiment of the derogatory and yet also envied stereotypical figure of the "shiksa," while, at the same time, an embodiment of the equally derogatory stereotype of the "JAP" (Jewish American princess) in disguise. Like a doll, DiDi is also drawn to elaborate costumes. In another remarkable panel, this one from Noomin's 1993 "Back to the Bagel Belt with DiDi Glitz," she is shown talking with Noomin, who is in a closet, while DiDi looks at herself in the mirror, holding an item of clothing that looks like a tallis (fig. 5).

The elaborate cross patterns in Noomin's images reflect her love of surface, difference, and dissonance. Kominsky-Crumb characterizes

Figure 5. Diane Noomin. "Back to the Bagel Belt with DiDi Glitz." *Glitz-to-Go*, Fantagraphics, 2011, p. 106. Reprinted by permission of Fantagraphics.

Noomin's palette as "so kitsch, so stupefyingly overdone, something like a mixture of Liberace, Joan Rivers and Jackie Mason—Graceland on the Borscht Belt" (Noomin, *Glitz* 7). This description captures Noomin's radicalness, the extent to which she was willing to destabilize both Jewishness and gender by treating them as mere costume and performance. As such her work adds a striking component to the genre of Jewish American female autographics begun by Kominsky-Crumb, drawing more on post-1990s notions of performativity than 1970s and 1980s notions of authenticity and de-idealization. I've had great success in the classroom pairing Noomin's comics with Judith Butler's work on performativity, especially when foregrounding the point that Butler's engagement with performativity is partially tied, as Butler once explained to a colleague of mine, to her engagement with her self-identification as a Jew.

As I hope I have demonstrated, Kominsky-Crumb's and Noomin's works have much to offer Jewish American literature courses. In addition to the works themselves, a teacher might explore their influence on later developments in Jewish American women's autographics and graphic novels by such contemporary writers as Joyce Brabner, Leela Corman, Vanessa Davis, Liana Finck, Sarah Glidden, Miriam Katin, Ariel Schrag, Lauren Weinstein, and others. One might also use the texts to underscore and enhance issues discussed throughout this essay, from visibility and representation to insider/outsider perspectives to the contested links between Jewishness and feminism. Above all, one can use these materials to draw on students' receptivity to visual texts to give them a critical awareness of the visual worlds in which Jewishness and gender intersect with particular and peculiar power.

Notes

1. To mention just a few influences: literary works by Philip Roth, Irena Klepfisz, Erica Jong, and Kate Millet; stand-up comedy by Joan Rivers, Don Rickles, and Jackie Mason; comics in *Mad Magazine* and by Jules Feiffer in the *Village Voice*; magazine articles by Gloria Steinem (in *Ms.*) and Helen Gurley Brown (in *Cosmopolitan*); photography by Diane Arbus and Cindy Sherman; movies by Woody Allen and Joan Micklin Silver; and art by Judy Chicago and Carolee Schneeman.

2. Following standard usage, this essay will use "comics" when referring to the form generally and "comix" when referring to works associated with the underground movement beginning in the 1960s, including works by Kominsky-Crumb and Noomin.

3. The more spiritually oriented group included such figures as Rachel Adler, E. M. Broner, Aviva Cantor, Blu Greenberg, and Judith Plaskow; and the more secular group included Evelyn Torton Beck, Melanie Kaye/Kantrowitz, Grace Paley, and Letty Cottin Pogrebin.

4. See McCloud; Madden; Chute and Jagoda; and Newgarden and Karasik for a general introduction to comics form. See Sabin and also Rosenkranz for an introduction to comix form, and Noomin's 1991 anthology *Twisted Sisters* and Groth for an introduction to women's comix forms and artists in particular. See Baskind and Omer-Sherman; Lightman; Oksman; and Royal for a reading of Jewish comics and comix texts.

5. While the works of both authors are readily available, they are also dispersed. Most of them can be found in the authors' most recent collections—Kominsky-Crumb's 2018 *Love That Bunch* and Noomin's 2011 *Glitz-2-Go*.

6. While the autobiographical figure of Goldie was quickly replaced in Kominsky-Crumb's comix by a figure named "The Bunch," one can see in the later character the same satirical autobiographical elements.

Works Cited

Antler, Joyce. *The Journey Home: Jewish Women and the American Century*. Free Press, 1997.

Baskind, Samantha, and Ranen Omer-Sherman, editors. *The Jewish Graphic Novel: Critical Approaches*. Rutgers UP, 2008.

Beck, Evelyn Torton. "The Politics of Jewish Invisibility." *NWSA Journal*, vol. 1, no. 1, 1996, pp. 93–102.

Brauner, David. "The Turd That Won't Flush: The Comedy of Jewish Self-Hatred in the Work of Corinne Pearlman, Aline Kominsky-Crumb, Miss Lasko-Gross, and Ariel Schrag." *Graphic Details*, McFarland, 2014, pp. 131–48.

Butler, Judith. "Imitation and Gender Insubordination." *Inside/Out: Lesbian Theories, Gay Theories*, edited by Diana Fuss, Routledge, 1991, pp. 13–25.

Chute, Hillary L. *Graphic Women: Life Narrative and Contemporary Comics*. Columbia UP, 2010.

Chute, Hillary L., and Patrick Jagoda. Introduction. *Comics and Media*, special issue of *Critical Inquiry*, edited by Chute and Jagoda, vol. 40, no. 3, pp. 1–10.

Diner, Hasia R, et al., editors. *A Jewish Feminine Mystique? Jewish Women in Postwar America*. Rutgers UP, 2010.

Friedan, Betty. *The Feminine Mystique*. Edited by Kirsten Fermaglich and Lisa M. Fine, W. W. Norton, 2013.

Groth, Gary, editor. *The Complete Wimmen's Comix*. Fantagraphics, 2016. 2 vols.

Horowitz, Daniel. "Jewish Women Remaking American Feminism / Women Remaking American Judaism: Reflections on the Life of Betty Friedan." *A Jewish Feminine Mystique*, Rutgers UP, 2010, pp. 235–56.

———. "Rethinking Betty Friedan and *The Feminine Mystique*: Labor Union Radicalism and Feminism in Cold War America." *The Feminine Mystique*, W. W. Norton, 2013, pp. 454–65.

Hyman, Paula E. "Jewish Feminism Faces the American Women's Movement: Convergence and Divergence." *American Jewish Identity Politics*, edited by Deborah Dash Moore, University of Michigan Press, 2008, pp. 221–40.

Kominsky-Crumb, Aline. "The Aline Kominsky-Crumb Interview." Interview by Peter Bagge. *The Comics Journal*, no. 139, Dec. 1990, www.tcj.com/the-aline-kominsky-crumb-interview/.

———."Goldie: A Neurotic Woman." *Wimmen's Comix*, no. 1, Last Gasp, 1972.

———. Interview by Hillary L. Chute. *Outside the Box: Interviews with Contemporary Cartoonists*, by Chute, U of Chicago P, 2010.

———. *Love That Bunch*. Drawn and Quarterly, 2018.

———. "Nose Job." *Wimmen's Comix*, no. 15, Last Gasp, 1989.

———. "Public Conversation: Schilt and Kominsky-Crumb." Interview by Kristen Schilt. *Critical Inquiry*, vol. 40, no. 3, 2014, pp. 118–31.

Kominsky-Crumb, Aline, and Diane Noomin. *Twisted Sisters Comics*. Last Gasp, 1976.

Leonard, Joanne. "Fetal Attractions: Diane Noomin's 'Baby Talk: A Tale of 3 4 Miscarriages' (1995) and *My Journal of a Miscarriage*, 1973." Lightman, pp. 79–97.

Lightman, Sarah, editor. *Graphic Details: Jewish Women's Confessional Comics in Essays and Interviews*. McFarland, 2014.

Madden, Matt. *Ninety-Nine Ways to Tell a Story: Exercises in Style*. Penguin Books, 2005.

McCloud, Scott. *Understanding Comics*. Harper Perennial, 1993.

Newgarden, Mark, and Paul Karasik. "How to Read Nancy." *The Best of Ernie Bushmiller's Nancy*, edited by Brian Walker, Holt/Comicana, 1988, www.laffpix.com/howtoreadnancy.pdf.

Noomin, Diane. "The Agony and Ecstasy of a Shayna Madel." *Wimmen's Comix*, no. 3, Last Gasp, 1973.

———. "Back to the Bagel Belt with DiDi Glitz." *Verre D'Eau*, no. 28, Last Gasp, 1993.

———. *Glitz-2-Go*. Fantagraphics, 2011.

———. "'I Felt Like I Didn't Have a Baby but At Least I'd Have a Book': A Diane Noomin Interview." Interview by Nicole Rudick. *The Comics Journal*, 8 May 2012, www.tcj.com/i-felt-like-i-didn't-have-a-baby-but-at -least-I'd-have-a-book-a-diane-noomin-interview/.

———. Interview with Andrea Juno. *Dangerous Drawings: Interviews with Comix and Graphic Artists*, by Juno, Juno, 1997.

———. "I Was a Red Diaper Baby." *Glitz-2-Go*, Fantagraphics, 2011, pp. 122–23.

———, editor. *Twisted Sisters: A Collection of Bad Girl Art*. Penguin Books, 1991.

Oksman, Tahneer. *"How Come Boys Get to Keep Their Noses?" Women and Jewish American Identity in Contemporary Graphic Memoirs*. Columbia UP, 2016.

Prell, Riv-Ellen. *Fighting to Become Americans: Assimilation and the Trouble between Jewish Women and Jewish Men*. Beacon Press, 1999.

Robbins, Trina. "Graphic Details: Interview with Trina Robbins." Interview by Leah Berkenwald. *Jewish Women's Archive*, 7 Feb. 2011, jwa.org/blog /graphic-details-interview-with-trina-robbins.

———, editor. *It Aint Me Babe: Women's Liberation*. Last Gasp, 1970.

———. "The Triangle Fire." *Lilith: The Jewish Women's Magazine*, no. 7, 1980.

Robbins, Trina, and Sharon Rudahl. "Zog Nit Keyn Mol: The Partisans Song." *Wimmen's Comix*, no. 10, 1985.

Rosenkranz, Patrick. *Rebel Visions: The Underground Comix Revolution, 1963–1975*. Fantagraphics, 2002.

Royal, Derek, editor. *Visualizing Jewish Narrative: Jewish Comics and Graphic Novels*. Bloomsbury, 2016.

Sabin, Roger. "Going Underground." *Comics, Comix and Graphic Novels: A History of Comic Art*. Phaidon, 1996, pp. 92–129.

Works Consulted and Reprints

Kominsky-Crumb, Aline. "Goldie: A Neurotic Woman." Reprinted in *Complete Wimmen's Comix*, vol. 1, Fantagraphics, 2016, pp. 39–43.

———. "Grief on Long Island." *The Bunch's Power Pak Comics*, no. 2, Kitchen Sink, 1981. Reprinted in *Love That Bunch*, Fantagraphics, 1990, pp. 57–61; in *Love That Bunch*, Drawn and Quarterly, 2018, pp. 72–76; and, in color and excerpted, in *Need More Love*, Fantagraphics, 1990, pp. 196–97.

———. *Love That Bunch*. Fantagraphics, 1990.

———. *Need More Love*. MQ Publications, 2007.

———. "Nose Job." *Wimmen's Comix*, no. 15, Last Gasp, 1989. Reprinted, in color, in *Need More Love*, MQ Publications, 2007, p. 86; in black and white in *Twisted Sisters*, Penguin Books, 1991, pp. 154–56; in *Complete Wimmen's Comix*, vol. 2, Fantagraphics, 2016, p. 564–66; and in *Love That Bunch*, Drawn and Quarterly, 2018, pp. 105–07.

———. "The Saga of Stuie Spitzer." *The Bunch's Power Pak Comics*, no. 2, Kitchen
Sink, 1981. Reprinted in *Love That Bunch*, Fantagraphics, 1990, pp.
82–86; in *Love That Bunch*, Drawn and Quarterly, 2018, pp. 98–102; and, in color, in
Need More Love, Fantagraphics, 1990, pp. 66–70.

Noomin, Diane. "The Agony and Ecstasy of a Shayna Madel." Reprinted in
Complete Wimmen's Comix, vol. 1, Fantagraphics, 2016, p. 128–29.

———. "Back to the Bagel Belt with DiDi Glitz." Reprinted in *Glitz-2-Go*,
Fantagraphics, 2011, pp. 106–08.

———. "A Blond Grows in Brooklyn in 3 DiDi." *True Glitz*, Rip Off Press,
1987. Reprinted in *Glitz-2-Go*, p. 136; and in *Complete Wimmen's Comix*,
vol. 2, Fantagraphics, 2016, p. 471.

———. "Coming of Age in Canarsie." *Wimmen's Comix*, no. 14, 1989. Reprinted
in *Twisted Sisters*, Penguin Books, 1991, p. 72; in *Glitz-2-Go*, Fantagraphics,
2011, p. 109; and in *Complete Wimmen's Comix*, vol. 2, Fantagraphics, 2016,
p. 557.

———. "The Fabulous World of DiDi Glitz." *Twisted Sisters*, Last Gasp, 1976.
Reprinted in *Glitz-2-Go*, Fantagraphics, 2011, pp. 68–79.

———. "Life in the Bagel Belt with DiDi Glitz." *True Glitz*, Rip Off Press,
1990. Reprinted in *Twisted Sisters*, Penguin Books, 1991, pp. 63–67; and in
Glitz-2-Go, Fantagraphics, 2011, pp. 102–05.

———. "Meet Debbie Dahlowitz." *Glitz-2-Go*, Fantagraphics, 2011, p. 163.

———. "Meet Marvin Mensch." *Wimmen's Comix*, no. 16, 1990. Reprinted in
Twisted Sisters, Penguin Books, 1991, pp. 76–77; in *Glitz-2-Go*, Fantagraphics, 2011, pp. 154–55; and in *Complete Wimmen's Comix*, vol. 2, Fantagraphics, 2016, pp. 588–89.

———. "Wimmin and Comix." *ImageTexT: Interdisciplinary Comics Studies*,
vol. 1, no. 2, 2004, www.english.ufl.edu/imagetext/archives/v1_2/noomin
/index.shtml?print.

Robbins, Trina, and Sharon Rudahl. "Zog Nit Keyn Mol: The Partisans Song."
Reprinted in *Complete Wimmen's Comix*, vol. 2, Fantagraphics, 2016,
pp. 378–79.

Linda Schlossberg

Teaching *Angels in America* in the Twenty-First Century: Memory, Mourning, and Meaning

Teaching Tony Kushner's *Angels in America, Part I: Millennium Approaches* and *Part II: Perestroika* presents myriad challenges. For today's college students, the Reagan era is history—as seemingly distant as the Holocaust and McCarthyism. The play's complex invocations of the past, along with the fact that the play's actors perform multiple roles (some based on real historical figures, such as Roy Cohn and Ethel Rosenberg), require the instructor to move between 1950s cultural discourses of anti-Semitism, homophobia, and McCarthyism and the Reagan-era policies and politics of the 1980s. Based on my experience of teaching the play in an introductory LGBT literature course, this essay offers strategies for bringing historical background to *Angels* in a way that not only fills in the blanks but also illuminates the relation between the play's moral themes and the Jewish ethic of remembrance.

Kushner's two-part play is set in New York City between 1985 and 1986, years of devastating loss and moral panic around the unfolding AIDS crisis. In addition to its religious connotations and promise of divine revelation, the title *Millennium Approaches* hints at recurring turn-of-the-century anxieties surrounding gender and sexuality (Showalter 4), and at broader apocalyptic fears of overpopulation, bioterrorism, and technological catastrophe. The title *Perestroika* not only refers to 1980s Soviet reforms but also suggests the metaphorical dissolution or restructuring of seemingly fixed realities, boundaries, and identities. In their movement from anxiety to openness, or glasnost, these titles map the emotional trajectory of the character Louis, whose lover Prior has HIV/ AIDS, as well as the larger moral lessons of the play.

Angels begins with the funeral of Louis's grandmother. In class, we ask why a play "about AIDS" opens with a Jewish funeral and the recitation of the Kaddish, a sanctioned, ritualized form of mourning. We examine the famous 1987 ACT UP (AIDS Coalition to Unleash Power) poster with the inverted pink triangle on a black background and the words "Silence = Death"—the iconic image of AIDS activism—and we review the ways in which AIDS went largely "unspoken" by the media and the Reagan administration (Crimp, "Cultural Analysis" 8). The most famous example of this, of course, was Reagan's own refusal to address the crisis publicly until 1987. Because students often are unfamiliar with this aspect of American history, we review 1980s metaphors of AIDS as a holocaust, plague, and curse visited upon those who did not conform to the ethos of the Christian right and political organizations such as the Moral Majority. For many Americans, caught up in a nationwide moral panic built from ignorance and fear, AIDS seemed to literalize the notion that gay people were morally sick, diseased, and defective. Taking note of the pink triangle's origination as a Holocaust symbol used to identify homosexuals, we discuss how the Reagan administration's disavowal of the AIDS crisis has been understood as a form of cultural genocide.

We then circle back to the beginning of the play, asking: Who gets to publicly honor their dead? Whose deaths are constituted as tragic and worthy of memorialization? In other words, how is mourning a privileged act? (Students may connect these questions to the work done by activist groups such as Black Lives Matter and Say Her Name.) Our students, who have come of age at a time when gay-straight alliances are common in schools and when positive media images of LGBT people are plentiful, may not understand the degree to which LGBT people in the 1980s were often closeted or estranged from their families, and the fact that deaths from AIDS were often attributed to other causes. Louis doesn't feel comfortable introducing Prior to his family at his grandmother's funeral: "I always get so closety at these family things" (*Angels* 25). People's suffering was often silenced, unrepresented, unspoken, left out of obituary notices, or not even shared with family members. By contrast, the ritual of reciting the Kaddish (not once, not twice, but daily, insistently, over and over) asks members of the Jewish community to collectively acknowledge and publicly mourn their dead. It is a moral mandate to the larger community to "never forget" and represents a sharp contrast to American culture's refusal, to this day, to fully mourn AIDS publicly. The continued sanctification of Reagan's presidential legacy (he was often referred to as "the great communicator," which is painfully ironic given his silence on AIDS) means that for many Americans their losses have never been culturally recognized. Regardless of the characters' religious backgrounds, in *Angels* Kushner presents us with a distinctive vision of Jewish morality accessible to all.

When reading the play, students are asked to identify moments that stage powerful links between 1950s and 1980s America, particularly in terms of cultural anxieties surrounding Jews, queerness, and communism. Kushner's play makes clear that the Cold War 1980s are haunted by the sins of the 1950s, just as the embittered Roy Cohn, dying of AIDS, is haunted by the ghost of Ethel Rosenberg, whom he sent to the electric chair. How do we understand these echoes? In class, we first discuss the concept of moral panic. We then review connections between these two historical periods. They are both animated by increased conservatism and a mythology of nationwide economic prosperity—a mythology that hides the lived reality of economic and racial segregation. They are also moments steeped in cultural anxieties about communism. Students generally know basic facts about McCarthyism and the Cold War, and about the fear of communism as a seductive, insidious, irreligious threat to a mythologized American way of life steeped in linked ideals of Christianity, the nuclear family, and private property. What may be less familiar to them are connections between cultural anxieties about homosexuality, Jewishness, and communism (all seen as threatening to the dominant culture of the 1950s) and the ways in which American Jews—many of whom were involved with labor organizing, trade unions, and the Communist Party—were perceived as possessing inviolable ethnic ties to the old country of Russia, then the Soviet Union, that rendered them implicitly traitorous (Suchoff 162). Anti-Semitic discourse has long constructed the Jew (especially the Jewish male) as sexually perverse, deviant, and other, yet somehow capable of wielding tremendous influence over centrally powerful institutions (such as the government and the media), a characterization we see in the play's depiction of Roy Cohn (Freeman 48–50). Moreover, Jews, we note in class, can pass and are often invisible, in the same way that homosexuals and communists figure as undetectable threats. The espionage trial of Julius and Ethel Rosenberg becomes a flash point for these anxieties. As Roy says of Ethel in the play, "That sweet unprepossessing woman, two kids, boo-hoo-hoo, reminded us all of our little Jewish mamas" (*Angels* 114). We discuss the Lavender scare and the ways in which communism and homosexuality are both constructed in the 1950s as invasive cancers that must be exorcized from the national body politic.[1]

Similarly, in the 1980s, HIV/AIDS, originally referred to as a "gay cancer" (and later Gay-Related Immune Deficiency [GRID]), was often constructed as a viral invasion spread by a secret, invisible community (Sontag 153). The dominant ideology was that gay men, through their aberrant lifestyle, were infecting the nation, and along the way taking innocent victims with them (such as thirteen-year-old Ryan White, a hemophiliac infected through a blood transfusion). AIDS was therefore a fitting punishment for an immoral lifestyle and identity. This ideology was articulated through both scientific and religious frameworks: as either the product of natural selection or a manifestation of a (Christian) God's will. The Reverend Jerry Falwell, for instance, argued that "AIDS is the wrath of a just God upon homosexuals." Pat Buchanan, Reagan's communications director, referred to AIDS as nature's "retribution" against gay men (qtd. in Shilts 311). Senator Jesse Helms (R-NC) and eight-time presidential candidate Lyndon LaRouche sought to impose a quarantine (Crimp, "How" 262); Helms and William F. Buckley thought HIV-positive people should have identifying tattoos (Crimp, "Cultural Analysis" 8; Bronski "Rewriting"). The threat of government-mandated quarantines and tattoos invoked the specter of the Holocaust. The sense that governmental indifference meant that American citizens were simply being left to die felt like the logical outcome of a new American political order characterized by free market individualism and the dictum "every man for himself." As Martin in *Angels* enthusiastically puts it, "It's a revolution in Washington . . . the end of Liberalism. The end of New Deal Socialism. . . . The dawning of a genuinely American political personality. Modeled on Ronald Wilson Reagan" (69).[2]

It is this neoliberal ethos that undergirds Louis's abandonment of Prior and animates his dread and shame. After leaving Prior, Louis asks, "Rabbi, what does the Holy Writ say about someone who abandons someone he loves at a time of great need? . . . [W]ho has this neo-Hegelian positivist sense of constant historical progress. . . . Maybe that person can't, um, incorporate sickness into his sense of how things are supposed to go." The Rabbi replies, "The Holy Scriptures have nothing to say about such a person" (31). Indeed, students generally don't like Louis—he abandons his boyfriend at his greatest moment of vulnerability—and are confused by his central role in the play. Louis is selfish and often unlikeable. In other words, he is flawed and human, presenting a challenging moral and theatrical role.

It's no secret that Louis is the character closest to Kushner in personal background and political outlook. Louis also arguably has a great deal in common with early 1990s New York City theatergoers, many of whom would have been Jewish and gay. Crucially, the play's moral critique is not, Look at those horrible people out there. Instead, it is, Look at these horrible people in here. The play asks Louis, and by extension the audience members, to question their own moral culpability in the world (a cornerstone of Jewish ethics).[3] *Angels* never lets the audience off the hook. It insists on complex self-reflection rather than easy moral or political answers (Omer-Sherman 97).

Along with this insistence on rigorous self-questioning, the play holds out the promise of radical forgiveness. Shockingly, powerfully, the play nears its end with Ethel and Louis reciting the Kaddish for Roy, suggesting that every death from AIDS is an innocent death, one that deserves to be sanctified. No one, even his most embittered enemies, gets to celebrate Roy's death from AIDS.[4] AIDS is never a punishment, and it is not something that people deserve because they are bad people—that is the rhetoric of the religious right. As Belize says, "He was a terrible person. He died a hard death. So maybe. . . . it's the hardest thing. Forgiveness. Which is maybe where love and justice finally meet. Peace, at least. Isn't that what the Kaddish asks for?" (*Angels* 256).

Because students have learned to interpret angels in literature and popular culture as symbols of goodness, it can be difficult for them to grasp their function in the play, especially since Kushner also makes them beautiful, polysexual, and seemingly fabulous. The fact that they choose Prior, a gay man with AIDS, as their prophet tempts students to see the angels as progressive figures whose values (of tolerance and sexual freedom) are in line with our own. But the Continental Angels choose Prior not because of his status as victim or martyr, but because of his social position as a man who comes from a long line (literally, a bloodline) of socially powerful white Christian men who have been in America for generations. To the angels, he represents not a future of sexual tolerance, multiracial harmony, and universal healthcare, but rather the past—of repression, slavery, and fatal illnesses.[5]

If Prior's life "stops"—that is, if he dies—the bloodline will be severed and the world (according to the angels' cosmology) will no longer "spin forward." It will no longer be wrecked by cultural "earthquakes"—social upheaval, migration, and racial integration. It will instead revert to "stasis"—becoming conservative and backward-looking. The angels' message to Prior—shut up and die—is effectively the same one communicated by the dominant culture of the 1980s to people with HIV/AIDS. As Prior says to the Angel of America: "Stop moving. That's what you want. Answer me. You want me dead!" She responds: "On you in your blood we have written: STASIS! THE END" (179–80). In sacrificing Prior, the angels have devised an answer to the social and political chaos that has plagued the earth—a final solution.

The temptation to give up, lie down, and die quietly must be resisted on the immediate level by Prior (he must survive) and, the play suggests, on a larger moral level, by the witnesses to history (we must never forget). As Prior says at the play's close, "We won't die secret deaths anymore." Prior demands, insists upon, "more life,"[6] while Belize reminds us that the world "only spins forward . . . the world doesn't spin backward. Listen to the world, to how fast it goes" (280, 266, 178–81). Kushner's mandate to "keep moving" is a corollary to "never forget"—the linking of past and present as a moral call to arms. Ultimately, *Angels* asks us to reject the conservatism and so-called stability of the 1950s and 1980s and keep moving forward. It is a play about refusing to live in the past. As Ethel (prophetically) tells Roy: "History is about to crack wide open. Millennium approaches" (118). The hateful racial, ethnic, sexual, religious, ideological, and geopolitical divisions of the 1980s are over, the play insists. Perestroika. Or are they?

In the same way that *Angels* is haunted by the 1950s, our current social and political climate is haunted by the 1980s. For my students, the historical figure of Roy Cohn was reanimated when they learned he had represented Donald Trump in court when Trump was accused in the 1990s of violating the Fair Housing Act (Brenner). Trump's call to "make America great again" resonates deeply with the cultural rhetoric and ideology of the 1980s. And Reagan is still invoked by political pundits as an aspirational figure. In a cultural moment characterized by political polarization, racial profiling, moral panic around immigration, and a newly empowered Far Right, the play's histories seem ever more relevant. Through memory and memorialization, we enact the Jewish ethical principle of *tikkun olam*—variously translated as to "heal" or "repair" the world (Omer-

Sherman 94). The promise of healing is specifically resonant in a play about AIDS; more broadly it enjoins us to mend the rifts of a divisive past. *Angels* is at once an impassioned reminder to never forget, to keep speaking the names of the dead, and to "keep moving"—just as the earth can only "spin forward"—and heal the world.

Notes

1. Recent revelations suggesting that Julius and Ethel Rosenberg may have been guilty of at least some of the charges brought against them do not change the fact that the public discourses surrounding the trial were steeped in anti-Semitism.

2. Theatergoers might hear in this line an ironic echo of "the dawning of the age of Aquarius" from the 1970s musical *Hair*.

3. The philosopher Maimonides's *The Guide for the Perplexed* is foundational in this regard. See Bicknell 534.

4. Many publications seemed to gloat over Cohn's death. See Cadden, "Strange Angel" 96.

5. Prior provides a lucid explication of the angels' cosmology in *Angels* 175–76.

6. In the afterword, Kushner states that he was inspired by Harold Bloom's translation of the Hebrew word for "blessing" as "more life" in Bloom's introduction to Olivier Revault d'Allonne's *Musical Variations on Jewish Thought* (Kushner 288).

Works Cited

Bicknell, Jeanette. "Self-Scrutiny in Maimonides' Ethical and Religious Thought." *Laval theologique et philosophique*, vol. 58, no. 3, 2002, pp. 531–43.

Brenner, Marie. "How Donald Trump and Roy Cohn's Ruthless Symbiosis Changed America." *Vanity Fair*, 28 June 2017, www.vanityfair.com/news/2017/06/donald-trump-roy-cohn-relationship.

Bronski, Michael. "Rewriting the Script on Reagan: Why the President Ignored AIDS." *The Forward*, 14 Nov. 2003, forward.com/news/7046.

Cadden, Michael. "Strange Angel: The Pinklisting of Roy Cohn." Garber and Walkowitz, pp. 93–105.

Crimp, Douglas, editor. *AIDS: Cultural Analysis / Cultural Activism*. October Books, 1988.

———. "Cultural Analysis / Cultural Activism." Crimp, *AIDS*, pp. 3–16.

———. "How to Have Promiscuity in an Epidemic." Crimp, *AIDS*, pp. 237–71.

Freeman, Jonathan. *Klezmer America: Jewishness, Ethnicity, Modernity*. Columbia UP, 2008.

Garber, Marjorie, and Rebecca L. Walkowitz, editors. *Secret Agents: The Rosenberg Case, McCarthyism and Fifties America*. Routledge, 1995.

Kushner, Tony. *Angels in America: A Gay Fantasia on National Themes*. Theatre Communications Group, 2010.

Omer-Sherman, Ranen. "Jewish/Queer: Thresholds of Vulnerable Identities in Tony Kushner's *Angels in America.*" *Shofar: An Interdisciplinary Journal of Jewish Studies*, vol. 25. no. 4, 2007, pp. 79–98.

Shilts, Randy. *And the Band Played On: Politics, People, and the AIDS Epidemic.* St. Martin's Press, 1987.

Showalter, Elaine. *Sexual Anarchy: Gender and Culture at the Fin-de-Siecle.* Penguin Books, 1990.

Sontag, Susan. *Illness as Metaphor and AIDS and Its Metaphors.* Doubleday, 1989.

Suchoff, David. "The Rosenberg Case and the New York Intellectuals." Garber and Walkowitz, pp. 155–69.

Part V

Multidisciplinary and Digital Humanities Approaches

Judah M. Cohen

Musical Theater as Literature: Art and Identity That Thrive on Change

The relation between musical theater and literature has a long and complicated history. When the Pulitzer committee awarded its drama prize to the musical satire *Of Thee I Sing* in 1932, it honored book and lyric writers George S. Kaufman, Morrie Ryskind, and Ira Gershwin but omitted composer George Gershwin, despite music's centrality to the show. Eighteen years later, the committee cited composer Richard Rodgers alongside lyricist Oscar Hammerstein II and book writer Joshua Logan for *South Pacific*, and it has cited the composers of winning musicals since. Yet even into the twenty-first century, literature's frequent integration with music—exemplified by the relation between the page and live performance—remains a subject of ambivalence. Recent Library of America editions compiling lyrics by Cole Porter and Ira Gershwin describe their subjects as "American Poets," while Lawrence Maslon's introduction to the Library's two-volume collection of classic musical theater scripts "celebrate[s] the gifted craftsmen who provided the words" (xii). Extricated from their musical settings, these well-deserved encomiums can nonetheless seem unsatisfying.

While perceptions of fundamental differences between music and literature may never resolve—note continued discussions about the choice of

Bob Dylan as the recipient of the 2016 Nobel Prize in Literature—musical theater presents opportunities to explore literature as a planned, interartistic partnership. This essay lays out an approach to musical theater as Jewish literature that speaks to broader, interdisciplinary expressions of identity and teamwork. As continuously changing fusions of verbal, sonic, and performative elements, musicals present literature as a multimediated process of narrative creation: ongoing, collaborative, and deeply dialogical.

Musical Theater as Literature

Scholarship on musical theater has grown immensely since the mid-1990s, building on central contributions from literature, performance studies, ethnic studies, American studies, and musicology. In addition to establishing a historical timeline and identifying canonical works and prominent creators, researchers have given questions of representation—including Jewish representation—a significant role. Andrea Most presented one key paradigm in her 2004 book *Making Americans: Jews and the Broadway Musical*, subjecting scripts and lyrics to literary and historical analyses to examine how Jewish authors created ethnic characters (whether Jews, African Americans, or Native Americans) that they produced on stage. Others, including John Bush Jones, Raymond Knapp (*American Musical and the Formation, American Musical and the Performance*), and Bruce Kirle, have taken similar approaches, exploring Jewish identity in musical theater as a flexible mode of expression that emphasizes the mediation between an active minority group and an art form often described as quintessentially American. Moreover, musicologists have undertaken intensive primary source studies and musical analyses of the work of individual composers or shows—including Philip Lambert's inquiry into the sounds of Jewishness in *Fiddler on the Roof* (138–81). More recent efforts have sought to bring these perspectives together, either through collected volumes (including Knapp et al.) or through increasingly nuanced essays in the journal *Studies in Musical Theatre*, resulting in vigorous academic forums that encourage interdisciplinary exchange, challenges, and reassessment.

Despite this scholarship, however, simplistic views of Jews and Broadway persist in popular media. Slickly produced works such as the 2013 documentary *Broadway Musicals: A Jewish Legacy* (directed by Michael Kantor) brashly overstate Broadway's "Jewish" character, juxtaposing images, anecdotes, and generalizations to reinforce myths of Jewish uniformity, achievement, and artistic dominance. Such attractive yet exaggerated perspectives require correctives that acknowledge musical theater's development in a Jewish population center (New York City) but avoid direct connections between artistic works and their creators' (presumed) identities in a broadly multiethnic environment.

Teaching Musicals as Jewish Literature in Process

The interest that musicals generate through high school and college drama programs opens the door to the course at the center of this essay, Musical Theater and Ethnic Representation: Jews and African Americans. Taught at Indiana University since 2009, the class balances broad perceptions of musicals as completed works with a more active view of these works as subject to constant change and modification over years of authorial collaboration. Kirle notes that even classic Jewish-themed musicals such as *Fiddler on the Roof* emerged from extensive negotiation among several collaborators, Jewish and otherwise, who intentionally sought to prioritize broad cultural appeal over Jewish specificity (144–52). Reviewing these negotiations, which continued well beyond the first performance, gives students a view of musicals as flexible containers of meaning that only appear to be frozen on the surface. By emphasizing how professionals craft and present musicals over time, the course looks at the form as a long-term, ongoing artistic dialogue.

To understand the broader artistic context in which this dialogue takes place, moreover, the course takes a comparative approach inspired by Adam Zachary Newton's concept of "facing" in literature, juxtaposing musicals reflecting black America and Jewish America into a progressive history across the twentieth and twenty-first centuries (see appendix). Students thereby learn how strategies of self-definition and self-realization are developed by artists in one often-marginalized American population through implied or direct interaction with artists in another. Exploring these two complementary histories together, moreover, gives students access to rich points of convergence, including the tendency of artists to adapt preexisting works into musical theater, their representations of communal trauma, and their comparative representations of the American South.

Preparing the Course: Harnessing Technology

While classroom discussion of conventional plays typically relies on published scripts, students examining works of musical theater require, at minimum, the coordination of text and music to gain entry into a meaningful experience. A high school or college course on musical theater thus faces two related challenges: teaching students how to "read" a musical in a classroom setting, and arranging available technology to make this process efficient.

Consumer technology both complements and complicates such matters. Whereas students in the 2000s could access a series of cast albums in the library reserves, digital streaming services increasingly allow students to listen almost anywhere, arguably making music more accessible than written texts. Instructors, consequently, face diverse and sometimes competing options. Some schools with dedicated music libraries have internal systems for digitizing and streaming music in their collections, allowing instructors to treat music and media as digital reserve materials. In the absence of such systems, however, instructors can access relatively low-cost commercial services such as *Spotify* or *Amazon Prime Music*, pay-based systems such as *iTunes* and *Amazon Music*, and sometimes university-based subscription services including the *Naxos Music Library* (which includes many cast albums). Subscription video channels, most notably the recent BroadwayHD, present another option with limited but growing resources at the time of this writing. Legally gray but easily accessible postings on *YouTube*, *Vimeo*, or other aggregate media services offer additional (if unreliable) options. Linking to these resources on password-protected instructional Web sites such as *BlackBoard* or *Canvas* allows students to access music alongside scripts, related Web sites, and supplementary materials. Maintaining these links requires vigilance, as materials get migrated to new internal course-management systems, legal standards change, and rights holders' agreements expire from one year to the next. Regular checks and work-arounds, however, have allowed the Indiana University course to include the same set of core works for over a decade.

Teaching students to integrate media with written scripts requires regular explanation and demonstration over the semester and helps students gain practical experience with a form of reading they typically find unfamiliar. Beyond mere mechanics, in-class demonstrations involving supplementary video where possible teach students to think more deeply about what a script actually signifies. Thus, early on the course takes students through a scene analysis—one good example is the filmed *Producers* number "The King of Broadway" to show how one performance brings together script-based, musical, choreographic, historical, and cultural conventions. As students move through the semester, this level of coordination between a show's study media (script, soundtrack) and its presentation in performance (video preserving live performance) becomes a symbol of the musical theater form, inuring students to the idea that literature inspires a search for experiences beyond the written word. By repeating this process with each featured show in the syllabus, the musical becomes to students both a definable work with permanent artifacts and a time-based work that changes with each staging.

Ancillary materials, posted by an enthusiastic fan community to a broad array of video and audio outlets, help to reinforce the balance between text and performance in the classroom. Discussions consequently can incorporate a large (if changing) array of video clips from Tony Award ceremonies, talk shows, promotional videos, and insider clearinghouses such as the Web site *American Theatre Wing* (www.americantheatrewing .org/). The vast amateur trade in noncommercial recordings can be helpful as well, with obvious caveats. When given clear viewing guidelines, students can use such video clips, in coordination with still images, as imperfect exemplars of the performed musical.

Musical Theater as Jewish Literature: The Parameters of Comparison

Musical theater histories by Larry Stempel, Raymond Knapp (*American Music and the Formation*), and others present the form as developing from loose collections of acts in the nineteenth century into increasingly unified, narrative-driven works (such as 1943's *Oklahoma*), with their cultural status rising accordingly. Adhering to this historical narrative, even with some skepticism, allows the course to establish its identity-based focus on Jews and African Americans in a period that covers more than a century: students examine the performance of ethnic stereotypes and then trace the legacy of such ubiquitous forms as the minstrel show and the ethnic impersonation act forward in time. Successive introductions to blackface and "Jewface" (a term recently popularized by Jody Rosen) create a baseline for evaluating the shows to come, while highlighting the persistence of these forms in American culture. Students learn, for example, the central role that Stephen Foster's minstrel songs such as "O Susannah" and "De Camptown Races" continue to hold in American society. Not only does this framing give students an idea of what to expect in the more unified works to come, but it also speaks to the richness of comparing works by Jewish and African American artists in parallel: students recognize the groups' different social standings and degrees of freedom of self-representation, while considering their common need to make artistic choices based on stereotypes—with subsequent repercussions. The musical art form thus emerges as a collection of representational strategies and responses to changing events rather than as a product of any one group's heritage or power. Students come to see a given work, moreover, as an outcome of artistic collaboration that reacts to what came before, further complicating the relation between themes of identity in the work and the identities of its creators.

Each of the twelve to fourteen shows that follow in the course adds its own layers of understanding, depicting new stages of self-realization (*Shuffle Along, Purlie*), massive pageants (*The Eternal Road*), African Americans through the eyes of a Jewish composer (*Porgy and Bess*), classic works in the form of African American–themed adaptations (*Carmen Jones, The Wiz*), the remembrance of past trauma (*Cabaret, Parade*), the biomusical in a new light (*Jelly's Last Jam*), nostalgia (*Fiddler on the Roof*), and the historical interactions of Jewish Americans and African Americans (*Caroline, or Change*). With occasional exceptions, each work receives a full week—two lectures—of consideration: one lecture providing context for the show, and a second focused on salient aspects of the show itself.

Here's one example using the 1937 show *The Eternal Road*—a work generally excluded from the standard musical theater canon. Introduced in the week after the musical or opera *Porgy and Bess* and before *Carmen Jones, The Eternal Road* exposes students to a neglected form of musical theater, the pageant, while exploring Jewish identity in the prewar Nazi era.

The week's first lecture familiarizes students with the pageant format, defined broadly by David Glassberg as a large-scale amateur "folk play" recounting local history and ending with a call for the community to embrace its past as it moves forward together (288). Students then learn about four major Jewish pageants in the 1930s and 1940s: *The Romance of a People*, which sold out Chicago's Soldier Field in July 1933, *The Eternal Road*, *We Will Never Die*, and the smaller piece *A Flag Is Born*. Newsreel footage of *Romance of a People* and excerpts from a Hollywood Bowl radio broadcast of *We Will Never Die*—both publicly available—address both the scale and the sound of these performances, affirming the significance of the pageant to Jewish American presentations of their own identity during a time of growing existential threat.

The second lecture launches into a discussion of *The Eternal Road*, which combined the talents of the major central European Jewish artists Meyer Weisgal, Max Reinhardt, Franz Werfel, and Kurt Weill. A Broadway show that reflects the vulnerability of the Jews in Europe, the nearly four-hour work uses an on-stage argument between a rabbi and a skeptic, who are hiding in their synagogue with other Jews from the pogrom outside, to present the broad expanse of Jewish biblical history. Grandiose in scale—requiring a complete reconstruction of the Manhattan Opera House stage—and philosophically dense, *The Eternal Road* challenges expectations of what musical theater is and what it can do. Recent recordings, including video of a 1999 production in Chemnitz, Germany, reinforce for students the challenges of staging the work, while helping them understand why it went untouched for sixty-two years after its premiere, despite critical acclaim (Weill et al.).

Repeated week to week, this format poses the musical as an endlessly shifting, heterogeneous range of expressions, with each show presenting a particular conception of the musical form rather than simply building a canon. This approach also opens deeper questions about the parameters of authentic representation, complicating an assumption that Jewish and African American artistic expression progressed from subordination to self-realization over the twentieth century. Ultimately, musicals present an imperfect solution to the quest for ethnic authenticity—where dialect, music, plot, and character react to old stereotypes but also establish new ones. Similarly valuable are the stories behind artists' creative choices: the relation between artists' personal backgrounds and their collaborative efforts, the ways artists harnessed different modes of expression to entertain and communicate, artists' interactions with critics and producers, and artists' changing relations to their own works from one staging to the next, or even one performance to the next.

Writing about Musical Theater

While students must learn to use a constellation of sensory modes to understand musicals, the course retains an emphasis on writing as a means of scholarly analysis and communication—but with the added challenge of translating multisensory experiences back into textual argument. Over the course of three short papers (about five pages each), students practice these skills by analyzing a single musical, comparing two musicals (or two versions of the same musical), and then choosing their own topic. Valuing creativity and risk-taking while promoting citation over implication, these paper assignments give students a chance to draw on the style of theater and art criticism that dominates popular journalism while also introducing an ethnographic level of observation. Students are also encouraged to consider musical theater as a lively ecosystem rather than a set of finished products.

Connecting to the Real World

The course benefits from musical theater's regular presence in the American cultural ecosphere, which opens a reliable connection between class material and contemporary events. Local touring companies and the campus theater department have brought musicals such as *Cabaret*, *The Producers*, and *The Wiz* to town, adding a level of relevance to class discussions. New musicals such as the short-lived *Soul Doctor*, which explores the lives of the "singing rabbi" Shlomo Carlebach and his friendship with the African American activist and jazz singer Nina Simone, have given students active works to monitor as they learn about the past. Recent live television musicals, including *The Wiz* and *Hairspray*, have shown how artists constantly update works for different media forms and audiences. And George C. Wolfe's ardent 2016 Broadway reconstruction of the story behind *Shuffle Along* added an invaluable perspective on the musical during the course's spring 2017 iteration. Combined with final lectures looking at materials from the most recent musical theater festivals, these contemporary productions emphasize the larger view of musicals as living creations that thrive on adaptation.

Musicals and the Flexibility of Jewish American Identity

When treated as a form of Jewish literature, musicals reveal the many dimensions inherent in reading, thinking about, and discussing the performance of identity in America in the twentieth and twenty-first centuries. While often directly linked to conventional literature—*Fiddler on the Roof* draws from Sholem Aleichem's Tevye stories, for example—the form embraces multisensory models of narrative creativity. Teaching this deep well of materials as the team-based, negotiated works that they are, particularly when done in conversation with works representing other groups such as African Americans, offers instructors of Jewish literature an ever-renewing way to address the narrative richness of Jewish American life as it expands beyond the page.

Works Cited

Gershwin, Ira. *Selected Lyrics*. Edited by Robert Kimball, The Library of America, 2009.

Glassberg, David. *American Historical Pageantry: The Uses of Tradition in the Early Twentieth Century*. U of North Carolina P, 1990.

Jones, John Bush. "Black and Jewish Musicals since the 1960s." *Our Musicals, Ourselves: A Social History of American Musical Theatre*, Brandeis UP, 2011, pp. 202–34.

Kantor, Michael, director. *Broadway Musicals: A Jewish Legacy*. 7th Art Releasing, 2013. DVD.

"The King of Broadway." *The Producers*, Columbia Pictures, 2006. DVD.

Kirle, Bruce. *Unfinished Business: Broadway Musicals as Works-in-Progress*. Southern Illinois UP, 2005.

Knapp, Raymond. *The American Musical and the Formation of National Identity*. Princeton UP, 2006.

———. *The American Musical and the Performance of Individual Identity*. Princeton UP, 2009.

Knapp, Raymond, et al., editors. *The Oxford Handbook of the American Musical*. Oxford UP, 2011.

Lambert, Philip. *To Broadway, to Life! The Musical Theater of Bock and Harnick*. Oxford UP, 2010.

Maslon, Lawrence. Introduction. *American Musicals, 1927–1949*, The Library of America, 2014, pp. xi–xiv.

Most, Andrea. *Making Americans: Jews and the Broadway Musical*. Harvard UP, 2004.

Newton, Adam Zachary. *Facing Blacks and Jews: Literature as Public Space in Twentieth-Century America*. Cambridge UP, 1999.

Porter, Cole. *Selected Lyrics*. Edited by Robert Kimball, The Library of America, 2006.

Rosen, Jody, compiler. *Jewface*. Reboot Stereophonic, 2006. Sound recording.

Shuffle Along; or, the Making of the Musical Sensation of 1921 and All That Followed. By George C. Wolfe, 26 March 2016, Music Box Theatre, New York.

Stempel, Larry. *Showtime: A History of the Broadway Musical Theater*. W. W. Norton, 2011.

Weill, Kurt, et al. *Der Weg der Verheissung: Ein biblisches Drama in vier Akten*. Arte, 2000. DVD.

Appendix: Recommended Musicals

Shuffle Along, Eubie Blake et al., 1921

Porgy and Bess, George Gershwin et al., 1935

The Eternal Road, Kurt Weill and Franz Werfel, 1937

Carmen Jones, Georges Bizet and Oscar Hammerstein II, 1943

Fiddler on the Roof, Jerry Bock and Sheldon Harnick, 1964

Cabaret, John Kander et al., 1966

Purlie, Gary Geld et al., 1970

The Wiz, Charlie Smalls and William F. Brown, 1975

The Grand Tour, Jerry Herman et al., 1979

Jelly's Last Jam, Jelly Roll Morton et al., 1994

Parade, Jason Robert Brown and Alfred Uhry, 1998

Caroline, or Change, Jeanine Tesori and Tony Kushner, 2004

Soul Doctor: Journey of a Rockstar Rabbi, Daniel S. Wise, 2013

Jennifer Caplan

Serious Fun: Teaching Jewish American Humor

Jewish humor sits at the nexus of Internet culture, social criticism, and gender politics in America. Humor is specific to both time and place, so the story of Jewish American humor is really the story of Jews in America, and the application of humor theory allows students to see the subversion inherent in most Jewish humor, as well as understand the social capital that has been garnered through the development of this mode of cultural expression. The course I teach on Jewish American humor begins and ends with questions about the nature of that humor: What is it? Who performs it? Is it the same today as a century ago? Can non-Jews do it? By the end, students recognize that these questions are as much about contemporary Jewish identity as they are about a specific medium. Early on we watch portions of *When Jews Were Funny*, a documentary in which most of the older generation of Jewish comics refuse the term "Jewish humor" altogether, while the younger comics embrace it. This conversation between older and younger comics sets up questions about the nature of Jewish humor and its origins in Jewish culture, selfhood, and community.

Because it is highly visible and has a canon that grows daily, thanks to the rapidity of Internet content delivery, Jewish humor is a popular course topic while also being difficult to define. The syllabus for this course needs updating regularly, and to teach it effectively I must pay attention to trends, since students will be aware of and excited to discuss media such as Web comics, *YouTube* sensations, memes, and viral videos. The course also works best when scheduled like a film studies class, with additional film-screening times separate from class sessions. The interdisciplinary nature of the subject makes it an excellent gateway course for both Jewish and religious studies, drawing in many students who would not ordinarily be interested in those topics. Every semester this course yields several new majors and minors. Drawing on iterations of the course taught at a range of institutions, this essay will offer some suggestions about course design, topic selection, assignments, and managing classroom discussions of volatile topics.

Course Structure

As with many courses, the syllabus for a course on Jewish American humor can be organized chronologically or thematically. The most successful approach is broadly chronological but also thematic, especially when covering the mid–twentieth century, when many different humor forms became popular. Nevertheless, this course is as much about Jewish immigration and Americanization as it is about humor, and the chronological approach helps students see the way Jewish humor has changed over time. The type of humor Jews produce is intrinsically tied to their place in America at a given moment in time. Showing that correlation requires a chronological scaffold for the course.

Beyond that scaffold, however, sessions can be focused around themes or ideas. To start the semester I work on creating a shared theoretical vocabulary, so that as a class we can meaningfully engage with the material. Students read foundational texts in humor theory (Freud's *Jokes and Their Relation to the Unconscious*, Bergson's *On Laughter*, and Oring's *Joking Asides*) as well as texts that will give them an introduction to American Judaism (Kaplan's *Judaism as a Civilization* and Glazer's *American Judaism*). I also assign readings that provide a broad analysis of Jewish humor, such as Telushkin's *Jewish Humor* or Alan Dundes's or Riv-Ellen Prell's work on Jewish mothers and the stereotype of the Jewish American princess. These early weeks are the most challenging for many students, as Freud's text is difficult, especially for students who have never previously read his work. While these texts risk discouraging students, they prepare them to treat the course seriously. Students produce higher-quality work when they understand that there is an academic language for discussing humor.

Around week four the course moves from theory to practice with a discussion of Yiddish theater and film. This is, of course, an arbitrary starting point. I reference works that draw on older humor traditions, such as the stories of Sholem Aleichem, but generally do not ask the students to read primary texts that are not American in origin. In part this is to avoid trying to include everything, or presenting a work as the ur-text of Jewish humor. Looking earlier than the nineteenth century, or branching out into places where the experience of Jews was quite different, would essentialize the notion of humor in a way that loses the distinctions vital for understanding humor's social function. Humor is culturally and linguistically specific; to include texts from too many times, places, or languages could cause students to see funniness as a sui generis category. This course asks them to turn a keen analytical eye on the material, and to do that it is important to limit the cultural variables at play. To provide students with better context for understanding Jewish humor cross-culturally without losing the focus on American culture, instructors could pair complementary secondary sources, such as portions of Ruth Wisse's *No Joke* and Jeremy Dauber's even more extensive *Jewish Comedy: A Serious History*, which look at Jewish humor broadly construed, with readings about specific elements of Jewish American life.

After introducing students to Yiddish theater, I can discuss the relation between it and vaudeville: Yiddish theater was designed for a parochial audience and largely focuses on trying to be high art, while vaudeville is consciously populist and middle- to lowbrow. I also introduce acts such as Fanny Brice, the Marx Brothers, and the Three Stooges. The Three Stooges' *You Nazty Spy* tends to come as a revelation to most students. The Stooges have not typically been seen as part of the tradition of Jewish humor in the same way the Marx Brothers have, but *You Nazty Spy* (and its sequel *I'll Never Heil Again*) demonstrate to students that their content is Jewish, as well as subversive. There is no single, agreed-upon definition of what makes a piece of humor Jewish, so part of the course is spent navigating that line, and students can use the tools of the course (i.e., Telushkin's concept of "Jewish sensibilities" [16], chapter 10 in Oring, or Freud's examples of jokes) to decide whether they believe a given piece of humor is Jewish.

From vaudeville the course moves to radio and television through *The Goldbergs*, a show that ran on both platforms. I then work thematically through the years between roughly 1950 and 1975, focusing on race, gender, class, and other social and cultural issues in mid-twentieth-century

America. These units help students understand the rapid changes that took place in Jewish American life after World War II. The opening of neighborhoods and towns that had been exclusively white caused a rapid demographic shift in where and how Jews were living. That shift trickled down into changes in synagogue attendance patterns, the growth of Jewish community centers and Jewish day schools, and a new attitude toward Jewish difference among Jewish humorists.

The unit on television includes not only *The Goldbergs* but also *Texaco Star Theatre*, *The George Burns and Gracie Allen Show*, *Your Show of Shows*, and others. Covering roughly the same time period, a unit on the history and development of Jewish life and culture in the Catskills explores both the post–World War II social changes that affected Jewish Americans and the way those changes were reflected in the humor being produced. Buddy Hackett's "Chinese Waiter Sketch" ("Original Chinese Waiter") works well here, as it clearly demonstrates to students the way that Jewish performers (like Sophie Tucker), who just a few years before had only been allowed to perform in blackface, now felt comfortable engaging with the white hegemonic superstructure of America and staked their claim as white performers able to mock not only their own ethnic qualities but other groups' as well. Lawrence Epstein's *The Haunted Smile* gives students a good overview of Jews' complicated social place in America after World War II, and for more depth it could be supplemented with selections from other texts, such as Eric Goldstein's *The Price of Whiteness* or Melanie Kaye/Kantrowitz's *The Colors of Jews*. From the Catskills I move to underground humor, or "sick humor," and the rise of political humor in the 1960s and 1970s. One unit includes musical satire with selections from Mickey Katz, Allan Sherman, Tom Lehrer, and Kinky Friedman,[1] and another focuses on stand-up comedy, primarily on the work of Lenny Bruce and Mort Sahl.

The final third of the course covers the heyday of stand-up comedy through twenty-first-century humor and includes a focus on Neil Simon and Woody Allen and a unit on gender, which covers not only the women involved in humor but the ongoing toxic nature of Jewish humor regarding women. There are an increasing number of Jewish women in comedy, but the majority of men and women comics still find Jewish women, and their bodies, an easy source of laughs (Amy Schumer, for example). Although only one week is specifically devoted to gender, it is a theme throughout the semester—for instance, Dundes's essay, which students read in the first two weeks of the semester, introduces them to gender dynamics in Jewish humor. This is followed by a unit on the resurgence of Jews on television, focused mainly on *Seinfeld* and Larry David. Also included is a unit on Jews and pornography, which explores where the line between blue, or risqué, humor and pornography is and why so many Jewish comedians work in this area. Howard Stern, Sarah Silverman, and *Broad City* provide good examples during this unit. The course concludes with a discussion of humor, politics, and Jewishness using the work of Jon Stewart, Bill Maher, and Al Franken.

Assignments

Several types of writing-focused assignments work well for this course. I assign traditional papers with prompts that ask students to think about humor in its social context. These focus on gender, politics, embodiment, assimilation, and other broad topics related to Jewish American life. Additionally, students produce "humor analyses," which are formal close readings of the humor itself. Students apply the terminology and tools of humor theory to a joke, scene, sketch, song, or other piece of humor. The terminology comes from Freud (*innocent* versus *tendentious*), Oring (*benign violation, defense mechanism, superiority*), and lecture (*verbal wit, incongruity*). In this way students are able to formally break down the specific mechanisms of humor and speak cogently about them, while also placing Jewish humor in a larger conversation about Jews in America.

The important thing is to ensure that students are watching the films and episodes together. Previously, the course was offered twice a week, and clips were shown in class, but students were asked to view complete works on their own. This was generally unsuccessful because there is something psychologically important about watching humor in a group; individuals laugh more and differently in a group than alone. Without this feedback, students lose important analytical data. Scheduling an additional afternoon or evening film session is vital. Throughout the semester there will be some students each week who can't make a particular session, and I try to organize them into a secondary small group, so they still have the experience of watching the material with others.

This course in Jewish humor is very adaptable. I first taught it as a small advanced seminar and then twice more as an introductory course at a large research university with a sizeable Jewish population. I taught it at a small, private liberal arts college in the South with a very small Jewish population as well as at a small, private liberal arts university in the Northeast. I have found that it does not matter whether the school has a Jewish population; this subject appeals to students broadly. And teaching the course to a predominantly non-Jewish student population does not change the amount of background material the class needs to succeed. Many Jewish college students who enroll in my course tend not to know the history of the Jews in America, especially the early history. Material about the Catskills may overlap with stories some students have heard from their grandparents, but even those instances are fewer each year. The best approach is to pitch the course at an introductory level regardless of the students' Jewish literacy or the ethnic makeup of the students at that institution—assume nothing and be prepared to unpack even basic Jewish terms.

One caveat is that the instructor must stay abreast of current conversations about controversial artists or texts, and be prepared for students to struggle with challenging material. Some examples, such as Woody Allen, are perhaps easy to spot; instructors will have to decide for themselves whether to include Allen's work and how to frame the conversation around him, his art, and the accusations against him. But keeping up with Amy Schumer's racist comments, Jeffrey Ross's most recent off-color roast, or current views of Joan Rivers's internalized misogyny requires ongoing work. The inclusion of politically or socially challenging material is vital to the course, and students seem very interested in, and divided about, the question of comedic immunity and the comic's role as a social observer. Staying ahead of the conversation on as many comedians as possible will allow the instructor to craft more meaningful class discussions.

This course on Jewish American humor can be tailored to specific interests. The course lends itself to sophisticated discussions about the relation between popular culture and race, gender, sexuality, class, and many other socially relevant issues. Humor feels familiar to students, and students from a range of backgrounds approach it as something they both understand and want to know more about. A course on Jewish American humor is an important addition to a Jewish studies curriculum because it allows students to explore so many of the fundamental questions about the relation between Judaism and Jewishness in America through a medium that also asks them to engage with psychology, sociology, literary criticism, film studies, cultural studies, gender theory, and many other disciplinary approaches. There are almost limitless theoretical and methodological approaches to the subject.

Note

1. I tend to focus on songs that have explicit Jewish religious or cultural references. See, for example, Katz, "Duvid" and "She'll"; Sherman's "Harvey and Sheila," "Hello Muddah, Hello Fadduh," "The Streets of Miami," and "The Twelve Gifts of Christmas" in *My Son, the Greatest*; Lehrer's "Hanukkah in Santa Monica," "National Brotherhood Week," and "Vatican Rag" in *The Tom Lehrer Collection*; and Friedman's "Ride 'Em Jewboy," "They Ain't Makin' Jews Like Jesus Anymore," and "We Reserve the Right to Refuse Service to You" in *The Best of Kinky Friedman*.

Works Cited

Bergson, Henri. *Laughter: An Essay On the Meaning of the Comic*. Arc Manor, 2008.

Dauber, Jeremy. *Jewish Comedy: A Serious History*. W. W. Norton, 2017.

Dundes, Alan. "The Jewish American Princess and the Jewish American Mother in American Jokelore." *Cracking Jokes*, by Dundes, Ten Speed Press, 1987, pp. 62–81.

Epstein, Lawrence. *The Haunted Smile*. PublicAffairs, 2001.

Freud, Sigmund. *Jokes and Their Relation to the Unconscious*. W. W. Norton, 1990.

Friedman, Kinky. *The Best of Kinky Friedman*. Shout! Factory, 2006.

Glazer, Nathan. *American Judaism*. U of Chicago P, 1988.

Goldstein, Eric. *The Price of Whiteness*. Princeton UP, 2006.

Hackett, Buddy. "The Original Chinese Waiter." *The Original Chinese Waiter Comedy Album*, Pickwick Records, 1961.

Kaplan, Mordechai. *Judaism as a Civilization*. Jewish Publication Society, 2010.

Katz, Mickey. "Duvid Crockett." *Greatest Shticks*, Koch Records, 2000.

———. "She'll Be Coming 'Round the Katzkills." *Greatest Shticks*. Koch Records, 2000.

Kaye/Kantrowitz, Melanie. *The Colors of Jews*. Indiana UP, 2007.

Lehrer, Tom. *The Tom Lehrer Collection*. Shout! Factory, 2010.

Oring, Elliott. *Joking Asides: The Theory, Analysis, and Aesthetics of Humor*. Utah State UP, 2016.

Prell, Riv-Ellen. *Fighting to Become Americans: Jews, Gender, and the Anxiety of Assimilation*. Beacon Press, 1999.

Sherman, Allan. *My Son, the Greatest*. Rhino Records, 1988.

Telushkin, Joseph. *Jewish Humor*. Quill Press, 1992.

The Three Stooges. *I'll Never Heil Again*. Columbia Pictures, 1941.

———. *You Nazty Spy*. Columbia Pictures, 1940.

When Jews Were Funny. Directed by Alan Zweig, First Run Features, 2013.

Wisse, Ruth. *No Joke: Making Jewish Humor*. Princeton UP, 2015.

Laini Kavaloski

Digital Jews: Questioning Borders in Jewish American Literature

Representations of history, literature, and even national identity in Jewish contexts are being mediated in new ways, yet teaching practices in Jewish studies do not always reflect these shifts. Emerging media genres such as digital games and hybrid activist Web sites are changing definitions of literature as well as perceptions of diaspora and homeland in the twenty-first century. Benedict Anderson's theory of print-based communities has been revised to reflect human-machine interactions based on highly networked forms of media that instantaneously travel across borders. Not only do computer-based media reshape the ways that communities are constructed, but these media also represent real-world geographies that shift the ways we think about borders and boundaries (Murray 6). The conceptual and spatial questions of homeland (both Jewish and otherwise) intersect in these new forms in profound ways. My course Digital Jews explores the ways that established and emerging digital forms shift our relation to borders. First, it introduces a wide geographical and theoretical context for thinking about the boundaries of Jewish American literature, one that I argue necessarily moves Jewish American literature beyond the confines of the United States and the field of Jewish studies.[1] Second, the course explores the ways that the devices and rhetorics of digital media produce alternative understandings of Jewish homeland, particularly in relation to Israel.[2] Third, as a course based in digital design, Digital Jews asks students to produce digital works that engage with the issues we examine in class. The critical digital practices that are used in the creative process allow students to reimagine definitions of homeland and narratives of conflict and territoriality.

This course explores these pertinent contemporary questions through multiple literary forms such as the novel, the graphic narrative, experimental Web sites, digital games, and hypertext fiction. In doing so, it challenges the national, theoretical, and formal boundaries of Jewish literature. Questions include: In what ways do various literary forms engage intersecting identities and representations of nationhood? How do digital works challenge traditional boundaries of Jewish American literature? How are texts about Jewish issues shaped or illuminated by larger theoretical frameworks? The first part of this course asks how individual and public memory and emotions move through objects, places, and institutions and examines the repercussions of these circulations. The second part of the course explores the ways memory and structures of territoriality move into digital texts, and the third and final unit of the course asks students to create media artifacts that take up the issues raised in class. By addressing some of the most pressing issues of our time head on, students begin to understand the ways that Jewish American literature is inseparable from wider questions of historiography, transnationalism, and literary form.

Transnational Memory and Identity

The first part of the course uses contemporary literature (two novels and a graphic memoir) to open up questions about Jewish memory and its relation to the Holocaust, feelings of Jewish insecurity (both inside and outside of the United States), and the ways that gender identity, religious practice, and nationalism complicate memory and insecurity. Though all written in English, these works are transnational: Nicole Krauss's *Great House* (written in London, Israel, and the United States and published in the United States); Miriam Libicki's graphic novel *Jobnik!: An American Girl's Adventure in the Israeli Army* (written in Israel, Canada, and the United States and published in the United States); and Shani Boianjiu's *The People of Forever Are Not Afraid: A Novel* (written and published in the United States by an Israeli author).

Krauss's *Great House* introduces the themes we explore in the course. Krauss's novel centers on the life of a desk that deeply affects four families. The huge writing desk originates in the pre–World War II Weisz family study in Hungary and later enters the lives of three other Jewish families in London, New York, and Israel. The seemingly disconnected chapters of the book become intertwined through the characters' relation to the desk. For one of the characters, Weisz, the desk becomes a symbol of an intense desire to return to an impossible state of wholeness—to a time and place before the Holocaust and to a stable and uncomplicated Jewish existence. Reading and discussing the novel, students explore how feelings and desires can become attached to external objects that are representative of a collective Jewish consciousness and the repercussions of these attachments.

Weisz's lifework is to recreate his father's study in a house on the outskirts of Jerusalem by retrieving the original furniture that was confiscated by the Nazis in the 1940s. The act of bringing the furniture to Jerusalem displaces these returned objects from their country of origin, and the process of recreating the study subverts the traditional Jewish notion of diaspora. As Weisz gathers the furniture in Jerusalem, he recognizes that the recovery of lost objects has failed to return him to a prior reality; instead, the attempt reveals a destructive temptation to counter the dispossession of his family by possessing or regaining material objects, including the desk. When Weisz first enters the Jerusalem house, the man he bought it from tells him, "When I came here the floor was still littered with pistachio shells the Arab had eaten before he fled with his wife and children" (285). So the house that contains the recreated study, a potential symbol of Jewish wholeness, has also witnessed a dispossession. The Jerusalem to which Weisz comes is not a redemptive space—instead, it is marked by territorialization. In class we discuss the ways that the novel frames the collapse of ancient and modern desires to return to wholeness in settings in Hungary, London, New York, and Israel.[3]

The desk in Krauss's text introduces and connects the various media forms and theoretical threads studied in this course. In the context of the discussion of mediated homelands and return, the diasporic desk symbolizes the limited story of Jewish return, an impossible ultimate arrival. Yet the function of the desk also suggests that the process through which memory gains resonances through objects is inextricably intertwined with the creative act of assembling histories, identities, and political processes. In the context of emerging computer-based media, the desk takes on further resonances, symbolizing not only loss but also creative potential.

The desk comes to stand in for the mediated future—for the computer world as well as its storehouse of memory.[4]

Krauss's novel, too, illustrates the ways that Jewish American literature is inseparable from narratives of memory, power, and militarism that circulate in the global arena. As students read this work, they engage with representations of Jewish exile and return that are inextricable from the memories and feelings that are tied to places and events. These intensities shape the characters' relations to national spaces, communities, and governments, as well as to other individuals.[5]

Libicki's graphic memoir moves the class from questions about the ways that emotion and memory flow through objects and nationalist narratives to questions of belonging and gender identity in Israel. *Jobnik!* synthesizes Libicki's imaginary conception of Israel as the Jewish homeland with her lived experience in the Israeli army during 2000 and 2001. Libicki's memoir complicates the rhetoric of homeland and return that surrounds the Israeli-Palestinian conflict, and the narratives of gendered nationalism that are prevalent in the military.

One of the pedagogical benefits of teaching Libicki's text is that it spatializes Miriam's complex identity positions in ways that are visually tangible for students. So too, analyzing the visual medium gives students practice with rhetorical devices that are present in digital form as well. The spatial representations of Miriam's memories in this work reveal the difficulty Miriam has reconciling state violence with her identities. Her position as a woman, a low-status *jobnik* ("office worker") in the army, an American, and a nonnative Hebrew speaker put her in a position of relative powerlessness in a system that values physical strength, masculinity, military status, and native language ability. While she positions herself as a citizen of both the United States and Israel, the graphic renderings of her ambivalence toward Israeli power create another story of identity, one that suggests a connection between her own gendered identity position in the Israeli Defense Forces (IDF) and larger systems of violence and territorial division (Kavaloski, "Contested Spaces"). The panels in figure 1 show how Miriam's memories of Yitzhak Rabin's assassination intersect with her feelings about Israel and Jewish insecurity in the larger world, as well as with her feelings about her position in the IDF.

By examining these complex and often contradictory narratives of identity and belonging in graphic form, students engage with various definitions of Jewishness and are able to discuss the ways that intersecting identity positions such as Miriam's are part of larger conversations in gender studies, ethnic studies, critical security studies, and new media studies, among others.

Figure I. Libicki, *Jobnik!*, p. 73.

Digital Homelands

The second part of the course explores the ways that digital literary works such as interactive games, activist Web sites, and hypertext fiction are shifting definitions of identity, history, and territory. Course texts may include *Zochrot.org*, an Israeli activist Web site; *PeaceMaker*, an interactive political game by ImpactGames; and *The Jew's Daughter*, an experimental hypertext fiction by Judd Morrissey.

The experimental approaches of *Zochrot.org* are particularly helpful for thinking about the ways that theory, identity, and historiography affect and shape physical landscapes. This hybrid Web project, first created by Eitan Bronstein in 2002, has come to include a digital and virtual interactive mapping project, an archive of testimonies by Israeli military leaders and Palestinian refugees, a gallery of digitized art installations, and an interactive GPS-based augmented-reality application. The site is concerned with revising the dominant history of the founding of Israel, Jewish identity, and prescriptive ideas of belonging. *Zochrot.org* does not eclipse the Jewish story; rather, the site respatializes the Jewish story in the wider context of a land-based history.

The networked and hypertext models on the *Zochrot* site complicate fixed perceptions of Israeli and Palestinian terrain. For example, the "Testimonies" tab on the site includes stories in the form of images, texts, video files, and interviews. The testimonies are narrated by Jewish immigrants, displaced Palestinians, and second-generation Israeli citizens (among others). By including this wide range of land-based stories told by Jews, Christians, Muslims, and Bedouins, the Web site reveals a longer and more extensive shared history. Stories across what are often seen as religious and ethnic divisions reveal common experiences of everyday life.

Indeed, the *Zochrot* site illustrates the new ways in which representations of history, literature, and even national identity in Jewish contexts are being mediated. Emerging media genres like the one represented by this Web site are changing the ways users understand the concepts of diaspora and homeland.[6] Stories that are told through multimedia digital forms and accessed by computer have a unique ability to represent space and spatial properties. These stories may present real-world spaces, as in the video interviews on *Zochrot.org*, or simulated spaces that depict either real or imaginary locations, as in video games. In literary narrative games like *Gone Home*, *Dear Esther*, and *1979 Revolution*, the user can navigate through virtual landscapes and maps that mark terrain. The player moves north or south on the screen to "walk" or carry out an action. The *Zochrot* Web site does not offer the same degree of spatial mimicry as games like these, but it does allow the user to navigate the screen "maps" that make visible common Israeli and Palestinian histories. The layers of hyperlinks within the site, in the form of images, maps, and text, create complex assemblages of memories and narratives that defy singular exclusionary histories.

The intertwining human histories, network aesthetics, and technological potentials within the *Zochrot* site reveal that a person is not insulated from outside forces but constantly influenced by them. The *Zochrot* Web site illustrates the interdependency of those who reside together on common territory, despite their perceived differences. Here, subjects and objects are both recalibrated as assemblages that are animate, entangling, and never inert passivities.

Critical Digital Practices

Students spend the third part of the course designing and creating digital works that engage with issues we have discussed in class, so that they not only read, interact with, and critique texts but also participate in the knowledge-making process. As students create digital stories such as comics, blogs, and games for readers, the class reflects on the knowledge-making processes that affect the ways they think about and perceive the world around them. In doing so, they grapple with how literature and media represent and challenge questions of Jewish identity, memory, and geopolitical power. Through this process, students encounter the affective, aesthetic, and technical aspects of the literature and technologies studied in class. Thus, students reflect on ways that their digital practices contribute to wider theoretical and institutional conversations.

The collaborative process of making media spans a five-to-six-week period and extends the formal and analytic frames of the course to include critical design frames for critique and for creative building practices. During this period, students work in groups based on common research interests, which they develop around topics and readings from the earlier part of the course. Each group creates five deliverables: the media object itself (a digital game, blog, digital story, or graphic narrative); an illustrated proposal of the project; a team Web site for uploading the proposal, team information, story link, and self-critique; a trailer for the story (a one-to-two-minute video teaser); and a five-to-seven-minute formal presentation of the digital story or game. By working in collaborative groups that produce artifacts for public audiences, students often invest in the project in a way that is unusual in the literature or writing classroom.

Not only do students find designing media and games exciting, but the process also facilitates deeper understandings of narrative structure and gives students a rare opportunity to participate in the process of knowledge production. As students create these mini–knowledge machines, they become cognizant of the learning outcomes for the digital story users. In the process of creating their projects, students pay particular attention to the ways that the story structure (the narrative development, the pathways of the game, and the conceptual architecture) and the design elements (sounds, images, and colors) affect the themes of the game or story, the story arc, the user environment, and the learning outcomes. When students craft stories and experiences for other users, they are able to reflect on the historical and narrative processes that affect the ways they perceive the world around them.

Digital Jews highlights pertinent issues in contemporary Jewish life through close reading and active, collaborative work. Through textual analyses of contemporary print works, students are introduced to questions of Jewish memory and identity. By interacting with digital works, students are able to experience the ways that feelings and memories associated with Jewish identity move into nonlinear, hyperlinked, or palimpsestic forms. In the final part of the course, students research, design, and build layered, networked narratives to reimage the boundaries of Jewish American literature to include wider geographical and theoretical spaces.

Notes

1. Benjamin Schreier argues in *Impossible Jew* that Jewish American literature must necessarily be situated within the larger context of critical literary studies.

2. There is a history of Jewish homeland that refers not to Israel per se, but to theoretical spaces, texts, and geographical locations outside of Israel.

3. For a further discussion of the ways that feelings are connected to particular lost objects and worlds in Krauss's *Great House*, see Kavaloski, "Territorializing the Good Life."

4. Just after World War II, the Cold War scientist Vannevar Bush, frustrated by the limited human ability to access information, imagined an early form of desktop computer based on a writing desk. In a 1945 article, Bush describes his invention as including mechanized storage for books, records, and communications: "it consists of a desk, and while it can be presumably operated from a distance, it is primarily a piece of furniture at which [people] work" (104).

5. Gilles Deleuze describes intensity as a principle of production that detects difference or rupture (*Repetition*).

6. The intersection of textual, visual, spatial, and aural and affective affordances in emerging media create an alternative expressive discourse, one that "refuses the modern occidental separation of ethics and aesthetics, culture and politics" (Gilroy 38–39).

Works Cited

Anderson, Benedict. *Imagined Communities: Reflections of the Origin and Spread of Nationalism*. Verso, 1983.

Boianjiu, Shani. *The People of Forever Are Not Afraid*. Hogarth Press, 2013.

Bush, Vannevar. "As We May Think." *Atlantic Monthly*, vol. 176, July 1945, pp. 101–08.

Dear Esther. Created by Dan Pinchbeck, The Chinese Room, 2016.

Deleuze, Gilles. *Repetition and Difference*. Translated by Paul Patton, Columbia UP, 1994.

Gilroy, Paul. *The Black Atlantic*. Harvard UP, 1993.

Gone Home. Created by Steve Gaynor, Fullbright, 2013.

The Jew's Daughter. Created by Judd Morrissey, 2000, www.thejewsdaughter.com.

Kavaloski, Laini. "Contested Spaces in Graphic Narrative: Refiguring Intersecting Homelands through Miriam Libicki's *Jobnik! An American Girl's Adventures in the Israeli Army*." *Studies in Comics*, vol. 6, no. 2, 2015, pp. 231–51.

———. "Territorializing the Good Life: Fetishism of Commodity and Homeland in Nicole Krauss's *Great House*." *The Good Life and the Greater Good in a Global Context*, edited by Laura E. Savu, Rowman and Littlefield, 2015, pp. 123–36.

Krauss, Nicole. *Great House*. W. W. Norton, 2010.

Libicki, Miriam. *Jobnik! An American Girl's Adventures in the Israeli Army*. Real Gone Girl, 2008.

Murray, Janet. "Inventing the Medium." *The New Media Reader*, edited by Noah Wardrip-Fruin and Nick Montfort, MIT Press, 2003.

1979 Revolution: Black Friday. Created by Navid Khonsari, iNK Studios, 2016.

PeaceMaker. Created by Asi Burak and Eric Brown, Impact Games / MIT, 2007.

Schreier, Benjamin. *Impossible Jew: Identity and the Reconstruction of Jewish American Literary History*. New York UP, 2015.

Zochrot. "Testimonies." *Zochrot.org*, 2014–present, zochrot.org/en/testimony/all.

Temma Berg

After the Golem: Teaching Golems, Kabbalah, Exile, Imagination, and Technological Takeover

The golem is an elusive creature. From a religious perspective it enacts spirit entering matter, a creation story of potential salvation crossed with reprehensible arrogance. As a historical narrative, the golem story becomes a tale of Jewish powerlessness and oppression, of pogroms and ghettoization, of assimilation and exile, and, sometimes, of renewal. As the subject of a course in women, gender, and sexuality studies, the golem narrative can be seen as a relentless questioning of otherness and identity and as a revelation of the complex intersectionalities of gender, class, sexuality, race, disability, and ethnicity. As a philosophical motif, the ambiguous figure of the golem represents our human fears that we are not the autonomous individuals we believe ourselves to be. Haunted by specters of artificiality and automatism, we wonder whether we are unique individuals or inexorably programmed by social, cultural, psychological, and biological forces we are just beginning to fathom. As a Jewish story, the golem narrative illuminates the relentless history of anti-Semitism and resistance to blood libels of all sorts, hope for the future as well as despair, and, most of all, the need for questioning any narrative we are given if we want to uncover its potential significances.

The course The Dream of the Artificial Wo/Man: Golems and Cyborgs from Adam to *Ex Machina*[1] fulfills Gettysburg College's science, technology, and society requirement, so conversations about technology permeate the course: the class explores the possibilities of human enhancement, the ways technology transforms our lives for better and for worse, and the blurring borders between humans and their machines.

The course is designed to empower students to question rather than passively receive information. Because students are encouraged to offer unusual, even fantastic ideas, they become the primary means of bringing the unexpected into the class. Most importantly, this is an English course, and as such, it traces a reception history of the golem story. As a result, this body of Jewish literature becomes the shifting ground of a persistent, indeed universal, trope rather than simply a signifier of Jewish difference.

The Course: Texts, Themes, Topics

The course begins with "Kaddish," an episode from the 1996–97 season of the television series *The X-Files*, and two essays of Gershom Scholem, "Tradition and New Creation in the Ritual of the Kabbalists" and "The Idea of the Golem." "Kaddish" and the Scholem essays not only present the Jewish mystical tradition in radically different ways but also immediately demonstrate the mercurial quality of the golem story, which is easily adapted from a medieval morality tale to a narrative about the FBI investigation of supernatural phenomena.

The next text is Curt Leviant's 2007 edition of Yudl Rosenberg's *The Golem and the Wondrous Deeds of the Maharal of Prague*, which first appeared in 1909.[2] Class discussion revolves around early Jewish history, the blood libel, Kabbalah and mysticism, and the structural intricacies of Rosenberg's text. Two early films—Paul Wegener and Henrik Galeen's *The Golem: How He Came into the World* and Julien Duvivier's *Le golem*—illuminate different ways of rearranging the elements of the story, thus serving as an excellent introduction to the explanatory power of structuralism.

The class then reads texts that preceded Rosenberg's classic tale of the golem of Prague: Shakespeare's *The Tempest* and Mary Wollstonecraft Shelley's *Frankenstein*. Close reading of *The Tempest* provides an opportunity to investigate possible biographical connections between Shakespeare, John Dee, and the Maharal of Prague, as well as thematic connections between the fictional Ariel, Caliban, and the Prague golem. According to legend, the Maharal, a magician rabbi, created the Prague golem in 1580; according to Benjamin Woolley, John Dee's biographer, Dee was in Prague during the 1580s. Perhaps Dee brought stories of a mythical clay creature back to England from Prague, and these stories influenced Shakespeare when he created the ethereal Ariel and the tellurian Caliban, both of whom, like the golem, must obey their master.[3]

While golem stories are often written by men and about male golems and golem makers, golem stories written by women and about female golems and golem makers enrich the genre and enable students to think about the ways texts are gendered. Issues of gender also intersect with questions of literary authority.[4] Sara Ruddick's "Maternal Thinking" is key to unraveling the complexities of the mother-daughter bond in Cynthia Ozick's "Puttermesser and Xanthippe" and Marge Piercy's *He, She and It*. Donna Haraway's "A Cyborg Manifesto" not only inspired but also quietly permeates Piercy's novel, which raises critical questions about the blurring boundaries between animal and human, organism and machine, and physical and nonphysical in the new world of computer technology. Piercy and Haraway envision the possibilities of a cyborg world in which people are not afraid of their joint kinship with animals and machines and look forward to "a monstrous world without gender" (Haraway 181).

Because the course does not follow chronological order, and because the class discusses *The Tempest* and *Frankenstein* after Rosenberg's golem story, students see more clearly the extraordinary power of literary influence. They can ponder whether Mary Shelley knew about the golem story and suppose that she did. And they can imagine that Shakespeare might have used the Maharal as a prototype for Prospero,[5] just as Shelley tells us in her preface that reading German ghost stories sparked her tale of Victor Frankenstein (6).

Next students read Gustav Meyrink's *The Golem*. This work, which appeared serially from 1913 to 1914 and draws on many different sources (folkloric as well as occult), places the golem story firmly at its center. Alchemy, tarot, German expressionism, ghettoes, and the rise of modernism play an important part in class conversation. Sigmund Freud's "The 'Uncanny'" is introduced here, but the uncanny remains an important concept throughout the course, which deals with what is and is not human, what is and is not imaginary, what is repressed and returns, and the unexpected pleasures of involuntary repetition.

Michael Chabon's *The Amazing Adventures of Kavalier and Clay* brings in the cultural work of comic book superheroes and their close proximity to the Holocaust. The class talks about Walter Benjamin's "The Work of Art in the Age of Mechanical Reproduction," crypto-Jews, and homosexuality, and the discussion touches on different film versions of *Superman*. In fall 2015, students brought in the latest *Superman* film (*Man of Steel*) as part of their group presentation and emphasized that in this cinematic iteration Superman becomes an illegal alien and thus ironizes contemporary xenophobia in the United States. The 2017 film *Wonder Woman*, which stars the Israeli Gal Gadot, raises questions about the politics of acknowledging or obscuring one's identity, a subject relevant to crypto-Judaism.[6]

Avram Davidson's "The Golem," which is set in Los Angeles, the city of make-believe, comes toward the end of the course. The funniest, most ironic, and, at six pages, shortest text on the syllabus, it brilliantly demonstrates the malleability of the golem story and picks up on almost every theme that permeates the course and its texts, especially performativity (which has been defined as the construction of identity, particularly gender, through repetitive performance) and the importance of recasting familiar narratives to realize new possibilities. Volunteers from the class act out the tale, which has, in addition to its narrator, three characters—Mr. and Mrs. Gumbeiner and a golem. "The gray-faced person" the Gumbeiners encounter could be either an angry Frankenstein-like monster, who might have escaped from a nearby University of California, Los Angeles, laboratory after attacking his creator, or an actor, who, unable to separate himself from his role, has wandered away from his studio to bring his tragic tale into the sitcom world of the Gumbeiners. Full of questions about identity, mimicry, agency, and authenticity, the story mocks both sitcom complacency and romantic excess and underscores our inability to decide, once and for all, what the golem represents. "The Golem" is a horror story, a vision of human fallibility, and a hopeful look at the possibilities that emerge if we are willing to play with the themes of the golem narrative.

Over the years, the course has concluded with different texts: Margaret Atwood's *Oryx and Crake*, Kazuo Ishiguro's *Never Let Me Go*, Max Barry's *Machine Man*, and E. L. Doctorow's *Andrew's Brain*. Published by *The Tablet* in 2012, Liana Finck's serial graphic novel or blog "The Modern Golem" transports the golem and his creator to contemporary New York City. Written in ten installments and using graphics superimposed on actual photographs, Finck's wry concoction brings the golem to the world of social media. From medieval story to modern blog, the golem remains irrepressible.

Assignments

There are three assignments for this course: biweekly midrashim, a group presentation, and a research project. A midrash is textual commentary, usually biblical, that emphasizes dialectical disputation and creative interpretation. Working in pairs, students write seven midrashim over the course of the semester. Students are encouraged to be adventurous, playful, and outrageous as they make connections. Inevitably, as the course proceeds, interconnections proliferate.

Students organize themselves into presentation groups to work on one of five topics: intertextuality and influence (using Shelley's work and *Frankenstein* films); alchemy, German expressionism, and modernism (using work by Meyrink, Wegener and Galeen, and Duvivier); computers, artificial intelligence, and human-robot relations (using work by Piercy and by Haraway); comic books, the business of artistic reproduction, and artistic authenticity (using work by Chabon, work by Benjamin, and *Superman* films); and bioethics and transhumanism (using work by either Atwood, Ishiguro, Barry, or Doctorow as well as *Ex Machina* and the proliferation of online videos and Web sites describing and selling technological enhancements). Group presenters determine the particular direction of their hour-long presentation. This course tends to attract more English majors than students in any other major, but science majors form an important minority that enriches the scientific and technological content in presentations as well as in the course as a whole. In an early iteration of the course, a computer science major explained how computers create a fourth dimension; in later iterations, a biology major researched the science in *Frankenstein* and in Shelley's early-nineteenth-century world, and a chemistry major explained the continuities and discontinuities between alchemy and chemistry; he even produced small amounts of gold in class.

The final assignment is the research project, which can further develop ideas explored in the midrashim or group presentations, though students often prefer to pursue something new. One science major, Luke, wrote a moving paper about the need for scientists to read literary texts about scientists, so they might see themselves as others see them. He analyzed Frankenstein and other fictional scientists and explained his literary analysis this way:

I decided to take the approach of reviving the golem, putting my spirit into the body of the text and seeing how my own literary interpretation would behave once it was there. I'm not used to the technique of using one's humanity, one's subjectivity, to analyze a subject; however, after gathering a better understanding of the similarities between science and the humanities, it seems extraordinarily appropriate.

By identifying with the golem, Luke was, paradoxically, able to get in touch with his human subjectivity. In science classes, he saw himself as drawing upon his objectivity and saw science as completely different from the humanities. But by using his imagination he better understood the similarities between science and the humanities and the importance of subjectivity. Another student looked at Greek artificial humans and compared them to golems; a third explored Karel Čapek's robots and the way processes of "identity differentiation" otherize and separate humans from mechanical beings and golems.

Mel, a student who wanted to hone their creative writing skills, decided to write a golem story.[7] They wrote a tale of an android named Sephi. The story ends with Sephi's response to Disney's *Pinocchio*, in which he expresses the hope that his maker was more like Geppetto than Frankenstein:

> "I'm considering the plausibility that my maker was a misguided Geppetto. Do you think they miss me?" Sephi looks to Michael for an answer, assuming he has some insight into the psyche of madness and heart that must have rendered Sephi so finely. The questions knock words from Michael, scatter them so he's mute. Sephi carries on, voicing his quandaries. "I have always assumed my maker was a Victor Frankenstein figure, and I an abandoned monster. This movie offers an unforeseen alternative. Maybe I was a wish."
>
> Sephi looks down at his hands, neck bare of any slack strings to let his head hang so low and fast.
>
> "Sephi," Michael finally manages, saying his name before he has anything else in his throat. "Sephi." He reaches out, empty-handed.

Michael's empty-handedness is an eloquent reminder of how much is always left out of any reading of a text, whether that text is our own lives or a written text that helps us understand the trajectory and significance of our lives. Michael does not hold any strings, nor does the author or the reader. We seek out meanings, find them, feel dissatisfied, then seek out other meanings. The analysis is interminable, at once exhilarating and disorienting.

Golem Theory

In recent years, several important monographs have been published that deepen our thinking about the haunting figure of the golem. Cathy S. Gelbin's *The Golem Returns: From German Romantic Literature to Global Jewish Culture, 1801–2008* explores the golem myth as it draws on and influences German literary history and, through its various transformations, changes attitudes toward Jewish difference. Elizabeth R. Baer's *The Golem Redux: From Prague to Post-Holocaust Fiction* stresses the golem story's permeability, instability, and the need for revision over time. The most recent theoretical text about the golem, Maya Barzilai's *Golem: Modern Wars and Their Monsters*, explores the golem as a representation of our ongoing fascination, in the twentieth and twenty-first centuries, with war and its technological and human weapons. Born out of the crucible of World War I, with its clay trenches and devastating technologies, the modern and postmodern golem repeatedly enacts the horrors of war and conscription, of men being made into obedient soldiers.

All three theoretical texts, as indeed all golem stories, speak to the inextricable intertwining of violence and creation. But in that persistent braiding, the golem story offers redemption. Whether we see golem stories as evolving indicators of Jewish cultural authenticity (Gelbin), as an endlessly proliferating palimpsest of Jewish history (Baer), or as meditations on the horrors of weapons of mass destruction (Barzilai), they are also always a figuring forth of the creative powers of the imagination. Like Jewishness itself, the golem story seems indestructible. It returns despite being repressed. It might be buried for a time but eventually it reemerges with even greater force. A canny legend, it tells us who we are and who we are not, what we can and what we cannot do. It offers us many different alternatives. Alive with promise, it offers us hope.

Notes

1. Over the years, the title of the course has changed to include different contemporary films: *Superman, Blade Runner, A.I. Artificial Intelligence,* and, most recently, *Ex Machina.*

2. I was not able to use this work until the 2008 iteration of the course. In earlier versions of the course I used Gershon Winkler's *The Golem of Prague.*

3. See Woolley, 219–33.

4. A very useful text for this part of the course is Charles E. Robinson's two-volume edition of *The Frankenstein Notebooks*, which examines who wrote and

revised what parts of *Frankenstein* and how the partnership between Mary Shelley and Percy Bysshe Shelley might have evolved.

5. Eventually I was forced to discard *The Tempest* as a teaching text (there are always difficult choices to make when constructing syllabi), but the story of the Maharal and his possible connection to Prospero remain a part of the course.

6. I owe this insight to Mel, a student whose work is more fully discussed later in this essay.

7. Luke and Mel are pseudonyms for the students whose work I have included. They enthusiastically gave me permission to use their words.

Works Cited

A.I. Artificial Intelligence. Directed by Steven Spielberg, Warner Bros., 2001.

Atwood, Margaret. *Oryx and Crake*. Doubleday, 2005.

Baer, Elizabeth R. *The Golem Redux: From Prague to Post-Holocaust Fiction*. Wayne State UP, 2012.

Barry, Max. *Machine Man*. Random House, 2011.

Barzilai, Maya. *Golem: Modern Wars and Their Monsters*. New York UP, 2016.

Benjamin, Walter. "The Work of Art in the Age of Mechanical Reproduction." 1936. *Illuminations*, edited and introduced by Hannah Arendt, translated by Harry Zohn, Schocken Books, 1969, pp. 217–51.

Blade Runner. Directed by Ridley Scott, Warner Bros., 1982.

Chabon, Michael. *The Amazing Adventures of Kavalier and Clay*. Random House, 2000.

Davidson, Avram. "The Golem." 1955. *The Avram Davidson Treasury*, edited by Robert Silverberg and Grania Davis, Tom Doherty Associates, 1998, pp. 30–36.

Doctorow, E. L. *Andrew's Brain*. Random House, 2014.

Duvivier, Julien, director. *Le golem*. 1936. Ergo Media, 1991.

Ex Machina. Directed by Alex Garland, Universal Pictures, 2015.

Finck, Liana. "The Modern Golem." *The Tablet*, www.tabletmag.com/jewish -life-and-religion/89746/the-modern-golem.

Freud, Sigmund. "The 'Uncanny.'" 1919. *The Standard Edition of the Complete Psychological Works of Sigmund Freud*, general editor, James Strachey, vol. 17, Hogarth Press, 1955, pp. 217–56.

Gelbin, Cathy S. *The Golem Returns: From German Romantic Literature to Global Jewish Culture, 1801–2008*. U of Michigan P, 2011.

Haraway, Donna J. "A Cyborg Manifesto: Science, Technology, and Socialist-Feminism in the Late Twentieth Century." *Simians, Cyborgs, and Women: The Reinvention of Nature*, Routledge, 1991, pp. 149–81.

Ishiguro, Kazuo. *Never Let Me Go*. Random House, 2005.

"Kaddish." *The X-Files: The Complete Fourth Season*, created by Chris Carter, performances by Gillian Anderson and David Duchovny, episode 15, Twentieth Century Fox Television, 1997, disc 4.

Man of Steel. Directed by Zack Snyder, Warner Bros., 2013.

Meyrink, Gustav. *The Golem*. Edited and introduced by E. F. Bleiler, translated by Madge Pemberton, Dover, 1976.

Ozick, Cynthia. "Puttermesser and Xanthippe." *The Puttermesser Papers*, by Ozick, Alfred A. Knopf, 1997, pp. 20–101.

Piercy, Marge. *He, She and It*. Ballantine Books, 1991.

Robinson, Charles E., editor. *The Frankenstein Notebooks*. By Mary Wollstonecraft Shelley, Garland Publishing, 1996. 2 vols.

Rosenberg, Yudl. *The Golem and the Wondrous Deeds of the Maharal of Prague*. 1909. Edited and translated by Curt Leviant, Yale UP, 2007.

Ruddick, Sarah. "Maternal Thinking." *Mothering: Essays in Feminist Theory*, edited by Joyce Trebilcot, Rowman and Allanheld, 1984, pp. 213–30.

Scholem, Gershom. "The Idea of the Golem." *On the Kabbalah and Its Symbolism*, translated by Ralph Manheim, New York, 1996, pp. 158–204.

———. "Tradition and New Creation in the Ritual of the Kabbalists." *On the Kabbalah and Its Symbolism*, translated by Ralph Manheim, New York, 1996, pp. 118–57.

Shakespeare, William. *The Tempest*. *The Complete Works*, edited by Alfred Harbage, Allen Lane The Penguin Press, 1969, pp. 1369–95.

Shelley, Mary Wollstonecraft. *Frankenstein*. 1816. 2nd ed., W. W. Norton, 2012.

Superman. Directed by Richard Donner, Warner Bros., 1978.

Wegener, Paul, and Henrik Galeen, directors. *The Golem: How He Came into the World*. Universum Film, 1920.

Winkler, Gershon. *The Golem of Prague*. 1980. Judaica Press, 1997.

Wonder Woman. Directed by Patty Jenkins, Warner Bros., 2017.

Woolley, Benjamin. *The Queen's Conjurer: The Science and Magic of Dr. John Dee, Adviser to Queen Elizabeth I*. Henry Holt, 2001.

Jennifer Lemberg

Teaching Contemporary Jewish American Holocaust Literature: Memory, "Fatigue," and Narratives of Post-Holocaust Return

Jewish American authors continue to examine the Holocaust in innovative and absorbing ways, but when teaching this literature, instructors may need to consider students' feeling, as one young woman once told me, that they have "done the Holocaust already." Indeed, a sense of what Simone Schweber has called "Holocaust fatigue" can be widespread among undergraduates who have studied the Holocaust earlier in their education and encountered it in popular media. For these students, the already immense difficulty of trying to understand the history and meaning of the Holocaust is further complicated by its having become overly familiar through what Schweber describes as "the near-explosion of Holocaust representations and invocations" of the past thirty years (49).

Jewish American literature that engages contemporary responses to the Holocaust, especially literature depicting travel to sites of memory, or heritage tourism, can help instructors respond to students' possible wariness about reading Holocaust literature. Because these works stage present-day encounters with sites of past trauma, Jewish American narratives of post-Holocaust return take on larger issues associated with the current state of Holocaust memory and its representations. The concerns they address are pertinent to understanding how we interact with Holocaust memory in

276

the present; raise new interdisciplinary questions about trauma, memory, identity, and place; and offer avenues for exploring ethical and political dilemmas. These narratives challenge students to think deeply about the Holocaust in a broad and multilayered context and to consider how, as developing thinkers and writers, they play an active role in making sense of its continued meanings.

Teaching post-Holocaust narratives of return also serves to familiarize students with some of the current trends in Jewish American literary studies, particularly regarding work by members of the second and third generations since the Holocaust. Exploring the concept of "postmemory" and the structures of multigenerational trauma that Marianne Hirsch defines in *The Generation of Postmemory* and other works, Jenni Adams observes that "the focus of theorizations of postmemory is . . . increasingly geographical and spatial" (239); for example, Victoria Aarons and Alan L. Berger identify "the literary conceit of the quest, a pursuit beginning and ending with the intersection of history and personal stories," as critical to the plot of much third-generation literature.[1] In these texts, they write, "personal narratives, individual stories of lost family members, become a way into the enormity of the historical reality of the Shoah" (12). For Monica Osborne, "[T]he acknowledgement that the combination of memories and archival documents still cannot tell the complete story of the Holocaust" in third-generation literature functions as a sign of the continuing effort of its authors to come to terms with the idea that "the story of the Holocaust is both theirs and not theirs" (155–56).

Reading post-Holocaust returns as a signifier for confronting the burdens of the past offers an important lens through which to view some of the major themes in Jewish American literature and to discover its connections to other forms of return depicted in the literature of different American ethnic or social groups. As Hirsch and Nancy K. Miller suggest, "[P]aradigms of place and displacement . . . shape the fields of diasporic studies" (6) during what they describe as "a present moment in which return has become a generative practice and paradigm" (7). Jewish American narratives dedicated to mapping geographical and temporal distances offer insights into this "paradigm" that may be useful in examining the memory work of other communities, and, conversely, attending to the presence of returns in other literatures deepens our understanding of Jewish American texts.

In my class Coming Home: Identity and Place, an interdisciplinary research seminar at New York University's Gallatin School of Individualized

Study, Jewish American Holocaust literature forms the middle section of a semester-long exploration of the theme of homecoming in the aftermath of historical trauma. The syllabus for the course consists of three parts, including representations of American veterans' homecomings, Jewish American narratives of post-Holocaust returns to Europe, and investigations into the history of and challenges to the repatriation of Native American objects and remains. We look at these subjects separately and consider each one in depth over several weeks. However, our study of these distinct literatures is defined by a sustained thematic focus on how narratives of return reveal traumatic memory to be a continuing source of personal and artistic struggle through their evocation of what Daniel Mendelsohn refers to as the "tantalizing proximity and unbridgeable distance" of the past ("What Happened").[2]

We begin the course by looking at accounts of veterans' homecomings in fiction and theory.[3] The figure of the traumatized (male) veteran is likely to be familiar to students through representations in popular media; as Allan Young observes, the "emotionally unstable" Vietnam veteran "had become an American archetype" by the 1970s (108). Though my students admit to not having read much literature by or about veterans, they easily recognize this archetype along with the personal crises veterans have suffered, which are related to the rupture between their pre- and postwar selves and the shattering of their beliefs about gender and national identity.[4] Starting with this subject allows students to examine their existing ideas about witnessing, storytelling, and the impact of historical trauma, work that helps to deepen their analysis of stories of Jewish American and Native American returns later in the semester.

The texts we read about returning veterans emphasize the inability of language to adequately bear witness to traumatic experience, and they frequently engage in "questioning the nature of their own narrative[s]," as one student, Emma, observed.[5] Analyzing depictions of the conflicts between veterans' experiences, the expectations of civilians, and national narratives prepares the class to think about these issues in other areas and establishes a useful foundation for our next unit, which takes up post-Holocaust narratives of return. Proceeding in this way, students are able to find links between post-Holocaust and other literatures that deal with the effects of historical trauma. This method is consistent with Michael Rothberg's concept of "multidirectional memory," or memory defined "as subject to ongoing negotiation, cross-referencing, and borrowing; as productive and not privative" (3), and provides students with the opportu-

nity to think about how various fields of inquiry have developed in relation to one another and to articulate their responses to studying literature
emerging from different communities and experiences.

In post-Holocaust narratives of return, the encounter with place presents a new way to contend with received ideas about the past. The practice of taking large, highly organized trips to sites of Holocaust memory has sometimes been criticized for its potential to reify a kind of
"Holocaust consciousness" that offers an "effective means of reinforc-
ing seemingly outworn paradigms" (Kugelmass 212). Literary accounts of
more individualized forms of travel, however, allow students to enter
sympathetically into the experience of grappling with this history. Like the
more individual quests undertaken by real-life heritage travelers who
eschew premade itineraries, these narratives "do not follow prescribed
paths" (Lehrer 93) and can surprise students with their renderings of
the difficulty of bearing the weight of Holocaust memory. Students are
moved, for example, by Mendelsohn's realization following his trip to
Ukraine that he "had been after the wrong story" about his relatives, "the
story of how they had died rather than the one of how they had lived,"
and by the way his insight causes readers to adjust their focus as well.

To deepen the responses of students to these latter-day quest narratives, instructors can first introduce them to theoretical approaches to
how the legacy of the Holocaust has been passed on. Critical to this un-
dertaking are essays by Nadine Fresco, Henri Raczymow, and Hirsch
("Objects") that help to define the multigenerational dimensions of Holocaust memory. Reading about the absence or sometimes overwhelming
presence of the past in the lives of later generations, students grasp more
fully the loss, longing, and curiosity that can impel post-Holocaust returns. Responding to Fresco's interviews with members of the second
generation who reported deep family silences in place of discussions about
the war, a student named Sam wrote: "I feel that these children must have
felt an overwhelming sense of loneliness in the face of this perturbing
quietness. It is something that has taken them a lifetime to begin to understand." In her comment, she registers a newfound awareness of the idea that
grappling with Holocaust memory takes place over time and demands a
dynamic relation to inherited ideas about the past.

Memoir and fiction by authors such as Mendelsohn, Eva Hoffman, and
Jonathan Safran Foer invite students to participate in this process of continuous unfolding. Each of these accounts of visiting landscapes of Holocaust memory makes coming to terms with the received narrative of the

Holocaust part of the story, locating traveler and reader within the ripples of post-Holocaust time. Describing herself as "wary of the ready-made metaphors and the prefabricated observations" that sometimes arise from heritage travel, for example, Hoffman states that "the urge to go is the next turn in a dialectic" that sends her to find her parents' village in Ukraine, a trip she takes after completing research intended "to supplement memory with history, to locate my family's story within the broader events" (204–05). Though my students learn to identify certain tropes in these works (e.g., friendly locals who appear to call long-held hatreds into question versus hostile ones who make those hatreds easier to imagine, and solemn arrivals at sites of memory), over weeks of intense discussion and analysis the most striking feature of their response is the differences they find in the readings.

Visual texts, including Menachem Daum's documentary *Hiding and Seeking: Faith and Tolerance after the Holocaust* and the Israeli author Rutu Modan's graphic novel *The Property*, with which we concluded the post-Holocaust section of the class, bring another element to our study. *Hiding and Seeking* follows Daum on a trip to Poland with his wife and sons to visit the farm where his wife's father and uncles hid during the Holocaust, a journey meant to broaden his sons' attitudes toward non-Jews. *The Property* imagines a return to Poland by an Israeli woman and her grandmother, a trip that the grandmother ostensibly undertakes to reclaim her family's apartment but that in reality allows her to attempt to reconnect with her former lover, the biological father of the son she bore after her escape. Both *Hiding and Seeking* and *The Property* feature tense exchanges between members of different generations over how the memory of the Holocaust as a personal story and a larger history should be understood and highlight relations between the Jewish returnees and the Poles who receive them. Through visual representations of gestures and expressions, sites of memory, and interactions between members of multiple generations, the film and the graphic novel assist students in recognizing the ongoing social, political, and psychological effects of the Holocaust.

The symbolic and actual importance of material claims in *The Property* form a thematic link to the last section of the course, which introduces students to some of the complex issues associated with the repatriation of Native American objects and remains.[6] As Hirsch points out, "[O]bjects, lost and again found, structure plots of return" in post-Holocaust and other literatures ("Objects" 200). In this final segment of our class, the subject of which is usually least familiar to my students, we consider some of the ways in which conflicts over stolen objects and remains are located at the center of complex narratives of nationhood, religion, and economic gain. Laurie Anne Whitt argues that "the politics of property is the central historical dynamic mediating Euro-American/Indigenous relations" (148), and though the looting of Native American objects and remains may be understood in the popular American imagination as an aftereffect of genocidal violence, it is more accurately viewed as a component of "empire building" (Fine-Dare 14). Learning about contemporary efforts to reclaim stolen property forces the class to contend with conflicts rooted in the past but also highly relevant to our time.

By the end of the course, my students feel deeply attuned to some of the agonizing questions that attach to Holocaust memory and demonstrate a more clearly defined sense of their individual and collective responsibility to the past. For their final projects, many students have researched how their personal stories are intertwined with ethnic, national, and political histories, while others have written about topics relevant to our current political moment. As a student named Abby shared in an online discussion forum:

> It was impossible for me, and probably many others, to read these pieces in a vacuum and ignore the context of our own lives. I am not the child of Holocaust survivors, so I cannot truly know the exact "grip of silence" that Fresco speaks of, the "silence that swallowed up the past, all the past, the past before death, before destruction" (419). I did, however, find myself lost in the memories I have of my own familial and cultural history.

Abby articulates the negotiations of proximity and distance that mark her thinking about the course material and acknowledges her place in relation to her classmates. Her statement, which recognizes the specificity of the Holocaust, the existence of our classroom community, and our shared status as citizens of a fragmented world, suggests not "fatigue" with the subject matter but connection to it. Schweber reminds us that "to teach about the past always and unavoidably implicates the present" (51). At its most imaginative and flexible, contemporary Jewish American Holocaust literature that takes readers on journeys of return acknowledges this truth. Teaching this literature alongside other narratives of posttraumatic return fosters students' interest in learning about the Holocaust and its contemporary representations, creating a classroom environment in which Holocaust memory is seen not as static or monumental but as critical to our ability to respond, in the present, to the complex resonances of the past.

Notes

1. In their discussion of the quest in third-generation literature, Aarons and Berger refer to David Roskies and Naomi Diamant's consideration of Daniel Mendelsohn's memoir *The Lost: A Search for Six of Six Million* in *Holocaust Literature: A History and Guide*.

2. Here my thinking is informed by Svetlana Boym's "typology" of nostalgia, in which she argues that "reflective nostalgia" can usefully "present an ethical and creative challenge" in response to a longing for home (xviii).

3. Toni Morrison's novel *Home* has been important to this section of the course.

4. For a discussion of the ways in which gender identity is negotiated through representations of the Vietnam War, see Jeffords.

5. I am grateful to my students for giving their permission for me to quote their work. All student names used in this essay have been changed.

6. I'd like to acknowledge the problems inherent in the efforts of a non-Native teacher to address this subject within a relatively short time frame. We approach this section of the course as a tentative introduction to new ideas rather than as a definitive overview.

Works Cited

Aarons, Victoria, and Alan L. Berger. *Third-Generation Holocaust Representation: Trauma, History, and Memory.* Northwestern UP, 2017.

Adams, Jenni. "Traces, Dis/Continuities, Complicities: An Introduction to Holocaust Literature." *The Bloomsbury Companion to Holocaust Literature*, edited by Adams, Bloomsbury Publishing, 2016, pp. 1–24.

Boym, Svetlana. *The Future of Nostalgia.* Basic Books / Perseus Books Group, 2001.

Fine-Dare, Kathleen S. *Grave Injustice: The American Indian Repatriation Movement and NAGPRA.* U of Nebraska P, 2002.

Foer, Jonathan Safran. *Everything Is Illuminated.* Houghton Mifflin, 2002.

Fresco, Nadine. "Remembering the Unknown." *International Review of Psycho-Analysis*, no. 11, 1984, pp. 417–27.

Hiding and Seeking: Faith and Tolerance after the Holocaust. Produced by Menachem Daum and Oren Rudavsky, First Run Features, 2004.

Hirsch, Marianne. *The Generation of Postmemory: Writing and Visual Culture after the Holocaust.* Columbia UP, 2012.

———. "Objects of Return." *After Testimony: The Ethics and Aesthetics of Holocaust Narrative for the Future*, edited by Jakob Lothe et al., Ohio State UP, 2012, pp. 198–220.

Hirsch, Marianne, and Nancy K. Miller. Introduction. *Rites of Return: Diaspora Poetics and the Politics of Memory*, edited by Hirsch and Miller, Columbia UP, 2011, pp. 1–20.

Hoffman, Eva. *After Such Knowledge: Memory, History, and the Legacy of the Holocaust*. Perseus Books Group, 2004.

Jeffords, Susan. *The Remasculinization of America: Gender and the Vietnam War*. Indiana UP, 1989.

Kugelmass, Jack. "Missions to the Past: Poland in Contemporary Jewish Thought and Deed." *Tense Past: Cultural Essays in Trauma and Memory*, edited by Paul Antze and Michael Lambek, Routledge, 1996, pp. 199–214.

Lehrer, Erica T. *Jewish Poland Revisited: Heritage Tourism in Unquiet Places*. Indiana UP, 2013.

Mendelsohn, Daniel. *The Lost: A Search for Six of Six Million*. HarperCollins, 2006.

———. "What Happened to Uncle Shmiel?" *The New York Times*, 14 July 2002, www.nytimes.com/2002/07/14/magazine/what-happened-to -uncle-shmiel.html.

Modan, Rutu. *The Property*. Translated by Jessica Cohen, Drawn and Quarterly, 2013.

Morrison, Toni. *Home*. Random House, 2012.

Osborne, Monica. "Representing the Holocaust in Third-Generation American Jewish Writers." *The Edinburgh Companion to Modern Jewish Fiction*, edited by David Brauner and Axel Stahler, Edinburgh UP, 2015, pp. 149–60.

Raczymow, Henri. "Memory Shot Through with Holes." Translated by Alan Astro, *Yale French Studies*, no. 85, 1994, pp. 98–105.

Roskies, David G., and Anita Diamant. *Holocaust Literature: A History and Guide*. Brandeis UP, 2012.

Rothberg, Michael. *Multidirectional Memory: Remembering the Holocaust in the Age of Decolonization*. Stanford UP, 2009.

Schweber, Simone. "'Holocaust Fatigue': Teaching It Today." *Social Education*, January-February 2006, pp. 48–55.

Whitt, Laurie Anne. "Cultural Imperialism and the Marketing of Native America." *Natives and Academics: Researching and Writing about American Indians*, edited by Devon A. Mihesuah, U of Nebraska P, 1998, pp. 139–71.

Young, Allan. *The Harmony of Illusions: Inventing Post-Traumatic Stress Disorder*. Princeton UP, 1995.

Part VI

New Approaches
and Key Texts

Karen E. H. Skinazi and Lori Harrison-Kahan

The Surprising Versatility of
Israel Zangwill's *The Melting Pot*

By the time they arrive in college, most students are familiar with the concept of the melting pot, a seemingly timeless idea that encapsulates for them a national ideal, simultaneously connoting unity and difference. Some students recall debates from high school about whether America can best be described as a melting pot or a salad bowl. Several can even recite the lyrics of *Schoolhouse Rock!*'s "The Great American Melting Pot" ("You simply melt right in / It doesn't matter what your skin"), which has reached new audiences on *YouTube* decades after initially airing on ABC in the late 1970s. Yet few are familiar with the literary text that popularized this enduring metaphor for American identity: Israel Zangwill's 1908 play *The Melting Pot*.

This essay argues that *The Melting Pot* is a key text for students of American literature and culture as well as of Jewish literature. While *The Melting Pot*'s use of symbolism and dramatic form offers many opportunities for literary interpretation, its varied cultural contexts allow students to engage in wide-ranging conversations about topics such as immigration and assimilation, multilingualism, interfaith and interethnic romance, transnationalism, American identity, and Jewishness. In addition to situating students within a distinct period in American and literary history and providing historical background for understanding how "the melting pot" entered the national lexicon, Zangwill's play offers lenses for interpreting contemporary texts, from current political rhetoric about immigration to works of popular culture.

The writings of Zangwill, a British Jewish writer whose literary legacy rests largely on his 1890s Dickensian tales about Jewish immigrants in the London ghetto, may seem an unusual option for an American literature course. But his books *Children of the Ghetto: A Study of a Peculiar People* and *The King of the Schnorrers* had a strong influence on Jewish American writing at the turn of the twentieth century. A Christian-Jewish romance set in New York, *The Melting Pot*, in turn, attests to America's influence on Zangwill's ideology and imagination.[1] Like much of late-nineteenth- and early-twentieth-century Jewish American literature, *The Melting Pot* explores transnational dynamics between old-world customs and new-world values. Moreover, as a British-authored play that premiered in Washington, DC, and centers on a Jewish American immigrant family, *The Melting Pot* is a product of transatlantic exchanges that shaped Anglophone literary culture of the Jewish Diaspora. While instructors can adapt the strategies outlined below by Karen Skinazi (in "Stirring the Pot") and Lori Harrison-Kahan (in "Mixing Metaphors") for Jewish American literature courses, they can also find frameworks for teaching this versatile text in the context of Jewish literary and cultural studies in the concluding section of this essay.

Stirring the Pot: Provoking Critical Thinking

Although the following oft-cited passage from Zangwill's *Melting Pot* appeared as the epigraph on the syllabus for my first-year seminar America and the Melting Pot, I initially resisted assigning the play itself:

> America is God's Crucible, the great Melting-Pot where all the races of Europe are melting and re-forming! Here you stand . . . think I, when I see them at Ellis Island . . . in your fifty groups, with your fifty languages and histories, and your fifty blood hatreds and rivalries. But you won't be long like that. . . . A fig for your feuds and vendettas! Germans and Frenchmen, Irishmen and Englishmen, Jews and Russians—into the Crucible with you all! God is making the American. (Zangwill 288)

Still, the text exerted a ghostly presence over the course material, whether we were discussing the 1927 film *The Jazz Singer*, in which Jack Robin (formerly Jakie Rabinowitz) woos American audiences and his gentile girl-friend with Jewish-inflected ragtime, or the chapter "Henry Ford's English-Language Melting Pot" in Jeffrey Eugenides's 2002 novel *Middlesex*. Reading texts that ranged the course of a century, students grappled with the significance of an individual possessing multiple identities in a country that continues to call itself a product of the melting pot. This metaphor ended up having a pivotal role in students' understanding of twentieth-century American culture at large—and so, ultimately, I knew I had to assign the play that first articulated it.

To counter a tendency to refer to the melting pot as an amorphous intellectual idea, rather than a rhetorical term with its own history, students should confront Zangwill's *Melting Pot* as a literary and historical artifact, rather than as a spectral ur-text hovering at the top of the syllabus. In Zangwill's drama, the star-crossed lovers, David Quixano, a Jew who lost his parents to the Kishinev pogrom, and Vera Revendal, a Christian whose father incited the anti-Semitic violence, leave hate and bloodshed in the past, presenting for the reader a romantic image of one nation united by God. Although various characters espouse contradictory ideas about ethnoreligious and national identity over the course of the play, the work concludes not only with the union of the lovers but also with David's triumphant prophecy: "What is the glory of Rome and Jerusalem where all nations and races come to worship and look back, compared with the glory of America, where all races and nations come to labour and look forward!" (363).

Despite its histrionic ending, the play proves a rich text for generating critical thinking, as is evident in class discussions. In conjunction with *The Melting Pot*, students read philosopher Horace Kallen's "Democracy versus the Melting Pot," which articulates the theory of cultural pluralism using the metaphor of America as a "symphony of civilization" (220). This pairing allows students to draw connections and question disparities between Zangwill's play and Kallen's critique. Although Kallen imagined cultural pluralism in opposition to the melting pot, which he viewed as a threat to democracy, students noted his and Zangwill's similar use of the metaphor of a symphony as well as correspondences between their overall visions. In Zangwill's play, David is, after all, in the process of composing an "American Symphony" to express his love for his adopted country and his utopian dream of the nation's diverse peoples coming together as one. Furthermore, some students remarked on Vera's biblical reference in the play's fourth act to Ruth's conversion to Judaism: "David, I come to you, and I say in the words of Ruth, thy people shall be my people and thy God my God!" (Zangwill 347). Students argued against the standard interpretation of the play as a rejection of religious identity and a vehicle of Americanization. Instead, our discussions opened up the possibility that the play offered a bold vision of a Judaized America.

Students' essays on *The Melting Pot* show how critical thinking can be parlayed into good academic writing. Consider, for example, the opening of an essay in which the student writes that the play "has been . . . lauded for what is, on its face, a feel-good story of a Jewish-Russian immigrant, David Quixano, who forgets his troubled past in becoming purely American."[2] The essay then goes on to remind us that "David Quixano, as his surname implies, is quixotic" and that we should thus be skeptical of "his unrestrained optimism" about America. Continuing to train his critical eye on the play's protagonist, the student notes that David's initial words in the play are "Isn't it a beautiful world, uncle?" (284). "Indeed," argues the student, "the protagonist's way of embracing this 'beautiful' new world, America, is to try to forget the past—that the father of his betrothed, Christian-Russian immigrant Vera Revendal, was instrumental in murdering his parents in the 1903 pogrom in Kishinev, Russia—and to forsake his Jewish background: he forgets the Jewish holiday of Purim, plays the violin on the Sabbath, and becomes engaged to a non-Jew." This student resists the romantic message of the play and its romanticizing of America, questioning what is "beautiful" about turning one's back on thousands of years of tradition and whether the protagonist should be understood as a mouthpiece for the author. In his conclusion, the student builds upon a passage from the play's final scene, in which the stage directions instruct that, as David tells Vera to kiss him, ominous "Cathedral music from 'Faust' surg[es] up softly" before the patriotic song "My Country, 'Tis of Thee" is heard, undercutting the happy ending (362–63).

Essays like this one demonstrate how close examination of the text by students challenges their preconceptions, encouraging them to rethink the relations between author and character, text and context, and expectations and discoveries. Zangwill's play provokes critical thinking, reading, and writing, defamiliarizes a commonplace concept, and propels undergraduates toward fresh and nuanced understandings of a supposedly well-worn metaphor.

Mixing Metaphors:
The Melting Pot as Interracial Literature

Persuaded by Werner Sollors's analysis of *The Melting Pot* in *Beyond Ethnicity: Consent and Descent in American Culture* and by the fact that the play script was newly available in Edna Nahshon's edition, I, too, overcame my initial resistance to teaching the play. Like Karen Skinazi, I discovered that the play's pedagogical value lies in its capacity for surprising readers.

The Jewishness of the protagonist was one such surprise. Based on the excerpts of the play I had read, I figured that his Jewishness was incidental, part of the representation of a generic immigrant character. Reading the play in its entirety, I was unprepared for David's historically specific backstory (i.e., the loss of his parents in the Kishinev pogrom), and for the characters of Mendel and Frau Quixano, David's uncle and grandmother, whose lines of dialogue challenge David's assimilationist rhetoric and who embody different versions of Jewish identity. I was surprised by the play's use of Yiddish, its references to religious practices, and the symbolic setting of act 2, which takes place during Purim. Unexpected, too, was the comic character of Kathleen, the Irish maid, who evolves over the course of the play, forming a partnership with Frau Quixano and adopting the signs of Jewishness of her employers. "I won't be the joke of Jews, no, begorra, that I won't" (274), she says at the beginning, invoking an Irish oath to express her confusion over the kosher dietary laws she is expected to maintain. By the end, Kathleen has learned to avoid mixing meat and dairy; instead, she is mixing colloquial ethnic dialects. Spoken in "Irish-sounding Yiddish," her final lines assert her identification with the Jewish Diaspora rather than with the dominant American culture: "Houly Moses, *komm' zurick!* Begorra, we Jews never know our way" (355). It turns out that the play that has provided a shorthand term for the Rooseveltian ideal of the unhyphenated American is actually a testament to cultural hybridity.[3] *The Melting Pot*'s nonstereotypical performances of Jewishness and narrative of cross-cultural pollination, rather than unidirectional Americanization, provide fertile ground for teaching the comparative study of race and ethnicity. The play now regularly appears on my syllabi alongside the work of writers such as W. E. B. Du Bois, Anzia Yezierska, Sui Sin Far, and Nella Larsen.

Before students read *The Melting Pot*, they are asked to reflect on their understanding of the melting pot as a metaphor for America, consider how they arrived at that understanding, discuss other such metaphors they have encountered, and describe what they find effective or ineffective about the melting pot as a concept. In discussing their responses, students say they are struck by the malleability of the metaphor. Some associate it with deracination and homogeneity. Others view the melting pot as an expression of heterogeneity, pluralism, or multiculturalism. Many were taught that the melting pot celebrates diversity. Even before reading *The Melting Pot* then, students become aware of the metaphor's instability; this supposedly shared notion of Americanness is host to contradictory meanings that shift depending on who one is and where one is educated.

Nor does the text neatly resolve what the metaphor means. Instead, it produces further complexity. Once students have read the play, they are asked to consider why Zangwill's text was so effective at popularizing the notion of America as a melting pot and how the play deviates from or complicates that notion. These questions generate discussion material about a range of topics, including the relation between art and propaganda (mirroring initial reviews of the play, some students argue for its aesthetic value, while others see it as a contrived social document); performance and theatrical form; the construction of national literary canons (whether a work by a British author can count as American literature, and why the canonization of Anglophone literatures might exclude works by Jews); disciplinary differences between the work done in literature classes and in history and sociology classes; and the relations between religion, race, ethnicity, culture, and nation.

Provocative discussions focus on the efficacy of figurative language as a means of constructing national identity and ideology. Students assume that the melting pot is a culinary metaphor, but as references to the "crucible" (287) make clear, Zangwill's metaphor is drawn from alchemy, the process by which base metals are transformed into gold: God is "the great Alchemist [who] melts and fuses" different races and nations "with his purging flame," declares David (363). Through close attention to Zangwill's diction ("seething" [287], "roaring" [297]), students discuss the implications of this metaphor and why popular discourse transformed the violent imagery of David's monologues into an ethnic stew whose exotic ingredients can be pleasurably consumed. Students are also attuned to the fact that the melting pot is not the only metaphor for America in the play. They observe that Zangwill, in making David a composer, employs the musical metaphor of a symphony, mixing the science of alchemy with the beauty of high art. The marriage plot provides another opportunity for students to unpack Zangwill's competing and complementary symbols

and metaphors. David and Vera's union, with its promise of future prog-
eny, becomes the play's most tangible embodiment of American ideology,
but why then are we apt to describe America as a melting pot rather than
as a metaphorical intermarriage? Contributing to the play's textual, con-
textual, and performative hybridity, this mixing of metaphors raises challenging questions that make *The Melting Pot* a valuable addition to American literary study.

Finding a Home for *The Melting Pot* in Jewish Literature Classes

Although the approaches outlined above could be adapted for classes in
Jewish American literature, this essay ends with some additional frameworks for teaching the play in Jewish studies contexts. *The Melting Pot*
provides an entrée into interrogating cultural representations of interfaith relationships, particularly in light of the 2013 survey by the Pew
Research Center that showed rises in intermarriage among Jews in the
last few decades and led to heated debates in the Jewish press.[4] The
play encourages consideration of the prevalence of intermarriage narratives in literature by and about Jews. It pairs well, for example, with fiction by well-known Jewish writers like Philip Roth and by lesser-known
ones like Emma Wolf, whose correspondence with Zangwill indicates
that Zangwill read and was influenced by Wolf's novels *Other Things Being Equal* and *Heirs of Yesterday*.[5] In addition, the iconic status of Zangwill's metaphor makes the play a fitting counterpart to Mary Antin's autobiography *The Promised Land* and poetry by Emma Lazarus, whose
"New Colossus" appears on a bronze plaque inside the base of the Statue
of Liberty. Together, these texts raise questions about how Jews, writing
in various genres, have contributed to the discourse of American exceptionalism.

As a response to the Kishinev pogrom, the play can also be taught as
part of a tradition of artistic attempts to grapple with the violent history
of anti-Semitism, a tradition that ranges from works by Yiddish writers
such as Sholem Aleichem and Isaac Bashevis Singer to Laura Z. Hobson's *Gentleman's Agreement*. In this respect, *The Melting Pot* prefigures
works of Holocaust literature, such as Edward Lewis Wallant's *The
Pawnbroker*, Art Spiegelman's *Maus I* and *II*, and Jonathan Safran Foer's
Everything Is Illuminated, which examine the effects of historical trauma
on Jewish American identity.

Finally, as Meri-Jane Rochelson notes in her edition of *The Melting Pot*, the text is "significantly connected" to the vicissitudes of Zangwill's relation with the Zionist movement (Introduction, 15). In the aftermath of the Kishinev pogrom, Zangwill broke with fellow Zionists over their failure to support the Uganda plan, which would have set aside territory in East Africa for a new Jewish homeland. Students can examine the cable Zangwill sent to the Federation of American Zionists in Pittsburgh following the pogrom to see his shift in allegiance. In 1903, Zangwill viewed America as a conduit to a Zionist future, suggesting that "the strenuous town of fire and steel in which" Jewish refugees met would "inspire [them] to build a great bridge over which Israel shall pass to his ancient home" ("To American Zionists").[6] These metaphors contrast significantly with the rhetoric of *The Melting Pot*, published five years later, in which David foretells an America that surpasses Jerusalem in glory.

Teaching *The Melting Pot* as a consequence of Zangwill's relation to Zionism rehistoricizes the text and extends its diasporic and transnational reach. In Jewish literature courses, the play could be placed in conversation with Theodor Herzl's 1902 utopian *Altneuland* (*Old New Land*) as well as with Michael Chabon's speculative *The Yiddish Policemen's Union*. Including this text in a unit on literary Zionism allows students to reframe it as a call for a Jewish, rather than a deracinated, homeland. This approach relocates *The Melting Pot* in Jewish, American, and global history and identifies it as part of a transnational network of Jewish and American literatures.

Notes

1. For more on Zangwill's biography, see Rochelson, *Jew*.

2. Thanks to former Princeton University student Mackenzie Berman for permission to excerpt his essay.

3. On the relationship between Zangwill and Theodore Roosevelt, see Nahshon 241–43. Students familiar with American history could be encouraged to consider why Zangwill dedicated the first printed edition of *The Melting Pot* to Roosevelt.

4. For a summary of the Pew survey results, see "Portrait." For a response that addresses *The Melting Pot*, see Skinazi.

5. See Harrison-Kahan and also Cantalupo.

6. See also Faris.

Works Cited

Aleichem, Sholem. *Collected Stories of Sholom Aleichem.* Crown, 1949.

Antin, Mary. *The Promised Land.* 1912. Penguin Books, 2012.

Cantalupo, Barbara. "The Letters of Israel Zangwill to Emma Wolf: Transatlantic Mentoring in the 1890s." *Resources for American Literary Study,* vol. 28, 2002, pp.121–38.

Chabon, Michael. *The Yiddish Policemen's Union.* Harper Perennial, 2008.

Faris, Hani. "Israel Zangwill's Challenge to Zionism." *Journal of Palestine Studies,* vol. 4, no. 3, 1975, pp. 74–90.

"The Great American Melting Pot." *Schoolhouse Rock!,* season 3, episode 6, ABC, 1 May 1976.

Harrison-Kahan, Lori. "'A Grave Experiment': Emma Wolf's Marriage Plots and the Deghettoization of American Jewish Fiction." *American Jewish History,* vol. 101, no. 1, 2017, pp. 5–34.

Herzl, Theodor. *Old New Land (Altneuland).* Translated by Lotta Levensohn, Herzl Press / Markus Wiener Publishing, 1987.

Hobson, Laura Z. *Gentleman's Agreement.* Simon and Schuster, 1947.

Kallen, Horace. "Democracy versus the Melting-Pot: A Study of American Nationality: Part Two." *The Nation,* vol. 100, no. 2591, 25 Feb. 1915, pp. 217–22.

Lazarus, Emma. *Selected Poems and Other Writings.* Edited by Gregory Eiselein, Broadview, 2002.

Nahshon, Edna. "Introductory Essay." *The Melting Pot. From the Ghetto to the Melting Pot: Israel Zangwill's Jewish Plays: Three Playscripts by Israel Zangwill,* edited by Nahshon, Wayne State UP, 2006, pp. 211–63.

"A Portrait of Jewish Americans." *Pew Research Center,* 1 Oct. 2013, www.pewforum.org/2013/10/01/jewish-american-beliefs-attitudes-culture-survey/.

Rochelson, Meri-Jane. Introduction. *The Melting-Pot,* by Israel Zangwill, Broadview, 2017, pp. 13–48.

———. *A Jew in the Public Arena: The Career of Israel Zangwill.* Wayne State UP, 2008.

Singer, Isaac Bashevis. *Satan in Goray.* 1935. Vintage, 2014.

Skinazi, Karen E. H. "Diving into the Melting Pot for Answers on Pew Survey on Jewish America." *The Forward,* 4 Nov. 2013, forward.com/opinion/186839/diving-into-the-melting-pot-for-answers-on-pew-sur/.

Sollors, Werner. *Beyond Ethnicity: Consent and Descent in American Culture.* Oxford UP, 1986.

"To American Zionists: Greetings from Eminent Jews Refer to Kishineff Horrors and Indorse Zionism." *The New York Times,* 9 June 1903, p. 5.

Zangwill, Israel. *The Melting Pot. From the Ghetto to the Melting Pot: Israel Zangwill's Jewish Plays: Three Playscripts by Israel Zangwill,* edited by Edna Nahshon, Wayne State UP, 2006, pp. 267–363.

John Wharton Lowe

Teaching Abraham Cahan's *Yekl* as a Comedy of Arrival and Dislocation

Abraham Cahan, Russian Jewish immigrant, pioneering editor of New York's Yiddish *Jewish Daily Forward*, and innovative creator of novels and short stories, was a dynamic catalyst for Americanization; in advice columns and articles, he counseled readers to learn English and fit into society in the United States. Simultaneously, however, he was a moving elegist for the language, social customs, and folk traditions that were being lost in the pell-mell race of new citizens for financial success and social acceptance. His novella *Yekl* offers a touching, often amusing, and vibrant portrait of what I call the comedy of arrival, tracing the bittersweet relationships of the eponymous Yekl Podgorny—now called Jake in New York—with his new, Americanized sweethearts, and his troubled relationship with Gitl, the wife he left behind in Russia along with their son, Yossele. When Yekl learns of his father's death back home, his conscience is disturbed, and he sends for his family, which curtails his amorous exploits in New York. Stung by the revelation that Jake has a family from Russia, Fanny, one of Jake's girlfriends, warns Gitl about another rival, Mamie (who is also Fanny's rival). Confronted with his infidelity, Jake leaves the family and arranges a divorce paid for from Mamie's savings; this money will then be used by Gitl and her new husband, Bernstein, previously the family's studious boarder, to open a grocery. Jake and Mamie open a dancing school. The novella ends with Jake and Mamie on their way to their wedding: "Each time the car came to a halt he wished the pause could be prolonged indefinitely; and when it resumed its progress, the violent lurch it gave was accompanied by a corresponding sensation in his heart" (89). As these words indicate, the comedy of arrival has a darker underside, the comedy of dislocation.

I stress two facets of the novella when teaching it: the uncanny ability of Cahan to infuse ethnic humor into sometimes grim material, and his sensitive portrait of Jewish ghetto women, their concerns, and their contributions to the process of acculturation. Indeed, Cahan would create a popular column in the *Forward* in 1906 that continued for sixty years. The Bintel Brief (Bundle of Letters) column consisted of letters to the editor, originally mostly by immigrant Jewish women, detailing problems and woes (Metzger). Cahan issued advice, establishing an early, Jewish version of the "Dear Abby" tabloid tradition.

The early reviews of *Yekl* were mixed, but the most positive and prescient appeared in *The New York Times*, which praised Cahan's "keen sense of humor" (qtd. in Lipsky 70) and the sharply sketched characters. Cahan had a keen eye for detail that extends to the novella's settings (crowded streets, tenement kitchens, sweatshops, dance halls, and parks) and to the realistic dialogue in key scenes, particularly those that involve verbal teasing, dueling, banter, and invective. His impressive use of detail came from his background as a reporter, which made him an expert in both visual detail and the accurate rendition of speech and dialect. This role enabled Cahan to acquire an encyclopedic range of experiences on the Lower East Side. Accordingly, when I teach this novel, I always provide an overview of the flood tide of immigration that occurred during the late nineteenth and early twentieth centuries, including a description of the hardships Jews experienced in eastern European cities and shtetls, such as pogroms and forced enlistment in the Czar's army. Two key resources for this period are Irving Howe's invaluable *World of Our Fathers* and Hamilton Holt's collection of immigrant biographies, *The Life Stories of Undistinguished Americans*.

Yekl probes exactly these issues, and the pressures of Americanization generate most of the events of the tale, including a divorce and two new marriages. The novel possesses the classic elements of comedy: order, disorder, and the restoration of order, which is often expressed through marriage. Yekl, a blacksmith in Russia, but an expert tailor in New York, begins his American career in Boston, where he learns American slang and quickly embraces English as a key to acculturation. New York, however, expands his horizons, introducing him to the enticements of the ghetto dancing schools, where he quickly acquires admirers of his virile frame and sweet talk. He has not one but many love interests including the trusting Fanny and the svelte and canny Polish seamstress Mamie, whose careful savings might come in handy if he does not send for his wife and son; his coworkers and acquaintances assume he is single.

Cahan takes care to show that Jews are not all alike; they come from many lands and backgrounds; some are pious and traditional, while others, like Jake and Mamie, are more secular and eager to cast off old customs. As my students examine the differences between life in Europe and New York, they see the myriad ways in which things in the Old World get turned upside down in the New, as is the case with Bernstein, who goes from revered scholar in Russia to lowly shop owner in New York, but also with Jake, whose peasant background is no barrier to his rapid rise in the Garment District and in American popular culture. Gitl, a model wife in the shtetl, becomes an embarrassing greenhorn to Jake when she arrives in New York. Mikhail Bakhtin's concept of carnivalization applies to the Jewish Diaspora as depicted by Cahan, where everything is turned upside down; everyone participates in the disruption, willingly or not; and "what is suspended first of all is hierarchical structure . . . all distance between people is suspended. . . . Carnival is the place for working out, in a concretely sensuous, half-real and half-playacted form, a *new mode of interrelationship between individuals*" (Bakhtin 123). Inevitably, this social environment enables comedy and ironic observations.

Cahan's story opens in the sweatshop with Jake surrounded by admiring lady seamstresses and the stolid Bernstein. Jake indulges in a good-natured verbal duel with his colleagues, code-switching between broken, heavily accented English and Yiddish (which Cahan conveniently translates for us). Anthropologists have found that many cultures feature this kind of linguistic combat, one based on the correct use of language and ritual insults.[1] Jewish culture draws on the heritage of the rural shtetl and the ghetto marketplace, where insults are used for attack or correction, but also for pleasure.[2] My students focus on another early scene in the dancing school that features a smorgasbord of code-switching, which is inextricably connected to dual-language societies and to multidialect cultures; the New York Jewish ghetto is both.

Cahan uses dialect in a variety of clever ways, working from the pattern that sociolinguists have observed in all multilingual speech communities—

the functional differentiation of languages.[3] Cahan's immigrants use Yiddish to communicate but liberally punctuate it with Russian or Polish epithets and curses, while sprinkling their speech with American slang or phrases to intimidate verbal opponents and to exhibit advanced acculturation. This code-switching is useful for framing verbal messages, identifying them as particular kinds of discursive work. Language shifts enable jokers to make temporary playthings of their targets and to change their relationships with the people spoken to, a valuable ability in an immigrant community. All these elements appear in Jake's initial scenes with Mamie at the dance hall, where she uses the resources of Yiddish, English, ritual curses, and slang interchangeably. When Jake asks her for a kiss and takes one without getting a reply, she slaps his arm. "'May the Angel of Death kiss you!' said her lips in Yiddish. 'Try again!' her glowing face overruled them in a dialect of its own" (23). Jake obviously prizes Mamie's verbal skill, and Gitl's initial failure to demonstrate similar linguistic ability is largely responsible for his scornful rejection of his wife as a hopeless greenhorn.

When Gitl arrives at Ellis Island, things again get turned upside down. In Russia, this traditional wife and mother, pious and skilled in the kitchen, would be considered a paragon; here, however, she is at a disadvantage when compared to women like Mamie, who dress as Americans, dance, flirt, and make money side by side with men. Gitl, dressed in heavy peasant garb, sporting the *shaytl*, or traditional black wig, and smelling of the steerage, repels Jake, who thinks his swarthy wife looks like a "squaw" (34), a sign he has picked up racial biases in America. She is shocked that Jake is clean-shaven and that they break the Sabbath by driving in cars.

In the fine film Joan Micklin Silver made of the novel, *Hester Street*, these biases are even more apparent. Silver emphasizes the comedy of arrival in Gitl's opening scenes; the contrast between Gitl's own hair and the wig is heightened, as the actress who plays Gitl, Carol Kane, has blond hair (unlike Gitl in the novel). In the movie, Jake sports an upturned, luxurious mustache, which heightens both his sexual nature and his role as a comic villain.

In his classic study of humor, Sigmund Freud emphasized the importance of displacement and absurdity, and the unification of apparent opposites (bisociation) in the creation of humor. He believed the basic components of humor include "playful judgement, the coupling of dissimilar things, contrasting ideas, 'sense in nonsense,' the succession of bewilderment and enlightenment, the bringing forward of what is hidden, and the peculiar brevity [or condensation] of wit" (Freud 14).

Cahan clearly recognized that the process of Americanization was rich in these qualities, as they are all abundantly present in the comedy of arrival portrayed in *Yekl*, especially in the humor directed at greenhorns, which formed a type of initiatory immigrant rite. This comedy of dislocation is by definition cruel, for it relies on the momentary contrast of what immigrants were and are, as they are transposed into a new culture. Thus the scene at Ellis Island becomes a comic juxtaposition of opposites, of Europe and America, of Jewish and gentile values—all rendered in speech, dress, action, and dramatic incident.

The painful process of Americanization is personified in *Yekl* by Mrs. Kavarsky, a well-meaning neighbor who takes an interest in poor Gitl. Childless herself, she takes on the characteristics of the stereotypical Jewish mother in her adoption of Gitl, and those of the scolding mother-in-law in her relationship with Jake. Like him, however, she comically ridicules Gitl to get her to assimilate, and it is interesting to note that one of this market woman's favorite tricks is to mimic idiosyncratic dialect and clumsy mannerisms; Mrs. Kavarsky pushes Gitl to Americanize because she sees this process as necessary to save Gitl's marriage, particularly after Jake's affair with Mamie, "a thief" and a Polish "serpent" (64), becomes known. As Cahan knew, ghetto mothers like Gitl, tied to the home and the immediate neighborhood, had little opportunity to mix with Americans and thereby learn English, or to attend language classes. In this respect Gitl's socially mobile husband and children—and independent women like Mamie and Fanny—have an advantage over Gitl.

Mrs. Kavarsky, however, is not the overbearing, whining, self-pitying Jewish mother of Woody Allen films or Philip Roth's early novels; she is more of a detached educator, who impatiently pushes her charge out of the nest. Many of her comments are ostensibly addressed to an unseen auditor, rather than to Gitl, a common—and comic—practice in Jewish culture of the time: "One might as well talk to the wall as to her! . . . I am working and working for her, and here she appreciates as much as the cat. Fie!" (57). But Gitl relishes Mrs. Kavarsky's damning portrait of Mamie: "that piece of ugliness should *try* and come to *my* house. Then she would know the price of a pound of evil. . . . Let her go to where she came from!" (56). Despite her complaint that America is to blame for Jake's lax morals, Mrs. Kavarsky urges Gitl to discard her wig, cut her hair in bangs, wear a corset, and compete sexually for Jake's loyalty. She affectionately showers down maledictions on Gitl but saves the rawest of them for "that Polish piece of disturbance" (64), Mamie, and for her spirited verbal duels with the errant husband, Jake.

In her inevitable final confrontation with him, Mrs. Kavarsky uses Yiddish to communicate, English to intimidate and remind him that she was in America "while you were hauling away at the bellows in Povodye," and finally, ritual gestures of insult to deliver her climactic blow. Gitl, however, knows how to toss an insult too; stung when she overhears Jake raise the issue of divorce to Mrs. Kavarsky, she bursts out of the bedroom, screaming: "May you and your Polish harlot be jumping out of your skins and chafing with wounds as long as you will have to wait for a divorce!" prompting an amazed Jake to marvel, "Look at the Cossack of straw. . . . Such a piece of cholera!" (71). Here the comic invective is from the Old World rather than the New. In the penultimate scene, in which the divorce is settled at the rabbi's home, we learn that Mrs. Kavarsky has also functioned as a *shadchen* ("matchmaker"), for she has been instrumental in arranging Gitl's coming marriage with Bernstein. She scolds Gitl for crying and code-switches into Yiddish: "foolish face that you are! Another woman would thank God for having at last got rid of the lump of leavened bread. . . . A rowdy, a sinner of Israel, a *regely loifer*, may no good Jew know him!" (87).

The Comedy of Arrival and Dislocation

My students usually note that while Jake is the pivotal figure in the tale, the story is actually dominated by the strong cast of women characters: Gitl, Mrs. Kavarsky, Mamie, and Fanny. The comedy of arrival and its sequel of success, where immigrants get the status and possessions they have desired, has a melancholy underside, in that all the things of the Old World have been lost—religious customs, relatives, holidays, landscapes— "tradition," as Tevye of *Fiddler on the Roof* puts it. Again and again, Cahan's characters think they know what they want, pursue their goals, and achieve them, only to find their victories hollow, thereby learning that their own desires make them their own worst enemies. This casts an ironic light on the American dream. Yekl, Gitl, Bernstein, and Mamie all achieve what they desire, but in victory they also find defeat. Here we find the comedy of dislocation, the obverse of the comedy of arrival. A good illustration of this comes in the rooftop scene where Jake and Mamie pledge their commitment to each other, an act that Jake knows is a betrayal not just of his wife and son but of his cultural tradition. The scene offers a comic contrast between the melodramatic plighting of troth scenario and the quake of Jake's conscience. Jules Chametzky notes that Jake interprets laundry blowing in the wind as a funeral shroud (64): "his attention had been attracted to a loosened pillow case ominously fluttering and flopping a yard or two off. The figure of his dead father, attired in burial linen, uprose to his mind" (Yekl 164).

Cahan himself had experienced the joy of arrival and the dejection of dislocation. He rejoiced in his American success, but like David Levinsky, the hero of his greatest novel, he knew he had lost much as well. At the end of *The Rise of David Levinsky*, David, who has risen to the summit of the garment industry but failed to achieve love or happiness, muses: "I am now worth more than two million dollars. . . . And yet when I take a look at my inner identity it impresses me as being precisely the same. My present station, power, the amount of worldly happiness at my command . . . seem void of significance. . . . There are cases when success is a tragedy" (3).

Cahan, though a nonbeliever himself, nevertheless valued, as Levinsky does, the Jewish heritage he had largely rejected, and his buoyant, hopeful imagination found ironic laughter in the pains, pleasures, and pitfalls of the immigrant experience. He clearly admired immigrant women like the ones in *Yekl* who were able to preserve traditional values of the Jewish home while simultaneously learning how to become modern American women. As my students come to see, the comic creativity and adaptations of both men and women animate Cahan's fiction and continue to entertain and instruct us today, in a new age of immigration, when similar patterns of acculturation and preservation are being enacted daily.

Notes

1. For two anthropological analyses of joking relationships and verbal dueling, see Apte 55 and Radcliffe-Brown 107.

2. For examples, see Reik.

3. For examples of this, see Raskin.

Works Cited

Apte, Mahadev. *Humor and Laughter: An Anthropological Approach.* Cornell UP, 1985.

Bakhtin, Mikhail. *Problems of Dostoevsky's Poetics.* Translated by Caryl Emerson, U of Minnesota P, 1984.

Cahan, Abraham. *The Rise of David Levinsky.* Harper, 1917.

———. Yekl *and "The Imported Bridegroom" and Other Stories of Yiddish New York.* Dover Publications, 1970.

Chametzky, Jules. *From the Ghetto: The Fiction of Abraham Cahan.* U of Massachusetts P, 1977.

Freud, Sigmund. *Jokes and Their Relation to the Unconscious.* Translated by James Strachey, W. W. Norton, 1960.

Hamilton, Holt. *The Life Stories of Undistinguished Americans As Told by Themselves.* 1906. Introduction by Werner Sollors, Routledge, 2000.

Howe, Irving. *World of Our Fathers.* Harcourt Brace Jovanovich, 1976.

Lipsky, Seth. *The Rise of Abraham Cahan.* Schocken Books, 2013.

Metzger, Isaac, editor. *A Bintel Brief: Sixty Years of Letters from the Lower East Side to the* Jewish Daily Forward. Schocken Books, 1971.

Radcliffe-Brown, A. R. "A Further Note on Joking Relationships." 1949. *Structure and Function in Primitive Society,* by Radcliffe-Brown, Cohen West, 1954, pp. 105–16.

Raskin, Victor. *Semantic Mechanisms of Humor.* D. Reidel, 1985.

Reik, Theodor. *Jewish Wit.* Gamut, 1962.

Silver, Joan Micklin, director. *Hester Street.* Midwest Films, 1975.

Judith R. Phagan

Displacement and Identity in the Work of Anzia Yezierska and Helena Maria Viramontes

Gloria Anzaldúa's seminal poem "To Live in the Borderlands" provides readers with an introduction to the concept of contested spaces in our daily lives. Anzaldúa states, "[Y]ou're a burra, buey, scapegoat, / forerunner of a new race, / half and half—both woman and man, neither—a new gender." "Borderlands" refers to the invisible borders that we live with, including those that divide us according to ethnicity, religion, sexuality, and family tradition. In my undergraduate course Rainbow of Voices, students read twentieth- and twenty-first-century works that explore the concept of borderlands. These works are written by Asian American, African American, Nuyorican, and Chicana writers and include narratives on LGBTQ, Jewish, and Muslim experience and experiences of disability. The course's goal is to listen carefully to marginalized voices and hear them as fully human members of a heterogeneous American society. For individuals in marginalized groups, the path toward adulthood is rarely easy. Anzia Yezierska's 1925 novel *Bread Givers*, Helena Maria Viramontes's 1995 novel *Under the Feet of Jesus*, and the 2007 independent film *Arranged*, directed by Stefan C. Schaefer and Diane Crespo, offer diverse coming-of-age narratives that negotiate these porous borderlands and that portray young people challenging their family traditions while also defending those traditions to the larger society.

In each work a young female protagonist comes of age in a different decade and culture while facing similar hurdles. These protagonists elicit empathy from students, who may face similar hurdles to self-actualization in the form of their parents' conservative worldviews. These protagonists also experience pressure from their peers to abandon traditional ways and be more modern.

We read *Bread Givers* as a defense of turn-of-the-century immigration to the United States in response to the historical backlash against "dirty immigrants" (17). The book begins in medias res with the Smolinsky family facing eviction from their cramped, dirty Hester Street tenement apartment. The myth of America ("it's always summer in America") and Reb Smolinsky's Orthodox Jewish belief that "the prayers of his daughters didn't count because God didn't listen to women" (9) are introduced early. One of those daughters, Sara Smolinsky, is the protagonist and battles dirt and hunger as well as her tyrannical father.

Inevitably my students hate Reb Smolinsky for denying his daughter an education, but Sara's mother and sisters feel that Sara should obey the father. Family is just one of the contested spaces in this novel: Sara is desperate to "make herself for a person," to become an educated person with a room of her own. One irony is that her temperament is remarkably similar to that of her father, whom she despises. Sara leaves home, gets a job and a basement apartment, and suffers from hunger while getting her education. She earns her high school diploma and graduates from college as a teacher. Ultimately she has a clean, bright room of her own and reconciles with her father. This reconciliation is problematic for many students, who resent the oppressive father, but Sara's forgiveness leads to such questions as, To what extent can one truly leave one's roots (religious in this case) behind? To what extent are economic issues present in the story, and how do they influence choices? Would Orthodox Jewish practice feel less confining for Sara if money were not an issue?

In *Under the Feet of Jesus*, the thirteen-year-old protagonist, Estrella, the daughter of undocumented workers, tries to survive as an outlaw in her own country. Like Sara, she faces hunger and poverty. While protagonists in the other books we read have homes with varying degrees of comfort, Estrella lives in the back seat of an old station wagon or in a migrant shack. The novel introduces the motif of dirt, which appears in the car and in cabins, fields, and a barn. Dirt is not the enemy of Estrella and the migrants she lives among, but part and parcel of their lives. Indeed the novel refers to the barn as a "cathedral" (9), conflating it and its dirt with religion. Estrella even experiences her sexual awakening and loses her virginity in the dirt under a truck during a respite from work.

Estrella is frequently hungry, which is particularly ironic because she and her family harvest the crops that other people eat. They do not make enough money to purchase quality produce and are occasionally reduced to stealing a peach that falls to the ground. Estrella, like Sara, desires an education, but her teachers are far more concerned with her dirty fingernails and the lice in her hair than with teaching her anything. Estrella is a strong girl who becomes a surrogate mother to her four younger siblings when her mother, who has been deserted by Estrella's father, has a nervous breakdown. The borderlands discussed in this novel are both figurative and literal. Estrella must always keep an eye out for *la migra* (United States immigration and border control services) and remember that her citizenship "papers" are under the feet of Jesus in her mother's makeshift altar in the migrant shack. Estrella is instructed: "Don't run scared. You stay there and look them in the eye. . . . If they stop you, if they try to pull you into the green vans, you tell them the birth certificates are under the feet of Jesus, just tell them" (63). Estrella must act like an adult, as must Sara in parts of *Bread Givers*. Many of my students, raised as latchkey children, know the challenges of self-protection at a young age. Students may discuss whether this need to adopt an adult role is limited by class or religion, and whether a statue of Jesus can protect Latino/as from the authorities.

In *Under the Feet of Jesus* the children are bathed daily despite the fact that the mother, Petra, works from before sunrise until after sundown. The motif of cleanliness is also stressed in the film *Arranged*, where both the Muslim and the Jewish fathers take great care with their daily ablutions. *Arranged* introduces challenges for its middle-class protagonists, Rochel and Nasira, who come from an Orthodox Jewish and a Muslim family respectively. Neither woman is uncomfortable with her religion, but they are both unhappy with the tradition of arranged marriage observed by their families.

Nasira is horrified at her father's apparent choice of an old friend for her husband (he is too old and ugly for her) but is heartened when she is presented to a Muslim family with an educated, handsome son with a master's degree. Nasira is excited and hopeful about this match and shares this excitement with Rochel. Both women value their religious heritage and some of their parents' old customs. However, each girl hungers for individuality and a love match. Rochel bears up during the process of meeting a dozen humorously inappropriate matches and then decides to take a "time out" from meetings with the *"shadchen"* ("matchmaker"). Her mother chides her for diminishing her sister's "prospects."

At the end of the film, however, Rochel is successfully married, as is Nasira, and both women are caught at the fragile border between tradition and modernity, where they must negotiate a compromise. The middle-class status the women enjoy removes class as a barrier to self-actualization but places religious tradition firmly in the center. How are Rochel's and Nasira's struggles different from those of Sara, whose story takes place more than fifty years earlier? Is the quandary of having to choose between the old and new ways inevitable for young people in all households (regardless of income or education)?

Each of the three books in *Bread Givers* marks a period of Sara's growth. Similarly, each of the five sections in *Under the Feet of Jesus* ends with a new development in Estrella's maturation. Despite differences in the characters' ethnicity, race, and religion and in the time periods in which the stories are set, reading these two novels and viewing *Arranged* raise questions that make for fertile classroom discussion and an opportunity for the cultivation of empathy and understanding. Anzaldúa reminds us that "to survive the Borderlands / you must live *sin fronteras* / be a cross-roads." Sara, Estrella, Rochel, and Nasira are examples of empowered women who are stronger for their struggles.

Works Cited

Anzaldúa, Gloria. "To Live in the Borderlands." *Power Poetry*, www.powerpoetry .org/content/live-borderlands.

Arranged. Directed by Stefan C. Schaefer and Diane Crespo, Film Movement, 2007.

Viramontes, Helena Maria. *Under the Feet of Jesus*. Plume Books, 1995.

Yezierska, Anzia. *Bread Givers*. Doubleday Page, 1925.

Sarah Gleeson-White and Lucas Thompson

Teaching Anzia Yezierska's
Bread Givers in Australia

We teach Anzia Yezierska's 1925 novel *Bread Givers* to upper-level undergraduates at the University of Sydney, Australia, as part of a survey course exploring literature of the United States through noncanonical texts. Included within a broader modernism module, *Bread Givers* allows us to explore representations of Jewish American identity in early-twentieth-century fiction, as well as the interaction between literary modernism and Hollywood cinema.

One of the challenges in teaching *Bread Givers* to Australian undergraduates pertains to their relative dearth of previous knowledge of ethnic American literature and its geographies. Their understanding of American fiction of this period tends to center on a small set of canonical authors, such as Ernest Hemingway, F. Scott Fitzgerald, and William Faulkner, which means that the semiautobiographical novel of a female Jewish immigrant may strike some students as an object of study whose value is not self-evident. Moreover, students may find Yezierska's prose as difficult to read as the work of other experimental modernists, because of its fragmented narrative strands, dislocated presentation of consciousness, cut-up-like techniques of narration, and intentionally jarring and choppy descriptive passages. The novel's idiosyncratic style, which a contemporary reviewer described as "raw, uncontrollable poetry" ("Turbulent Folk-ways"), can cause students to quickly feel lost within an unfamiliar textual landscape. We therefore introduce students to David Damrosch's theory on reading "distant" texts in ways that avoid "the twin perils of exoticism and assimilation," where exoticism implies a fetishization of the text's al-terity, and assimilation implies a stance taken by the reader that is overly familiar in its assumptions of similarity (13). In essence, the challenge is one of scale: exoticism keeps the text at too great a distance from the reader; assimilation moves it too near. Of course, the temporal and geo-graphic distance between the students' world and the world of the novel is indeed significant, yet the emotional resonances and bildungsroman structure through which Sara Smolinsky finds her place in the world offer deep forms of identification and "recognition" (Felski 23) for many stu-dents. Keeping these scales in constant tension allows students to develop a properly critical perspective on the novel.

After foregrounding this interpretive approach, we explore how Yezier-ska's novel tracks Sara's path from a seemingly "problematic overemotional-ity" (Ngai 94) to some degree of containment as she enters both a stable profession and a romantic relationship, which register her becoming Ameri-can, a trajectory common across so much ethnic—and especially Jewish American—literature. Yezierska's rather feverish prose style and narrative voice provide a second challenge: to orient the students' readings of the novel away from the problematic racialization of overemotionality that Si-anne Ngai identifies across a vast historicocultural plane, "from Harriet Beecher Stowe's ebullient Topsy (1852) to Warner Brothers' hyperactive Speedy Gonzales (1950), to the hand-wringing Jews, gesticulating Italians, and hot-tempered Greeks in films ranging from *The Jazz Singer* to *My Big Fat Greek Wedding*" (93). To interrogate this association, we situate the novel in its mass-cultural context, considering whether Yezierska might have written *Bread Givers* with motion pictures in mind. As one of the best-known writ-ers of the Jewish ghetto during the 1910s and 1920s, Yezierska came to the attention of Hollywood in 1920 when Samuel Goldwyn hired her to co-write the scenario for his film adaptation of her short-story cycle, *Hungry Hearts*; the film was released in 1922, three years before the publication of *Bread Givers*.[1] Given this context, we encourage students to consider the cinematic possibilities of *Bread Givers*. Might Yezierska have written *Bread Givers* using strategies she learned during her time in Hollywood?

Ngai also describes *Bread Givers* as "animated," a descriptor that use-fully invokes two seemingly antithetical concepts—the mechanical and the emotional—and thus provides a way of theorizing the transmedial potential of the novel (95). Indeed, many editions of *Bread Givers* include stills from the motion-picture adaptation of *Hungry Hearts*, which we use to frame students' reading of the novel in its mass-cultural context, particularly as a silent-film melodrama. Because the narrative of silent cinema relies heavily on nonverbal modes of communication (barring intertitles and diegetic print texts, such as letters), its visual language—facial expressions, gesticulations, and so on—needs to be writ large to ensure meaning is relayed. *Bread Givers*, we argue, embodies a similar aesthetic of gesticulation and emotionality. We go still one step further and encourage students to experiment with reading (or rereading) the novel as the literary analogue to a silent film. Responding to the fact that several students have told us that they imagine the events of the novel taking place in black and white, we encourage the class to use the book as a set of imaginative instructions for generating a silent film, using carefully selected extracts on literary imagination from Elaine Scarry's *Dreaming by the Book* as a guide. Inviting students to read in this way invariably opens up fruitful conversations around literary reception, and the ways in which aesthetic encounters are often built around specific imaginative acts. Moreover, this mode of reading preserves a certain amount of historical and cultural distance, once again helping students resist an easy "assimilation" of Yezierska's characters.

We also situate the novel within a broader discourse of ethnicity, noting that *Bread Givers* appeared during something of a boom in the representation of the Jewish immigrant in a range of popular cultural venues, including newspapers, cartoons, songs, the vaudeville stage, and of course motion pictures. At the same time, several prominent Jewish entrepreneurs, like Goldwyn, began to dominate the commercial entertainment industry. As Lester Friedman notes, "Between 1900 and 1929 alone, approximately 230 films featured clearly discernable Jewish characters," with a substantial number of these films exploring immigrant themes (9). And according to Patricia Erens, nearly forty films about the Jewish ghetto were released in the 1920s alone, some of which attempted to depict Jewish immigrants in relatively nuanced ways beyond the stereotypes of the villain and the miser (77). In lectures and tutorials, we screen brief scenes depicting the Jewish ghetto from *Hungry Hearts* and *Salome of the Tenements* (a 1925 adaptation of Yezierska's novel of the same name), as well as from *The Jazz Singer*, before asking students to consider *Bread Givers*' modal affinities with these cinematic representations of Jewishness. The novel's engagements with mass culture register its modernness: its participation in new technologies and their expressive forms. In this way, we encourage students to consider the association of the term *animatedness* with the technological, and the ways it might be imbricated with affect. Over the course of the module, which also considers African American and Native American modernisms, we put various other questions to students, which they can choose to take up in an extended essay. We encourage them to consider, for instance, questions of canonicity and countermodernisms, and the ways in which ethnic writers refracted modernist concerns through their unique encounters with American culture.[2] Published in the same year as Fitzgerald's *The Great Gatsby*, Yezierska's novel opens up productive discussions about literary value and the broader cultural and institutional structures that enshrine certain American novels in a canon. We invite students interested in literary style to map Yezierska's shifting stylistic terrain and to fold their close readings into a wider discussion of the novel's thematic concerns. We show how interpreting *Bread Givers* in the light of Damrosch's negotiation of exoticism and assimilation can allow for productive ways of reading, not merely this novel, but Jewish American and ethnic American fiction more broadly.

Notes

1. Famous Players–Lasky Corporation produced the 1925 film version of Yezierska's novel *Salome of the Tenements*; Yezierska had nothing to do with this production.

2. Sollors and also Konzett are indispensable in framing this part of the module.

Works Cited

Damrosch, David. *What Is World Literature?* Princeton UP, 2003.

Erens, Patricia. *The Jew in American Cinema*. Indiana UP, 1985.

Felski, Rita. *The Uses of Literature*. Blackwell Publishing, 2008.

Fitzgerald, F. Scott. *The Great Gatsby*. 1925. Penguin Books, 1990.

Friedman, Lester. *Hollywood's Image of the Jew*. Frederick Ungar, 1982.

The Jazz Singer. Directed by Alan Crosland, performance by Al Jolson, Warner Bros., 1927.

Konzett, Delia Caprosa. *Ethnic Modernisms: Anzia Yezierska, Zora Neale Hurston, Jean Rhys, and the Aesthetics of Dislocation*. Palgrave-Macmillan, 2002.

Ngai, Sianne. *Ugly Feelings*. Harvard UP, 2005.

Scarry, Elaine. *Dreaming by the Book*. Princeton UP, 1999.

Sollors, Werner. *Ethnic Modernism*. Harvard UP, 2008.

"Turbulent Folkways of the Ghetto in a New Novel." *The New York Times*, 13 Sept. 1925, www.nytimes.com/1925/09/13/archives/turbulent-folkways-of -the-ghetto-in-a-new-novel-bread-givers-by.html.

Yezierska, Anzia. *Bread Givers*. 1925. Persea Books, 2003.

———. *Hungry Hearts*. 1920. Penguin Classics, 1997.

———. *Salome of the Tenements*. 1923. U of Illinois P, 1996.

Catherine Rottenberg

Anzia Yezierska and
the Changing Fortunes of Jewishness

Anzia Yezierska's literary corpus has generated increasing scholarly interest over the past few decades. Yezierska's best-known novel, *Bread Givers*,
is today considered by many to be a modern classic, and within Jewish
American studies, students are very often required to read her work. Yet the
last of her four surviving novels, *All I Could Never Be*, was only recently
rediscovered and has been republished by Persea Books after being out of
print for decades. While this 1932 novel shares many narrative similarities
with Yezierska's previous full-length fiction, *All I Could Never Be* also di-
verges significantly from *Salome of the Tenements*, *Bread Givers*, and *Arrogant Beggar* in its portrayal of Jewishness. Precisely because it both reflects
and reproduces the unmooring of Jewishness from a racial category, *All I
Could Never Be* is a fascinating text that promises to change how Yezierska's
corpus is understood and taught, while simultaneously enabling scholars and
instructors to better understand the complex processes that have facilitated
the transformation of Jewishness into a white ethnicity.[1]

The novel tells the story of Fanya Ivanowna, who, raised in dire poverty in Poland, eventually finds her way to the Lower East Side. Electri-
fied by a settlement-house lecture given by a well-known educator, Henry
Scott, Fanya is impetuous enough to seek Scott out and ask him to read

her autobiography.[2] Scott is immediately impressed and offers her a job as a translator with a group of sociologists studying Polish immigrant life in the United States. Eventually, Scott makes sexual advances to his young protégé, and although Fanya loves him, she is confused and rejects these advances. This marks the end of their intimate relationship. For years afterward, Fanya imagines herself still in love with Scott, and following her success as an author she even attempts to rekindle the relationship. This attempt fails miserably, and Fanya decides to start her life anew by leaving the Lower East Side and New York City behind her. She buys a house in a small New England town, where eventually Vladimir Pavlowich, a painter-turned-hobo, enters her life. This non-Jewish fellow immigrant ignites Fanya's passion, and the reader is made to understand that after so many years of feeling like a rootless outsider, Fanya has finally created a home for herself in America.

All of the more formal elements that characterize Yezierska's novels can be found in *All I Could Never Be*: the unique mix of melodrama, sentimental romance, and realism, the relatively loose form and plot structure, the grittiness and peculiar pace of her prose, and, finally, the obsessive theme that drives so many of her narratives, namely, the desire of the female immigrant protagonist to "make herself for a person" (*Bread Givers* 66). In addition, the novel has many narrative aspects that are reminiscent of Yezierska's earlier works. Fanya is yet another one of Yezierska's indomitable female protagonists. Not unlike the stories of Sara Smolinsky in *Bread Givers* and Sonya Vrunsky in *Salome of the Tenements*, Fanya's story underscores the potential payoff of perseverance, independence, and hard work while simultaneously highlighting the profound loneliness of an immigrant and female rebel. Fanya's overall trajectory is, in effect, nearly identical to that of Sara's and Sonya's: they all manage to fulfill themselves professionally or artistically and ultimately find like-minded men who support their life decisions as well as their ambitions.

In Yezierska's earlier novels, however, the female protagonists end up working and living side by side with their Jewish partners, while *All I Could Never Be* presents us with a female protagonist who, in the end, is not poised to marry a Jewish soulmate but, rather, to consummate a union with a non-Jewish immigrant in a small New England town. This is a striking difference. Indeed, if Yezierska's writing has, in many ways, come to represent early-twentieth-century Jewish American fiction, then it seems particularly important for scholars and students to investigate Yezierska's changing depictions of Jewishness and Jewish otherness.

Yezierska's earlier fiction, and most particularly her first novel, *Salome of the Tenements*, clearly articulates Jewish difference in racialized terms. The Jewish protagonist Sonya Vrunsky's marriage to the Anglo-Saxon millionaire philanthropist John Manning is described not in terms of interfaith matrimony but in terms of racial mixing. In sharp contrast, *All I Could Never Be* identifies the partnership between Jewish and gentile immigrants in small-town America not only as possible but as perhaps the only bridge to a more integrated and accepting society. Though the text intimates that the cultural gulf between Scott (a native-born Anglo-Saxon American) and Fanya (an immigrant Jew) may still be too wide, barring any possibility of intimate union at least for the moment, the ostensible Jewish-gentile divide is ultimately overcome by the affinity between Fanya and Vladimir (both Russian-Polish immigrants). Nationality rather than racial similarity takes precedence, complicating the notion of Jewishness as a distinct racial category while concurrently stressing the way in which America promises the transcendence of old-world enmities and prohibitions against interfaith marriages.

Furthermore, the text raises the question of Jewish difference throughout the narrative only to displace it in the end by raising the specter of "something deeper, more far-reaching than the race barrier" (231). This elusive "something" materializes in Oakdale, the small New England town where Fanya finally settles. This something, which is deeper than race, is never defined, yet it is related in some way to class status and more specifically to downward mobility. While Fanya, the now middle-class Jewish immigrant, has been accepted into the New England town, others have been ostracized by the respectable inhabitants of Oakdale. The despised other in the town is not the Jew, it turns out, but rather the previously upper-middle-class woman Jane, who once belonged to the wealthiest and best family in town but has since spiraled into abject poverty (224). It is almost as if the novel positions the determined and active Jewish immigrant as the one (best) able to fulfill the promise of the American dream, while contrasting her with the once privileged "native aristocrat of Oakdale" (241) who has passively accepted her bad fortune. Ultimately, the narrative deflects attention away from the question of Jewish otherness by positing a more profound difference than the (Jewish) race barrier. Moreover, if intermarriage between Jew and gentile can become desirable, and if Jewishness is no longer irreconcilable with quintessential small-town American life, then Jewish difference, whether conceived in racial or national terms, no longer seems to make much difference at all. This, in turn, suggests that Yezierska, whose popularity and later canonicity were arguably based on her ability to capture the Jewish, and in particular the female Jewish, immigrant experience on the Lower East Side, was already distancing herself from that narrative by the 1930s.

Yezierska's Depression-era novel offers the New England town rather than the iconic Lower East Side as potentially better-suited to fashioning a new mode of Jewish Americanness. For teachers and scholars of Jewish American literary studies, then, *All I Could Never Be* can be a particularly useful text for interrogating shifting perceptions, depictions, and framings of Jewishness, since Jewish racial otherness is no longer taken for granted or at least does not signify in the same way in this 1932 novel as it does in Yezierska's earlier fiction. Indeed, it may be that *All I Could Never Be* presages and even participates in the transmutation of Jewishness into a white ethnic identity, a complex and contested notion that, as Lori Harrison-Kahan and Jennifer Glaser have separately demonstrated, continues to spark debate and preoccupy Jewish American literary scholars to this day.

Notes

1. For a discussion of the shifting signification of Jewishness, see Brodkin; Goldstein; and Jacobson.

2. As the few scholars who have written about this novel in any detail have demonstrated, the irony here is that the story of the relationship between Fanya and Scott is autobiographical, bearing a striking resemblance to Yezierska's relationship with John Dewey. See Dayton-Wood 216; see also Henriksen as well as Dearborn for biographical accounts of Yezierska's life.

Works Cited

Brodkin, Karen. *How Jews Became White Folks and What That Says about Race in America.* Rutgers UP, 1998.

Dayton-Wood, Amy. "What College Has Done for Me: Anzia Yezierska and the Problem of Progressive Education." *College English*, vol. 74, no. 3, 2012, 215–33.

Dearborn, Mary. *Love in the Promised Land: The Story of Anzia Yezierska and John Dewey.* Macmillan, 1989.

Glaser, Jennifer. *Borrowed Voices: Writing and Racial Ventriloquism in the Jewish American Imagination.* Rutgers UP, 2016.

Goldstein, Eric. *The Price of Whiteness: Jews, Race, and American Identity.* Princeton UP, 2006.

Harrison-Kahan, Lori. "Drunk with the Fiery Rhythms of Jazz." *MFS: Modern Fiction Studies*, vol. 51, no. 2, 2005, pp. 416–36.

Henriksen, Louise Levitas. *Anzia Yezierska: A Writer's Life*. Rutgers UP, 1988.

Jacobson, Matthew Frye. *Whiteness of a Different Color*. Harvard UP, 1998.

Yezierska, Anzia. *All I Could Never Be*. 1932. Persea Books, 2019.

———. *Arrogant Beggar*. 1927. Duke UP, 1996.

———. *Bread Givers*. 1925. Persea Books, 2002.

———. *Salome of the Tenements*. 1923. U of Illinois P, 1995.

Four Approaches to Teaching "Goodbye, Columbus"

Introduction

Josh Lambert

Philip Roth's novella "Goodbye, Columbus" first appeared in *The Paris Review*, in an issue dated Autumn-Winter 1958–59. Though Roth was not yet twenty-six years old, it was hardly his first publication: a few of his stories had been published four years earlier, and one had even been selected for the 1955 edition of *The Best American Short Stories*. Still, most critics agree that the appearance of "Goodbye, Columbus" marked Roth's emergence as a major writer. No wonder the author selected it as the title story for his first book, which was published as *"Goodbye, Columbus" and Five Stories* on 7 May 1959. That book went on to win both the National Book Award for Fiction and the National Jewish Book Award, to sell well in paperback, and to attract scathing criticism from some rabbis and reviewers for Jewish publications who objected to its unflattering portraits of American Jews; one such critic called it "a book that drips with disrespect and detestation of Jewish life" (Ziprin).

Most readers and critics disagreed, and Roth defended himself from such accusations skillfully in lectures and in print. Still, it is thanks in part to such controversies, as well as a 1969 Hollywood film adaptation of the novella, that "Goodbye, Columbus" has remained one of Roth's most widely read, admired, and discussed works.[1] The novella's brevity and

317

humor make it an easy text to position on a syllabus, and while it tells a relatively simple story about two young people's summer romance, it manages to do so in a way that evokes both its historical period and broad questions about Jews, gender, sexuality, race, class, suburbanization, and more. The short statements that follow, contributed by scholars working in different disciplines and teaching in different departments at different institutions, outline some of the ways in which Roth's novella can be taught effectively. While not aiming to be exhaustive, these statements survey a variety of approaches and suggest both the many kinds of courses in which the text works well and the tactics scholars have employed in teaching it. It is hoped that these contributions will be helpful for anyone considering how best to use "Goodbye, Columbus" in a course.

Understanding the Jewish 1950s

Rachel Gordan

Bringing together sex, religion, class, and Jews, "Goodbye, Columbus" is an invaluable text for teaching the post–World War II Jewish American experience. Roth's novella can be productively read as a primary source for understanding the Jewish 1950s alongside excerpts from key sociological and historical works from the 1950s, including sociologist Nathan Glazer's *American Judaism*, especially chapters 6 and 7, and theologian and sociologist Will Herberg's *Protestant-Catholic-Jew*, especially chapters 3 and 8.

Roth vividly portrays the relation between postwar Jewish religious life and socioeconomic shifts of this era. The year before "Goodbye, Columbus" was published, sociologist Nathan Hurvitz remarked that "American Jews have climbed the social ladder more quickly and have achieved middle-class status more widely than any other ethnic group during the same period of American history" (117). In the novella, the Patimkin family's move from Newark to Short Hills, New Jersey, during Brenda Patimkin's childhood, represents this major socioeconomic shift. But not all Jews were equally affected by these changes. As Brenda and Neil Klugman become acquainted, Brenda's offhand remark, "We lived in Newark when I was a baby," ruffles Neil, who still lives there (12). This tension between the two lovers reminds readers that postwar American Jewry, with all its rapid changes, was far from monolithic in its experience.

"Goodbye, Columbus" also demonstrates how postwar socioeconomic changes affected religion. Herberg wrote of the Jewish migration to suburbia that it was "not merely an alternation in place of residence; it involved a certain transformation in the entire outlook and mode of life" (189). Ascending the socioeconomic ladder, postwar middle-class Jews now shared a perspective on religion with their fellow middle-class Americans, and religion became a marker, a way to fit in. In Herberg's formulation, not to attend church or synagogue was to take oneself outside the mainstream of middle-class America.

The implicit critique that Roth's protagonist, Neil, directs at the Patimkins' affluent life is echoed in sociological literature on 1950s Jews. For instance, if the fictional Neil had read Glazer's study, published two years before Roth's novella, he likely would have nodded along in agreement with Glazer's observations about postwar suburban Jews. In describing the challenges of studying his subject, Glazer writes: "Were we to limit ourselves to what American Jews say about their religion, or to what they carry on the surface of their minds, how confused and banal a picture we would carry away! We would find, on the one hand, the clichés of liberal religion and, on the other, a kind of confusion in which loyalty to the Jewish people is identified with Jewish religion" (131).

In a conversation with Brenda's mother, Mrs. Patimkin, about her synagogue, Neil comes away with similar views. Mrs. Patimkin asks Neil what kind of Jew he is, and he answers, "I'm just Jewish," but, trying to find common ground, asks if she knows "Martin Buber's work": "'Buber . . . Buber,' she said, looking at her Hadassah list. 'Is he orthodox or conservative?'" Neil replies, "He's a philosopher" (88). Mrs. Patimkin cares about which synagogue one attends—and its affiliation with Reform, Conservative, or Orthodox Judaism—and seems to have little interest in Jewish thought. While Mrs. Patimkin's Judaism is tied to the synagogue, Neil's Jewishness finds its center in Jewish culture and thought. In Roth's presentation of these two characters, Mrs. Patimkin's Judaism, reflecting affluent suburbia, is portrayed as concerning appearances and fitting in; Neil's Jewishness, still tied to urban, working-class experience, has more intellectual substance. But in truth, Neil, too, is portrayed as choosing a third way: an alternative to the materialism of the Patimkins and the working-class concerns of his own parents. Neil's character augurs alternative ways of being Jewish that are rooted in an outsider perspective on the middle-class materialism that the Patimkins represent.

These and many other themes of "Goodbye, Columbus" echo Herman Wouk's bestselling *Marjorie Morningstar*, published earlier in the decade: in both novels a geographic move is attended by socioeconomic changes in Jewish life, and in both a female Jewish protagonist's sexuality is positioned at the center of the narrative. Notably, the reception of the two texts was similar, too: both were made into movies with leading Hollywood actors, and both novelists were criticized by rabbis and Jewish leaders for mocking Jewish religion in their fiction.[2]

By reading such literary texts as primary sources, students examining postwar American religion or Jewish history gain substantial insight into the period and into the ways different kinds of Jews thought about Judaism and one another. There is a tendency among undergraduates to think that only later generations thought critically about 1950s suburbanites. Roth's novella is a valuable reminder that even during these years of change, Jews such as Roth were aware of how shifts in Jewish socioeconomics intersected with shifts in the status of religion. Jews' economic ascent helped make possible the acceptance of postwar Judaism as a middle-class American religion, alongside Protestantism and Catholicism—exactly the change that Herberg and Glazer describe in their sociology. These economic and religious developments, in turn, made Roth's biting depictions of middle-class Jews palatable to an American audience: if Jews had successfully integrated into middle-class American society by 1959, what was the harm in a piece of fiction that was not entirely flattering? As noted earlier, many American Jews were indeed uneasy about Roth's less than flattering portrayals, suggesting that socioeconomic changes could only take Jews so far—maybe not much farther than the distance between Newark and Short Hills, New Jersey.

"Goodbye, Columbus" and the Production of Postwar Identity

Benjamin Schreier

I'm sure I'm not alone in landing in the profession having already formed a personal attachment to Roth's "Goodbye, Columbus"; some might say this affection circumscribes my teaching of the novella, but I like to think of it as a resource for my pedagogy. I've been teaching "Goodbye, Columbus" for as long as I've been teaching, and one of its strengths is that it can be taught in many different contexts.

I find the book quite useful in surveys. In an American literature survey organized around the idea of frontiers, which I taught early in my career, Roth's novella was able to do a lot of work, as it is intimately concerned with all sorts of borders and border crossings—between city and suburb, between classes, and between identity groups. Reading "Goodbye, Columbus" alongside texts like James Fenimore Cooper's *The Last of the Mohicans*, Frederick Douglass's autobiographies, Willa Cather's *The Professor's House*, Allen Ginsberg's "Howl," and Toni Morrison's *Beloved*, students focused on Neil's ability to cross borders even as he defends a concept of authenticity: think of the novella's preoccupation with scenes of movement, Neil's talk with Ben Patimkin at the factory, and Neil and Brenda's uncle Leo at Ron's wedding. In a course on post-1865 American literature taught with texts like Henry James's *Washington Square*, Zora Neale Hurston's *Their Eyes Were Watching God*, Frank O'Hara's *Lunch Poems*, and Sandra Cisneros's *The House on Mango Street*, Roth's novella tells a literary historical tale about post–World War II style and multiculturalism. In this context, it makes sense to attend to Neil's work as narrator, and also to the novella's differentiation of identities—Jewish, black, and unmarked but white goy.[3]

In an internationally focused, comparative Jewish literature course or a domestically oriented Jewish American literature course, discussion can turn to the novella's production of Jewish identity, in particular by encouraging students to think of the work as something more than a mere historical document. In that context, students might focus on the pages describing Neil's drive into Newark, with his meditation about how neighborhoods that were once Jewish have become black, and on how this meditation serves his own labor of identification vis-à-vis the Patimkins, Neil's aunt Gladys, and postwar America. Ethnic literature in the United States provides one more productive rubric. In a course I organized around the theme "the ethnicity of class," which looks at how racial and ethnic difference in literature in the United States often encodes—and displaces— class difference, Roth's novella, which is so good on postwar American threats to ethnic identification, showed how class helps make identity visible: if working-class Aunt Gladys embodies an outdated Jewish stereotype, and rich Brenda never seems securely Jewish, then Neil embodies a search for postwar Jewish American possibility.

When teaching—especially authors or books easily taken hold of by the machinery of ethnic recognition—I try to steer clear of using literary texts primarily to make sociological observations and instead emphasize texts as making possible or acting on forms of thought. In this context, and given my own interest in thinking critically about the kind of work done by concepts of identity, "Goodbye, Columbus" is a great text.

One way to read the novella is as an exploration of identity—the narrative is a tangle of vectors through and away from Jewishness, and the book's settings showcase Jewishness's waning persuasiveness. A close reading exposes the mechanisms that allow Neil, and readers, to think about these ideas. Roth, like other postwar writers, shows how new modes of thinking about American identity were becoming possible. Indeed, the novella can be used to show those mechanisms in action, not simply presumed to be a representation of them, as Neil's primary activity in the story involves differentiating himself from atavistic and assimilatory modes of Jewishness, even though no other obvious mode of positive identification appeals to him. The novella provides an interesting way of looking at a curious machinery of identification, whereby Neil can imagine himself to be Jewish but without any self-evident religious or practical content. Here individual knowledge replaces communitarian practice. In contrast, much of the Jewish literature of a generation before Roth and a generation after him seems more invested in a community-based concept of identity. It's as if, to make an acrobatic use of Sartre, "Goodbye, Columbus" suggests that Jewishness as an identity belongs to Neil and cannot belong to other people. In this sense, the book shines a light at once on cultural narratives about and incitements to containment and conformity and on how ideas about Americanness were invested and reinscribed during the decades after World War II. Students in a graduate seminar I taught on Cold War literature in the United States were especially interested in how the Patimkins carried their Jewish past with them but secured it, out of sight, in a storage room, a contrast with the uncontained and overflowing, and now anachronistic, expressions of Jewish identity by Aunt Gladys and Uncle Leo.

Teaching "Goodbye, Columbus" in Germany

Bettina Hofmann

Teaching Philip Roth and other Jewish American writers in international contexts poses particular challenges, and the use of a foreign language is not the greatest obstacle. To become teachers of English, students in Germany study American literature along with British literature and English linguistics, and they take practical language courses. Thus, studying literature makes up only a small part of their curriculum. Typically, the students have little systematic knowledge of the United States, and no background in Judaism or Jewish American culture. Their primary source of knowledge about American civilization is American popular culture. Their reading skills—which include paying attention to subtle differences in meaning and applying theoretical concepts—need to be practiced continually. With "Goodbye, Columbus" they can effectively practice these skills in classroom discussions. The novella is attractive to nonnative speakers because of its length, yet it offers a complexity that is usually associated with novels. Written by one of the great stylists of the English language, the text is both accessible and challenging. It is an excellent example of American writing of the twentieth century with regard to vocabulary, grammar, syntax, and stylistics, and it exhibits features of both formal writing and American vernacular. Therefore, one goal for a teacher in this context is to have students decipher the apparent simplicity of the text to discover its complexity.

In my many years of teaching I have positioned Roth's text in different ways, contrasting the novella with that of other Jewish American authors or placing it in the context of ethnic literatures, religion in the United States, and the 1950s. These reference points pertain to a feature shared by all of Roth's writing, namely, his interest in the sociohistorical and political dimensions of American and Jewish American life. German students generally exhibit little knowledge of Jewish history, probably with the exception of the Holocaust. Thus teaching Roth's text with an emphasis on, for instance, the motif of food directs their attention away from death and destruction and toward life-affirming principles. International students more broadly also tend to know little about Jewish traditions or the denominations and movements within Judaism. Teachers can assign David Biale's *Insider/Outsider: American Jews and Multiculturalism* as secondary reading to help illuminate the position of Jews in America.

Often, when students focus on the protagonist Neil, to whom they can relate because they are about his age, they talk about what he experiences as if it were something that happened to a real person. Here is the opportunity to teach them that a writer can successfully use a boy-meets-girl romance to introduce contrasting ideas. After it has been established that Neil is looking for forbidden fruit, literally in the fridge and metaphorically in Brenda, the class analyzes the different ways food is presented in the story. A focus on food proves especially rewarding, as this motif contains references to Judaism as an ethnicity. Fabio Parasecoli's article "Food: Identity and Diversity" has served as a comprehensive starting point for a discussion of the various social functions of food. Parasecoli's article contains examples only from Europe, so students are challenged to make the transfer to American foods. This way, students learn that items of food in texts are not simply realist props but indicators of location, time, power structures, ethnic consciousness, and (historical) identity.[4]

Surprisingly for many students, subtle references in "Goodbye, Columbus" also link food to Judaism as a religion. The allusion to Elijah, in which the religious ritual of the Seder is secularized through the dedication of Elijah's cup to Mickey Mantle (19), is especially hard for students to grasp. A few times I have observed an almost epiphanic moment when students suddenly understand that a seemingly innocuous detail that they had regarded as a descriptive element intended to make the scene realistic now offers them, with the knowledge of the Passover ritual, a new dimension to the text. This is a lasting learning experience that helps students develop a new sensitivity to difference and see that they can access other religious and cultural traditions by studying them. When they read, they may direct this awareness of difference to the representation of ethnic groups in American literature as well as in other literatures.

Using Film to Teach "Goodbye, Columbus"

Julian Levinson

Although students may be sensitive to the ways images reframe and distort reality, they are still sometimes dismayed when they discover that a movie has deviated from the work of fiction on which it is based. This affective response can provide useful energy for classroom discussions about the adapted text and about the problem of adaptation more generally.

Teaching the film *Goodbye, Columbus*, adapted from Roth's novella, works particularly well when it is introduced in lessons devoted to the novella, specifically its denouement. One of 1969's biggest box-office draws and an Academy Award nominee for Best Adapted Screenplay, this movie exploited the novella's romantic plot to indulge audiences with sumptuous scenes of postadolescent eros. The final scene offers a fascinating example of Hollywood's preference for unambiguous closure. In Roth's original text, some critical questions are left unanswered. First, while Neil insists that Brenda deliberately left her diaphragm for her mother to discover, this is by no means confirmed. Indeed, Brenda may be correct when she accuses Neil of shrouding his paranoia and fear of rejection in "psychoanalytic crap" (132). Second, ambiguity surrounds Brenda's feelings about the breakup. As their argument heats up, Neil imagines that Brenda is hiding her face because she is crying, but then the text notes that "in Brenda's face there was positively no threat of tears; she looked, suddenly, solid and decisive" (133). When Neil walks out, we know that he is crying, though Brenda's reactions remain mysterious: "I *think* Brenda was crying *too* when I went out the door" (135, italics added). Finally and more generally, it is not altogether clear what conclusions Neil has drawn from the breakup. The long paragraph following his departure from the hotel finds him asking himself fundamental questions about love, desire, and his identity, leaving the final sequence about Neil's return to Newark ambiguous in its tone and import.

The movie's version of this sequence reproduces much of Roth's dialogue verbatim but uses nonverbal cues to create a much more straightforward account of Neil and Brenda's breakup, featuring Neil as a much stronger masculine figure. Hence, in the movie it is Brenda, not Neil, who breaks down in tears—and she is near hysterics. Neil's affect moves from principled rage (he shouts "No! No! No!" when Brenda says she can no longer return home) to calm resolution as he lays out for Brenda a clearcut choice between her family and him. The camera's slow approach toward Neil's face, ending in a close-up, reveals his dawning recognition that she is simply not courageous enough to choose passion over material comfort.

Thus, the movie delivers an unalloyed condemnation of Brenda, whose irredeemable materialism fits the stereotype of a Jewish American princess—and who serves as a foil to Neil, who becomes the footloose and fancy-free young bachelor, off to new adventures. To be sure, this reading is warranted by the text; Roth's portrait of Brenda played no small part in codifying and disseminating the stereotype of the Jewish American princess (Prell). But when juxtaposed with the film's version of the last scene, Roth's work appears less certain about where and how to allocate blame.

This becomes clearer when we notice how the novella's final sequence is handled. When Neil leaves the hotel room, the camera shows him from behind as he strolls confidently down a rain-soaked street. We do not see Neil staring in confusion at his reflection, nor do we see him return, chastened, to the library. Instead the credits roll down, and as Neil wanders into the evening we hear the mellow sounds of the soundtrack, played by a sunshine pop band from California called the Association. The song, which features a graceful electric organ à la the Beach Boys, describes a boy-meets-girl scenario as a tricky game of masquerade and covert pursuit. As we watch Neil disappear down the street, it is clear that he understands the game now, and that he will be playing it with greater mastery from here on out. This conclusion reflects not only Hollywood's preference for conventional gender roles but also late 1960s cultural ideals, according to which domesticity is a trap and male freedom is a tangible goal (think of the film *Easy Rider*, also released in 1969).

This is one reading of the movie's conclusion, but other readings are possible as well. Some students may find Neil's condemnation of Brenda so harsh that he appears monstrously out of control. Some may see his rage as a symptom of weakness. For a class exercise, students reread the final sequence of the text closely, responding to a series of simple questions: Who, if anyone, is primarily responsible for the breakup? How do Neil and Brenda each feel about the breakup? What has Neil learned from his summer romance? Then they watch the final scene of the movie and consider how its version of the breakup differs from Roth's with respect to these questions. To account for these differences, students should consider how novelists and filmmakers work with different kinds of resources—how, for example, Roth can write from Neil's perspective, while it is more difficult for filmmakers to reproduce such an effect. Students should also consider how these two depictions are informed by the values and expectations of two different cultural moments (the late 1950s and the late 1960s). After the class considers how the movie betrays the biases of its cultural moment, the instructor can ask how students' readings of the movie reflect contemporary concerns. Fruitful discussions can also focus on casting decisions and questions about how Jewishness is portrayed in visual culture. Here students can be asked how they would cast the movie today. Lessons focused on the movie can thus raise numerous questions about Roth's text as well as broader questions about the ways different media and different historical moments shape acts of interpretation.

Notes

1. For an overview of Roth's works that pays special attention to "Goodbye, Columbus," see Gooblar.

2. Several of the criticisms of "Goodbye, Columbus" are cited by Silvey; the example of Rabbi Theodore Lewis, who condemned Roth's portrayal of Jews as depraved and lecherous, is typical. In his 1959 nonfiction book *This Is My God*, Herman Wouk described the criticism he received for his humorous depiction of a bar mitzvah in *Marjorie Morningstar*, written four years earlier.

3. The term *goy*, referring to gentiles, is used regularly by Roth, and in particular it appears in "Goodbye, Columbus," in plural form (as "goyim"), on page 94.

4. For students who want to pursue this line of thought, Diner may be recommended; further reading may include Heinze.

Works Cited

Biale, David. *Insider/Outsider: American Jews and Multiculturalism.* U of California P, 1998.

Cather, Willa. *The Professor's House.* Vintage, 1990.

Cisneros, Sandra. *The House on Mango Street.* Vintage, 1991.

Cooper, James Fenimore. *The Last of the Mohicans.* Penguin Classics, 1986.

Diner, Hasia R. *Hungering for America: Italian, Irish, and Jewish Foodways in the Age of Migration.* Harvard UP, 2001.

Douglass, Frederick. *Autobiographies.* Library of America, 1994.

Ginsberg, Allen. "Howl." *"Howl" and Other Poems*, City Lights Publishers, 2001.

Glazer, Nathan. *American Judaism.* U of Chicago P, 1957.

Gooblar, David. *The Major Phases of Philip Roth.* Continuum Books, 2011.

Goodbye, Columbus. Directed by Larry Peerce, Paramount Pictures, 1969.

Heinze, Andrew R. *Adapting to Abundance: Jewish Immigrants, Mass Consumption, and the Search for American Identity.* Columbia UP, 1990.

Herberg, Will. *Protestant-Catholic-Jew: An Essay in American Religious Sociology.* U of Chicago P, 1955.

Hurston, Zora Neale. *Their Eyes Were Watching God.* Harper Perennial, 2006.

Hurvitz, Nathan. "Sources of Middle-Class Values of American Jews." *Social Forces*, vol. 37, no. 2, Dec. 1958, pp. 117–23.

James, Henry. *Washington Square.* Penguin Classics, 2007.

Morrison, Toni. *Beloved.* Vintage, 2004.

O'Hara, Frank. *Lunch Poems.* City Lights Publishers, 2001.

Parasecoli, Fabio. "Food: Identity and Diversity." *Culinary Cultures of Europe: Identity, Diversity and Dialogue*, edited by Darra Goldstein and Kathrin Merkle, Council of Europe Publishing, 2005, pp. 11–37.

Prell, Riv-Ellen. *Fighting to Become Americans: Jews, Gender, and the Anxiety of Assimilation.* Beacon Press, 1999.

Roth, Philip. "Goodbye, Columbus." *"Goodbye, Columbus" and Five Short Stories.* 1959. Vintage Books, 1987, pp. 3–136.

Silvey, Patrick. "'I'm Just Jewish . . .': Defining Jewish Identity in Philip Roth's 'Goodbye, Columbus' and Five Short Stories." *Philip Roth Studies*, vol. 10, no. 1, 2014, pp. 59–76.

Wouk, Herman. *Marjorie Morningstar.* Doubleday, 1955.

———. *This Is My God.* Doubleday, 1959.

Ziprin, Nathan. "Book of Jewish Value." *The Jewish Floridian*, 3 June 1960, p. 10-A.

Part VII

Resources

**Roberta Rosenberg and
Rachel Rubinstein**

Primary Source Anthologies

Aarons, Victoria, et al., editors. *The New Diaspora: The Changing Landscape of American Jewish Fiction*. Wayne State UP, 2015.

Antler, Joyce, editor. *America and I: Short Stories by American Jewish Women Writers*. Beacon Press, 1990.

Blair, Sarah, and Jonathan Freedman, editors. *Jewish in America*. U of Michigan P, 2004.

Bukiet, Melvin, and David Roskies, editors. *Scribblers on the Roof: Contemporary Jewish Fiction*. Persea Books, 2006.

Chametzky, Jules, et al., editors. *Jewish American Literature: A Norton Anthology*. W. W. Norton, 2001.

Charyn, Jerome, editor. *Inside the Hornet's Head: An Anthology of Jewish American Writing*. Da Capo Books, 2005.

Hoberman, Michael, et al., editors. *Jews in the Americas, 1776–1826*. Routledge, 2017.

Rubin, Derek, editor. *Who We Are: On Being (and Not Being) a Jewish American Writer*. Schocken Books, 2005.

Solotaroff, Ted, and Nessa Rappaport, editors. *Writing Our Way Home: Contemporary Stories by American Jewish Writers*. Knopf Doubleday, 1992.

Staub, Michael. *The Jewish 1960s: An American Sourcebook*. Brandeis UP, 2004.

Wenger, Beth, editor. *The Jewish Americans: Three Centuries of Jewish Voices in America*. Doubleday, 2007.

Zakrzewski, Paul, editor. *Lost Tribe: Jewish Fiction from the Edge*. Harper Perennial, 2003.

Zangwill, Israel. *From the Ghetto to the Melting Pot: Israel Zangwill's Jewish Plays*. Edited by Edna Nahshon, Wayne State UP, 2005.

Literary Criticism Monographs, 1959–99

Alter, Robert. *After the Tradition: Essays on Modern Jewish Writing*. E. P. Dutton, 1969.

Baumgarten, Murray. *City Scriptures: Modern Jewish Writing*. Harvard UP, 1982.

Bloom, Alexander. *Prodigal Sons: The New York Intellectuals and Their World*. Oxford UP, 1986.

Budick, Emily Miller. *Blacks and Jews in Literary Conversation*. Cambridge UP, 1998.

Fiedler, Leslie. *The Jew in the American Novel*. Herzl Institute, 1959.

Furman, Andrew. *Israel through the Jewish-American Imagination*. State U of New York P, 1997.

Guttman, Alan. *The Jewish Writer in America: Assimilation and the Crisis of Identity*. Oxford UP, 1971.

Harap, Louis. *Creative Awakening: The Jewish Presence in Twentieth-Century American Literature, 1900s to 1940s*. Greenwood Press, 1987.

———. *The Image of the Jew in American Literature: From Early Republic to Mass Immigration*. Jewish Publication Society of America, 1974.

————. *In the Mainstream: The Jewish Presence in Twentieth-Century American Literature, 1950s–1980s*. Greenwood Press, 1987.

Lichtenstein, Diane. *Writing Their Nations: The Tradition of Nineteenth-Century American Jewish Women Writers*. Indiana UP, 1992.

Mersand, Joseph E. *Tradition in American Literature: A Study of Jewish Characters and Authors*. 1939. Revised ed., Modern Chapbooks, 1968.

Newton, Adam Zachary. *Facing Black and Jew: Literature as Public Space in Twentieth-Century America*. Cambridge UP, 1999.

Pinsker, Sanford. *The Schlemiel as Metaphor: Studies in Yiddish and Jewish American Fiction*. 1971. Revised ed., Southern Illinois UP, 1991.

Rogin, Michael. *Blackface, White Noise: Jewish Immigrants in the Hollywood Melting Pot*. U of California P, 1998.

Schechner, Mark. *After the Revolution: Studies in the Contemporary Jewish American Imagination*. Indiana UP, 1987.

Sherman, Bernard. *The Invention of the Jew: Jewish American Education Novels, 1916–1964*. T. Yoseloff, 1969.

Sollors, Werner. *Beyond Ethnicity: Consent and Descent in American Culture*. Oxford UP, 1987.

Whitfield, Stephen J. *In Search of American Jewish Culture*. Brandeis UP, 1999.

Wisse, Ruth R. *The Schlemiel as Modern Hero*. U of Chicago P, 1980.

Literary Criticism Monographs, 2000–Present

Bornstein, George. *The Colors of Zion: Blacks, Jews, and Irish from 1845 to 1945*. Harvard UP, 2011.

Cappell, Ezra. *American Talmud: The Cultural Work of Jewish American Fiction*. State U of New York P, 2007.

Casteel, Sarah Phillips. *Calypso Jews: Jewishness in the Caribbean Literary Imagination*. Columbia UP, 2016.

Eichler-Levine, Jodi. *Suffer the Little Children: Uses of the Past in Jewish and African-American Children's Literature*. New York UP, 2013.

Franco, Dean. *Ethnic American Literature: Comparing Chicano, Jewish, and African American Writing*. U of Virginia P, 2006.

————. *Race, Rights and Recognition: Jewish American Literature since 1969*. Cornell UP, 2012.

Freedman, Jonathan. *Klezmer America: Jewishness, Ethnicity, Modernity*. Columbia UP, 2008.

Garrett, Leah. *Young Lions: How Jewish Authors Reinvented the American War Novel*. Northwestern UP, 2015.

Glaser, Jennifer. *Borrowed Voices: Writing and Racial Ventriloquism in the Jewish American Imagination*. Rutgers UP, 2016.

Goffman, Ethan. *Imagining Each Other: Blacks and Jews in Contemporary American Literature*. State U of New York P, 2000.

Harrison-Kahan, Lori. *The White Negress: Literature, Minstrelsy, and the Black-Jewish Imaginary*. Rutgers UP, 2010.

Hoffman, Warren. *The Passing Game: Queering Jewish American Culture*. Syracuse UP, 2009.

Kandiyoti, Dalia. *Migrant Sites: America, Place, and Diaspora Literatures.* Dartmouth College P, 2009.

Kent, Alicia. *African, Native, and Jewish American Literature and the Reshaping of Modernism.* Palgrave Macmillan, 2007.

Lambert, Josh. *Unclean Lips: Obscenity, Jews, and American Culture.* New York UP, 2014.

Levinson, Julian. *Exiles on Main Street: Jewish American Writers and American Literary Culture.* Indiana UP, 2008.

Meyers, Helene. *Identity Papers: Contemporary Narratives of American Jewishness.* State U of New York P, 2011.

Omer-Sherman, Ranen. *Diaspora and Zionism in Jewish American Literature.* Brandeis UP, 2002.

Rottenberg, Catherine. *Performing Americanness: Race, Class, and Gender in Modern African-American and Jewish-American Literature.* Dartmouth College P / UP of New England, 2008.

Rubinstein, Rachel. *Members of the Tribe: Native America in the Jewish Imagination.* Wayne State UP, 2010.

Schlund-Vials, Cathy J. *Modeling Citizenship: Jewish and Asian-American Writing.* Temple UP, 2011.

Schreier, Ben. *The Impossible Jew: Identity and the Reconstruction of Jewish American Literary History.* New York UP, 2015.

Shreiber, Maeera. *Singing in a Strange Land: A Jewish American Poetics.* Stanford UP, 2007.

Weber, Donald. *Haunted in the New World: Jewish American Culture from Cahan to the Goldbergs.* Indiana UP, 2005.

Wirth-Nesher, Hana. *Call It English: The Languages of Jewish American Literature.* Princeton UP, 2006.

Essay Collections on Criticism and Theory

Aarons, Victoria, editor. *The New Jewish American Literary Studies.* Cambridge UP, 2019.

Avery, Evelyn, editor. *Jewish Women Writers in America.* Palgrave Macmillan, 2007.

Baskind, Samantha, and Ranen Omer-Sherman, editors. *The Jewish Graphic Novel: Critical Approaches.* Rutgers UP, 2008.

Bauman, Mark K., editor. *Dixie Diaspora: An Anthology of Southern Jewish History.* U of Alabama P, 2007.

Biale, David, et al., editors. *Insider/Outsider: American Jews and Multiculturalism.* U of California P, 1998.

Boyarin, Daniel, et al., editors. *Queer Theory and the Jewish Question.* Columbia UP, 2003.

Brook, Vincent, editor. *You Should See Yourself: Jewish Identity in Postmodern American Culture.* Rutgers UP, 2006.

Budick, Emily Miller, editor. *Ideology and Jewish Identity in Israeli and American Literature.* State U of New York P, 2001.

Cammy, Justin, et al., editors. *Arguing the Modern Jewish Canon: Essays on Literature and Culture in Honor of Ruth Wisse.* Harvard UP, 2008.

Fried, Lewis, editor. *Handbook of American-Jewish Literature: An Analytical Guide to Topics, Themes, and Sources.* Greenwood Press, 1988.
Jelen, Sheila, et al., editors. *Modern Jewish Literatures: Intersections and Boundaries.* U of Pennsylvania P, 2011.
Kugelmass, Jack, editor. *Key Texts in American Jewish Culture.* Rutgers UP, 2003.
Lambert, Josh, and Lori Harrison-Kahan, editors. *Finding Home: The Future of Jewish American Literacy Studies.* Special issue of *MELUS*, vol. 37, no. 2, 2012.
Malin, Irving, editor. *Contemporary American-Jewish Literature: Critical Essays.* Indiana UP, 1973.
Rottenberg, Catherine, editor. *Black Harlem and the Jewish Lower East Side: Narratives out of Time.* State U of New York P, 2013.
Shatzky, Joel, and Michael Taub, editors. *Contemporary Jewish-American Novelists: A Bio-Critical Sourcebook.* Greenwood Press, 1997.
Wirth-Nesher, Hana, editor. *The Cambridge History of Jewish American Literature.* Cambridge UP, 2016.
———, editor. *New Essays on Roth's* Call It Sleep. Cambridge UP, 1996.
———, editor. *What Is Jewish Literature?* Jewish Publication Society, 1994.
Wirth-Nesher, Hana, and Michael P. Kramer, editors. *The Cambridge Companion to Jewish American Literature.* Cambridge UP, 2003.

Sources on the Holocaust in Jewish American Literature

Aarons, Victoria, editor. *Third-Generation Holocaust Narratives.* Lexington Books, 2016.
Aarons, Victoria, and Holli Levitsky, editors. *New Directions in Jewish American and Holocaust Literatures: Reading and Teaching.* State U of New York P, 2019.
Berger, Alan L. *Crisis and Covenant: The Holocaust in American Jewish Fiction.* State U of New York P, 1985.
Berger, Alan L., and Gloria Cronin. *Jewish American and Holocaust Literature: Representation in the Postmodern World.* State U of New York P, 2004.
Budick, Emily Miller. "The Holocaust in the Jewish American Literary Imagination." *Cambridge Companion to Jewish American Literature,* edited by Hana Wirth-Nesher and Michael P. Kramer, Cambridge UP, 2003, pp. 212–30.
Eaglestone, Robert, and Barry Langford, editors. *Teaching Holocaust Literature and Film.* Palgrave Macmillan, 2008.
Hirsch, Marianne, and Irene Kacandes. *Teaching the Representation of the Holocaust.* Modern Language Association of America, 2004. Options for Teaching 18.
"The Holocaust Resource Center." *Yad Vashem,* www.yadvashem.org/yv/en /holocaust/resource_center/index.asp.
Langer, Lawrence. *The Holocaust and the Literary Imagination.* Yale UP, 1975.
Lipstadt, Deborah. *Beyond Belief: The American Press and the Coming of the Holocaust.* Free Press, 1986.
Norich, Anita. *Discovering Exile: Yiddish and Jewish American Culture during the Holocaust.* Stanford UP, 2007.

Novick, Peter. *The Holocaust in American Life*. New York: Free Press, 1986.
"Resources for Educators." *United States Holocaust Memorial Museum*, www
.ushmm.org/educators.
"Search Our Collection." *Facing History and Ourselves*, www.facinghistory.org
/resource-library?search=holocaust.
Shandler, Jeffrey. *While America Watches: Televising the Holocaust*. Oxford UP,
2000.
Wyman, David S. *The Abandonment of the Jews: America and the Holocaust,
1941–1945*. Pantheon, 1984.

Jewish American Literatures in Other Languages: Translations, History, and Criticism

Astro, Alan, editor. *Yiddish South of the Border: An Anthology of Latin Ameri-
can Yiddish Writing*. U of New Mexico P, 2003.
Bachman, Merle L. *"Yiddishland": Threshold Moments in American Literature*.
Syracuse UP, 2008.
Bejarano, Margalit. *Contemporary Sephardic Identity in the Americas: An
Interdisciplinary Approach*. Syracuse UP, 2012.
Ben-Ur, Aviva. *Sephardic Jews in America: A Diasporic History*. New York UP,
2009.
Berkowitz, Joel. *Shakespeare on the American Yiddish Stage*. U of Iowa P,
2002.
Cassedy, Steven. *Building the Future: Jewish Immigrant Intellectuals and the
Making of Tsukunft*. Holmes and Meiers Publishers, 1999.
Cohen, Julia Philips, and Sarah Abrevaya Stein. *Sephardi Lives: A Documentary
History, 1700–1950*. Stanford UP, 2014.
Forman, Frieda, et al., editors. *Found Treasures: Stories by Yiddish Women
Writers*. Second Story Press, 1994.
Gittleman, Sol. *From Shtetl to Suburbia: The Family in Jewish Imagination*.
Beacon Press, 1978.
Glaser, Amelia, and David Weintraub, editors. *Proletpen: America's Rebel
Yiddish Poets*. U of Wisconsin P, 2012.
Glatstein, Jacob. *The Glatstein Chronicles*. Edited by Ruth R. Wisse, Yale UP, 2010.
Hadda, Janet. *Isaac Bashevis Singer: A Life*. Oxford UP, 1997.
Harshav, Benjamin, editor. *Sing, Stranger: A Century of American-Yiddish
Poetry: A Historical Anthology*. Stanford UP, 2006.
Harshav, Benjamin, and Barbara Harshav, editors. *American-Yiddish Poetry:
A Bilingual Anthology*. 1986. Stanford UP, 2007.
Hellerstein, Kathryn, editor. *Paper Bridges: Selected Poems of Kadya Molodowsky*.
Wayne State UP, 1999.
———. *A Question of Tradition: Women Poets in Yiddish, 1586–1987*. Stanford
UP, 2014.
Howe, Irving. *World of Our Fathers: The Journey of the East European Jews to
America and the Life They Found and Made*. Harcourt Brace Jovanovich, 1976.
Howe, Irving, et al., editors. *The Penguin Book of Modern Yiddish Verse*.
Penguin Books, 1988.

Howe, Irving, and Eliezer Greenberg, editors. *A Treasury of Yiddish Stories.* 1954. Revised ed., 1990.

Katz, Stephen. *Red, Black, and Jew: New Frontiers in Hebrew Literature.* U of Texas P, 2009.

Kronfeld, Chana. *On the Margins of Modernism: Decentering Literary Dynamics.* U of California P, 1996.

Kumove, Shirley, editor and translator. *Drunk from the Bitter Truth: The Poems of Anna Margolin.* State U of New York P, 2005.

Margolis, Rebecca. *Jewish Roots, Canadian Soil: Yiddish Culture in Montreal, 1905–45.* McGill-Queen's UP, 2011.

Matza, Diane, editor. *Sephardic-American Voices: Two Hundred Years of a Literary Legacy.* Brandeis UP, 1997.

Metzker, Isaac, editor. *A Bintel Brief: Sixty Years of Letters from the Lower East Side to the* Jewish Daily Forward. Schocken Books, 1990.

Michels, Tony. *A Fire in Their Hearts: Yiddish Socialists in New York.* Harvard UP, 2005.

Mintz, Alan, editor. *Hebrew in America: Perspectives and Prospects.* Wayne State UP, 1993.

———. *A Sanctuary in the Wilderness: A Critical Introduction to American Hebrew Poetry.* Stanford UP, 2011.

Molodowsky, Kadia. *A Jewish Refugee in New York: Rivke Zilberg's Journal.* Translated by Anita Norich. Indiana UP, 2019.

Norich, Anita. *Writing in Tongues: Translating Yiddish in the Twentieth Century.* U of Washington P, 2013.

Rosenwald, Laurence. *Multilingual America: Language and the Making of American Literature.* Cambridge UP, 2008.

Sandrow, Nahma. *Vagabond Stars: A World History of Yiddish Theatre.* Syracuse UP, 1996.

Shandler, Jeffrey. *Adventures in Yiddishland: Postvernacular Language and Culture.* U of California P, 2005.

Shapiro, Lamed. *"The Cross" and Other Jewish Stories.* Edited by Leah Garrett, Yale UP, 2007.

Shell, Marc, and Werner Sollors, editors. *The Multilingual Anthology of American Literature: A Reader of Original Texts with English Translations.* New York UP, 2000.

Singer, Isaac Bashevis. *The Collected Stories.* Edited by Ilan Stavans, Library of America, 2004. 3 vols.

Sollors, Werner, editor. *Multilingual America: Transnationalism, Ethnicity, and the Languages of American Literature.* New York UP, 1998.

Stavans, Ilan, editor. *The Schocken Book of Modern Sephardic Literature.* Schocken Books, 2005.

———, editor. *The Scroll and the Cross: A Thousand Years of Jewish-Hispanic Literature.* Routledge, 2002.

Weingrad, Michael. *American Hebrew Literature: Writing Jewish National Identity in the United States.* Syracuse UP, 2011.

———, editor. *Letters to America: Selected Poems of Reuven Ben-Yosef.* Syracuse UP, 2015.

Wisse, Ruth. *A Little Love in Big Manhattan: Two Yiddish Poets*. Harvard UP, 1988.

Yiddish Book Center. www.yiddishbookcenter.org.

Yiddish Radio Project. Sound Portraits Productions, 2002, www .yiddishradioproject.org/.

Yiddish Radio Project: Stories from the Golden Age of Yiddish Radio. Read by Carl Reiner et al., National Public Radio, 2002. CD.

Reference Materials on Jewish American History

American Jewish Desk Reference: The Ultimate One-Volume Reference to the Jewish Experience in America. Random House, 1999.

Antler, Joyce. *You Never Call, You Never Write: A History of the Jewish Mother*. Oxford UP, 2007.

Buhle, Paul. *Jews and American Popular Culture*. Praeger Publishers, 2007. 3 vols.

Diner, Hasia. *The Jews of the United States, 1654–2000*. U of California P, 2004.

Diner, Hasia, et al. *A Jewish Feminine Mystique? Jewish Women in Postwar America*. Rutgers UP, 2010.

Dinnerstein, Leonard. *Anti-Semitism in America*. Oxford UP, 1994.

Fader, Ayala. *Mitzvah Girls: Bringing Up the Next Generation of Hasidic Jews in Brooklyn*. Princeton UP, 2009.

Feingold, Henry, et al. *The Jewish People in America*. Johns Hopkins UP / American Jewish Historical Society, 1992. 5 vols.

Glenn, Susan A. *Daughters of the Shtetl: Life and Labor in the Immigrant Generation*. Cornell UP, 1990.

Goldstein, Eric. *The Price of Whiteness: Jews, Race, and American Identity*. Princeton UP, 2006.

Greenberg, Cheryl. *Troubling the Waters: Black-Jewish Relations in the American Century*. Princeton UP, 2006.

Hoberman, J., and Jeffrey Shandler. *Entertaining America: Jews, Movies, and Broadcasting*. Jewish Museum / Princeton UP, 2003.

Hyman, Paula E., and Deborah Dash Moore, editors. *Jewish Women in America: An Historical Encyclopedia*. Routledge Press / American Jewish Historical Society, 1997. 2 vols.

Joselit, Jenna Weissman. *The Wonders of America: Reinventing Jewish Culture, 1880–1950*. Hill and Wang, 1994.

Leibman, Laura. *Messianism, Secrecy, and Mysticism: A New Interpretation of Early American Jewish Life*. Vallentine Mitchell, 2013.

Mintz, Jerome R. *Hasidic People: A Place in the New World*. Harvard UP, 1992.

Moore, Deborah Dash. *At Home in America*. Columbia UP, 1981.

———, editor. *City of Promises: A History of the Jews of New York*. New York UP, 2012. 3 vols.

Pinsker, Sanford. *Jewish American History and Culture: An Encyclopedia*. Taylor and Frances, 1992.

Prell, Riv-Ellen. *Fighting to Become Americans: Assimilation and the Trouble between Jewish Women and Jewish Men*. Beacon Press, 1999.

———. *Women Remaking American Judaism*. Wayne State UP, 2007.

Raphael, Marc Lee. *Profiles in American Judaism: The Reform, Conservative, Orthodox, and Reconstructionist Traditions in Historical Perspective.* Harper and Row, 1988.

Rischin, Moses. *The Promised City: New York's Jews, 1870–1914.* Harvard UP, 1977.

Sarna, Jonathan D. *American Judaism: A History.* Yale UP, 2004.

Sarna, Jonathan D., and Adam Mendelsohn, editors. *Jews and the Civil War: A Reader.* New York UP, 2010.

Wenger, Beth. *History Lessons: The Creation of American Jewish Heritage.* Princeton UP, 2010.

Teaching Jewish Studies

Freedman, Samuel G. "Classes in Judaic Studies, Drawing a Non-Jewish Class." *The New York Times*, 3 Nov. 2004, www.nytimes.com/2004/11/03 /education/classes-in-judaic-studies-drawing-a-nonjewish-class.html.

Garber, Zev, editor. *Academic Approaches to Teaching Jewish Studies.* UP of America, 2000.

Loveland, Kristen. "The Association for Jewish Studies: A Brief History." *Association for Jewish Studies*, www.associationforjewishstudies.org/docs /default-source/ajs-history/ajs-history.pdf?sfvrsn=2. PDF.

Ritterband, Paul, and Harold S. Wechsler. *Jewish Learning in American Universities: The First Century.* Indiana UP, 1994.

Encyclopedias, Handbooks, and Readers' Guides on Jewish Culture, History, Literature, and Religion

Bush, Andrew, et al., editors. *Key Words in Jewish Studies.* Rutgers UP, 2012–18.

Cronin, Gloria, and Alan Berger, editors. *Encyclopedia of Jewish-American Literature.* Facts on File, 2009.

Davies, W. D., and L. Finkelstein, general editors. *The Cambridge History of Judaism.* Cambridge UP, 2008–18. 8 vols.

Encyclopedia Judaica. Keter, 1994. 16 vols.

Goodman, Martin, editor. *The Oxford Handbook of Jewish Studies.* Oxford UP, 2005.

Jewish Women: A Comprehensive Historical Encyclopedia. Jewish Women's Archive, 1998–2019, jwa.org/encyclopedia.

Lambert, Josh. *American Jewish Fiction: A JPS Guide.* Jewish Publication Society, 2009.

Reisner, Rosalind. *Jewish American Literature: A Guide to Reading Interests.* Libraries Unlimited, 2004.

YIVO Encyclopedia of Jews in Eastern Europe. YIVO Institute for Jewish Research, 2010, www.yivoencyclopedia.org/.

Major Jewish American Studies Archives

American Jewish Committee Archives (New York, NY), www.ajcarchives.org /main.php.

Asher Library, Spertus Institute for Jewish Learning and Leadership (Chicago, IL), www.spertus.edu.

Center for Jewish History (New York, NY), www.cjh.org.

Dorot Jewish Division, New York Public Library, www.nypl.org/locations /divisions/jewish-division#!.

Jacob Rader Marcus Center of the American Jewish Archives, Hebrew Union College–Jewish Institute of Religion (Cincinnati, OH), americanjewish archives.org.

Jewish Studies Collection, Harry Ransom Center, University of Texas, Austin, hrc.utexas.edu/collections/guide/jewish/.

Jewish Women's Archive (Brookline, MA), jwa.org.

Judaica Collection, Harvard University Library (Cambridge, MA), library .harvard.edu/collections/judaica-collection.

Judaica Collections, University of Pennsylvania (Philadelphia, PA), www.library .upenn.edu/collections/judaica/judaicacollection.html.

Magnes Collection of Jewish Art and Life, University of California, Berkeley, www.magnes.berkeley.edu/.

Selected Periodicals Focusing on Jewish American Literature and Culture

AJS Review: The Journal of the Association for Jewish Studies
American Jewish Archives Journal
American Jewish History
Canadian Jewish Studies / Études juives canadiennes
Commentary Magazine
The Forward
In Geveb: A Journal of Yiddish Studies
Jewish Film and New Media: An International Journal
Jewish Quarterly Review
The Jewish Review of Books
Jewish Social Studies
Journal of Jewish Identities
MELUS
Moment Magazine
Prooftexts: A Journal of Jewish Literary History
Raíces: Revista judía de cultura
Shofar: An Interdisciplinary Journal in Jewish Studies
Studies in American Jewish Literature
Tablet Magazine

Additional Online Resources

Digital Yiddish Theater Project, yiddishstage.org.
Ergo Media Jewish Video Catalog, www.ergomedia.com/.
H-Judaic: Jewish Studies Network, networks.h-net.org/h-judaic.
Jewish Atlantic World, rdc.reed.edu/c/jewishatl/home/.
The Jewish Museum, thejewishmuseum.org.

Milken Archive of Jewish Music: The American Experience, www.milkenarchive
    .org/.
National Center for Jewish Film, jewishfilm.org/.
National Museum of American Jewish History, www.nmajh.org.
RAMBI—Index of Articles on Jewish Studies, web.nli.org.il/sites/NLI/English
    /infochannels/Catalogs/bibliographic-databases/rambi/.
Steven Spielberg Jewish Film Archive, en.jfa.huji.ac.il.

Notes on Contributors

Peter Antelyes is associate professor of English at Vassar College. He is the author of "'Haim Afen Range': The Jewish Indian and the Redface Western" (2009), "Red Hot Mamas: Sophie Tucker, Bessie Smith, and the Ethnic Maternal Voice in American Popular Song" (1994), and *Tales of Adventurous Enterprise: Washington Irving and the Poetics of Western Expansion* (1990).

Temma Berg is professor emerita of English, Judaic studies, and women, gender, and sexuality studies at Gettysburg College. She is the author of "Taking the Baltic Merchant: At Sea through the Archives" (2013), *The Lives and Letters of an Eighteenth-Century Circle of Acquaintance* (2006), "Reading Amazon Fragments: Queering *Shirley*" (2016), and "The Business of Coquetting" (2018). She is currently working on a study of the lives and works of the Brontë sisters, which focuses on reading as represented in their novels and in their reading responses to their predecessors as well as to one another.

Corinne E. Blackmer is professor of English and Judaic studies at Southern Connecticut State University. She is the author of "A Traumatic Professorial Education: Anti-Zionism and Homophobia in a Serial Campus Hate Crime" (2018), "Teaching Race, Gender, and Narrative Form in Gertrude Stein's 'Melanctha'" (2018), and *Queering Anti-Zionism: LGBTQ Academics' BDS Activism* (forthcoming).

Justin Cammy is associate professor of Jewish studies and comparative literature at Smith College. His book on Young Vilna, the last major Yiddish literary group in interwar Poland, is forthcoming. He is currently completing an English translation of Abraham Sutzkever's *Vilna Ghetto*, one of the earliest Holocaust memoirs to describe the destruction of a Jewish city.

Jennifer Caplan is assistant professor and program director of Jewish studies at Towson University. She is the author of "The Nebbish in Popular Culture; or, How the Underdog Can Win" (2016); "Nebbishes, New Jews, and Humor: The Changing Image of American Jewish Masculinity Post-Holocaust" (February 2020); and "The Past, Lived and Imagined: Nostalgia in Jewish Women's Comics" (forthcoming).

Sarah Phillips Casteel is professor of English at Carleton University. She is the author of *Calypso Jews: Jewishness in the Caribbean Literary Imagination* (2016) and *Second Arrivals: Landscape and Belonging in Contemporary Writing of the Americas* (2007) and coeditor of *Canada and Its Americas: Transnational Navigations* (2010).

Judah M. Cohen is Lou and Sybil Mervis Professor of Jewish Culture and professor of Jewish studies and musicology at Indiana University, Bloomington. He is the author of *Jewish Religious Music in Nineteenth-Century America: Restoring the Synagogue Soundtrack* (2019), *The Making of a Reform Jewish Cantor* (2009), and *Through the Sands of Time: A History of the Jewish Community of St. Thomas, U.S. Virgin Islands* (2004).

Jodi Eichler-Levine is Philip and Muriel Berman Professor of Jewish Civilization and associate professor of religion studies at Lehigh University. She is the author of *Suffer the Little Children: Uses of the Past in Jewish and African American Children's Literature* (2013). Her *Crafting Judaism: Gender, Creativity, and Jewish Americans* is forthcoming.

Dean Franco is professor of English and director of the Humanities Institute at Wake Forest University. He is the author of *The Border and the Line: Race, Literature, and Los Angeles* (2019); *Race, Rights, and Recognition: Jewish American Literature since 1969* (2012); and *Ethnic American Literature: Comparing Chicano, Jewish, and African American Writing* (2006).

Sarah Gleeson-White is associate professor of American literature at the University of Sydney. She is the editor of *William Faulkner at Twentieth Century-Fox: The Annotated Screenplays* (2017) and *Strange Bodies: Gender and Identity in the Novels of Carson McCullers* (2003). Her current book project explores the interactions of print and motion picture cultures of the silent film era.

Rachel Gordan is assistant professor of religion and Jewish studies at the University of Florida. Her research and teaching interests include American religious history, Jewish history, Judaism, and midcentury Jewish American religion and culture. Her current projects address postwar American Judaism and the making of the novel and film *Gentleman's Agreement*.

Louis Gordon is adjunct lecturer at California State University, San Bernardino. He is the author, with Ian Oxnevad, of *Middle East Politics for the New Millennium* (2016) and the author of "Updike's Middle East: A Neoliberal Approach to Conflict Resolution" (2019), "Two Voices or One? Philip Roth and Zionism" (2017), "Jewish Graphic Gangsters" (2008), and "Arthur Koestler and His Ties to Zionism and Jabotinsky" (1991).

Lori Harrison-Kahan is associate professor of the practice of English at Boston College. She is the author of *The White Negress: Literature, Minstrelsy, and the Black-Jewish Imaginary* (2010), the editor of *The Superwoman and Other Writings by Miriam Michelson* (2019), and the editor, with Josh Lambert, of *The Future of Jewish American Literary Studies*, a special issue of *MELUS*.

Kathryn Hellerstein is professor of Germanic languages and literatures and the Ruth Meltzer Director of the Jewish Studies Program at the University of Pennsylvania. She is the author of *A Question of Tradition: Women Poets in Yiddish, 1586–1987* (2014) and a coeditor of *Jewish American Literature: A Norton Anthology* (2001).

Bettina Hofmann is senior lecturer at the University of Wuppertal. She is the author of "Outcast: About the Fate of Japanese Americans after World War II" (2017), "Popular Culture: Ethnicity, Ethnic Stereotyping and U.S. History in Graphic Novels" (2014), and "Ha Jin's *A Free Life*: Revisiting the *Künstlerroman*" (2010).

Dalia Kandiyoti is associate professor of English at the College of Staten Island, City University of New York. She is the author of *Migrant Sites: America, Place, and Diaspora Literatures* (2009) as well as articles on Latina/o, Sephardic, diasporic, and world literatures. Her book, *The Converso's Return*, about Sephardic and converso history in contemporary world literature, is under contract from Stanford University Press.

Laini Kavaloski is assistant professor of English and humanities at the State University of New York, Canton. She is the author of articles in *Studies on Critical Security*, *Studies in Comics*, and *Comparative Drama* and in the collection *Pioneers in Digital Teaching Practices*. Her current project is a book titled "The In/Security of Digital Form: Network, Palimpsest, Procedure."

Josh Lambert is academic director of the Yiddish Book Center and visiting assistant professor of English at the University of Massachusetts, Amherst. He is the author of *Unclean Lips: Obscenity, Jews, and American Culture* (2014) and *American Jewish Fiction: A JPS Guide* (2009).

Lori Hope Lefkovitz is Ruderman Professor of Jewish Studies, professor of English, and director of the Humanities Center at Northeastern University. She is the author of *In Scripture: First Stories of Jewish Sexual Identities* and *The Character of Beauty in the Victorian Novel*, editor of *Textual Bodies: Changing Boundaries of Literary Representation*, and coeditor of *Shaping Losses: Cultural Memory and the Holocaust*.

Laura Arnold Leibman is professor of English and humanities at Reed College. She is the author of *Indian Converts* (2008) and *Messianism, Secrecy, and Mysticism: A New Interpretation of Early American Jewish Life* and a coeditor of *Jews in the Americas, 1776–1826* (2017). Her book *The Art of the Jewish Family: A History of Women in Early New York in Five Objects*, is forthcoming from the Bard Graduate Center (2020).

Jennifer Lemberg is an instructor at New York University's Gallatin School of Individualized Study and associate director of the Olga Lengyel Institute for Holocaust Studies and Human Rights. She is the author of essays in *The Edinburgh Companion to Modern Anglophone Jewish Fiction*, *Women's Studies Quarterly*, and *Studies in American Indian Literatures*.

Julian Levinson is Samuel Shetzer Professor of American Jewish Studies and associate professor of English at the University of Michigan. He is the author of *Exiles on Main Street: Jewish American Writers and American Literary Culture*. His current book project is "Reclaiming Scripture: Jewish Self-Fashioning in Protestant America."

Judith Lewin is associate professor of English at Union College. She is the author of essays in *The Cambridge Dictionary of Judaism and Jewish Culture*, *Shofar*, and *Nashim: A Journal of Jewish Women's Studies and Gender Issues*. She is currently serving on the editorial board updating the online *Shalvi/Hyman Encyclopedia of Jewish Women* at the Jewish Women's Archive and writing an essay on Allegra Goodman.

John Wharton Lowe is Barbara Methvin Distinguished Professor of English at the University of Georgia. He is the author of *Jump at the Sun: Zora Neale Hurston's Cosmic Comedy* (1996) and *Calypso Magnolia: The Crosscurrents of Caribbean and Southern Literature* (2016). He coedited *Approaches to Teaching Gaines's* The Autobiography of Miss Jane Pittman *and Other Works* (2019).

Joanna Meadvin is program manager for the Sobrato Early Academic Language Program, a comprehensive school-change model of intensive, enriched language and literacy education. She is the author of "Searching for Home: Henry Roth's Spanish American Turn" (2017) and "At Heym in the Joyf: Mimi Pinzon's Argentine Yiddish World" (2017) and the translator of Pablo Albacares's "The Popular Culture Turn" (2018).

Nadia Fayidh Mohammed is an Arabic language and culture researcher based in London. She is the author of "Multiculturalism and Feminism in Arab-American Poetry" (2017), "One Poem, Two Translations: Between Translation and Cultural Adaptation in Translating Whitman's 'Song of Myself' to Arabic" (2019), and "Lifting Off Scheherazade's 'Orientalist' Veil" (2003).

Yaron Peleg is Kennedy-Leigh Reader in Modern Hebrew Studies at the University of Cambridge. He is the author of *Directed by God: Jewishness in Contemporary Israeli Film and Television* (2016), *Israeli Culture between the Two Intifadas* (2008), and *Derech Gever: Homoeroticism in Modern Hebrew Literature, 1880–2000* (2003, in Hebrew).

Judith R. Phagan is associate professor of English and English Department chair at St. Joseph's College. She is the author of "Passing in the Age of Rachel Dolezal" (2016). Her research addresses disability narratives, the LGBTQ community, marginalized voices, passing, and eugenics. Her current project is titled "Colson Whitehead's *Underground Railroad*: A Look at Eugenics and White Male Passing."

Meri-Jane Rochelson is professor emerita of English at Florida International University. She is the author of *A Jew in the Public Arena: The Career of Is-*

rael Zangwill (2008) and a biography of her father, *Eli's Story: A Twentieth-Century Jewish Life* (2018); the editor of *Children of the Ghetto*, by Israel Zangwill (1998); and a coeditor of *Transforming Genres: New Approaches to British Fiction of the 1890s* (1994).

Roberta Rosenberg is professor emerita at Christopher Newport University. She is the author of "The Importance of Jewish Ritual in the Secular, Postmodern World of *Transparent*" (2017) and "Larry David's 'Dark Talmud'; or, Kafka in Prime Time" (2013) and a coeditor of *Service Learning and Literary Studies in English* (2015), winner of the 2017 Teaching Literature Book Award from Idaho State University.

Catherine Rottenberg is associate professor in the Department of American and Canadian Studies at the University of Nottingham. She is the author of *Performing Americanness: Race, Class, and Gender in Modern African-American and Jewish-American Literature* (2008) and *The Rise of Neoliberal Feminism* (2018) and the editor of *Black Harlem and the Jewish Lower East Side: Narratives out of Time* (2013).

Rachel Rubinstein taught at Hampshire College until 2019 and currently serves as vice president of Academic and Student Affairs at Holyoke Community College. She is the author of *Members of the Tribe: Native America in the Jewish Imagination* (2010) and the coeditor of *Arguing the Modern Jewish Canon: Essays on Literature and Culture in Honor of Ruth R. Wisse* (2008). Her current research focuses on Yiddish and translation in the Americas.

Linda Schlossberg is associate director of undergraduate studies in the Program in Women, Gender, and Sexuality Studies at Harvard University. She is the author of the novel *Life in Miniature* (2010) and the editor, with Maria C. Sanchez, of *Passing: Identity and Interpretation in Sexuality, Race, and Religion* (2001). She was awarded the 2016 Emerging Writer's Fellowship from the Writer's Center and a 2019 Literary Arts Fellowship from the Somerville Arts Council.

Benjamin Schreier is Mitrani Family Professor of Jewish Studies and professor of English and Jewish studies at Pennsylvania State University. He is the author of *The Impossible Jew: Identity and the Reconstruction of Jewish American Literary History* (2015) and *The Power of Negative Thinking: Cynicism and the History of Modern American Literature* (2009) and the editor, with Jonathan P. Eburne, of *The Year's Work in Nerds, Wonks, and Neocons* (2017). He is currently finishing a book titled *The Rise and Fall of Jewish American Literature*.

Sasha Senderovich is assistant professor of Russian, Jewish, and international studies at the University of Washington, Seattle. He is the author of articles on Isaac Babel, David Bergelson, Moyshe Kulbak, and contemporary Soviet-born émigré Jewish American writers. Together with Harriet Murray, he translated, from the Yiddish, David Bergelson's *Judment: A Novel* (2017). He is working on his first book, *How the Soviet Jew Was Made: Culture and Mobility after the Revolution.*

Karen E. H. Skinazi is senior lecturer and director of the liberal arts program at the University of Bristol. She is the author of *Women of Valor: Orthodox Jewish Troll Fighters, Crime Writers, and Rock Stars in Contemporary Literature and Culture* (2018) and the editor of *Marion: The Story of an Artist's Model: A Novel,* by Winnifred Eaton (pseud. Onoto Watanna) (2012). Her current project, with Rachel S. Harris, is titled "With a Headscarf: The Art of Religious Women's Feminisms."

Naomi B. Sokoloff is professor of Near Eastern languages and civilization and of comparative literature, cinema, and media at the University of Washington, Seattle. She is the author of *Imagining the Child in Modern Jewish Literature* (1992) and the coeditor of *Gender and Text in Modern Hebrew and Yiddish Literature* (1992), *Boundaries of Jewish Identity* (2010), and *What We Talk about When We Talk about Hebrew* (2018).

Ilan Stavans is Lewis-Sebring Professor of Humanities and Latin American and Latino Culture at Amherst College. He is the author of *On Borrowed Words* (2001), *Dictionary Days* (2008), and *Quixote: The Novel and the World* (2015) and the editor of *The Oxford Book of Jewish Stories* (1998) and *Oy Caramba! An Anthology of Jewish Stories from Latin America* (2016).

Lucas Thompson is a lecturer in the English Department at the University of Sydney. He is the author of *Global Wallace: David Foster Wallace and World Literature* (2016) and articles in *New Literary History, Comparative Literature Studies, Texas Studies in Literature and Language,* and *Journal of American Studies.*

Katharine G. Trostel is assistant professor of English at Ursuline College and codirector of the Venice Ghetto Collaboration. She is the author of "Memoryscapes: Urban Palimpsests and Networked Jewish Memory in the works of Tununa Mercado (Argentina) and Karina Pacheco Medrano (Peru)" (2016) and "City of (Post) Memory: Memory Mapping in Nona Fernández's 2002 *Mapocho*" (2018) and the coauthor of "Reading-in-Place and Thick Mapping the Venice Ghetto at 500" (2018).

Zohar Weiman-Kelman is assistant professor of foreign literatures and linguistics at Ben Gurion University in the Negev. They are the author of *Queer Expectations: A Genealogy of Jewish Women's Poetry* (2018) and articles in *Criticism, Prooftexts, Journal of Lesbian Studies,* and *Orbis Litterarum.* Their current project, "Un(Archiving) Yiddish Sex," looks at Yiddish sexology, philology, and poetry.

Donna Aza Weir-Soley is associate professor of English and an affiliate faculty member in African and African diaspora studies and women's studies at Florida International University. She is the author of *Eroticism, Spirituality, and Resistance in Black Women's Writings* (2009) and of two poetry collections, *First Rain* (2006) and *The Woman Who Knew* (2016), and the coeditor of *Caribbean Erotic* (2011).

Lucas Wilson, a PhD candidate at Florida Atlantic University, is studying Canadian literature and literature of the United States; the Holocaust, particularly the literature of children of Holocaust survivors; religion and literature; and American Evangelicalism.

Hana Wirth-Nesher is professor emerita of English and American studies and Samuel L. and Perry Haber Chair on the Study of the Jewish Experience in the United States at Tel Aviv University. She is the author or editor of *Call It English: The Languages of Jewish American Literature* (2006), *The Cambridge History of Jewish American Literature* (2016), and *City Codes: Reading the Modern Urban Novel* (1996).